MW01105181

# Gazetteer and Business Directory of Cortland County, New York, for 1869

## Date Due

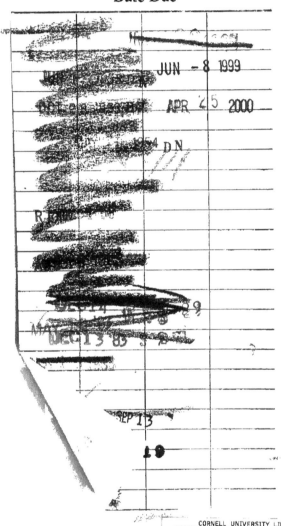

JUN − 8 1999

APR 25 2000

E. E. Edwin

# GAZETTEER

AND

# BUSINESS DIRECTORY

OF

## CORTLAND COUNTY, N. Y.,

FOR

## 1869.

COMPILED AND PUBLISHED BY

# HAMILTON CHILD.

AUTHOR OF WAYNE, ONTARIO, SENECA, CAYUGA, TOMPKINS, ONONDAGA, MADI-
SON, ONEIDA, CHEMUNG, SCHUYLER, NIAGARA, STEUBEN, CHE-
NANGO, ORLEANS AND OTHER COUNTY DIRECTORIES.

Permanent Office, 23 & 24 E. Washington St , Syracuse, N. Y.

## HANG UP THIS BOOK FOR FUTURE REFERENCE.

SYRACUSE:
PRINTED AT THE JOURNAL OFFICE, 23 & 24 E WASHINGTON STREET.
1869

# THE REYNOLDS

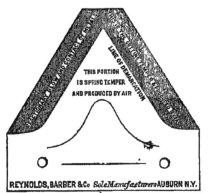

REYNOLDS, BARBER & Co. *Sole Manufacturers* AUBURN N.Y.

# Mower & Reaper
# KNIVES.

**MANUFACTURED EXCLUSIVELY BY US, UNDER REYNOLDS' PATENTS** for Tempering Steel without the aid of any liquids, received the only award at the Great National Implement Trial, held at Auburn, in 1866    They possess the following superior qualities.

1. They are made with a fine Cutlery Temper at the edges
2. They hold only a Spring Temper at the center and at the heel
3. They are warranted perfectly uniform, every knife being exactly alike in temper
4. We warrant they can be ground from 8 to 10 times without losing their cutting edge
5. Finally, we will warrant them to cut from 40 to 50 acres of grain or grass without being once ground

We are the sole Manufacturers of these Knives in the United States

---

# REYNOLDS, BARBER & CO.,

## Steel Tempering Works, Auburn, N. Y.

# INTRODUCTION.

In presenting the initial number of the "Gazetteer and Directory of Cortland County" to the public, the publisher desires to return his sincere thanks to all who have so kindly assisted in obtaining the valuable information which it contains, and without whose aid it would have been impossible to collect, in the brief space of time in which it is essential that all such works should be completed. Especially are our thanks due to the several editors of the *Cortland Co. Republican, Cortland County Standard, Cortland County Democrat, Gazette and Banner*, and the *Marathon News*, for the uniform kindness which has been evinced in calling public attention to the author's efforts; and to them and the following persons, Hon. Horatio Ballard, Hon. Chas. Foster, and Hon. H. S. Randall, and Frank Place, Esq., Co. Clerk, of Cortlandville; Daniel E. Whitmore, of Marathon, and Shubal Carver, of Homer, school commissioners of the County, for essential aid in furnishing material for the work. Many others have kindly volunteered their aid, to all of whom we return sincere thanks.

The following works were consulted in its preparation: "Goodwin's Pioneer History of Cortland Co ;" "French's Gazetteer of the State of New York;" "Documentary History of New York;" "Hotchkin's History of the Presbyterian Church in Western New York;" "Census Reports of 1865;" and "Proceedings of the Board of Supervisors in 1867."

That errors may have occurred in so great a number of names and dates as are here given, is probable, and that names have been omitted that should have been inserted is quite certain. We can only say that we have exercised more than ordinary diligence and care in this difficult and complicated feature of book-making. To such as feel aggrieved in consequence of error or omission, we beg pardon, and ask the indulgence of the reader in marking such as had been observed in the subsequent reading of the proofs, and which are noted in the *Errata*, following the Introduction.

It is also suggested that our patrons observe and become familiar with the explanations at the commencement of the Directory.

The Map of the County was engraved with great care by Messrs. "Weed, Parsons & Co ," of Albany, and, it is believed, will prove a valuable acquisition to the work

The *Advertisers* represent some of the leading business men and firms of the County, and also many enterprising and reliable dealers in other parts of the State. We most cheerfully commend them all to the patronage of those under whose observation these pages may come.

With thanks to friends generally, we leave our work to secure the favor which earnest endeavor ever wins from a discriminating business public

HAMILTON CHILD.

# ERRATA.

---

## ADDITIONS AND CORRECTIONS.

---

**Postal Rates and Regulations.**—The new Postal Convention with the United Kingdom, which went into operation on January 1, 1869, establishes the following rates of international postage

1 Letters twelve cents per single rate of fifteen grammes, one half ounce, In the United States, and six pence (twelve cents), in the United Kingdom, pre-payment optional A fine of five cents in the United States, and two pence (four cents) in the United Kingdom, is, however, to be levied and collected, in addition to the deficient postage, on each unpaid or insufficiently pre-paid letter received by one country from the other

2 Newspapers, two cents each in the United States, and one penny each in the United Kingdom, if not exceeding four ounces in weight

3 Book packets, including printed papers of all kinds, and patterns or samples of merchandise, including seeds and grain, when not exceeding one ounce in weight, two cents in the United States, and one penny in the United Kingdom, when exceeding one ounce, and not exceeding two ounces in weight, four cents in the United States, and two pence in the United Kingdom, when exceeding two ounces, and not exceeding four ounces in weight, six cents in the United States, and three pence in the United Kingdom, and when exceeding four ounces in weight, an additional rate of six cents in the United States, and three pence in the United Kingdom, will be charged for every additional four ounces, or fraction thereof The postage chargeable as above upon all articles of printed matter, including patterns or samples of merchandise, must be fully prepaid at the mailing office in either country, and is in full to destination, the receiving country delivering the same in all cases without any charge whatever

After the 1st of January 1869, the registry fee for letters in the United States will be 15 cents, instead of 20 cents as heretofore

## GAZETTEER.

**County.**—THE CORTLAND DEMOCRAT was started in 1845 by Seth Haight. It subsequently passed into the hands of H G Crouch In 1856 it passed into the hands of E F Gould, and was published by him for two years as the *Cortland American* In 1857 it was purchased by C P Cole, and issued under the name of the *Cortland Gazette* In 1861 Mr Cole went over to the Republican party, and gave it his support In 1864 the *Democrat* was revived and published by H G Crouch and M P Calender Mr Crouch subsequently sold his interest to C A. Rohler, who soon after purchased the interest of Mr Calender In 1865 L S Crandall purchased an interest in the *Democrat*, and afterwards became sole proprietor In 1868 the *Democrat* was purchased by Benton B Jones, who, on taking possession, enlarged the paper Recently he has purchased a new press and made a still further enlargement It is now one of the first-class papers, and is one of the best advertising mediums in Central New York. The name of the paper has been changed to THE CORTLAND COUNTY DEMOCRAT —[H. C GOODWIN

The publishers of the following papers have failed to furnish the necessary statistics for a history of their several papers, probably on account of absence from home, or a press of other duties

THE MARATHON NEWS, published at Marathon by C Dwight Smith

THE GAZETTE AND BANNER, published at Cortland Village by Chas P Cole

THE CORTLAND COUNTY STANDARD, published at Cortland Village by F. G Kinney

**Cortlandville.**—In the Gazetteer of Cortlandville, the following villages were omitted with the hope of obtaining further statistics

*McGrawville*, (p o) four and a half miles east of Cortland Village, contains three churches, an academy and union school, a hotel, several stores, a saw mill, a grist mill, a stone pump manufactory, a tannery and about 500 inhabitants

*Blodget Mills*, (p o) is the south-east part, on the Tioughnioga River, is a station on the Syracuse, Binghamton and N Y R R, and contains a Methodist church a steam saw mill, planing and bracket sawing, &c, a wool carding mill, a grist mill, several stores and about twenty dwellings

*South Cortland*, (p v) in the south-west part of the town, contains two churches and about thirty dwellings

**Cuyler.**—In our sketch of this town, Muncey Hill is stated to be poorly adapted to cultivation This is an error, as it contains several farms as good as any upon the uplands One of them is owned by Arza Muncey, Esq , son of one of the first settlers, after whom the hill was named

*Keeney's Settlement* is a post village

## DIRECTORY.

**Cincinnatus.**—BARNES N ROUNDS, is also a coroner

**Cortlandville.**—Burr & McGraw, general insurance agents, have sold out to A M Ford and Frank W Freeman, since our canvass

FORD & FREEMAN (Cortland Village,) (*Abram M Ford and Frank W Freeman,*) general insurance agents, Masonic Hall Block, successors to Burr & McGraw whose interest they have purchased since our canvass

AARON SAGER, (Cortland Village,) druggist, has taken a partner since our canvass, and the business is now conducted under the firm name of SAGER & DALTON, (*Aaron Sager and Thos Dalton* )

Perkins, Jarvis & Co , (Cortland Village,) grocers and provision dealers, have dissolved, and the business is now carried on by G N Copeland & Co , (*G N Copeland and James A Schermerhorn*)

JONES, GEO B , is also excise commissioner

Kingman, Orrin, (McGrawville,) hotel keeper, commenced business since our canvass

Pomeroy, Theodore C , M D , is also a coroner

WATERS, ALVAH D , is also district attorney

Webster, Geo W , (Cortland Village,) county treasurer, was omitted

**Homer.**—Bowen, Ira, (Homer,) excise commissioner was omitted

Barber, Geo J J , (Homer,) general merchant, is also postmaster

**Marathon.**—Isaacs, Wm H , (Texas Valley,) postmaster, was omitted

Carley, E C , (Marathon,) has retired from the firm of Carley & Burch, and Charles C Adams has entered into partnership with Mr Burch, under the firm name of Burch & Adams

Oscar Wildey and Daniel D Hunt have formed a partnership since our canvass

Willard, R F , (Marathon,) jeweler and watchmaker, has opened business since our canvass

**Scott.**—Babcock, Hervey W , (Scott,) merchant, was erroneously printed Babcock Henry W ; he is also postmaster

Churchill, Sylvester C , (East Scott,) is also postmaster

**Taylor.**—Angel, Jerome W , is also a coroner.

---

**E. M. Van Hoesen & Brother,** General Merchants, Preble, N Y , publish a card on page 132 Messrs. Van Hoesen keep a good assortment of all articles necessary for a first-class country store, and he must be very fastidious who cannot find something to his taste Everything to clothe a man from head to foot and to furnish his pantry can be found here and will be sold at low prices

**Dodge & Lord,** manufacturers of Melodeons and Reed Organs, at Ithaca, N Y , were formerly connected with Syracuse manufactories They have since moved their business where lumber is cheap, and expenses less than in the larger cities, like New York, Boston, Albany or Syracuse The styles of their organs are particularly their own, possessing all modern improvements, and some unknown to other manufacturers. They have found market for their instruments in every county of the State, and in Northern Pennsylvania and New Jersey, and have an increasing trade with the West, in all of which places they are brought into successful competition with the first Eastern manufacturers They are both practical men, and have secured workmen of long experience and tried abilities Situated midway between the Erie and N Y C railroads, they can ship conveniently to all parts of the country. See card, page 201

**A. Mahan,** dealer in Books, Stationery and Music, Cortland, N Y , advertises facing pages 100-1 This large establishment was started as a Book Store by Mr Geo Apgar, Oct 1st, 1865 He was succeeded Jan 1st, 1868, by Mr A Mahan, who has by his characteristic energy added largely to the business of the concern In addition to the large stock of Books, Stationery, Paper Hangings, &c , kept on hand, Mr Mahan has a large and valuable stock of Musical Instruments and general musical merchandise As he buys largely and of importers and manufacturers, dealers can rely upon getting goods of him as low as at any house in Central New York Mr M makes a specialty of fine goods suitable for Holiday, Wedding and other Gifts. We predict for him a prosperous business career

**Allen Potter** is prepared to do Planing, Matching, Wool Carding &c , at Blodget's Mills The old Carding Machine has been remodeled and fitted up in good style, and he is now prepared to execute all work intrusted to his care in the best manner The new Planing and Matching Machine recently put into his mill are just the things wanted to make the establishment first class, while his Bracket Sawing cannot be beat in these parts. Hoe handles and all sorts of turned work kept constantly on hand and for sale at low prices See card, page 114

# GENERAL CONTENTS.

| | PAGE |
|---|---|
| Addenda, Redington & Howe's Musical Catalogue, | latter part of book |
| Almanac or Calendar for 20 years | 62 |
| Board of Supervisors, | 15 |
| Brilliant Whitewash | 59 |
| Business Directory | 111-195 |
| Capacity of Cisterns or Wells | 58 |
| Census Report | 18-19 |
| Chemical Barometer | 59 |
| County Officers | 15 |
| Courts in Cortland County | 15 |
| Discount and Premium | 58 |
| Distance Table, | 200 |
| Errata | 9-10 |
| Facts on Advertising | 58 |
| French Decimal System of Weights and Measures | 53-57 |
| Gazetteer of County. | 63-70 |
| Gazetteer of Towns | 71-110 |
| Government Land Measure | 52 |
| How to get a Horse out of a Fire | 59 |
| How to Judge a Horse | 61 |
| How to Secure the Public Lands | 47-48 |
| How to Succeed in Business | 45-47 |
| Interest Table | 57 |
| Law Maxims | 48-52 |
| Leech Barometer | 59 |
| Lodges, Associations, &c. | 197-198 |
| Measurement of Hay in the Mow or Stack | 51 |
| Postal Rates and Regulations | 41-43 |
| Post Offices and Postmasters. | 19 |
| Rules for Detecting Counterfeit or Spurious Bank Notes. | 44-45 |
| School Statistics, | 19 |
| Stamp Duties | 34-40 |
| Table of Weights of Grain, Seeds, &c | 58 |
| The States, their Settlement, &c | 21-32 |
| The Territories, their Area, Boundaries, Population, &c. | 32-34 |
| To measure Grain in a Bin | 59 |
| U S Internal Revenue Officers | 15 |
| Valuable Recipes. | 60-61 |

* ◆ *

# INDEX TO BUSINESS DIRECTORY.

| | PAGE | | PAGE, |
|---|---|---|---|
| Cincinnatus, | 111 | Preble, | 165 |
| Cortlandville, | 115 | Scott, | 169 |
| Cuyler, | 130 | Solon, | 171 |
| Freetown, | 137 | Taylor, | 175 |
| Harford, | 141 | Troxton, | 177 |
| Homer, | 143 | Virgil, | 183 |
| Lapeer, | 155 | Willet, | 193 |
| Marathon, | 160 | | |

# INDEX TO ADVERTISEMENTS.

**Agricultural Implements.**
*(See also Mowers and Reapers )*
Gregg, Plyer & Co , Trumansburgh   202

**Bill Poster.**
VanSlyck, W H , Cortland ... .. . . 150

**Book Binder.**
Miller, Jacob, Syracuse   . . 178

**Boots and Shoes.**
Bennett, Edwin A., Syracuse,   facing 168–9
Smith, Alfred G , Marathon   150

**Bracket Sawing.**
Potter, Allen, Blodget Mills   .   .. 114

**Business College.**
Meads, C P , Bryant & Stratton's Commercial College, Syracuse on 1st cover

**Cancer Doctor.**
Kingsley, Dr , Rome   ..   1

**Cigar Manufacturer.**
Brinck, Chas G , Marathon .   .182

**Cloak and Dress Maker.**
Adams, Geo A. Mrs., Homer   ..192

**Clothier.**
Goldsmith, I I , Cortland   .   151

**Cooper.**
Kinne, Chas W , Cortland   .. 133

**Dry Goods.**
Burke, Fitzsimons, Hone & Co , Rochester   .   2
Wildey, Oscar, Marathon   . 158

**Engraver and Printer.**
Silcox, Geo W , Syracuse   . 192

**Flax and Cordage Mills.**
Boorom, John L , Homer   150

**General Merchants.**
Carr, D W , McGrawville   .   .. 201
Tanner, J. H , Blodget Mills   . 128
VanHoesen, H M & Bro , Preble   132
Wiles, Clifton W , Freetown   114

**Gents' Furnishing Goods.**
Goldsmith, I I , Cortland   .151

**Groceries, Provisions Etc.**
Burt, J , Homer   .. 140

**Hats, Caps and Furs.**
Bonner, W J , Homer   151
Spendley, R H & Co , Cortland   150

**Howe's Ague Cure Etc.**
Howe, C B , Seneca Falls   . 20

**Human Hair Goods.**
Adams, Geo. A. Mrs , Homer   .. 192
Loftus, Henry, Syracuse   ... 140

**Jewelry, Watches Etc.**
Gray, J C , Marathon   .   .   . 134

**Marble Works.**
Francis & Duffy, Syracuse   . 162
Watson, Joseph, Homer   .   124

**Melodeons and Organs.**
Dodge & Lord, Ithaca   .201

**Merchant Millers.**
Carley, A & Son, Marathon   123

**Mowers and Reapers**
*(See also Agricultural Implements )*
Gregg, Plyer & Co , Trumansburgh . 202

**Mower and Reaper Knives.**
Reynolds, Barber & Co , Auborn   6

**Music and Musical Instruments.**
Gray, J C , Marathon   134
Redington & Howe, Syracuse   on map
See also *Addenda* at end of volume

**Oriental Syrup and Balm of Gilead Ointment.**
Taft, G T & Co , Seneca Falls.   20

**Painter.**
*(House, Sign Etc )*
Shirley, Henry F , Cortland .   .. 128

**Paints, Oils Etc.**
Shirley, Henry F , Cortland   128

**Paper Dealers.**
Garrett, J & F B , Syracuse.   ..... 162
Shumway, E A , Syracuse   . . . 186

**Paper Hangers.**
Shirley, Henry F,, Cortland   .. 128
VanSlyck, W H., Cortland ..   ... 150

**Paper Makers.**
Tremain, Chas & Co , Manlius   146

**Photograph Artists.**
Gray, J C , Marathon   134
Ranger, W. V , Syracuse   18

**Physicians.**
Baker, E L , Marathon   . . 132
Kingsley, Dr , Rome   1

**Planing Mills.**
Potter, Allen, Blodget Mills   .   114

**Printers' Supplies.**
Garrett, J & F B , Syracuse.   162
Shumway, E A , Syracuse   186

**Printing Offices.**
Cortland Co Democrat, Cortland .   .184
Cortland Co Republican, Homer.   120
Cortland Co Standard, Cortland .   . 14
Gazette and Banner, Cortland   . 194
Journal, Syracuse   . .... 188
Marathon News   ..... 174
Silcox, Geo W , Syracuse ..   192
Smith, B Hermon, Syracuse,   facing 84–85

**Produce Dealer.**
Hoag, A H , Preble .    186

**Raspberry Plants.**
Wight, Warren, Waterloo    146

**Satchels and Traveling Bags.**
Bonner, W J , Homer    151

**Sewing Machines.**
Marvin & Bishop, Syracuse    16
Orcutt, W C , Syracuse    152

**Slat Window Shades.**
Cone, H S , Marathon    124

**Taxidermist.**
Haight, James M , East Homer,    186

**Tobacconist.**
Fralick, Louis, Homer    132

**Toys and Fancy Goods.**
Gray, J C., Marathon    134

**Umbrellas.**
Bonner, W J , Homer    151

**Wood Turning.**
Potter, Allen, Blodget Mills    114

**Wool Carding.**
Potter, Allen, Blodget Mills    114

**Woolen Mills.**
Burke, Fitzsimons, Hone & Co , Rochester    2
Hayden Bros , Port Byron and Syracuse    203

---

**Chas. G. Brinck,** Wholesale dealer and manufacturer of Cigars, Brinck Block, Marathon, N Y , publishes a card on page 132 Those who want a genuine article will of course call on Brinck, and we can assure the public that his Cigars are made of *tobacco* and not of some other substance in a thin covering of Connecticut leaf

**Edwin A. Bennett & Co.,** of the Parlor Boot and Shoe store, 62 South Salina St , Syracuse, N Y , has recently opened to the public one of the largest and best selected stocks of boots and shoes to be found in Central New York In the custom department the best workmen that can be found are employed, and those who want a really elegant and easy fitting boot will do well to call at this establishment, a cut of the interior of which appears in connection with the advertisement on folded leaf, op pages 168-9 From long experience Mr Bennett thoroughly understands his business, and his increasing trade compelled him to remove to more extensive quarters, where the public can be better accommodated

**Louis Fralick,** No 2 Wall street, Homer, N Y , keeps constantly on hand a large assortment of the best brands of Tobacco, Snuff, Cigars and other articles found at a first class store of this kind We take pleasure in calling the attention of the public to his store, as it is centrally located and dealers will find a complete assortment to suit the taste of the most fastidious Give him a call ye lovers of the weed and test the truth of our statement His card appears on page 132

**A. H. Hoag,** dealer in Butter, Cheese, and all kinds of Farm Produce, Preble, N. Y , publishes a card on page 186 Mr Hoag understands his business and keeps thoroughly posted respecting the markets, and is able to pay the highest price for grain and other produce Dealers as well as producers will also find it for their advantage to give him their orders

**C. P. Mead's Business College** is advertised inside front cover This is one of the Chain of Bryant & Stratton's Colleges, so well known throughout the country. Young men who desire a thorough, practical, business education, will do well to call at the Pike Block and receive all the information required A separate department for young ladies, where they will receive instruction in the same course prescribed for young men For particulars see card as above

**Ranger's Photograph Parlors,** No 28 East Genesee St , Syracuse, have become a favorite resort for those desiring first class likenesses Mr Ranger has for a long time been noted as being a superior artist Parties calling on Mr Ranger at his rooms in the Franklin Buildings, will find him ever ready to accommodate See card, page 16

**D. W. Carr,** dealer in Foreign and Domestic Dry Goods, McGrawville, N Y , publishes a card on colored page 201 Mr Carr keeps a good assortment of Hats and Caps, Ready-made Clothing, Groceries, and everything usually found in a country store He deals upon the one price system, which is rapidly growing in favor with the public. Give him a call

**A. Carley & Son,** proprietors of the Marathon Mills, publish a card on colored page 133 This is both a flouring and a custom mill and is capable of grinding 500 bushels daily The proprietors deal largely in Grain of all kinds, Flour, Meal, Feed &c , a large stock of which is kept constantly on hand Messrs Carley are enterprising business men, and, by fair and honorable dealing, are extending their trade into Chenango, Broome and other Counties, while in Cortland it is also rapidly extending The Mill gives constant employment to six or eight men and employs a capital of $40,000.

# COURTS IN CORTLAND COUNTY, 1869.

### TO BE HELD AT THE COURT HOUSE IN CORTLAND VILLAGE

### SPECIAL TERMS OF THE SUPREME COURT, CIRCUIT COURTS AND COURTS OF OYER AND TERMINER.

First Monday in January, 1869, . . . . . . . . . . . . BOARDMAN, Justice
Last Monday in June, 1869,. .. . . . . . . . . . . . PARKER, Justice

### ADDITIONAL SPECIAL TERM, WITHOUT A JURY

First Tuesday in April, 1869, . . . . . PARKER, Justice

## COUNTY OFFICERS.

### Coroners.

P O ADDRESS

Angell, Jerome, .. Union Valley,
Barnes, N Rounds,. Cincinnatus
Pomeroy, T C , . Cortland Village

### County Clerk.

Place, Frank,. . Cortland Village

### County Judge.

Smith, Abram P , Cortland Village

### County Treasurer.

Webster, George W , .. Cortland Village

### District Attorney.

P O ADDRESS

Waters, Alvah D , Cortland Village

### Excise Commissioners.

Bowen, Ira, . Homer
Burgess, Lewis A , Marathon
Jones, George B , . Cortland Village

### Loan Commissioners.

Clark, A W , Scott
Green, Page, . . Virgil

### Sheriff

Brown, Isaac W , Cortland Village

## BOARD OF SUPERVISORS.

Cincinnatus, . Monroe E. Smith.
Cortlandville, Samuel E Welch
Cuyler, . . .. Alex Dunce
Freetown, . Hiram Hall
Harford, . . Samuel H Steel
Homer, . Geo W Phillips
Lapeer, Dann C Squires
Marathon, . Chas A Bouten

Preble, Matthias Van Hoesen
Scott, Isaac N Bellows
Solon, Johnson Wheeler.
Taylor, . . Oramel F Forbes
Truxton, . . . Joel McCall
Virgil, .. Roswell M. Price
Willet, .. .. ... Elisha F Nichols

## List of U. S. Internal Revenue Officers.

P. O ADDRESS

B F Tillinghast, . ... . Assistant Assessor, ... . Cincinnatus,
J P Holmes, . ... .. " " ... .... .. Cortland Village
B W Payne, .. . " " ... .. Homer
Harrison Hoyt, .Deputy Collector, . . ... . Homer

## GET THE BEST,
## IT COSTS NO MORE!

# HOWE'S
## NEW IMPROVED
## Family Sewing Machine!

THE SIMPLEST,
THE HANDSOMEST,
THE MOST COMPLETE,
THE BEST,

## SEWING MACHINE IN THE WORLD.

The Genuine has no Medallion Head.

## MARVIN & BISHOP,

**General Agents, 66 South Salina Street,**

# SYRACUSE, N. Y.

# RANGER'S PHOTOGRAPH PARLORS!

**Franklin Buildings,**

**28 E. Genesee St.,**

**SYRACUSE, N. Y.**

SOLAR PICTURES, CABINET CARDS, CARTES-DE-VISITE PICTURES, in the most elegant styles. Pictures Copied and Enlarged. Pictures Painted. First-Class Work only made at this Gallery. SARONY'S POSING APPARATUS, for making Graceful and Fancy Positions, has been added to this Gallery. Particular attention paid to COPYING, ENLARGING AND PAINTING OLD PICTURES.

**D. B. SPOONER,** a celebrated Painter from the Eastern States, has a Studio in connection with the Gallery.

The public are invited to call and examine specimens. Remember the place. I irst class work only made at this Gallery.

# W. V. RANGER.

**Henry F. Shirley,** Painter, Paper Hanger and Decorator, Cortland, N Y., publishes a card on page 128  Those who are acquainted with Mr Shirley and with his style of work will need no urging to continue their patronage  To others we say if you want your work done well, give him a call  If you wish to have your house painted or a beautiful sign, give the job to Shirley  He keeps on hand paints and varnishes for sale

**I. I. Goldsmith,** Tailor and dealer in Ready Made Clothing and Furnishing Goods, Cortland N Y , is constantly giving *fits* to the multitude who are thronging the Young America Clothing Store  First-class workmen employed and good materials used  The obliging proprietor of this establishment will spare no pains to give entire satisfaction in all cases  Give him a call  His card appears on colored page 151

**The Marathon News,** published at Marathon, Cortland Co , N Y , by C Dwight Smith, is a family paper replete with news and miscellaneous matter that render it an acceptable visitor to the homes of its patrons throughout the county  The variety contained in its local columns is an important feature of the paper, and one that adds materially to its interest as a local paper  Book and Job Printing is executed at the same office  See card, page 174

**Howe's New Improved Family Sewing Machine** is advertised on page 16 by Marvin & Bishop, General Agents, 66 South Salina Street, Syracuse, N Y  This machine is rapidly growing in favor with the public as its merits become known  The recent improvements made in this machine render it invaluable  Its simplicity, durability, ease of operation and perfection of mechanical construction are unsurpassed by any machine in the country  Try the Improved Howe before purchasing elsewhere

**Hayden Brothers,** proprietors of the Retail Woolen Mills, at Port Byron, have long been celebrated as being manufacturers of desirable and reliable goods  The establishment was started in 1824 as a small custom mill  Since then the greatly increased business has called for extensive additions and improvements, which have been made, and to day their cloth is known and worn in every county in the State and every State in the Union  They use only the best qualities of wool, entirely free from waste or shoddy, and employ only experienced and careful workmen who strive to maintain the reputation their goods have ever borne among their retail customers  A few months since they opened a store at No 29 Warren street, Syracuse, where they keep full lines of all goods of their manufacture  Farmers, mechanics and business men generally, can make good bargains by calling at the store, where Mr J W Gates, the manager, will be pleased to give them good goods at advantageous terms  See card, page 203

**Gregg Iron Works,** at Trumansburgh, Tompkins County, owned by Gregg, Plyer & Co., successors to James A Clapp, of Farmer Village, who established the first manufactory of agricultural implements in the southern part of Seneca Co , about the year 1847  Gregg, Plyer & Co removed to Trumansburgh in 1865  During that year they erected a substantial and commodious brick building in which to conduct their rapidly increasing business  It is a two story building, 101 feet long and 90 feet wide  Located in the western part of the village, it attracts the notice of all coming into town from that section  At these works are manufactured the celebrated Iron Mower, patented by Daniel H Thayer, of Ludlowville, in Tompkins Co  They are celebrated for their strength, simplicity and durability  They also manufacture Sharp's Patent Wheel Horse Rake, besides Threshing Machines, Clover Machines, and other agricultural implements  In the various departments the Company work up about 500 tons of cast and wrought iron, and 200 tons of coal annually

The works are admirably conducted — Only experienced and competent workmen, (of whom, when in full operation, there are about 55,) are employed, and the farmer who purchases a machine of this firm may rely on the investment s being a good one  See card, page 202

**Burke, Fitzsimons, Hone & Co.,** Importers, Jobbers and Retailers of Dry Goods, Fancy Goods and Woolens, No 53 Main street, Rochester, publish a card on page 2  This House was established in 1849, since which time its success has been uninterrupted, each year increasing its amount of business  Their annual sales amount to the enormous sum of near $1,500,000, their trade extending from the Eastern portions of the State to the "Far West"  Occupying, as they do, fully 25,000 feet of flooring in actual business departments, every portion of which is crowded with immense piles of goods from foreign countries, as well as of domestic manufacture, renders the facilities of this house for Jobbing equal to any in the country  The firm are also proprietors of the "Genesee Falls Woolen Mills," where they manufacture 100,000 yards of goods annually.

**The Daily Journal Steam Book & Job Printing Establishment,** 24 East Washington Street, Syracuse, advertises on page 188  We take pleasure in calling the attention of our patrons to this establishment as it is the largest Book and Job office in Central New York  Their great variety of type and materials enables the proprietors, Truair & Smith, to execute all kinds of plain and fancy work in a style excelled by none  A large corps of experienced workmen are always employed, and the ability and good taste of the Foreman of the office is a sufficient guaranty that all work will be executed in the best style of the art

# ABSTRACT FROM CENSUS REPORT
## OF 1865.
### CORTLAND COUNTY.

---

#### POPULATION

| TOWNS | Population in 1865. | Changes since 1855 | | VOTERS, 1865 | | | Aliens, 1865 | Colored persons not taxed, 1865 | Number, deducting aliens and colored persons not taxed |
|---|---|---|---|---|---|---|---|---|---|
| | | Increase | Decrease | Native | Naturalized | Total. | | | |
| Cincinnatus, | 1169 | 50 | | 333 | 7 | 340 | 4 | 1 | 1164 |
| Cortlandville, | 5008 | 679 | | 1251 | 109 | 1360 | 107 | 12 | 4889 |
| Cuyler,* | 1447 | 1447 | | 341 | 33 | 374 | 20 | | 1427 |
| Freetown, | 942 | | 13 | 247 | 19 | 266 | 16 | 1 | 923 |
| Harford, | 888 | | 38 | 235 | 5 | 240 | 4 | 1 | 883 |
| Homer, | 3856 | 71 | | 913 | 70 | 983 | 141 | 5 | 3710 |
| Lapeer, | 782 | 12 | | 198 | | 198 | | | 762 |
| Marathon, | 1485 | 144 | | 357 | 28 | 385 | 29 | 1 | 1455 |
| Preble, | 1267 | 48 | | 305 | 33 | 338 | 30 | | 1237 |
| Scott, | 1149 | | 144 | 319 | 12 | 331 | 12 | | 1137 |
| Solon, | 905 | | 62 | 242 | 29 | 271 | 7 | | 988 |
| Taylor, | 1107 | | 84 | 306 | 4 | 310 | 2 | 1 | 1164 |
| Truxton,* | 1689 | | 1755 | 331 | 78 | 409 | 112 | | 1577 |
| Virgil, | 2009 | | 222 | 499 | 21 | 520 | 28 | | 1981 |
| Willett, | 962 | 67 | | 259 | 8 | 267 | 19 | | 963 |
| Total, | 24815 | 240 | | 6136 | 456 | 6592 | 533 | 22 | 24260 |

#### AGRICULTURAL, ETC

| TOWNS. | Winter Wheat— bushe's harvested 1864 | Oats, bushels harvested 1864 | Indian Corn, bushels harvested 1864 | Potatoes, bushels harvested 1864 | Toba co, pounds harvested 1864 | Hops, pounds harvested 1864 | Apple , bushels, rvested 1864 | Milc , Cows, number of, 1865. | Butter, pounds made 1864 | Horses, two years old and over, 1865 | Sheep, number shorn 1865 |
|---|---|---|---|---|---|---|---|---|---|---|---|
| Cincinnatus, | 30 | 8871 | 6059 | 7689 | | 4450 | 11880 | 1408 | 160350 | 337 | 1146 |
| Cortlandville, | 1601 | 25510 | 40743 | 53488 | 4745 | 11790 | 42097 | 2915 | 335587 | 773 | 7302 |
| Cuyler, | 63 | 16575 | 6119 | 14658 | 900 | 21947 | 21893 | 2599 | 68862 | 404 | 2463 |
| Freetown, | | 7675 | 3220 | 7334 | 250 | 6100 | 15741 | 1744 | 131298 | 285 | 1296 |
| Harford, | 129 | 8768 | 4988 | 7247 | | | 11374 | 735 | 102000 | 217 | 1206 |
| Homer, | 2022 | 35727 | 28841 | 23888 | 5400 | 660 | 41261 | 3606 | 259289 | 749 | 5338 |
| Lapeer, | | 5067 | 3904 | 4572 | | | 8825 | 970 | 93039 | 388 | 1837 |
| Marathon, | 85 | 5517 | 4922 | 8293 | 2400 | 610 | 13328 | 1263 | 127000 | 829 | 1435 |
| Preble,. | 3178 | 26589 | 16170 | 11871 | 3751 | | 15855 | 1503 | 150547 | 884 | 2167 |
| Scott, | 555 | 18549 | 9257 | 10870 | 200 | 60862 | 12550 | 968 | 105450 | 356 | 3195 |
| Solon, | | 9217 | 4344 | 9570 | 500 | 6878 | 13669 | 6488 | 167668 | 365 | 1835 |
| Taylor, . | | 8964 | 4359 | 8525 | | 9641 | 11989 | 1499 | 165385 | 286 | 1484 |
| Truxton, | 90 | 13472 | 7554 | 17029 | 6800 | 19790 | 25187 | 8186 | 316260 | 483 | 1103 |
| Virgil, .. | 469 | 16221 | 13074 | 16514 | 150 | 2388 | 27167 | 2109 | 269095 | 664 | 4531 |
| Willett, . | | 3693 | 4037 | 9158 | | | 10621 | 977 | 136428 | 246 | 1515 |
| Total, | 6217 | 208981 | 151592 | 211196 | 25096 | 145317 | 282424 | 31920 | 2688778 | 6256 | 37732 |

*Cuyler, erected from Truxton in 1858

## ADDITIONAL STATISTICS FROM CENSUS OF 1865.

In addition to the above extracts we give the following *totals* for the County, as per returns for the several heads mentioned —
*Cash Value of Farms*, 1865, $10,629,627; of *Stock*, 1865, $2,295,608, of *Tools and Implements*, 1865, $439,819, *Acres Plowed*, 1865, 27,952¼; *Tons of Hay*, 1864, 75,451, *Winter Rye*, bushels harvested in 1864, 856; *Barley*, bushels harvested in 1864, 11,096¾; *Flax*, acres sown in 1865, 204; *Pounds of Lint*, 1864, 31,198, *Honey*, pounds collected in 1864, 17,112; *Working Oxen*, number in 1865, 945, *Neat Cattle*, number killed for beef in 1864, 3,042, *Swine*, number of pigs in 1865, 6,364, one year old and over, 1865, 7,226; slaughtered in 1864, 6,964; pounds of pork made, 1864, 1,567,973, *Wool*, pounds shorn, 1865, 137,291¼, *Sheep*, number of lambs raised, 1865, 20,579, number killed by dogs, 1864 240, *Poultry*, value owned, 1865, $16,979 30, value of eggs sold in 1864, $12,032 84 *Fertilizers* value bought, 1864, $2,385 40, *Domestic Manufactures*, 1864, yards of fulled cloth 2,791, yards of flannel, 13,427, yards of linen, 5,182; yards of cotton and mixed goods, 705; *Apples*, number of trees in fruit, 1864, 168,967, barrels of cider, 1864, 4,620

# SCHOOL STATISTICS,

## FOR THE YEAR ENDING SEPTEMBER 30, 1868

| TOWNS | No of Dists | No of Teachs | No of Pupils | Average Attendance | Amount Expended for year ending Sept 30, 1868 |
|---|---|---|---|---|---|
| Cincinnatus | 8 | 7 | 395 | 164 | $ 2030 05 |
| Cortlandville | 23 | 25 | 1616 | 565 | 10118 92 |
| Cuyler | 19 | | 473 | 194 | 2628 28 |
| Freetown | 8 | 8 | 366 | 127 | 2494 83 |
| Harford | 7 | 8 | 268 | 103 | 1873 78 |
| Homer | 21 | | 1104 | 369 | 5661 70 |
| Lapeer | 9 | 8 | 292 | 127 | 1391 34 |
| Marathon | 7 | 8 | 477 | 160 | 1984 70 |
| Preble | 12 | | 430 | 146 | 2210 85 |
| Scott | 9 | | 335 | 143 | 1825 65 |
| Solon | 10 | | 322 | 127 | 1663 24 |
| Taylor | 11 | | 369 | 160 | 2872 26 |
| Truxton | 15 | | 558 | 213 | 8116 50 |
| Virgil | 20 | 21 | 606 | 275 | 4108 25 |
| Willet | 8 | 8 | 276 | 122 | 1676 01 |
| Total | 187 | | 7786 | 2995 | |

# Post Offices and Post Masters in Cortland Co.

| POST OFFICE | TOWN | POST MASTER |
|---|---|---|
| Blodget Mills, | Cortlandville, | Peter R Tanner |
| Cincinnatus, | Cincinnatus, | N Rounds Barnes |
| Cortland Village, | Cortlandville, | Horace A Jarvis |
| Cuyler, | Cuyler, | Marshall Blanchard |
| East Homer, | Homer, | Luther H Rose |
| East Scott, | Scott, | Sylvester C Churchill. |
| East Virgil, | Virgil, | Alex McVean |
| Freetown Corners, | Freetown, | Jonathan J Hoxie |
| Harford, | Harford, | Samuel W Nelson |
| Harford Mills, | Harford, | David Wilcox |
| Homer, | Homer, | Geo J J Barber |
| Hunt's Corners, | Lapeer, | Wm E Hunt. |
| Keeney's Settlement, | Cuyler, | Wesley Fox |
| Lapeer, | Lapeer, | Royal Johnson |
| Little York, | Homer, | James E Corbing |
| Marathon, | Marathon, | Gabriel L Oakley |
| McGrawville, | Cortlandville, | Moses G Smith |
| Messengerville, | Virgil, | Bradley M House |
| Preble, | Preble, | Chester Markham |
| Scott, | Scott, | Hervey W Babcock. |
| Solon, | Solon, | Rufus T Peck. |
| South Cortland, | Cortlandville, | A P Rowley |
| Taylor, | Taylor, | Edmond Potter. |
| Texas Valley, | Marathon, | Wm H Isaacs |
| Truxton, | Truxton, | Geo H Arnold |
| Union Valley, | Taylor, | Nelson L Brooks |
| Virgil, | Virgil, | Elisha Winslow |
| Willet, | Willet, | David A. Wiles |

# THE STATES,

### THEIR SETTLEMENT, ADMITTANCE TO THE UNION, POPULATION,

#### SUFFRAGE LAWS, ETC

*ALABAMA* was settled near Mobile, in 1702, by the French; was formed into a Territory by act of Congress, approved March 3, 1817, from the eastern portion of the Territory of Mississippi, framed a Constitution August 2, 1819, and was admitted into the Union December 14 of the same year.  Area 50,722 square miles, or 32,462,080 acres — Population in 1860, 964,201, of whom 435,080 were slaves  It is the chief cotton growing State of the Union  White male citizens who have resided one year in the State and three months in the county, are entitled to vote  An election for a Convention was held December 24, 1860, and a majority of over 50,000 votes cast for secession , the Convention met January 7, 1861, and on the 11th passed the ordinance of secession, by a vote of 61 to 39, which was followed on the 21st by the resignation of its members of Congress.

*ARKANSAS* was settled at Arkansas Post in 1685, by the French, and was part of the Louisiana purchase ceded by France to the United States, April 30, 1803.  It was formed into a Territory by act of Congress, March 2, 1819, from the southern part of the Territory of Missouri; its western boundary was settled May 26, 1824, and its southern, May 19, 1828   Having adopted a Constitution, a memorial was presented in Congress, March 1, 1836, and an act for its admission into the Union passed June 15 of the same year  Area 52,198 square miles, or 33,406,-720 acres.  In 1860 its population was 435,450, of whom 111,115 were slaves.  It is an agricultural State, its staples being corn and cotton — Citizenship and residence in the State for six months, qualify voters in the county and district where they reside.  January 16, 1861, its Legislature ordered a State Convention, which assembled, and on May 6, voted to secede, 69 to 1   January 4, 1864, a Convention assembled in Little Rock, which adopted a new Constitution, the principle feature of which consisted in a clause abolishing slavery.  The Convention adjourned January 22   This body also inaugurated a Provisional Government  The Constitution was submitted to the people, and 12,177 votes cast for it, to 226 against it.  The State was re-organized under the plan contained in the Amnesty Proclamation of President LINCOLN, in pursuance of which an election was held March 14, 1864.  The vote required under the Proclamation was 5,405.  About 16,000 votes were cast.

B

*CALIFORNIA* was settled at Diego in 1768, by Spaniards, and was part of the territory ceded to the United States by Mexico, by the treaty concluded at Guadaloupe Hidalgo, February 22, 1848. After several ineffectual attempts to organize it as a Territory or admit it as a State, a law was passed by Congress for the latter purpose, which was approved September 9, 1850 Area 188,981 square miles, or 120,947,784 acres Population in 1860, 305,439. It is the most productive gold mining region on the continent, and also abounds in many other minerals — White male citizens of the United States, and those of Mexico who may choose to comply with the provisions of the treaty of Queretaro, of May 30, 1848, who have resided in the State six months and in the county or district thirty days, are entitled to vote.

*CONNECTICUT* was settled at Windsor, in 1633, by English Puritans from Massachusetts, and continued under the jurisdiction of that Province until April 23, 1662, when a separate charter was granted, which continued in force until a Constitution was formed, September 15, 1818 It was one of the original thirteen States, and ratified the United States Constitution, January 9, 1788 Area 4,674 square miles, or 2,991,360 acres. Population in 1860, 460,147. It is one of the most densely populated and principal manufacturing States in the Union Residence for six months, or military duty for a year, or payment of State tax, or a freehold of the yearly value of seven dollars, gives the right to vote

*DELAWARE* was settled at Wilmington, early in 1638, by Swedes and Finns; was granted to William Penn, in 1682, and continued under the government of Pennsylvania until the adoption of a Constitution, September 20, 1776, a new one was formed June 12, 1792 It was one of the original thirteen States, and ratified the United States Constitution, December 7, 1787. Area 2,120 square miles, or 1,356,800 acres — Population, in 1860, 112,216, of whom 1,798 were slaves. It is a grain and fruit growing State, with some extensive manufactories. Residence in the State one year, and ten days in the election district, with payment of a State or county tax assessed ten days prior to an election, gives the right to vote, except that citizens between twenty-one and twenty-two years of age need not have paid the tax.

*FLORIDA* was settled at St Augustine, in 1565, by Spaniards, was formed from part of the territory ceded by Spain to the United States by treaty of February 22, 1819; an act to authorize the President to establish a temporary government was passed March 3, 1819, articles of surrender of East Florida were framed July 10, and of West Florida, July 17, 1821, and it was then taken possession of by General Jackson as Governor An act for the establishment of a Territorial Government was passed March 30, 1822, and by act of March 3, 1823, East and West Florida were constituted one Territory. Acts to establish its boundary line between Georgia and Alabama were passed May 4, 1826, and March 2, 1831 After several ineffectual attempts to organize it into two Territories, or into a State and Territory, an act for its admission into the Union was passed March 3, 1845. Area 59,268 square miles, or 37,930,520 acres. Population, in 1860, 140,425, of whom 61,745 were slaves. It is an agricultural State, tropical in its climate and products. Every free white male citizen, who has resided in the State two years and in the county six months, and has been enrolled in the militia (unless exempt by law,) is qualified to vote; but no soldier, seaman or marine can vote unless qualified before enlistment. Its Legislature called a Convention, December 1, 1860, which met January 3, 1861, and passed a secession ordinance on the 10th by a vote of 62 to 7.

*GEORGIA* was settled at Savannah, in 1733, by the English under General Oglethorpe  It was chartered June 9, 1782, formed a Constitution February 5, 1777, a second in 1785 and a third May 30, 1798.— It was one of the original thirteen States, and ratified the United States Constitution January 2, 1788.  Area 58,000 square miles, or 37,120,000 acres  Population, in 1860, 1,057,286, of whom 462,198 were slaves  It is a large cotton and rice growing State  Citizens of the State, six months resident of the county where voting, who have paid taxes the year preceding the election, are entitled to vote.  November 18, 1860, its Legislature ordered an election for a State Convention, which assembled and passed a secession ordinance January 19, 1861, by a vote of 208 to 89, and on the 23d of the same month its members of Congress resigned　　*

*ILLINOIS* was settled at Kaskaskia, in 1683, by the French, and formed part of the northwestern territory ceded by Virginia to the United States.  An act for dividing the Indiana Territory and organizing the Territory of Illinois, was passed by Congress, February 3, 1809 , and an act to enable it to form a State Constitution, Government, &c , was passed April 18, 1818; a Constitution was framed August 26, and it was admitted into the Union December 23 of the same year.  Area 54,405 square miles, or 64,819,200 acres  Population, in 1860, 1,711,951  It is the chief "prairie" State, and the largest grain growing and second largest cattle raising State in the Union  All white male inhabitants, who have resided in the State one year and election district sixty days, can vote in the district where actually residing

*INDIANA* was settled at Vincennes, in 1690, by the French, and formed part of the northwestern territory ceded by Virginia to the United States.  It was organized into a Territory May 7, 1800, from which the Territory of Michigan was set off in 1805, and Illinois in 1809.  An act was passed to empower it to form a State Constitution, Government, &c , April 19, 1816, and it was admitted into the Union December 11 of the same year  Area 33,809 square miles, or 21,637,760 acres.  Population, in 1860, 1,350,428  It is an agricultural State, chiefly devoted to grain growing and cattle raising  A residence of one year in the State entitles males of 21 years of age to vote in the county of their residence.

*IOWA* was first settled at Burlington by emigrants from the Northern and Eastern States  It was part of the region purchased from France , was set off from the Territory of Wisconsin and organized as a separate Territory June 12, 1838; an act for its admission as a State was passed and approved March 3, 1845, to which the assent of its inhabitants was to be given to be announced by Proclamation of the President, and on December 28, 1846, another act for its admission was passed  Area 50,914 square miles or 32,584,960 acres.  Population, in 1860, 674,913  It is an agricultural State, resembling Illinois, and contains important lead mines. White male citizens of the United States, having resided in the State six months and county twenty days, are entitled to vote.

*KANSAS* was formed out of the original Louisiana purchase, and organized into a Territory by act of Congress, May 30, 1854, and after several ineffectual attempts was finally admitted into the Union in January, 1861 Area 78,418 square miles, or 50,187,520 acres Population, in 1860, 107,-206 It is an agricultural State, with a soil of rich and deep black loam, except the central portion, which is partly a desert The western portion is a fine grazing country, well wooded Residence in the State six months, and in the township or ward thirty days, confers the right of suffrage on white male citizens It also abounds in minerals.

*KENTUCKY* was settled in 1775, by Virginians; formed into a Territory by act of the Virginia Legislature, December 18, 1789, and admitted into the Union June 1, 1792, by virtue of an act of Congress passed February 4, 1791 Area 37,680 square miles, or 24,115,200 acres.— Population in 1860, 1,155,684, of whom 225,483 were slaves. It is an agricultural State, raising more flax and hemp than any other Loyalty, a residence of two years in the State and one in the county are the requirements to vote "Any citizen of this State who shall enter the service of the so-called Confederate States, in either a civil or military capacity, or into the service of the so-called Provisional Government of Kentucky, in either a civil or military capacity; or having heretofore entered such service of either the Confederate States or Provisional Government, shall continue in such service after this act takes effect, (March 11, 1862,) or shall take up or continue in arms against the military forces of the United States or State of Kentucky, or shall give voluntary aid and assistance to those in arms against said forces, shall be deemed to have expatriated himself, and shall no longer be a citizen, except by permission of the Legislature by a general or special statute."

*LOUISIANA* was settled at Iberville, in 1699, by the French, and comprised a part of the territory ceded by France to the United States, by treaty of April 30, 1803, which purchase was erected into two Territories by act of Congress March 26, 1804, one called the Territory of Orleans, the other the District of Louisiana, afterwards changed to that of Missouri.— Congress, March 2, 1806, authorized the inhabitants of Orleans Territory to form a State Constitution and Government when their population should amount to 60,000, a Constitution was adopted January 22, 1812, and the State admitted into the Union April 8 of the same year, under the name of Louisiana Area 41,255 square miles, or 26,403,200 acres. Population in 1860, 708,002, of whom 331,726 were slaves It is the chief sugar producing State of the Union Two years' residence in the State and one in the parish are the qualifications of voters December 10, 1860, the Legislature ordered a State Convention to be held, which assembled and passed an ordinance of secession January 26, 1861, by a vote of 113 to 17 The people voted on the question, and on March 28 the following was announced as the result For, 20,448, against, 17,296, a majority of 3,152 The Convention ratified the 'Confederate' Constitution March 11, 1861, by avote of 107 to 7, and refused to submit it to the people by 94 to 10 On the 11th day of January, 1864, Maj. Gen. Banks issued a Proclamation for an election of State officers and delegates to a Constitutional Convention, for the purpose of affecting a reconstruction of the State Government under the plan suggested in the Amnesty Proclamation of President Lincoln. The election was held on the 22d day of February, 1864 The officers thus elected were installed March 4 The total vote cast was 10,725. The vote requisite under the Proclamation was 5,051. The Convention amended the Constitution so as to abolish slavery. The new Constitution was adopted by the people by a vote of 6,836 for, to 1,566 against.

*MAINE* was settled at York, in 1623, by the English, and was formerly under the jurisdiction of Massachusetts. October 29, 1819, the inhabitants of the District of Maine framed a Constitution, applied for admission December 8, 1819. Congress passed an act March 3, 1820, and it was admitted as a State March 15, of the same year. Area 31,766 square miles, or 20,330,240 acres. Population, in 1860, 628,279. It is largely engaged in the lumber trade and ship building. Citizens of the United States, except paupers and persons under guardianship, who have resided in the State for three months next preceding the election, are entitled to vote.

*MARYLAND* was settled at St Mary, in 1634, by Irish Roman Catholics, having been chartered June 20, 1632. It was one of the original thirteen States; formed a Constitution August 14, 1776, and ratified the Constitution of the United States April 28, 1788. Area 11,124 square miles, or 7,119,260 acres. Population in 1860, 687,049, of whom 87,189 were slaves. It is mainly an agricultural State, producing grain and tobacco. A residence of one year in the State, and six months in the county, gives the right to vote to every white male citizen who takes the oath of allegiance prescribed in the Constitution. January 28, 1864, a bill passed the Legislature submitting to the people the question of a Convention to revise the Constitution of the State. The popular vote on the question was as follows · For Convention, 32,203; against, 18,337. The Convention assembled and adopted a Constitution abolishing slavery, which was submitted to and adopted by the people, and in accordance with its provisions, on the 29th of October, 1864, the Governor issued his Proclamation declaring the slaves in that State free from the 1st day of November.

*MASSACHUSETTS* was settled at Plymouth, November 3, 1620, by English Puritans, and Charters were granted March 4, 1629, January 13, 1630, August 20, 1726, and October 7, 1731. It was one of the original 13 States, adopted a Constitution March 2, 1780, which was amended November 3, 1820, and ratified the Constitution of the United States February 6, 1788. Area 7,800 square miles, or 4,992,000 acres. Population in 1860, 1,231,066. It is a largely commercial, the chief manufacturing and most densely populated State in the Union. A residence of one year in the State, and payment of State or county tax, gives the right to vote to male citizens of 21 years and upward, except paupers and persons under guardianship.

*MICHIGAN* was settled at Detroit in 1670, by the French, and was part of the territory ceded to the United States by Virginia. It was set off from the territory of Indiana, and erected into a separate Territory January 11, 1805, an act to attach to it all the territory of the United States west of the Mississippi river, and north of the State of Missouri, was passed June 28, 1834. Wisconsin was organized from it April 30, 1836. In June of the same year an act was passed to provide for the admission of the State of Michigan into the Union, and a Constitution having been adopted, it was admitted January 26, 1837. Area 56,243 square miles, or 35,995,552 acres. Population in 1860, 749,113. It is a grain growing and cattle rearing State, with rich and extensive mines of copper and iron in the Northern Peninsula. A residence in the State of six months preceding the election, entitles white male citizens to vote

*MINNESOTA* was settled about 1846, chiefly by emigrants from the Northern and Western States  It was organized as a Territory by act of Congress approved March 3, 1849, and admitted into the Union February 26, 1857.  Area 95,274 square miles, or 60,975,536 acres  Population in 1860, 172,123 whites, and about 25,000 Indians, many of the tribes being of a warlike character.  It is an agricultural State, chiefly devoted to Northern grains  The right to vote is extended to male persons of 21 years of age, of the following classes, if they have resided in the United States one year, the State four months, and the election district ten days·  White citizens of the United States, and those of foreign birth who have declared their intention to become citizens ; persons of mixed white and Indian blood who have adopted the customs of civilization, and those of pure Indian blood who have been pronounced capable by any district court of the State

*MISSISSIPPI* was settled at Natchez, in 1716, by the French, and was formed out of part of the territory ceded to the United States by South Carolina in 1787, and Georgia in 1802.  It was organized as a Territory by act of Congress, April 7, 1789, and enlarged on the north March 27, 1804, and on the south May 14, 1812  After several unsuccessful attempts to enter the Union, Congress finally passed an act March 1, 1817, enabling the people of the western part of the Territory to form a State Constitution and Government, which being complied with August 15, it was admitted December 10 of the same year  Area 47,156 square miles, or 30,179,840 acres  Population in 1860, 791,305, of whom 436,631 were slaves  It is the second cotton growing State of the Union  Citizens who have resided one year in the State, and four months in the county, and having performed military duty or paid taxes, are entitled to vote  A Convention met January 7, 1861, and on the 9th passed an ordinance of secession by a vote of 84 to 15.

*MISSOURI* was settled at Genevieve in 1763, by the French, and was part of the territory ceded by France by treaty of April 30, 1803  It was created under the name of the District of Louisiana, by an act approved March 26, 1804, and placed under the direction of the officers of the Indiana Territory, and was organized into a separate Territory June 4, 1812, its name being changed to that of Missouri, and was divided March 2, 1819, the Territory of Arkansas being then created.  An act authorizing it to form a State Constitution and Government was passed March 6, 1820, and it was admitted into the Union December 14, 1821  Area 67,380 square miles, or 43,123,200 acres  Population in 1860, 1,182,012, of whom 114,931 were slaves  An act of gradual emancipation was passed July 1, 1863, by a vote of 51 to 30.  On the 6th of January, 1865, a Constitutional Convention assembled in St. Louis, and on the 8th of April adopted a new Constitution, declaring the State free, prohibiting compensation for slaves, and adopting many other radical changes  On the 6th of June the Constitution was adopted by the people by a vote of 43,670 to 41,808, and pursuant to a Proclamation issued on the 1st of July, the Constitution went into effect July 4, 1865.  It is an agricultural and mining State.  Citizens of the United States who have resided in the State one year, and county three months, are entitled to vote  By an act passed by the Legislature of 1863, voting by ballot was adopted, and the *viva voce* system abolished.

*NEBRASKA* was settled by emigrants from the Northern and Western States, and was formed out of a part of the territory ceded by France, April 30, 1803  Attempts to organize it were made in 1844 and 1848, but it was not accomplished until May 30, 1854  Area 75,955 square miles, or 44,796,160 acres  Population 28,841, besides a few roving tribes of Indians.  A Convention adopted a State Constitution February 9, 1866, which was submitted to the people on the 22d of June, and adopted by a vote of 3,938 for, to 3,838 against, and State officers were elected.' A bill was passed by Congress, July 27th, admitting the State, but the President withheld his signature.  In February, 1867, Congress passed an act imposing certain conditions to admission, which were promptly accepted, and the territory became a State.  It is an agricultural region, its prairies affording boundless pasture lands

*NEVADA* was organized as a Territory March 2, 1861  Its name signifies snowy, and is derived from the Spanish word *nieve* (snow.)  It comprises 81,539 square miles, or 52,184,960 acres, lying mostly within the Great Basin of the Pacific coast.  Congress, at its session in 1864, passed an act which was approved March 21, to enable the people of the Territory to form a Constitution and State Government, in pursuance of which a Government was organized and the Territory admitted as a State by Proclamation of the President, October 31, 1864  At the time of its organization the Territory possessed a population of 6,857 white settlers  The development of her mineral resources was rapid and almost without parallel, and attracted a constant stream of immigration to the Territory  As the population has not been subject to the fluctuations from which other Territories have suffered, the growth of Nevada has been rapid and steady  At the general convention election of 1863, 10,934 votes were cast  During 1864 great accessions to the population were made.  It is probably the richest State in the Union in respect to mineral resources.  No region in the world is richer in argentiferous leads  It also contains an immense basin of salt, five miles square.  Quartz mills are a very important feature in mining operations  The State is barren for agricultural purposes, and is remarkably healthy

*NEW HAMPSHIRE* was settled at Dover, in 1623, by English Puritans, and continued under the jurisdiction of Massachusetts until September 18, 1679, when a separate charter was granted.  It was one of the original thirteen States, and ratified the United States Constitution June 21, 1788; its State Constitution was framed January 5, 1776, and amended in 1784 and 1792.  Area 9,280 square miles, or 5,939,200 acres. Population in 1860, 326,073.  It is a grazing and manufacturing State  All male citizens, except paupers, are allowed to vote.

*NEW JERSEY* was settled at Bergen, in 1624, by the Dutch and Danes , was conquered by the Dutch in 1655, and submitted to the English in 1664, being held thereafter under the same grants as New York, until it was surrendered to the Crown in 1702.  It was one of the original thirteen States, adopted a State Constitution July 2, 1776, and ratified the United States Constitution December 18, 1787  Area 8,320 square miles, or 5-, 824,800 acres  Population in 1860, 672,035.  It is a grain and fruit growing region, its orchard and market products being relatively greater than those of any other State.  A residence of one year in the State gives the right to vote, except to paupers, &c.

*NEW YORK* was settled at Manhattan, in 1614, by the Dutch ; was ceded to the English by grants to the Duke of York, March 20, April 26, and June 24, 1664 , was retaken by the Dutch in 1673, and surrendered again by them to the English, February 9, 1674. It was one of the original thirteen States ; ratified the United States Constitution July 26, 1788 ; framed a Constitution April 20, 1777, which was amended October 27, 1801, and November 10, 1821 ; a new one was adopted November 3, 1846 Area 47,000 square miles, or 30,080,000 acres. Population in 1865, 3,831,777 It is the most populous, wealthy and commercial of the States. White male citizens of the United States, who have resided in the State one year, in the county four months, and election district thirty days, are entitled to vote ; and all men of color who have resided in the State three years, and own and pay taxes on a freehold assessed at $250

*NORTH CAROLINA* was settled at Albemarle, in 1650, by the English, and was chartered March 20, 1663 It was one of the original thirteen States, and ratified the United States Constitution, November 21, 1789 , its State Constitution was adopted December 18, 1776, and amended in 1835 Area 50,704 square miles, or 32,450,560 acres Population in 1860, 992,622, of whom 331,059 were slaves It as an agricultural State, with some mines and extensive pine forests Every freeman of 21 years of age, having resided one year in any county in the State, may vote for a member of the House of Commons, but must own fifty acres of land to vote for a Senator A State Convention passed an ordinance of secession May 21, 1861 An election for delegates to a State Convention took place September 21, 1865. The Convention assembled October 2. On the 2d of October it passed an ordinance forever prohibiting slavery The Legislature ratified the Constitutional amendment December 1. An election was held on the first Thursday of November, for Governor, Members of Congress and the Legislature.

*OHIO* was settled at Marietta, in 1788, by emigrants from Virginia and New England ; was ceded by Virginia to the United States October 20, 1783 ; accepted by the latter March 1, 1784, and admitted into the Union April 30, 1802. Area 39,964 square miles, or 25,576,960 acres. Population in 1860, 2,339,511. It is the most populous and wealthy of the agricultural States, devoted principally to wool growing, grain and live stock A male of 21 years of age, who has resided in the State one year, and has paid or been charged with a State or county tax, is eligible to vote.

*OREGON,* although it had previously been seen by various navigators, was first taken possession of by Capt. Robert Gray, who entered the mouth of its principal river May 7, 1792, naming it after his vessel, the Columbia, of Boston. Exploring expeditions soon followed, and fur companies sent their trappers and traders into the region. In 1811 a trading post was established at the mouth of the Columbia river by the American Fur Company, who named it Astoria For some time a Provisional Territorial Government existed, but the boundary remained unsettled until the treaty with Great Britain in 1846, when the 49th parallel was adopted. It was formally organized as a Territory August 14, 1848 , was divided March 2, 1853, on the 46th parallel, the northern portion being called Washington and the southern Oregon. November 9, 1857, a State Constitution was adopted, under which it was admitted February 14, 1859, about one-third of it on the east being added to Washington Territory, its northern boundary following the Columbia river until its intersection with latitude 46° north. Area 102,606 square miles, or 65,667,840 acres. Population in 1860, 52,465. It is an agricultural State, possessed of a fertile soil, extensive pastures, genial climate, and is well wooded. Gold and other precious metals are found in considerable abundance.

*PENNSYLVANIA* was settled at Philadelphia, in 1681, by English Quakers, and was chartered February 28 of the same year. It was one of the original thirteen States, ratifying the United States Constitution December 12, 1787, adopted a State Constitution September 28, 1776, and amended it September 2, 1790. Area 46,000 square miles, or 29,440,000 acres. Population in 1860, 2,906,115. It is the second State in wealth and population, and the principal coal and iron mining region in the Union. Residence in the State one year, and ten days in the election district, with payment of a State or county tax assessed ten days prior to an election, gives the right to vote, except that citizens between 21 and 22 years of age need not have paid the tax.

*RHODE ISLAND* was settled at Providence in 1636, by the English from Massachusetts, under Roger Williams. It was under the jurisdiction of Massachusetts until July 8, 1662, when a separate charter was granted, which continued in force until the formation of a Constitution in September, 1842. It was one of the original thirteen States, ratifying the United States Constitution May 29, 1790. Area 1,306 square miles, or 835,840 acres. Population in 1860, 174,620. It is largely engaged in manufactures. A freehold possession of $13; or, if in reversion, renting for $7, together with a residence of one year in the State and six months in the town, or, if no freehold, then a residence of two years in the State and six months in the town, and payment of $1 tax or military service instead, are the qualifications of voters.

*SOUTH CAROLINA* was settled at Port Royal, in 1670, by the English, and continued under the charter of Carolina, or North Carolina, until they were separated in 1729. It was one of the original thirteen States, ratifying the United States Constitution May 23, 1798, it framed a State Constitution March 26, 1776, which was amended March 19, 1778, and June 3, 1790. Area 29,385 square miles, or 18,806,400 acres. Population in 1860, 703,708, of whom 402,406 were slaves, an excess of 101,270 over the whites. It is the principal rice-growing State. Whites, who have resided in the State two years and district six months, and have a freehold of fifty acres of land, or have paid a State tax, are entitled to vote. December 17, 1860, a Convention assembled in Columbia, adjourned to Charleston, and on the 24th unanimously adopted an ordinance of secession, which was followed the next day by a Declaration of Causes claimed to be sufficient to justify the act. An election for delegates to a State Convention was held September 4, 1865. The Convention assembled September 13, and adjourned on the 28th. It repealed the ordinance of secession, abolished slavery, equalized the representation of the Senate and taxation throughout the State, giving the election of Governor and Presidential electors to the people, ordered voting in the Legislature by *viva voce*, endorsed the Administration unanimously, and directed a commission to submit a code to the Legislature for the protection of the colored population. The Legislature ratified the Constitutional Amendment November 13, 1865.

*TENNESSEE* was settled at Fort Donelson, in 1756, by emigrants from Virginia and North Carolina; was ceded to the United States by North Carolina, December, 1789, conveyed by the Senators of that State February 25, 1790, and accepted by act of Congress April 2 of the same year, it adopted a Constitution Feb. 6, 1796, and was admitted into the Union the 1st of June following. Area 45,600 square miles, or 29,184,000 acres  Population in 1860, 1,109,601, of whom 275,179 were slaves  It is a mining and agricultural State, and is largely productive of live stock. Citizens of the United States who have resided six months in the county are entitled to vote.  A military league was formed between the Governor, Isham G. Harris, and the rebel States, May 7, 1861, ratified the same day by the Senate by a vote of 14 to 6, and a Declaration of Independence submitted to the people, the election to be held June 8, the result of which was declared by the Governor, June 24, to be 104,913 for, and 47,238 against  This movement not being acceptable to the people of East Tennessee, which had declared against separation by a vote of 32,923 to 14,780, they, in a Convention held at Greenville, June 18–21, repudiated it.  Andrew Johnson, Provisional Governor of the State, called a State Convention to be held in Nashville the second Monday in January.  Delegates were elected, the Convention met, declared slavery forever abolished, prohibited compensation to owners of slaves, and abrogated the secession ordinances  These amendments of the Constitution were submitted to the people 22d of February, 1865, with the following result  For ratification, 22,197, rejection, 63  The United States Constitutional Amendment was ratified April 5, 1865.

*TEXAS* was first settled at Bexar, in 1694, by Spaniards; formed a part of Mexico until 1836, when she revolted from that Republic and instituted a separate Government, under which she existed until admitted into the Union by a joint resolution approved March 1st, 1845, imposing certain conditions, which were accepted, and a Constitution formed July 4 of the same year, and another joint resolution adopted by Congress, consummating the annexation, was approved December 29, 1845.  Area 237,504 square miles, or 152,002,500 acres  Population in 1860, 604,215, of whom 182,566 were slaves.  It is an agricultural region, principally devoted to grain, cotton and tropical fruits  Free white male citizens of 21 years of age, who have resided in the State one year and district six months are entitled to vote.  A Convention assembled at Galveston January 28, 1861, and on February 1 passed an ordinance of secession, by a vote of 166 to 7, to be submitted to the people February 23, and on March 4 they declared the State out of the Union, and Gov. Houston issued a Proclamation to that effect.

*VERMONT* was settled in 1724, by Englishmen from Connecticut, chiefly under grants from New Hampshire; was formed from a part of the territory of New York, by act of its Legislature March 6, 1769, framed a Constitution December 25, 1777, and was admitted into the Union March 4, 1791, by virtue of an act of Congress passed February 18 of the same year  Area 10,212 square miles, or 6,535,680 acres.  Population in 1860, 315,098.  It is a grazing region, producing more wool, live stock, maple sugar, butter, cheese and hay, in proportion to its population, than any other State.  Any citizen of the United States who has resided in the State one year, and will take the oath of allegiance, is entitled to vote

*VIRGINIA* was settled at Jamestown, in 1607, by the English, and was chartered April 10, 1606, May 23, 1609, and March 12, 1612.  It was one of the original thirteen States, ratifying the United States Constitution June 25, 1788, it framed a State Constitution July 5, 1776, which was amended January 15, 1880. The State was divided in 1863 Present area 37,352 square miles. Population in 1860, 1,314,533, of whom 481,-410 weie slaves It is a large corn producing, and the chief tobacco grow-ing State Every white male citizen of the age of 21 years, who has been a resident of the State for one year, and of the county, city or town where he offers to vote for six months next preceding an election, and has paid all taxes assessed to him, after the adoption of the Constitution, under the laws of the Commonwealth after the re-organization of the county, city or town where he offers to vote, is qualified to vote for members of the General Assembly and all officers elective by the people A Convention sitting in Richmond on the 17th of April, 1861, passed an ordinance of secession, by a vote of 88 to 55, which was submitted to the people at an election held May 23, the result of which was announced June 25 to be 128,824 for, and 32,134 against. The State Government was re-organized by a Convention which met at Wheeling, May 11, 1861. Upon the divi-sion of the State in 1863, the seat of Government was removed to Alexan-dria A State Constitutional Convention, March 10, 1864, adopted a sec-tion abolishing slavery.

*WEST VIRGINIA.*—On the passage of the ordinance of se-cession by the Virginia Convention, a Convention of the western and other loyal counties of the State was held at Wheeling, which assembled May 11, 1861, and on the 17th nnanimously deposed the then State officers and organized a Provisional Government On the 26th of November, 1861, a Convention representing the western counties assembled in Wheeling and framed a Constitution for West Virginia, which was submitted to the people on the 3d of May, 1862, and adopted by them by a nearly unani-mous vote. The division of the State was sanctioned by the Legislature May 13, 1862, and ratified by Congress by an act approved December 31, 1862, conditioned on the adoption of an amendment to the Constitution providing for the gradual abolition of slavery, which was done on the 24th of March, 1863, by a vote of the qualified electors of the proposed State, 28,318 voting in favor of the amendment, and 572 against it. In pursu-ance of the act of Congress, the President issued a Proclamation, April 20, 1863, admitting the State sixty days from the date thereof, and on the 20th of June the new State Government was formally inaugurated Area 24,000 square miles Population in 1860, 350,599, of whom 12,754 were slaves It is a large corn producing State, and abounds in coal and other minerals The Alexandria Legislature adopted the United States Consti-tutional Amendment February 9, 1865 White male citizens, residents of the State one year and county thirty days, unless disqualified by rebellion, are entitled to vote.

*WISCONSIN* was settled at Green Bay, in 1669, by the French; was a part of the territory ceded by Virginia, and was set off from Mich-igan December 24, 1834, and was organized into a Territory April 30, 1836. Iowa was set off from it June 12, 1838, and acts were passed at various times setting its boundaries March 3, 1847, an act for its admis-sion into the Union was passed, to take effect on the issuing of a Procla-mation by the President, and by act of May 29, 1848, it was admitted into the Union Area 53,924 square miles, or 34,511,360 acres. Population in 1860, 775,881 It is an agricultural State, chiefly engaged in grain raising and wool growing Both white and colored citizens of the United States, or white foreigners who have declared their intention to become citizens, are entitled to vote Colored citizens were admitted to the franchise, by a decision of the Supreme Court, rendered the 27th day of March, 1866, holding that, whereas an election was held in 1849, under the provisions of chapter 137, of that year, at which election 5,265 votes were cast in favor of the extension of the right of suffrage to colored men, and 4,075 against such extension, therefore, the section of said law conferring such right had been constitutionally adopted and is the law of the land.

# THE  TERRITORIES,

### THEIR BOUNDARIES, AREA, PHYSICAL FEATURES, ETC

*ALASKA,* our new territory, recently purchased of Russia, comprehends all the north-west coast on the Pacific, and the adjacent islands north of the parallel of 50 degrees 40 minutes north, and the portion of the mainland west of the meridian (about 140° west) of Mount St. Elias.  The area is computed at 481,276 square miles.  The climate, although warmer than in the same latitude on the eastern coast, is too rigorous to admit of successful agricultural operations, and the chief value of the country and adjacent seas is derived from their fisheries and hunting grounds  The southern and central portions are mountainous; the northern portion along the Arctic ocean is quite flat, nowhere rising more than fifteen or twenty feet above the sea.  The population is estimated at about 80,000, mostly Esquimeaux

*ARIZONA* was organized by the Thirty-Seventh Congress, in the winter of 1863, out of the western half of New Mexico, the boundary between the two Territories being the 109th meridian (32d west from Washington,) and includes the greater portions of the valleys of Colorado and Gila, which two rivers drain its entire surface, with parts of Utah, New Mexico and Nevada, and yet convey, it is reported, a less volume of water to the sea than the Hudson at Albany.  The fertile Messilla Valley was left with New Mexico  The Territory forms a block nearly square, and contains 126,141 square miles, or 80,730,240 acres  Its white population is probably considerably less than  10,000  For agricultural purposes it is probably the most worthless on the Continent, owing to the absence of rains, but it is reputed to abound in silver mines.

*COLORADO* was organized March 2, 1861, from parts of Kansas, Nebraska and Utah, and is situated on each side of the Rocky Mountains, between latitude 37° and 41°, and longitude 25° and 32° west from Washington.  Area 104,500 square miles, or 66,880,000 acres.  Population 50,-000, besides numerous tribes of Indians.  By an enabling act passed March 21, 1864, the people of the Territory were authorized to frame a State Constitution and organize a State Government, and a Convention accordingly met in 1865, and on the 12th of August adopted a Constitution, which was submitted to and adopted by the people September 5, and State officers elected November 14.  A bill to admit the Territory as a State passed Congress, but was vetoed May 25, 1866.  It is said to be a superior grazing and cattle producing region, with a healthy climate and rich soil. An extensive coal bed, and also gold, iron and other minerals abound.

*DAKOTA* was first settled by emyloyees of the Hudson Bay Company, but is now being peopled by emigrants from the Northern and Western States. It was set off from the western portion of Minnesota when that Territory became a State in 1857, and was organized March 2, 1861. Area 148,932 square miles, or 95,316,480 acres Population 2 576 whites, and 2,261 Indians, besides the roving tribes.

*IDAHO* was organized by the Thirty-Seventh Congress, at its second session, in the winter of 1863. Its name means 'Bead of the Mountains,' and it embraces the whole breadth of the Rocky Mountain region, and has within its bounds the head waters of nearly all the great rivers that flow down its either slope, but the greater portion lies east of the mountains Its southern boundary is the 41st, its northern the 46th parallel of latitude. It extends from the 104th meridian on the east to the 110th on the west. Area 326,373 square miles, or 208,870,720 acres. For agricultural purposes it is comparatively worthless, but abounds in gold and other valuable mines

*MONTANA* was settled by emigrants from the Northern and Western States. Organized in 1864, with the following boundaries Commencing at a point formed by the intersection of the 27° L W. from Washington with the 45° N. L., thence due west on said 45th degree to a point formed by its intersection with the 34th degree W. from Washington, thence due south along said 34th degree of longitude to its intersection with the 44th degree and 30 minutes of N L , thence due west along said 44th degree and 30 minutes of N. L. to a point formed by its intersection with the crest of the Rocky Mountains; thence following the crest of the Rocky Mountains northward till its intersection with the Bitter Root Mountains; thence northward along the crest of said Bitter Root Mountains to its intersection with the 39th degree of longitude W. from Washington, thence along said 39th degree of longitude northward to the boundary line of the British possessions; thence eastward along said boundary to the 27th degree of longitude W from Washington; thence southward along said 27th degree to the place of beginning This makes it the northermost Territory next the States east of the Missouri Valley. It is a good mining and agricultural region The total population is put down at 15,822. Large accessions have been made since the census was taken.

*NEW MEXICO* was formed from a part of the territory ceded to the United States by Mexico, by the treaty of Guadaloupe Hidalgo, February 2, 1848, and was organized into a Territory September 9, 1850 — Area 121,201 square miles, or 77,568,640 acres. Population 83,000, besides large tribes of warlike Indians The principal resource of the country is its minerals.

*UTAH* was settled by the Mormons, and was formed from a part of the territory ceded to the United States by Mexico, by the treaty of Guadaloupe Hidalgo, February 2, 1848, and was organized into a Territory, September 9, 1850. Area, 106,382 square miles, or 68,084,480 acres Population, 40,273, of whom 29 were slaves Brine, sulphureous and chalybeate springs abound; limestone, granite, sandstone and marble are found in large quantities; iron is abundant, and gold, silver, copper, lead and zinc have been found. Not one-fiftieth part of the soil is fit for tillage, but on that which is, abundant crops of grain and considerable cotton are raised A Convention was held at Great Salt Lake City, January 22, 1862, and a State Constitution formed, but it has not been acted on by Congress.

*WASHINGTON* was settled by emigrants from the Northern and Western States, and was organized into a Territory, March 2, 1853, from the northern portion of Oregon, to which was added another portion from the eastern part when the latter Territory was admitted as a State, February 14, 1859  Area  69,994 square miles, or 48,636,800 acres.  Population 11,168, besides numerous tribes of Indians.

*WYOMING* was organized in July 1868  It lies between the 27th and 84th meridians of longitude west from Washington, and between the 41st and 45th parallels of latitude  The Territory is rich in mineral wealth, having large quantities of iron, coal, gypsum and building stone, besides vast quantities of gold, silver and copper.  Salt springs of great value are found within its limits.  The western portion of the Territory embraces what is generally known as the "Sweet Water Mines."  The climate is healthy, and the Territory is rapidly filling up with an enterprising and hardy population.  The act of Congress organizing the Territory, provides that "There shall be no denial of the elective franchise or any other right, on account of color or race, and all persons shall be equal before the law."

# STAMP DUTIES.

### SCHEDULE OF DUTIES ON AND AFTER MARCH 1, 1867

| | Stamp Duty. |
|---|---|
| Accidental injuries to persons,tickets, or contracts for insurance against, | exempt |
| Affidavite, | exempt. |
| Agreement or contract not otherwise specified: | |
| For every sheet or piece of paper upon which either of the same shall be written, | $0 5 |
| Agreement, renewal of,same stamp as original instrument. | |
| Appraisement of value or damage, or for any other purpose  For each sheet of paper on which it is written, | 5 |
| Assignment of a lease, same stamp as original, and additional stamp upon the value or consideration of transfer, according to the rates of stamps on deeds  (See Conveyance ) | |
| Assignment of policy of insurance, same stamp as original instrument.  (See Insurance.) | |
| Assignment of mortgage, same stamp as that required upon a mortgage for the amount remaining unpaid  (See Mortgage,) | |
| Bank check, draft or order for any sum of money drawn upon any | |

| | Stamp Duty |
|---|---|
| bank, banker or trust company at sight or on demand, | 2 |
| When drawn upon any other person or persons, companies or corporations, for any sum exceeding $10, at sight or on demand, | 2 |
| Bill of exchange, (inland,) draft or order for the payment of any sum of money not exceeding $100, otherwise than at sight or on demand, or any promissory note, or any memorandum, check, receipt, or other written or printed evidence of an amount of money to be paid on demand or at a time designated : For a sum not exceeding $100, | 5 |
| And for every additional $100 or fractional part thereof in excess of $100, | 5 |
| Bill of exchange, (foreign,) or letter of credit drawn in, but payable out of, the United States :  If drawn singly, same rates of duty as inland bills of exchange or promissory notes  If drawn in sets of three or more, for every bill of each set, where the sum made payable shall not | |

Stamp Duty.

exceed $100 or the equivalent thereof in any foreign currency And for every additional $100, or fractional part thereof in excess of $100, ......... 2

Bill of lading or receipt (other than charter party) for any goods, merchandise, or effects to be exported from a port or place in the United States to any foreign port or place, ......... 10

Bill of lading to any port in British North America, ......... exempt

Bill of lading, domestic or inland, ......... exempt.

Bill of sale by which any ship or vessel, or any part thereof, shall be conveyed to or vested in any other person or persons
When the consideration shall not exceed $500, ......... 50
Exceeding $500, and not exceeding $1,000, ......... 1 00
Exceeding $1,000, for every additional $500, or fractional part thereof, ......... 50

Bond for indemnifying any person for the payment of any sum of money When the money ultimately recoverable thereupon is $1,000 or less, ......... 50
When in excess of $1,000, for each $1,000 or fraction, ......... 50

Bond administrator or guardian, when the value of the estate and effects, real and personal, does not exceed $1,000, ......... exempt
Exceeding $1,000, ......... 1 00

Bond for due execution or performance of duties of office, ......... 1 00

Bond, personal, for security for the payment of money. (See Mortgage )

Bond of any description, other than such as may be required in legal proceedings, or used in connection with mortgage deeds, and not otherwise charged in this schedule, ......... 25

Broker's notes. (See Contract.)

Certificates of measurement or weight of animals, wood, coal or hay, ......... exempt.

Certificates of measurement of other articles, ......... 5

Certificates of stock in any incorporated company, ......... 25

Certificates of profits, or any certificate or memorandum showing an interest in the property or accumulations of any incorporated company If for a sum not less than $10 and not exceeding $50, ......... 10
Exceeding $50 and not exceeding $1,000, ......... 25
Exceeding $1,000, for every additional $1,000 or fractional part thereof, ......... 25

Certificate Any certificate of damage or otherwise, and all other certificates or documents issued by any port warden, ma-

Stamp Duty.

rine surveyor, or other person acting as such, ......... 25

Certificate of deposit of any sum of money in any bank or trust company, or with any banker or person acting as such. If for a sum not exceeding $100, ......... 2
For a sum exceeding $100 ......... 5

Certificate of any other description than those specified, ......... 5

Charter, renewal of, same stamp as an original instrument

Charter party for the charter of any ship or vessel, or steamer, or any letter, memorandum, or other writing relating to the charter, or any renewal or transfer thereof. If the registered tonnage of such ship, vessel, or steamer does not exceed 150 tons, ......... 1 00
Exceeding 150 tons, and not exceeding 300 tons, ......... 3 00
Exceeding 300 tons, and not exceeding 600 tons, ......... 5 00
Exceeding 600 tons, ......... 10 00

Check Bank check, ......... 2

Contract Broker's note, or memorandum of sale of any goods or merchandise, exchange, real estate, or property of any kind or description issued by brokers or persons acting as such:
For each note or memorandum of sale, ......... 10

Bill or memorandum of the sale or contract for the sale of stocks, bonds, gold or silver bullion, coin, promissory notes, or other securities made by brokers, banks, or bankers, either for the benefit of others or on their own account For each hundred dollars, or fractional part thereof, of the amount of such sale or contract, ......... 1

Bill or memorandum of the sale or contract for the sale of stocks, bonds, gold or silver bullion, coin, promissory notes, or other securities, not his or their own property, made by any person, firm, or company not paying a special tax as broker, bank or banker: For each hundred dollars, or fractional part thereof, of the amount of such sale or contract, ......... 5

Contract (See Agreement )

Contract, renewal of, same stamp as original instrument

Conveyance, deed, instrument or writing, whereby any lands tenements, or other realty sold shall be granted, assigned, transferred, or otherwise conveyed to or vested in the purchaser or purchasers, or any other person or persons, by his, her or their direction, when the consideration or value does not exceed $500, ......... 50

| | Stamp Duty |
|---|---|
| When the consideration exceeds $500, and does not exceed $1,000, | 1 00 |
| And for every additional $500, or fractional part thereof, in excess of $1,000, | 50 |
| Conveyance   The acknowledgment of a deed, or proof by a witness, | exempt |
| Conveyance   Certificate of record of a deed, | exempt |
| Credit, letter of.  Same as foreign bill of exchange | |
| Custom-house entry   (See Entry ) | |
| Custom-house withdrawals.  (See Entry ) | |
| Deed   (See  Conveyance — Trust deed ) | |
| Draft   Same as inland bill of exchange, | |
| Endorsement of any negotiable instrument, | exempt. |
| Entry of any goods, wares or merchandise at any custom-house, either for consumption or warehousing   Not exceeding $100 in value, | 25 |
| Exceeding $100, and not exceeding $500 in value, | 50 |
| Exceeding $500 in value, | 1 00 |
| Entry for the withdrawal of any goods or merchandise from bonded warehouse, | 50 |
| Gauger's returns, | exempt |
| Indorsement upon a stamped obligation in acknowledgment of its fulfillment, | exempt |
| Insurance (life) policy: When the amount insured shall not exceed $1,000, | 25 |
| Exceeding $1,000, and not exceeding $5,000, | 50 |
| Exceeding $5,000, | 1 00 |
| Insurance (marine, inland, and fire,) policies, or renewal of the same : If the premium does not exceed $10, | 10 |
| Exceeding $10, and not exceeding $50, | 25 |
| Exceeding $50, | 50 |
| Insurance contracts or tickets against accidental injuries to persons, | exempt |
| Lease, agreement, memorandum, or contract for the hire, use, or rent of any land, tenement, or portion thereof   Where the rent or rental value is $300 per annum or less, | 50 |
| Where the rent or rental value exceeds the sum of $300 per annum, for each additional $300, or fractional part thereof in excess of $300, | 50 |
| Legal documents : | |
| Writ, or other original process, by which any suit, either criminal or civil, is commenced in any court, either of law or equity, | exempt |
| Confession of judgment or cognovit, | exempt |
| Writs or other process on ap- | |

| | Stamp Duty |
|---|---|
| peals from justice courts or other courts of inferior jurisdiction to a court of record | exempt. |
| Warrant of distress | exempt. |
| Letters of administration.  (See Probate of will ) | |
| Letters testamentary, when the value of the estate and effects, real and personal, does not exceed $1,000, | Exempt |
| Exceeding $1,000, | 5 |
| Letters of credit   Same as bill of exchange, (foreign ) | |
| Manifest for custom-house entry or clearance of the cargo of any ship, vessel, or steamer, for a foreign port · | |
| If the registered tonnage of such ship, vessel, or steamer does not exceed 300 tons, | 1 00 |
| Exceeding 300 tons, and not exceeding 600 tons, | 3 00 |
| Exceeding 600 tons, | 5 00 |
| [These provisions do not apply to vessels or steamboats plying between ports of the United States and British North America ] | |
| Measurers' returns, | exempt. |
| Memorandum of sale, or broker's note   (See Contract.) | |
| Mortgage of lands, estate, or property, real or personal, heritable or movable, whatsoever, a trust deed in the nature of a mortgage, or any personal bond given as security for the payment of any definite or certain sum of money , exceeding $100, and not exceeding $500, | 50 |
| Exceeding $500, and not exceeding $1,000, | 1 00 |
| And for every additional $500, or fractional part thereof, in excess of $1,000, | 50 |
| Order for payment of money, if the amount is $10, or over, | 2 |
| Passage ticket on any vessel from a port in the United States to a foreign port, not exceeding $35, | 50 |
| Exceeding $35, and not exceeding $50, | 1 00 |
| And for every additional $50, or fractional part thereof, in excess of $50, | 1 00 |
| Passage tickets to ports in British North America, | exempt. |
| Pawner's checks, | 5 |
| Power of attorney for the sale or transfer of any stock, bonds or scrip, or for the collection of any dividends or interest thereon, | 25 |
| Power of attorney, or proxy, for voting at any election for officers of any incorporated company or society, except religious, charitable, or literary societies, or public cemeteries, | 10 |
| Power of attorney to receive or collect rent, | 25 |
| Power of attorney to sell and convey real estate, or to rent or | |

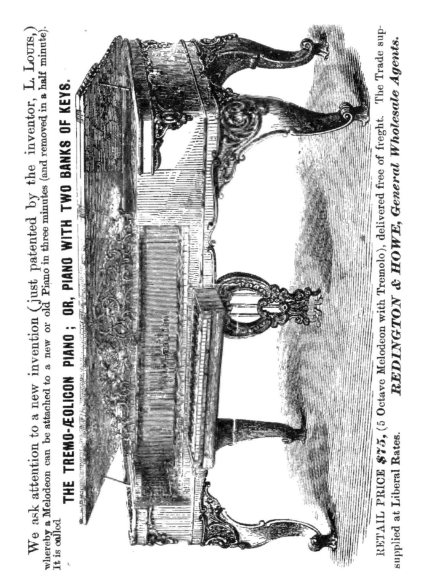

| | Stamp Duty. |
|---|---|
| lease the same, | 1 00 |
| Power of attorney for any other purpose, | 50 |
| Probate of will, or letters of administration, where the estate and effects for or in respect of which such probate or letters of administration applied for shall be sworn or declared not to exceed the value of $1,000, | exempt |
| Exceeding $1,000, and not exceeding $2,000, | 1 00 |
| Exceeding $2,000, for every additional $1,000, or fractional part thereof, in excess of $2,000, | 50 |
| Promissory note. (See Bill of exchange, inland.) | |
| Deposit note to mutual insurance companies, when policy is subject to duty, | exempt |
| Renewal of a note, subject to the same duty as an original note | |
| Protest of note, bill of exchange, acceptance, check, or draft, or any marine protest, | 25 |
| Quit-claim deed to be stamped as a conveyance, except when given as a release of a mortgage by the mortgagee to the mortgagor, in which case it is exempt, but if it contains covenants may be subject as an agreement or contract | |
| Receipts for satisfaction of any mortgage or judgment or decree of any court, | exempt |
| Receipts for any sum of money or debt due, or for a draft or other instrument given for the payment of money, exceeding $20, not being for satisfaction of any mortgage or judgment or decree of court, (See Indorsement.) | 2 |
| Receipts for the delivery of property. | exempt |
| Renewal of agreement, contract or charter, by letter or otherwise, same stamp as original instrument. | |
| Sheriff's return on writ or other process, | exempt |
| Trust deed, made to secure a debt, to be stamped as a mortgage | |
| Warehouse receipts, | exempt. |
| Warrant of attorney accompanying a bond or note, if the bond or note is stamped, | exempt. |
| Weigher's returns, | exempt |
| Official documents, instruments, and papers issued by officers of the United States Government, | exempt. |
| Official instruments, documents, and papers issued by the officers of any State, county, town, or other municipal corporation, in the exercise of functions strictly belonging to them in their ordinary governmental or municipal capacity, | exempt. |
| Papers necessary to be used for | |

the collection from the United States Government of claims by soldiers, or their legal representatives, for pensions, back pay, bounty, or for property lost in the service, **exempt.**

## CANCELLATION

In all cases where an *adhesive* stamp is used for denoting the stamp duty upon an instrument, the person using or affixing the same must write or imprint thereupon *in ink* the initials of his name, and the date (the year, month, and day) on which the same is attached or used. Each stamp should be separately cancelled. When stamps are printed upon checks, &c., so that in filling up the instrument, the face of the stamp is and must necessarily be written across, no other cancellation will be required.

All cancellation must be distinct and legible, and except in the case of proprietary stamps from private dies, no method of cancellation which differs from that above described can be recognized as legal and sufficient.

## PENALTIES.

A penalty of fifty dollars is imposed upon every person who makes, signs, or issues, or who causes to be made, signed, or issued, any paper of any kind or description whatever, or who accepts, negotiates, or pays, or causes to be accepted, negotiated, or paid, any bill of exchange, draft, or order, or promissory note, for the payment of money, without the same being duly stamped, or having thereupon an adhesive stamp for denoting the tax chargeable thereon, cancelled in the manner required by law, with intent to evade the provisions of the revenue act.

A penalty of two hundred dollars is imposed upon every person who pays, negotiates, or offers in payment, or receives or takes in payment, any bill of exchange or order for the payment of any sum of money drawn or purporting to be drawn in a foreign country, but payable in the United States, until the proper stamp has been affixed thereto.

A penalty of fifty dollars is imposed upon every person who fraudulently makes use of an adhesive stamp to denote the duty required by the revenue act, without effectually cancelling and obliterating the same in the manner required by law.

Attention is particularly called to the following extract from section 155, of the act of June 30, 1864, as amended by the act of July 13, 1866.

"If any person shall wilfully remove or cause to be removed, alter or cause to be altered, the cancelling or defacing marks on any adhesive stamp, with intent to use the same, or to cause the use of the same, after it shall have been used once, or shall knowingly or wilfully sell or buy such washed or restored stamps, or offer the same for sale, or give or expose the same to any per-

C

son tor use, or knowingly use the same or prepare the same with intent for the further use thereof, or if any person shall knowingly and without lawful excuse (the proof whereof shall lie on the person accused) have in his possession any washed, restored or altered stamps, which have been removed from any vellum, parchment, paper, instrument or writing, then, and in every such case, every person so offending, and every person knowingly and wilfully aiding, abetting, or assisting in committing any such offence as aforesaid, shall, on conviction thereof, * * * be punished by a fine not exceeding one thousand dollars, or by imprisonment and confinement to hard labor not exceeding five years, or both, at the discretion of the court."

It is not lawful to record any instrument, document, or paper required by law to be stamped, or any copy thereof, unless a stamp or stamps of the proper amount have been affixed and cancelled in the manner required by law, and such instrument or copy and the record thereof are utterly null and void, and cannot be used or admitted as evidence in any court until the defect has been cured as provided in section 158

All wilful violations of the law should be reported to the United States District Attorney within and for the district where they are committed

## GENERAL REMARKS

Revenue stamps may be used indiscriminately upon any of the matters or things enumerated in Schedule B, except proprietary and playing card stamps, for which a special use has been provided.

Postage stamps cannot be used in payment of the duty chargeable on instruments

The law does not designate which of the parties to an instrument shall furnish the necessary stamp, nor does the Commissioner of Internal Revenue assume to determine that it shall be supplied by one party rather than by another; but if an instrument subject to stamp duty is issued without having the necessary stamps affixed thereto, it cannot be recorded, or admitted, or used in evidence, in any court, until a legal stamp or stamps, denoting the amount of tax, shall have been affixed as prescribed by law, and the person who thus issues it is liable to a penalty, if he omits the stamps with an intent to evade the provisions of the internal revenue act.

The first act imposing a stamp tax upon certain specified instruments took effect, so far as said tax is concerned, October 1, 1862. The impression which seems to prevail to some extent, that no stamps are required upon any instruments issued in the States lately in insurrection, prior to the surrender, or prior to the establishment of collection districts there, is erroneous

Instruments issued in those States since October 1, 1862, are subject to the same taxes as similar ones issued at the same time in the other States.

No stamp is necessary upon an instrument executed prior to October 1, 1862, to make it admissible in evidence, or to entitle it to record

*Certificates of loan* in which there shall appear any written or printed evidence of an amount of money to be paid on demand, or at a time designated, are subject to stamp duty as "promissory notes"

When two or more persons join in the execution of an instrument, the stamp to which the instrument is liable under the law, may be affixed and cancelled by either of them; and "when more than one signature is affixed to the same paper, one or more stamps may be affixed thereto, representing the whole amount of the stamp required for such signatures"

No stamp is required on any warrant of attorney accompanying a bond or note, when such bond or note has affixed thereto the stamp or stamps denoting the duty required, and, whenever any bond or note is secured by mortgage, but one stamp duty is required on such papers—such stamp duty being the highest rate required for such instruments, or either of them. In such case a note or memorandum of the value or denomination of the stamp affixed should be made upon the margin or in the acknowledgement of the instrument which is not stamped.

Particular attention is called to the change in section 154, by striking out the words "or used," the exemption thereunder is thus restricted to documents, &c, *issued* by the officers therein named Also to the changes in sections 152 and 158, by inserting the words "and cancelled in the manner required by law."

The acceptor or acceptors of any bill of exchange, or order for the payment of any sum of money, drawn or purporting to be drawn in any foreign country, but payable in the United States, must, before paying or accepting the same, place thereupon a stamp indicating the duty.

It is only upon conveyances of realty *sold* that conveyance stamps are necessary A deed of real estate made without valuable consideration need not be stamped as a conveyance, but if it contains covenants, such, for instance, as a covenant to warrant and defend the title, it should be stamped as an agreement or contract.

When a deed purporting to be a conveyance of realty sold, and stamped accordingly, is inoperative, a deed of confirmation, made simply to cure the defect, requires no stamp In such case, the second deed should contain a recital of the facts, and should show the reasons for its execution.

Partition deeds between tenants in common, need not be stamped as conveyances, inasmuch as there is no sale of realty, as merely a marking out, or a defining, of the boundaries of the part belonging to each, but where money or other valuable consideration is paid by one co-tenant to another for equality of partition, there is a sale to the extent of such consideration, and the conveyance, by the party receiving it, should be stamped accordingly

A conveyance of lands sold for unpaid taxes, issued since August 1, 1866, by the officers of any county, town, or other municipal corporation in the discharge of their strictly official duties, is exempt from stamp tax

A conveyance of realty sold, subject to a mortgage should be stamped according to the consideration, or the value of the property *unencumbered.* The consideration in such case is to be found by adding the amount paid for the equity of redemption to the mortgage debt. The fact that one part of the consideration is paid to the mortgagor and the other part to the mortgagee does not change the liability of the conveyance.

The stamp tax upon a mortgage is based upon the amount it is given to secure The fact that the value of the property mortgaged is less than that amount, and that consequently the security is only partial, does not change the liability of the instrument When, therefore, a second mortgage is given to secure the payment of a sum of money partially secured by a prior mortgage upon other property, or when two mortgages upon separate property are given at the same time to secure the payment of the same sum, each should be stamped as though it were the only one

A mortgage given to secure a surety from loss, or given for any purpose whatever, other than as security for the payment of a definite and certain sum of money, is taxable only as an agreement or contract

The stamp duty upon a lease, agreement, memorandum, or contract for the hire, use, or rent of any land, tenement, or portion thereof, is based upon the *annual* rent or rental value of the property leased, and the duty is the same whether the lease be for one year, for a term of years, or for the fractional part of a year only.

Upon every assignment or transfer of a mortgage, a stamp tax is required equal to that imposed upon a mortgage for the amount remaining unpaid, this tax is required upon every such transfer in writing, whether there is a *sale* of the mortgage or not, but no stamp is necessary upon the endorsement of a negotiable instrument, even though the legal effect of such indorsement is to transfer a mortgage by which the instrument is secured

An assignment of a lease within the meaning and intent of Schedule B, is an assignment of the *leasehold*, or of some portion thereof, by the *lessee*, or by some person claiming by, from, or under him, such an assignment as subrogates the assignee to the rights, or some portion of the rights, of the *lessee*, or of the person standing in his place A transfer by the *lessor* of his part of a lease, neither giving nor purporting to give a claim to the leasehold, or to any part thereof, but simply a right to the rents, &c., is subject to stamp tax as a contract or agreement only

The stamp tax upon a fire insurance policy is based upon the *premium.*

Deposit notes taken by a mutual fire insurance company, not as payment of premium nor as evidence of indebtedness therefor, but to be used simply as a basis upon which to make rateable assessments to meet the losses incurred by the company, should not be reckoned as premium in determining the amount of stamp taxes upon the policies

When a policy of insurance properly stamped has been issued and lost, no stamp is necessary upon another issued by the same company to the same party, covering the same property, time, &c, and designed simply to supply the loss. The second policy should recite the loss of the first

An instrument which operates as the renewal of a policy of insurance, is subject to the same stamp tax as the policy

When a policy of insurance is issued for a certain time, whether it be for one year only or for a term of years, a receipt for premium, or any other instrument which has the legal effect to continue the contract and extend its operation *beyond that time,* requires the same amount of revenue stamps as the policy itself, but such a receipt as is usually given for the payment of the monthly, quarterly, or annual premium, is not a renewal within the meaning of the statute The payment simply prevents the policy from expiring, by reason of non performance of its conditions ; a receipt given for such a payment requires a two-cent stamp, if the amount received exceeds twenty dollars, and a two-cent stamp only When, however, the time of payment has passed, and a tender of the premium is not sufficient to bind the company, but a new policy or a new contract in some form, with the mutuality essential to every contract, becomes necessary between the insurer and the insured, the same amount of stamps should be used as that required upon the original policy

A permit issued by a life insurance company changing the terms of a policy as to travel, residence, occupation, &c, should be stamped as a contract or agreement.

A bill single or a bill obligatory, i e, an instrument in the form of a promissory note, *under seal,* is subject to stamp duty as written or printed evidence of an amount of money to be paid on demand or at a time designated, at the rate of five cents for each one hundred dollars or fractional part thereof

A waiver of protest, or of demand and notice, written upon negotiable paper and signed by the indorser, is an agreement, and requires a five-cent stamp

A stamp duty of twenty-five cents is imposed upon the "protest of every note, bill of exchange, check or draft," and upon every marine protest. If several notes, bills of exchange, drafts, &c, are protested at the same time and all attached to one and the same certificate, stamps should be affixed to the amount of twenty-five cents for each note, bill, draft, &c, thus protested

When, as is generally the case, the caption to a deposition contains other certificates in addition to the jurat to the affidavit of the deponent, such as a certificate that the parties were or were not notified, that they did or did not appear, that they did or did not object, &c, it is subject to a stamp duty of five cents

When an attested copy of a writ or other

process is used by a sheriff or other person in making personal service, or in attaching property, a five-cent stamp should be affixed to the certificate of attestation

A marriage certificate issued by the officiating clergyman or magistrate, to be returned to any officer of a State, county, city, town, or other municipal corporation, to constitute part of a public record, requires no stamp, but if it is to be retained by the parties, a five-cent stamp should be affixed

The stamp tax upon a bill of sale, by which any ship or vessel, or any part thereof, is conveyed to or vested in any other person or persons, is at the same rate as that imposed upon conveyances of realty sold ; a bill of sale of any other personal property should be stamped as a contract or agreement

An assignment of real or personal property, or of both, for the benefit of creditors, should be stamped as an agreement or contract

Written or printed assignments of agreements, bonds, notes not negotiable, and of all other instruments the assignments of which are not particularly specified in the foregoing schedule, should be stamped as agreements.

No stamp is necessary upon the registry of a judgment, even though the registry is such in its legal effect as to create a lien which operates as a mortgage upon the property of the judgment debtor

When a "power of attorney or proxy for voting at any election for officers of any incorporated company or society, except religious, charitable, or literary societies, or public cemeteries," is signed by several stockholders, owning separate and distinct shares, it is, in its legal effect, the separate instrument of each, and requires stamps to the amount of ten cents for each and every signature ; one or more stamps may be used representing the whole amount required.

A notice from landlord to tenant to quit possession of premises requires no stamp

A stamp tax is imposed upon every "manifest for custom-house entry or clearance of the *cargo* of any ship, vessel, or steamer for a foreign port " The amount of this tax in each case depends upon the registered tonnage of the vessel

If a vessel clears in ballast and has no cargo whatever, no stamp is necessary, but if she has any, however small the amount —a stamp should be used.

A bond to convey real estate requires stamps to the amount of twenty five cents

The stamp duty upon the probate of a will, or upon letters of administration, is based upon the sworn or declared value of all the estate and effects, real, personal, and mixed, undiminished by the debts of the estate for or in respect of which such probate or letters are applied for

When the property belonging to the estate of a person deceased, lies under different jurisdictions and it becomes necessary to take out letters in two or more places. the letters should be stamped according to the value of all the property, real, personal, and mixed, for or in respect of which the particular letters, in each case are issued

Letters *de bonis non* should be stamped according to the amount of property remaining to be administered upon thereunder, regardless of the stamps upon the original letters.

A mere *copy* of an instrument is not subject to stamp duty unless it is a certified one, in which case a five-cent stamp should be affixed to the certificate of the person attesting it, but when an instrument is executed and issued in duplicate, triplicate, &c., as in the case of a lease of two or more parts, each part has the same legal effect as the other, and each should be stamped as an original.

# POSTAL RATES AND REGULATIONS.

LETTERS —The law requires postage on all letters (including those to foreign countries when prepaid), excepting those written to the President or Vice President, or members of Congress, or (on official business) to the chiefs of the executive departments of the Government, and the heads of bureaux and chief clerks, and others invested with the franking privilege, to be prepaid by stamps or stamped envelopes, prepayment in money being prohibited

All drop-letters must be prepaid The rate of postage on drop-letters, at offices where free delivery by carrier is established, is two cents per half ounce or fraction of a half ounce , at offices where such free delivery is NOT established the rate is one cent.

The single rate of postage on all domestic mail letters throughout the United States is three cents per half ounce, with an additional rate of three cents for each additional half ounce or fraction of a half ounce. The ten cent (Pacific) rate is abolished

NEWSPAPERS, ETC —Letter postage is to be charged on all handbills, circulars, or other printed matter which shall contain any manuscript writing whatever

Daguerreotypes, when sent in the mail, are to be charged with letter postage by weight.

Photographs on cards, paper, and other flexible material, (not in cases), can be sent at the same rate as miscellaneous printed matter, viz, two cents for each four ounces or fraction thereof

Photograph Albums are chargeable with book postage—four cents for each four ounces or fraction thereof

NEWSPAPER POSTAGE —Postage on daily papers to subscribers when prepaid quarterly or yearly in advance, either at the mailing office or office of delivery, per quarter (three months), 35 cts , six times per week, per quarter 30 cts , for tri-weekly, per quarter 15 cts ; for semi-weekly, per quarter 10 cts. , for weekly, per quarter 6 cents

Weekly newspapers (one copy only) sent by the publisher to actual subscribers within the county where printed and published, FREE

Postage per quarter (to be paid quarterly or yearly in advance) on newspapers and periodicals issued less frequently than once a week, sent to actual subscribers in any part of the United States . Semi monthly, not over 4 oz , 6 cts , over 4 oz. and not over 8 oz , 12 cts , over 8 oz and not over 12 oz , 18 cts , monthly, not over 4 oz., 3 cts , over 4 oz and not over 8 oz , 6 cts ; over 8 oz and not over 12 oz., 9 cts.; quarterly, not over 4 oz , 1 cent; over 4 oz and not over 8 oz., 2 cts.; over 8 oz and not over 12 oz., 3 cts

TRANSIENT MATTER —Books not over 4 oz. in weight, to one address, 4 cts ; over 4 oz and not over 8 oz , 8 cts ; over 8 oz and not over 12 oz , 12 cts. , over 12 oz. and not over 16 oz., 16 cts.

Circulars not exceeding three in number to one address, 2 cts , over 3 and not over 6, 4 cts , over 6 and not over 9, 6 cts.; over 9 and not exceeding 12, 8 cts

On miscellaneous mailable matter, (embracing all pamphlets, occasional publications, transient newspapers, hand-bills and posters, book manuscripts and proof-sheets, whether corrected or not, maps, prints, engravings, sheet music, blanks, flexible patterns, samples, and sample cards, phonographic paper, letter envelopes, postal envelopes or wrappers, cards, paper, plain or ornamental, photographic representations of different types, seeds, cuttings, bulbs, roots and scions,) the postage to be pre-paid by stamps, is on one package, to one address, not over 4 oz in weight, 2 cts , over 4 oz and not over 8 oz , 4 cts ; over 8 oz and not over 12 oz , 6 cts , over 12 oz and not over 16 oz , 8 cts. The weight of packages of seeds, cuttings, roots and scions, to be franked, is limited to thirty-two ounces.

[ALL printed matter (except single copies of newspapers, magazines, and periodicals to regular subscribers) sent via overland mail, is to be charged at LETTER POSTAGE rates ]

Any word or communication, whether by printing, writing, marks or signs, upon the cover or wrapper of a newspaper, pamphlet, magazine, or other printed matter, other than the name or address of the person to whom it is to be sent, and the date when the subscription expires, subjects the package to letter postage

# FOREIGN POSTAGE.

| COUNTRIES. | Letters per one-half ounce. | | | | Newspapers if not over 4 oz., pre-payment compulsory. | | Books, Packets, Prints, Patterns, or Samples, per 4 ounces, pre-payment compulsory. | |
|---|---|---|---|---|---|---|---|---|
| | By Direct Mail | | Closed Mail via England | | By Direct Mail | Closed Mail via England | By direct Mail. | Closed Mail via England |
| | Paid | Unp'd | Paid | Unp'd | | | | |
| | Cents | Cents | Cents | Cents | Cents | Cents | Cents. | Cents |
| North German Union, (including all the German States and Austria) | 10 | 10 | 15 | 15 | 3 | 4 | 6 | 8 |
| Denmark | 13 | 14 | 18 | 19 | 5 | 6 | 8 | 10 |
| Sweden | 16 | 18 | 21 | 23 | 8 | 9 | 11 | 13 |
| Norway | 20 | 23 | 25 | 28 | 15 | 14 | 16 | 18 |
| Russia | 15 | 18 | 20 | 20 | 6 | 16 | 6 | 10 |
| Switzerland | 15 | 15 | 24 | 24 | 10 | 11 | 13 | 15 |
| Greece | 14 | 19 | 15 | | 17 | 18 | 20 | 22 |
| Italy (via Austria) | 14 | 14 | 19 | | 7 | 4 | 10 | 8 |
| Papal States | 13 | | 18 | 18 | 7 | 8 | 10 | 12 |
| Moldavia and Wallachia | | 18 | | 20 | 7 | 8 | 10 | 12 |
| Turkey | 18 | 15 | 20 | 20 | 7 | 8 | 10 | 12 |
| Egypt | 15 | 15 | 20 | 20 | 7 | 8 | 10 | 12 |

MONEY ORDERS —Absolute safety in sending money by mail is secured by obtaining a Money Order, on any Money Order Office, for which the fees are — Orders not exceeding $20, 10 cents  Orders not exceeding $50, 25 cents.  *NEVER PUT MONEY IN A LETTER—ALWAYS PROCURE A MONEY ORDER*

Valuable Letters should be carried to the Post-office  If money is to be remitted, a Postal Money Order should be obtained  If upon points where there is no Money Order Office, then the letter should be registered.  Money should never be enclosed in an ordinary letter

STAMPS AND ENVELOPES can be obtained at the BOX DELIVERY  Envelopes in numbers not less than 500 with the "address of the purchaser," and a "return request," across the end, can be procured (by leaving an order with the Post-master,) at the same prices as ordinary stamped envelopes.

REGISTERED LETTERS —Valuable Letters for any part of the United States, Holland, United Kingdom, Italian States, Africa, East Indies, Egypt, Falkland Islands, China, and Australia, will be registered on application at the office
Registry fee to the above foreign countries 16 cents  Registry fee in the United States, 20 cents, Canada and the British Provinces, 5 cents ,
North Germany, 8 cents.  *Letters addressed to POST-MASTERS must be prepaid at the usual rates*

RULES —1  Direct Letters plainly to the street and number, as well as the Post-office and State

2  Head  letters with the  name  of the writer's *Post Office and State, Street and Number*  Sign them with full name, and request that answers be directed accordingly

3  Letters sent to strangers or transient visitors in a town or city, whose special address may be unknown, should be marked on the lower left hand corner with the word "Transient"

4  *Place the postage stamp on the upper right hand corner,* and leave space between the stamp and direction for post marking, without interfering with the writing  N B —*A request for the return of a letter to the writer,* if unclaimed within thirty days or less, written or printed, with the writer's *name, Post Office and State* across the left hand side of the envelope, on the face side, will be complied with  Letters bearing such indorsements will be returned to the writer *free of charge*

# Additional Table of Foreign Postage.

The * indicates that, unless the letter is registered, pre-payment is optional; in all other cases it is required  § Pamphlets and Periodicals, ten cents per four ounces or fraction thereof  ‡ Pamphlets, Magazines, &c., two cents per four ounces or fraction thereof

| COUNTRIES. | Letters ¼oz | Letters ½oz | News papers | Pamphlets per oz |
|---|---|---|---|---|
| Acapulco | | 10 | 2 | ‡ |
| Argentine Republic, 22d each month from N Y | 18 | 25 | | |
| Aspinwall | | 10 | 2 | |
| Australia, British Mail, via Panama | | 22 | 6 | ‡ |
| Bahamas, by direct steamer from New York | | 5 | 2 | |
| Bogota, New Granada | | 18 | 6 | ‡ |
| Bolivia | | 34 | 6 | ‡ |
| Brazil, 22d each month from New York | | *10 | 2 | |
| Buenos Ayres, 22d each month from New York. | 18 | 25 | | |
| Canada, any distance, (if not prepaid, 10 cts) | | * 6 | 2 | |
| Central America, Pacific Slope, via Panama | | 10 | 2 | ‡ |
| Chili, British Mail, via Panama. | | 34 | 6 | ‡ |
| China, via San Francisco | | 10 | 2 | ‡ |
| Costa Rica | | 10 | 2 | ‡ |
| Cuba | | 10 | 2 | ‡ |
| Ecuador, British Mail, via Panama.. | | 34 | 6 | ‡ |
| Guatemala | | 10 | 2 | ‡ |
| Havana | | 10 | 2 | ‡ |
| Honduras | | 34 | 6 | ‡ |
| Hong Kong, via San Francisco | | 10 | 2 | ‡ |
| Japan, via San Francisco | | 10 | 2 | ‡ |
| Mexico | | 10 | 2 | ‡ |
| Montevideo, 22d each month from N Y | 18 | 25 | | |
| Nassau, N Prov, by direct steamer from N Y | | 5 | 2 | ‡ |
| New Brunswick | | *10 | 2 | ‡ |
| Newfoundland, (15 c if over 3,000 miles) | | 10 | 2 | ‡ |
| New Granada, (except Aspinwall and Panama) | | 18 | 6 | |
| Nicaragua, Pacific Slope, via Panama | | 10 | 2 | ‡ |
| do    Gulf Coast of | | 34 | 6 | |
| Novia Scotia (* 15 cts. if over 3,000 miles) | | *10 | 2 | ‡ |
| Panama | | 10 | 2 | ‡ |
| Peru, British Mail, via Panama | | 34 | 6 | ‡ |
| Porto Rico, Br'sh Mail, via Havana or San Juan | | 18 | 4 | |
| Prince Edward's Island. [under 3,000 miles] | | *10 | 2 | |
| Sandwich Islands, by mail to San Francisco | | 10 | 2 | ‡ |
| Turk's Island | | 10 | 2 | |
| Uruguay, by Am pkt 22d each month from N Y | 18 | 25 | | |
| Vancouver's Island | | 10 | 2 | |
| Venezuela, British Mail, via Aspinwall | | 18 | 4 | |
| do    by American Ven packet | | 10 | 3 | |

The recent postal treaty with Great Britain provides that besides letters and newspapers, "book packets," and "packets of patterns and samples," may be sent. Such packets—

1. Must contain no writing

2. Must be fully prepaid (6 cents per 4 ounces from the U S, or 3 pence sterling from Great Britain)

3. Must be open at the ends to allow inspection

Samples of merchandise must not be of intrinsic value.

Dutiable articles—books, music, &c, sent from Great Britain to the United States, must, in addition to the postage, pay the regular duties, which are—On books and engravings, 25 per cent; music and photographs, 20 per cent

If letters or articles sent to Italy are not prepaid, or are insufficiently paid, they will be charged with deficient postage, and subject to fine, on arrival at their destination

# Infallible Rules for Detecting Counterfeit or Spurious Bank Notes.

RULE 1st —Examine the shading of the letters in title of Bank called LATHEWORK, which in genuine notes presents an even, straight, light and silky appearance, generally so fine and smooth as to appear to be all in one solid, pale body. In the counterfeit the lines are coarse and irregular, and in many of the longer lines breaks will be perceived, thus presenting a very inferior finish in comparison to genuine work.

2d —Observe the dics, circles and ovals in the genuine, they are composed of a network of lines, which, by crossing each other at certain angles, produce an endless variety of figures, SEE THE ONE CENT STAMP ATTACHED The fine line alone is the unit which enables you to detect spurious work In the counterfeit, the REPRESENTED white lines are coarse, irregular, and cross each other in a confused, irregular manner, thus producing blurred and imperfect figures

3d —Examine the form and features of all human figures on the note In the genuine, the texture of the skin is represented by fine dots and lines intermixed In the eyes, the pupil is distinctly visible, and the white clearly seen ; the nose, mouth and chin, well formed, natural and expressive ; the lips are slightly pouting, and the chin well thrown out ; and the delicate shading of the neck perfectly harmonizes with the rest of the figure Observe the fingers and toes ; they should be clearly and accurately defined The hair of the head should show the fine strands and present a natural appearance The folds of the drapery of human figures should lay natural and present a fine, finished appearance In the counterfeit the female figure does not bear the natural prominence in outlines ; observe, the eyes and shading surrounding does not present the lifelike appearance it should. The fingers and toes are not properly and proportionately defined ; the hair does not bear that soft and finished appearance as in the genuine

4th —Examine the imprint or engraver's names in the evenness and shape of the fine letters Counterfeits never bear the imprint perfect This rule should be strictly observed, as it is infallible in detecting counterfeits

5th —In the genuine note the landscapes are well finished , trees and shrubs are neatly drawn , the limbs well proportioned, and the foliage presenting a fine natural appearance , clear sky is formed of fine parallel lines, and when clouds or heavy skies appear, they cross each other, and bear a soft, smooth and natural appearance The perspective, showing a view of the surrounding country, is always clear and distinct The small figures in the background are always plainly seen, and their outlines and general character recognized Ships are well defined and the canvass has a clear texture ; railroad cars are very accurately delineated ; in examining a train observe carefully the car most distant In the counterfeit the landscape is usually poorly executed , the leaves of trees poorly and unnaturally defined — The lines representing still water are scratchy rather than parallel, the sky is represented generally in like manner, and where rolling clouds are to be seen, the unnatural effect is obvious Domestic animals are generally poorly executed, particularly the head and limbs , the eyes are seldom clearly defined Ships are poorly drawn, the texture of the canvass coarse and inferior in style of workmanship, thus giving an artificial appearance Railroad cars are also poorly executed ; the car farthest from the eye is usually the most imperfect The perspective is always imperfect , the figures in the background can seldom be recognized.

6th —Bills altered from a smaller to a higher denomination, can readily be detected by a close observer, in consequence of the striking difference between the parts which have been extracted and the rest of the note. This difference is readily perceived in the lack of color, body and finish of the dye ; we have seen bills where the surrounding shading in altered dies was too dark, but from the back or finish of the white lines you have a sure test. Again observe particularly the words "Five" or "Ten Dollars" as the case may be, denoting the denomination of the note; the parallel outlines and shading (if any) are coarse and imperfect Alterations are frequently made by pasting a greater denomination over a smaller, but by holding the bill up to the light, the fraud will be perceived Another method resorted to is to cut out the figures in the dies as well as the words one dollar, or the words two or three as the case may be, and with a sharp eraser, scrape down the ends and also the edges of the pieces to be inserted, when the pieces thus prepared are affixed they are hardly perceivable, but by passing the note through the hand so as to feel the die both with the finger and thumb at the same time, the fraud will be detected by the stiffness of the outer edges, "occasioned by the gum or method adopted" in affixing the parts The letter S should always be examined, as in many alterations it is pasted or stamped at the end of the word "dollar;" and even when stamped there, the carrying out of the outlines for its shading will readily show the fraud Bills of broken banks are frequently altered by extracting the name of bank, state and town; they may readily be detected by observing first the state, second the title or name of the bank, third the town or location

GENERAL REMARKS IN REFERENCE TO COUNTERFEITS.—The paper on which they are printed is generally of a very inferior quality, with less body, finish and toughness than bank note paper has The ink generally lacks the rich luster of the genuine, the red letters and figures are generally imperfect, and the ink does not present the vermilion hue as it should The printing is generally inferior, usually exhibiting specks of white in the most prominent letters The date and filling up, and the President's and Cashier's names are generally written by the same person, although in many instances they present a different appearance There are bills in circulation bearing either genuine dies or vignettes; but upon close examination you will be enabled to detect any spurious bill, whether counterfeit or altered, by the instructions here given, if persevered in for a short time We beg to suggest, it time will admit, the learner should examine minutely every bill he receives A powerful pocket magnifying glass, which can be purchased for from fifty cents to one dollar at any of the opticians, will greatly enable you to see and comprehend the difference between genuine and spurious work

◆ ◆

# HOW TO SUCCEED IN BUSINESS.

What will my readers give to know how to get rich? Now, I will not vouch that the following rules will enable every person who may read them to acquire wealth, but this I will answer for, that if ever a man does grow rich by honest means, and retains his wealth for any length of time, he must practice upon the principles laid down in the following essay The remarks are not original with me, but I strongly commend them to the attention of every young man, at least as affording the true secret of success in attaining wealth A single perusal of such an essay at an impressible moment, has sometimes a very wonderful effect upon the disposition and character

Fortune, they say, is a fickle dame—full of her freaks and caprices, who blindly distributes her favors without the slightest discrimination So inconstant, so wavering is she represented, that her most faithful votaries can place no reliance on her promises Disappointment, they tell us, is the lot of those who make offerings at her shrine Now, all this is a vile slander upon the dear blind lady

Although wealth often appears the result of mere accident, or a fortunate concurrence of favorable circumstances without any exertion of skill or foresight, yet any man of sound health and unimpaired mind may become wealthy, if he takes the proper steps

Foremost in the list of requisites are honesty and strict integrity in every transaction of life Let a man have the reputation of being fair and upright in his dealings, and he will possess the confidence of all who know him Without these qualities every other merit will prove unavailing Ask concerning a man, "Is he active and capable?" Yes "Industrious, temperate and regular in his habits?"—Oh yes "Is he honest? Is he trustworthy?" Why, as to that, I am sorry to say that he is not to be trusted, he needs watching, he is a little tricky, and will take an undue advantage, if he can "Then I will have nothing to do with him," will be the invariable reply  Why, then, is honesty the best policy ?  Because, without it, you will get a bad name, and everybody will shun you

A character for knavery will prove an insurmountable obstacle to success in almost every undertaking  It will be found that the straight line is, in business, as in geometry, the shortest  In a word, it is almost impossible for a dishonest man to acquire wealth by a regular process of business, because he is shunned as a depredator upon society.

Needy men are apt to deviate from the rule of integrity, under the plea that necessity knows no law ; they might as well add that it knows no shame  The course is suicidal, and by destroying all confidence, ever keeps them immured in poverty, although they may possess every other quality for success in the world

Punctuality, which is said to be the soul of business, is another important element in the art of money getting  The man known to be scrupulously exact in the fulfillment of his engagements, gains the confidence of all, and may command all the means he can use with advantage, whereas, a man careless and regardless of his promises in money matters will have every purse closed against him.  Therefore be prompt in your payments.

Next, let us consider the advantages of a cautious circumspection in our intercourse with the world  Slowness of belief and a proper distrust are essential to success.  The credulous and confiding are ever the dupes of knaves and impostors  Ask those who have lost their property how it happened, and you will find in most cases that it has been owing to misplaced confidence  One has lost by endorsing, another by crediting, another by false representations; all of which a little more foresight and a little more distrust would have prevented.  In the affairs of this world men are not saved by faith, but by the want of it

Judge of men by what they do, not by what they say  Believe in looks rather than words  Observe all their movements  Ascertain their motives and their ends  Notice what they say or do in their unguarded moments, when under the influence of excitement  The passions have been compared to tortures which force men to reveal their secrets  Before trusting a man, before putting it in his power to cause you a loss, possess yourself of every available information relative to him  Learn his history, his habits, inclinations and propensities, his reputation for honor, industry, frugality and punctuality; his prospects, resources, supports, advantages and disadvantages, his intentions and motives of action, who are his friends and enemies, and what are his good or bad qualities  You may learn a man's good qualities and advantages from his friends—his bad qualities and disadvantages from his enemies  Make due allowance for exaggeration in both  Finally, examine carefully before engaging in anything, and act with energy afterwards  Have the hundred eyes of Argus beforehand, and the hundred hands of Briarius afterwards.

Order and system in the management of business must not be neglected  Nothing contributes more to dispatch  Have a place for everything and everything in its place , a time for everything, and everything in its time  Do first what presses most, and having determined what is to be done, and how it is to be done, lose no time in doing it  Without this method all is hurry and confusion, little or nothing is accomplished, and business is attended to with neither pleasure nor profit

A polite, affable deportment is recommended  Agreeable manners contribute powerfully to a man's success  Take two men, possessing equal advantages in every other respect, but let one be gentlemanly, kind, obliging and conciliating in his manners , the other harsh, rude and disobliging; and the one will become rich, while the other will starve

We are now to consider a very important principle in the business of money getting, namely—Industry—persevering, indefatigable attention to business  Persevering diligence is the Philosopher's stone, which turns everything to gold.  Constant, regular, habitual and systematic application to business, most in time, if properly directed, produce great results  It must lead to wealth, with the same certainty that poverty follows in the train of idleness and inattention  It has been truly remarked that he who follows his amusements instead of his business, will, in a short time, have no business to follow

The art of money-saving is an important part of the art of money-getting  Without frugality no one can become rich ; with it, few would be poor  Those who consume as fast as they produce, are on the road to ruin  As most of the poverty we meet with grows out of idleness and extravagance, so most large fortunes have been the result of habitual industry and frugality  The practice of economy is as necessary in the expenditure of time as of money  They say if " we take care of the pence the pounds will take care of themselves."  So, if we take care of the minutes, the days will take care of themselves.

The acquisition of wealth demands as much self-denial, and as many sacrifices of present gratification, as the practice of virtue itself  Vice and poverty proceed in some degree, from the same sources, namely—the disposition to sacrifice the future to the present; the inability to forego a small present pleasure for great future advantages  Men fail of fortune in this world, as they fail of happiness in the world to come, simply because they are unwilling to deny themselves momentary enjoyments for the sake of permanent future happiness

Every large city is filled with persons, who, in order to support the appearance of wealth, constantly live beyond their income, and make up the deficiency by contracting debts which are never paid  Others, there are, the mere drones of society, who pass their days in idleness, and subsist by pirating on the hives of the industrious. Many who run a short lived career of splendid beggary, could they be but persuaded to adopt a system of rigid economy for a few years, might pass the remainder of their days in affluence But no! They must keep up appearances, they must live like other folks.

Their debts accumulate, their credit fails, they are harassed by duns, and besieged by constables and sheriff In this extremity, as a last resort, they submit to a shameful dependence, or engage in criminal practices which entail hopeless wretchedness and infamy on themselves and families

Stick to the business in which you are regularly employed Let speculators make thousands in a year or a day; mind your own regular trade, never turning from it to the right hand or to the left. If you are a merchant, a professional man, or a mechanic, never buy lots or stocks, unless you have surplus money which you wish to invest Your own business you understand as well as other men; but other people's business you do not understand Let your business be some one which is useful to the community All such occupations possess the elements of profit in themselves

---

# How to Secure the Public Lands,

## OR THE ENTRY OF THE SAME UNDER THE PRE-EMPTION AND HOMESTEAD

### LAWS

The following circular gives all necessary information as to the procedure necessary in purchasing and securing the public lands

DEPARTMENT OF THE INTERIOR,    } 
GEN'L LAND OFFICE, July 19, 1865 }

Numerous questions having arisen as to the mode of procedure to purchase public lands, or acquire title to the same by bounty land locations, by pre-emptions or by homestead, this circular is communicated for the information of all concerned

In order to acquire title to public lands the following steps must be taken·

1 Application must be made to the Register of the district land office in which the land desired may be situated

A list of all the land offices in the United States is furnished by the Department, with the seats of the different offices, where it is the duty of the Register and Receiver to be in attendance, and give proper facilities and information to persons desirous of obtaining lands

The minimum price of ordinary public lands is $1,25 per acre. The even or reserved sections falling within railroad grants are increased to double the minimum price, being $2,50 per acre

Lands once offered at public sale, and not afterwards kept out of market by reservation, or otherwise, so as to prevent free competition, may be entered or located

2 By the applicant filing with the Register his written application describing the tract, with its area, the Register will then certify to the receiver whether the land is vacant, with its price, and when found to be so, the applicant must pay that price per acre, or may locate the same with land warrant, and thereafter the Receiver will give him a "duplicate receipt," which he is required to surrender previous to the delivery to him of the patent, which may be had either by application for it to the Register or to the General Land Office

3. If the tract has not been offered at public sale it is not liable to ordinary private entry, but may be secured by a party legally qualified, upon his compliance with the requirements of the pre-emption laws of 4th September, 1841, and 3d March, 1843, and after such party shall have made actual settlement for such a length of time as will show he designs it for his permanent home, and is acting in good faith, building a house and residing therein, he may proceed to the district land office, establish his pre-emption claim according to law, by proving his actual residence and cultivation, and showing that he is otherwise within the purview of these acts — Then he can enter the land at $1,25, either in cash or with bounty land warrant, unless the premises should be $2,50 acre lands In that case the whole purchase-money can be paid in cash, or one-half in cash, the residue with a bounty land warrant

4 But if parties legally qualified desire to obtain title under the Homestead Act of 20th May, 1862, they can do so on com-

plying with the Department Circular, dated 30th October, 1862

5 The law confines Homestead entries to surveyed lands; and although, in certain States and Territories noted in the subjoined list, pre-emptors may go on land before survey, yet they can only establish their claim after return of survey, but must file their pre-emption declaration within three months after receipt of official plat, at the local land-office where the settlement was made before survey Where, however, it was made after survey, the claimant must file within three months after date of settlement; and where actual residence and cultivation have been long enough to show that the claimant has made the land his permanent home, he can establish his claim and pay for the same at any time before the date of the public sale of lands within the range in which his settlement may fall

6 All unoffered surveyed lands not acquired under pre-emption, homestead, or otherwise, under express legal sanction, must be offered at public sale under the President's Proclamation, and struck off to the highest bidder, as required by act of April 24, 1820

J M EDMUNDS,
Commissioner General Land Office.

---

# LAW MAXIMS.

1 A promise of a debtor to give "satisfactory security" for the payment of a portion of his debt, is a sufficient consideration for a release of the residue by his creditor.

2 Administrators are liable to account for interest on funds in their hands, although no profit shall have been made upon them, unless the exigencies of the estate rendered it prudent that they should hold the funds thus uninvested

3 Any person who voluntarily becomes an agent for another, and in that capacity obtains information to which as a stranger he could have had no access, is bound in subsequent dealing with his principal, as purchaser of the property that formed the subject of his agency, to communicate such information

4 When a house is rendered untenantable in consequence of improvements made on the adjoining lot, the owner of such cannot recover damages, because it is presumed that he had knowledge of the approaching danger in time to protect himself from it.

5 When a merchant ship is abandoned by order of the master, for the purpose of saving life, and a part of the crew subsequently meet the vessel so abandoned and bring her safe into port, they will be entitled to salvage

6 A person who has been led to sell goods by means of false pretenses, cannot recover them from one who has purchased them in good faith from the fraudulent vendor.

7 An agreement by the holder of a note to give the principal debtor time for payment, without depriving himself of the right to sue, does not discharge the surety

8 A seller of goods who accepts, at the time of sale, the note of a third party, not endorsed by the buyer, in payment, cannot in case the note is not paid, hold the buyer responsible for the value of the goods

9 A day-book copied from a "blotter" in which charges are first made, will not be received in evidence as a book of original entries

10. Common carriers are not liable for extraordinary results of negligence that could not have been foreseen by ordinary skill and foresight

11 A bidder at a Sheriff's sale may retract his bid at any time before the property is knocked down to him, whatever may be the conditions of the sale

12. Acknowledgment of debt to a stranger does not preclude the operation of the statute

13 The fruits and grass on the farm or garden of an intestate descend to the heir

14 Agents are solely liable to their principals

15 A deposit of money in bank by a husband, in the name of his wife, survives to her

16. Money paid on Sunday contracts may be recovered

17 A debtor may give preference to one creditor over another, unless fraud or special legislation can be proved

18. A court cannot give judgment for a larger sum than that specified in the verdict

19. Imbecility on the part of either husband or wife, invalidates the marriage

20 An action for malicious prosecution will lie, though nothing further was done than suing out warrants

21 An agreement not to continue the practice of a profession or business in any specified town, if the party so agreeing has received a consideration for the same, is valid

22 When A consigns goods to B to sell on commission, and B delivers them to C, in payment of his own antecedent debts, A can recover their value

23 A finder of property is compelled to make diligent inquiry for the owner thereof, and to restore the same  If, on finding such property, he attempts to conceal such fact, he may be prosecuted for larceny

24 A private person may obtain an injunction to prevent a public mischief by which he is affected in common with others

25 Any person interested may obtain an injunction to restrain the State or a municipal corporation from maintaining a nuisance on its lands

26 A discharge under the insolvent laws of one State will not discharge the insolvent from a contract made with a citizen of another State

27 To prosecute a party with any other motive than to bring him to justice, is malicious prosecution, and actionable as such

28 Ministers of the gospel, residing in any incorporated town, are not exempt from jury, military, or fire service

29 When a person contracts to build a house, and is prevented by sickness from finishing it, he can recover for the part performed, if such part is beneficial to the other party

30 In a suit for enticing away a man's wife, actual proof of the marriage is not necessary  Cohabitation, reputation, and the admission of marriage by the parties, are sufficient

31 Permanent erections and fixtures, made by a mortgagor after the execution of the mortgage upon land conveyed by it, become a part of the mortgaged premises

32 When a marriage is denied, and plaintiff has given sufficient evidence to establish it, the defendant cannot examine the wife to disprove the marriage

33 The amount of an express debt cannot be enlarged by application.

34 Contracts for advertisements in Sunday newspapers cannot be enforced

35. A seller of goods, chattels, or other property, commits no fraud, in law, when he neglects to tell the purchaser of any flaws, defects, or unsoundness in the same

36 The opinions of witnesses, as to the value of a dog that has been killed are not admissible in evidence  The value of the animal is to be decided by the jury

37 If any person puts a fence on or plows the land of another, he is liable for trespass whether the owner has sustained injury or not

38 If a person, who is unable from illness to sign his will, has his hand guided in making his mark, the signature is valid

39 When land trespassed upon is occupied by a tenant, he alone can bring the action

40 To say of a person, "If he does not come and make terms with me, I will make a bankrupt of him and ruin him," or any such threatening language, is actionable, without proof of special damage.

41. In an action for slander, the party making the complaint must prove the words alleged; other words of like meaning will not suffice

42. In a suit of damages for seduction, proof of pregnancy, and the birth of a child, is not essential  It is sufficient if the illness of the girl, whereby she was unable to labor, was produced by shame for the seduction, and this is such a loss of service as will sustain the action

43. Addressing to a wife a letter containing matter defamatory to the character of her husband is a publication, and renders the writer amenable to damages

44 A parent cannot sustain an action for any wrong done to a child, unless he has incurred some direct pecuniary injury therefrom in consequence of some loss of service or expenses necessarily consequent thereupon

45 A master is responsible for an injury resulting from the negligence of his servant, whilst driving his cart or carriage, provided the servant is at the time engaged in his master's business, even though the accident happens in a place to which his master's business does not call him ; but if the journey of a servant be solely for a purpose of his own, and undertaken without the knowledge and consent of his master, the latter is not responsible

46 An emigrant depot is not a nuisance in law

47 A railroad track through the streets is not a nuisance in law

48　In an action for libel against a newspaper, extracts from such newspaper may be given to show its circulation, and the extent to which the libel has been published The jury, in estimating the damages, are to look at the character of the libel, and whether the defendant is rich or poor　The plaintiff is entitled, in all cases, to his actual damages, and should be compensated for the mental sufferings endured, the public disgrace inflicted, and all actual discomfort produced.

49　Delivery of a husband's goods by a wife to her adulterer, he having knowledge that she has taken them without her husband's authority, is sufficient to sustain an indictment for larceny against the adulterer

50　The fact that the insurer was not informed of the existence of impending litigation, affecting the premises insured, at the time the insurance was effected, does not vitiate the policy

51　The liability of an innkeeper is not confined to personal baggage, but extends to all the property of the guest that he consents to receive

52　When a minor executes a contract, and pays money, or delivers property on the same, he cannot afterwards disaffirm such contract and recover the money, or property, unless he restores to the other party the consideration received from him for such money or property

53.　When a person has, by legal inquisition been found an habitual drunkard, he cannot, even in his sober intervals, make contracts to bind himself or his property, until the inquisition is removed

54　Any person dealing with the representative of a deceased person, is presumed, in law, to be fully apprized of the extent of such representative's authority to act in behalf of such estate

55　In an action against a railroad company, by a passenger, to recover damages for injuries sustained on the road, it is not compulsory upon the plaintiff to prove actual negligence in the defendants, but it is obligatory on the part of the latter to prove that the injury was not owing to any fault or negligence of theirs

56　A guest is a competent witness, in an action between himself and an inn-keeper, to prove the character and value of lost personal baggage　Money in a trunk, not exceeding the amount reasonably required by the traveler to defray the expenses of the journey which he has undertaken, is a part of his baggage, and in case of its loss, while at any inn, the plaintiff may prove its amount by his own testimony

57.　The deed of a minor is not absolutely void　The court is authorized to judge, from the instrument, whether it is void or not, according to its terms being favorable or unfavorable to the interests of the minor

58.　A married woman can neither sue nor be sued on any contract made by her during her marriage, except in an action relating to her individual property　The action must be commenced either by or against her husband　It is only when an action is brought on a contract made by her before her marriage, that she is to be joined as a co-plaintiff, or defendant, with her husband

59　Any contract made with a person judicially declared a lunatic is void

60　Money paid voluntarily in any transaction, with a knowledge of the facts, cannot be recovered.

61　In all cases of special contract for services, except in the case of a minor, the plaintiff can recover only the amount stipulated in the contract.

62.　A wife is a competent witness with her husband, to prove the contents of a lost trunk, or when a party.

63.　A wife cannot be convicted of receiving stolen goods when she received them of her husband

64　Insurance against fire, by lightning or otherwise, does not cover loss by lightning when there is no combustion

65　Failure to prove plea of justification, in a case of slander, aggravates the offence

66　It is the agreement of the parties to sell by sample that constitutes a sale by sample, not the mere exhibition of a specimen of the goods

67　An agent is liable to his principals for loss caused by his misstatements, tho' unintentional

68　Makers of promissory notes given in advance for premiums on policies of insurance, thereafter to be taken, are liable thereon.

69　An agreement to pay for procuring an appointment to office is void

70　An attorney may plead the statute of limitations, when sued by a client for money which he has collected and failed to pay ever

71　Testimony given by a deceased witness on first trial, is not required to be repeated verbatim on the second.

72.　A person entitling himself to a reward offered for lost property, has a lien upon the property for the reward ; but only when a definite reward is offered

73　Confession by a prisoner must be voluntarily made, to constitute evidence against him

74　The defendant in a suit must be served with process, but service of such process upon his wife, even in his absence from the State, is not, in the absence of statutory provisions, sufficient

75 The measure of damages in trespass for cutting timber, is its value as a chattel on the land where it was felled, and not the market price of the lumber manufactured

76 To support an indictment for malicious mischief in killing an animal, malice towards its owner must be shown, not merely passion excited against the animal itself

77 No action can be maintained against a sheriff for omitting to account for money obtained upon an execution within a reasonable time He has till the return day to render such account

78. An interest in the profits of an enterprise, as profits, renders the party holding it a partner in the enterprise, and makes him presumptively liable to share any loss

79 Males can marry at fourteen, and females at twelve years of age

80 All cattle found at large upon any public road, can be driven by any person to the public pound

81. Any dog chasing, barking, or otherwise threatening a passer-by in any street, lane, road, or other public thoroughfare, may be lawfully killed for the same

82. A written promise for the payment of such amount as may come into the hands of the promisor, is held to be an instrument in writing for the payment of money

83 The declaration of an agent is not admissible to establish the fact of agency — But when other proper evidence is given, tending to establish the fact of agency, it is not error to admit the declarations of the agent, accompanying acts, though tending to show the capacity in which he acted When evidence is competent in one respect and incompetent in another, it is the duty of the court to admit it, and control its effects by suitable instructions to the jury

84 The court has a general power to remove or suspend an attorney for such immoral conduct as rendered him unworthy of confidence in his official capacity

85 Bankruptcy is pleadable in bar to all actions and in all courts, and this bar may be avoided whenever it is interposed, by showing fraud in the procurement of the discharge, or a violation of any of the provisions of the bankrupt act

86. An instrument in the form of a deed, but limited to take effect at the termination of the grantor's natural life, is held to be a deed, not a will

87 A sale will not be set aside as fraudulent, simply because the buyer was at the time unable to make the payment agreed upon, and knew his inability, and did not intend to pay

88 No man is under an obligation to make known his circumstances when he is buying goods

89 Contracting parties are bound to disclose material facts known to each, but of which either supposes the other to be ignorant, only when they stand in some special relation of trust and confidence in relation to the subject matter of the contract But neither will be protected if he does anything, however slight, to mislead or deceive the other.

90 A contract negotiated by mail is formed when notice of acceptance of the offer is duly deposited in the post-office, properly addressed This rule applies, although the party making the offer expressly requires that if it is accepted, speedy notice of acceptance shall be given him

91 The date of an instrument is so far a material part of it, that an alteration of the date by the holder after execution, makes the instrument void.

92. A corporation may maintain an action for libel, for words published of them and relating to its trade or business, by which it has incurred special damages

93 It is unprofessional for a lawyer who has abandoned his case without trying it, a term or two before trial, to claim a fee conditional upon the success of his client, although his client was successful

94 Although a party obtaining damages for injuries received through the default of another, was himself guilty of negligence, yet that will not defeat his recovery, unless his negligence contributed to cause the injury

95 A person may contract to labor for another during life, in consideration of receiving his support, but his creditors have the right to inquire into the intention with which such arrangement is made, and it will be set aside if entered into to deprive them of his future earnings

96 A grantor may by express terms exclude the bed of a river, or a highway, mentioned as boundary, but if without language of exclusion a line is described as 'along,' or ' upon,' or as ' running to ' the highway or river, or as ' by,' or ' running to the bank of' the river, these expressions carry the grantee to the center of the highway or river

97 The court will take pains to construe the words used in a deed in such a way as to effect the intention of the parties, however unskillfully the instrument may be drawn But a court of law cannot exchange an intelligible word plainly employed in a deed for another, however evident it may be that the word used was used by mistake for another

98 One who has lost his memory and understanding is entitled to legal protection, whether such loss is occasioned by his own misconduct or by an act of Providence

99 When a wife leaves her husband voluntarily, it must be shown, in order to make him liable for necessaries furnished to her, that she could not stay with safety Personal violence, either threatened or inflicted, will be sufficient cause for such separation.

100 Necessaries of dress furnished to a discarded wife must correspond with the pecuniary circumstances of the husband, and be such articles as the wife, if prudent, would expect, and the husband should furnish, if the parties lived harmoniously together.

101 A fugitive from justice from one of the United States to another, may be arrested and detained in order to his surrender by authority of the latter, without a previous demand for his surrender by the executive of the State whence he fled

102 A watch will not pass under a bequest of "wearing apparel," nor of "household furniture and articles for family use "

103 Money paid for the purpose of settling or compounding a prosecution for a supposed felony, cannot be recovered back by a party paying it.

104 An innkeeper is liable for the death of an animal in his possession, but may free himself from liability by showing that the death was not occasioned by negligence on his part

105 Notice to the agent of a company is notice to the company

106 An employer is not liable to one of his employees for an injury sustained by the latter in consequence of the neglect of others of his employees engaged in the same general business

107 Where a purchaser at a Sheriff's sale has bid the full price of property under the erroneous belief that the sale would divest the property of all liens, it is the duty of the court to give relief by setting aside the sale

108 When notice of protest is properly sent by mail, it may be sent by the mail of the day of the dishonor, If not, it must be mailed for the mail of the next day, except that if there is none, or it closes at an unseasonably early hour, then notice must be mailed in season for the next possible mail

109 A powder-house located in a populous part of a city, and containing large quantities of gunpowder, is a nuisance

110 When the seller of goods accepts at the time of the sale, the note of a third person, unindorsed by the purchaser, in payment, the presumption is that the payment was intended to be absolute, and though the note should be dishonored, the purchaser will not be liable for the value of the goods

111 A man charged with crime before a committing magistrate, but discharged on his own recognizance, is not privileged from arrest on civil process while returning from the magistrate's office

112. When one has been induced to sell goods by means of false pretences, he cannot recover them from one who has bona fide purchased and obtained possession of them from the fraudulent vendor

113. If the circumstances attendant upon a sale and delivery of personal property are such as usually and naturally accompany such a transaction, it cannot be declared a legal fraud upon creditors

114 A stamp impressed upon an instrument by way of seal, is good as a seal, if it creates a durable impression in the texture of the paper

115 If a party bound to make a payment use due diligence to make a tender, but through the payee's absence from home is unable to find him or any agent authorized to take payment for him, no forfeiture will be incurred through his failure to make a tender

## Government Land Measure.

A township, 36 sections, each a mile square

A section, 640 acres

A quarter section, half a mile square, 160 acres

An eighth section, half a mile long, north and south, and a quarter of a mile wide, 80 acres

A sixteenth section, a quarter of a mile square, 40 acres

The sections are numbered from one to thirty-six, commencing at the northeast corner, thus

| 6 | 5 | 4 | 3 | 2 | n w\|n e |
|---|---|---|---|---|---|
|   |   |   |   |   | s w\|s e |
| 7 | 8 | 9 | 10 | 11 | 12 |
| 18 | 17 | 16 | 15 | 14 | 13 |
| 19 | 20 | 21 | 22 | 23 | 24 |
| 30 | 29 | 28 | 27 | 26 | 25 |
| 31 | 32 | 33 | 34 | 35 | 36 |

The sections are all divided in quarters, which are named by the cardinal points, as in section one The quarters are divided in the same way The description of a 40 acre lot would read. The south half of the west half of the southwest quarter of section. in township 24, north of range 7 west, or as the case might be, and sometimes will fall short, and sometimes overrun the number of acres it is supposed to contain

# THE DECIMAL SYSTEM

### OF

# WEIGHTS AND MEASURES.

### As Authorized by Act of Congress--Approved July 28, 1866.

## STANDARDS.

In every system of Weights and Measures it is necessary to have what are called "*Standards*," as the pound, yard, gallon, &c , to be divided and multiplied into smaller and larger parts and denominations. The definition and construction of these Standards involve philosophical and scientific principles of a somewhat abstruse character, and are made and procured by the legislative department of the government. The nominal Standards in the new system are the METER, the ARE, the LITER, and the GRAM. The only *real* Standard, the one by which all the other standards are measured, and from which the system derives its name of "Metric," is the METER

## THE METER

Is used for all measures of length, distance, breadth, depth, heighth, &c., and was intended to be, and is very nearly, one ten-millionth of the distance on the earth's surface from the equator to the pole  It is about 39¾ inches, or 3 feet, 3 inches and 3 eighths, and is to be substituted for the yard

## THE ARE

Is a surface whose side is ten Meters, and is equal to 100 square Meters or about 4 square rods

## THE LITER

Is the unit for measuring solids and capacity, and is equal to the contents of a cube whose edge is one-tenth of a meter  It is about equal to 1 quart, and is a standard in cubic, dry and liquid measures

D

☞ A cubic Meter (or Kiloliter) is called a *stere*, and is also used as a standard in certain cubic measures

## THE GRAM

Is the Unit of *weight*, and is the weight of a cube of pure water, each edge of the cube being one one-hundredth of a Meter.  It is about equal to 15¼ grains.  It is intended as the Standard in *all* weights, and with its divisions and multiples, to supersede the use of what are now called Avoirdupois, Apothecaries and Troy Weights

Each of the foregoing Standards is divided decimally, and larger units are also formed by multiples of 10, 100, &c.  The successive subordinate parts are designated by the prefixes Deci, Centi and Milli, the successive multiples by Deka, Hecto, Kilo and Myria, each having its own numerical signification, as will be more clearly seen in the tables hereinafter given

The terms used may, at first sight, have a formidable appearance, seem difficult to pronounce, and to retain in memory, and to be, therefore, objectionable; but with a little attention and use, the apprehended difficulty will be found more apparent than real, as has been abundantly proved by experience  The importance, also, of conformity in the use of commercial terms, on the part of the United States, with the practice of the many nations in which the system, *with its present nomenclature*, has already been adopted, must greatly over-balance the comparatively slight objection alluded to.

# TABLES.

## MONEY

| OLD | | | NEW. | |
|---|---|---|---|---|
| 4 farthing make | 1 penny. | | 10 mills make | 1 cent |
| 12 pence | " | 1 shilling. | 10 cents " | 1 dime |
| 20 shillings | " | 1 pound. | 10 dimes " | 1 dollar. |

## LONG AND CLOTH MEASURE.—NEW.

| 10 | millimeters | make | 1 | centimeter |
|---|---|---|---|---|
| 10 | centimeters | " | 1 | decimeter |
| 10 | decimeters | " | 1 | METER |
| 10 | meters | " | 1 | dekameter |
| 10 | dekameters | " | 1 | hectometer. |
| 10 | hectometers | " | 1 | kilometer |
| 10 | kilometers | " | 1 | myriameter |

## SQUARE MEASURE —NEW

| 100 | square millimeters make | 1 | square centimeter. |
|---|---|---|---|
| 100 | square centimeters " | 1 | square decimeter |
| 100 | square decimeters " | 1 | square meter or CENTARE |
| 100 | centares " | 1 | ARE |
| 100 | ares " | 1 | hectare. |

☞ The denominations less than the Are, including the Meter, are used in specifying the contents of surfaces of small extent ; the terms *Centare, Are* and *Hectare*, in expressing quantities of land surveyed or measured

The above table may, however, be continued beyond the Meter, thus:

| 100 | square meters | make | 1 | square dekameter |
|---|---|---|---|---|
| 100 | square dekameters | " | 1 | square hectometer. |
| 100 | square hectometers | " | 1 | square kilometer |
| 100 | square kilometers | " | 1 | square myriameter. |

## CUBIC MEASURE —NEW.

### For Solids.

| 1000 | cubic millimeters | make | 1 | cubic centimeter. |
|---|---|---|---|---|
| 1000 | cubic centimeters | " | 1 | cubic decimeter or liter |
| 1000 | cubic decimeters | " | 1 | cubic meter or stere. |
| 1000 | cubic meters | " | 1 | cubic dekameter |
| 1000 | cubic dekameters | " | 1 | cubic hectometer |
| 1000 | cubic hectometers | " | 1 | cubic kilometer |
| 1000 | cubic kilometers | " | 1 | cubic myriameter |

### For Dry and Liquid Measures

| 10 | milliliters | make | 1 | centiliter. |
|---|---|---|---|---|
| 10 | centiliters | " | 1 | deciliter |
| 10 | deciliters | " | 1 | LITER |
| 10 | liters | " | 1 | dekaliter |
| 10 | dekaliters | " | 1 | hectoliter |
| 10 | hectoliters | " | 1 | kiloliter |
| 10 | kiloliters | " | 1 | myrialiter. |

[☞ A LITER, the standard of Measures of Capacity, usually in a cylindrical form, is equivalent to a cubic *Decimeter*, or the one-thousandth part of a cubic Meter, the contents of which are about one quart ]

The Kiloliter, or STERE, is a cubic Meter, and is used as a unit in measuring firewood and lumber.

| 10 | decisteres | make | 1 | stere |
|---|---|---|---|---|
| 10 | steres | " | 1 | dekastere. |

## ALL WEIGHTS —NEW

| 10 | milligrams | make | 1 | centigram |
|---|---|---|---|---|
| 10 | centigrams | " | 1 | decigram. |
| 10 | decigrams | " | 1 | GRAM |
| 10 | grams | " | 1 | dekagram. |
| 10 | dekagrams | " | 1 | hectogram |
| 10 | hectograms | " | 1 | kilogram |
| 10 | kilograms | " | 1 | myriagram. |
| 10 | myriagrams | " | 1 | quintal |
| 10 | quintals | " | 1 | millier or tonneau |

# PRONUNCIATION OF TERMS.

| TERMS | ENGLISH | TERMS | ENGLISH |
|---|---|---|---|
| Meter, | Mee-ter. | Stere, | Stars. |
| Millimeter | Mill-e-mee-ter | Are, | Are |
| Centimeter | Sent-e-mee-ter. | Centare, | Sent-are. |
| Decimeter, | Des-e-mee-ter | Hectare, | Hect-are. |
| Dekameter, | Dek-a-mea-ter | Gram, | Gram, |
| Hectometer, | Hec-to-mee-ter. | Milligram, | Mill-e-gram |
| Kilometer, | Kill-o-mee-ter | Centigram, | Sent-e-gram |
| Myriameter, | Mir-e-a mee-ter. | Decigram, | Des-e-gram |
| Liter, | Li-ter | Dekagram, | Dek-a-gram. |
| Milliliter, | Mill-e-li-ter. | Hectogram, | Hec-to-gram |
| Centiliter, | Sent-e-li-ter. | Kilogram, | Kill-o-gram |
| Deciliter, | Des-e-ll-ter | Myriagram, | Mir-e-a-gram |
| Dekaliter, | Dek-a-li-ter | Quintal, | Quin-tal |
| Hectoliter, | Hec-to-li-ter. | Millier, | Mill-i-er |
| Kiloliter, | Kill-o-li-ter | Tonneau, | Tun-no |
| Myrialiter, | Mir-e-a-ll-ter | | |

## Acts and Resolutions of Congress

### PUBLIC — No. 183.

AN ACT to authorize the use of the metric system of weights and measures

*Be it enacted by the Senate and House of Representatives of the United States of America in Congress assembled,* That from and after the passage of this act, it shall be lawful throughout the United States of America to employ the weights and measures of the metric system, and no contract or dealing, or pleading in any court, shall be deemed invalid or liable to objection, because the weights or measures expressed or referred to therein are weights or measures of the metric system

SEC 2 *And be it further enacted,* That the tables in the schedule hereto annexed, shall be recognized in the construction of contracts, and in all legal proceedings, as establishing, in terms of the weights and measures now in use in the United States, the equivalents of the weights and measures expressed therein in terms of the metric system, and said tables may be lawfully used for computing, determining and expressing, in customary weights and measures, the weights and measures of the metric system

## MEASURES OF LENGTH

| METRIC DENOMINATIONS AND VALUES. | | EQUIVALENTS IN DENOMINATIONS IN USE |
|---|---|---|
| Myriametre, | 10,000 metres, | 6 2137 miles. |
| Kilometre,.. | 1,000 metres, | 0 62137 mile, or 2,280 feet and 10 inches |
| Hectometre, .. | 100 metres, | 328 feet and one inch |
| Dekametre, | 10 metres, | 393 7 inches |
| Metre, .. ... | 1 metre, | 39 37 inches. |
| Decimetre, . | 1–10th of a metre, | 3 987 inches. |
| Centimetre, ..... | 1–100th of a metre, | 0 3937 inch. |
| Millimetre, . | 1–1000th of a metre, | 0 0394 inch. |

## MEASURES OF SURFACE.

| METRIC DENOMINATIONS AND VALUES | | EQUIVALENTS IN DENOMINATIONS IN USE |
|---|---|---|
| Hectare, ... .. | 10,000 square metres, | 2 471 acres |
| Are, ........ | 100 square metres, | 119 6 square yards |
| Centare, ... . .. | 1 square metre, | 1 550 square inches |

## MEASURES OF CAPACITY.

| METRIC DENOMINATIONS AND VALUES. | | | EQUIVALENTS IN DENOMINATIONS IN USE. | |
| --- | --- | --- | --- | --- |
| Names. | No. of liters. | Cubic Measure | Dry Measure | Liquid or Wine Measure. |
| Kilolitre or stere,..... | 1000 | 1 cubic metre, .. | 1.308 cubic yard, | 264 17 gallons |
| Hectolitre, ..... | 100 | .1 of a cubic metre,.. | 2 bus. and 3 35 pecks, .. | 26 417 gallons. |
| Dekalitre, .. .... | 10 | 10 cubic decimetres,.. | 9.08 quarts, | 2 6417 gallons |
| Litre, .. . .... | 1 | 1 cubic decimetre, | 0.908 quart, | 1 0567 quart. |
| Decilitre, .. ... | 0.1 | of a cubic decimetre, | 6.1022 cubic inches, .... | 0 845 gill |
| Centilitre, .. .. | 0 01 | 10 cubic centimetres, .. | 0.6102 cubic inch,. | 0 338 fluid ounce |
| Millilitre, . . .. | 0 001 | 1 cubic centimetre, | 0.061 cubic inch, .. | 0 27 fluid drachm |

## WEIGHTS.

| Metric Denominations and Values | | | Equivalents in Denominations in Use |
|---|---|---|---|
| Names | No of grams | Weight of what quantity of water at maximum density | Avoirdupois weight. |
| Millier or tonneau, | 1000000 | 1 cubic metre,... ... | 2204 6 pounds |
| Quintal, .... .. | 100000 | 1 hectolitre, . ........ | 220 46 pounds. |
| Myriagram, . . | 10000 | 10 litres, .... .... ... | 22 046 pounds |
| Kilogram, or kilo,. | 1000 | 1 litre, . .... ... | 2 2046 pounds. |
| Hectogram,.. . . . | 100 | 1 decilitre, . .... | 3 5274 ounces. |
| Dekagram, . ... | 10 | 10 cubic centimetres, . . | 0 3527 ounce |
| Gram, .... .. | 1 | 1 cubic centimetre, . | 15 432 grains |
| Decigram, . .. . . | 1-10 | 1 of a cubic centimetre . | 0 5432 grain |
| Centigram,... .. | 1-100 | 10 cubic millimetres, | 0 1543 grain |
| Milligram, .. .... . | 1-1000 | 1 cubic millimetre, | 0 0154 grain |

# INTEREST TABLE.

**At Seven per Cent. in Dollars and Cents, from $1 to $10,000.**

| AM'NT | 1 day. | 7 days. | 15 days. | 1 mo | 3 mos | 6 mos. | 12 mos |
|---|---|---|---|---|---|---|---|
| $ | $ C. | $ C | $ C. | $ C. | $ C | $ C. | $ C. |
| 1 | 00 | 00 | 00¼ | 00½ | 01¾ | 03½ | 07 |
| 2 | 00 | 00¼ | 00½ | 01¼ | 03½ | 07 | 14 |
| 3 | 00 | 00⅓ | 00¾ | 01¾ | 05¼ | 10½ | 21 |
| 4 | 00 | 00½ | 01 | 02⅓ | 07 | 14 | 28 |
| 5 | 00 | 00¾ | 01½ | 03 | 08¾ | 17½ | 35 |
| 6 | 00 | 00¾ | 01¾ | 03½ | 10½ | 21 | 42 |
| 7 | 00 | 01 | 02 | 04 | 12¼ | 24½ | 49 |
| 8 | 00 | 01 | 02¼ | 04⅔ | 14 | 28 | 56 |
| 9 | 00 | 01¼ | 02½ | 05¼ | 15¾ | 31½ | 63 |
| 10 | 00¼ | 01¼ | 03 | 5¾ | 17½ | 35 | 70 |
| 20 | 00⅓ | 02¾ | 06 | ⅔ | 35 | 70 | 1 40 |
| 30 | 00½ | 04 | 09 | 17½ | 52½ | 1 05 | 2 10 |
| 40 | 00¾ | 05½ | 12 | 23⅓ | 70 | 1 40 | 2 80 |
| 50 | 01 | 06¾ | 15 | 29¼ | 87½ | 1 75 | 3 50 |
| 100 | 02 | 13½ | 29 | 58⅓ | 1 75 | 3 50 | 7 00 |
| 200 | 04 | 27¼ | 58 | 1 16⅔ | 3 50 | 7 00 | 14 00 |
| 300 | 06 | 40¾ | 87½ | 1 75 | 5 25 | 10 50 | 21 00 |
| 400 | 08 | 54½ | 1 17 | 2 33⅓ | 7 00 | 14 00 | 28 00 |
| 500 | 10 | 68 | 1 46 | 2 91⅔ | 8 75 | 17 50 | 35 00 |
| 1000 | 19½ | 1 36 | 2 92 | 5 83⅓ | 17 50 | 35 00 | 70 00 |
| 2000 | 39 | 2 72¼ | 5 83 | 11 66⅔ | 35 00 | 70 00 | 140 00 |
| 3000 | 58 | 4 08¼ | 8 75 | 17 50 | 52 50 | 105 00 | 210 00 |
| 4000 | 78 | 5 44½ | 11 67 | 23 33⅓ | 70 00 | 140 00 | 280 00 |
| 5000 | 97 | 6 80½ | 14 58 | 29 16⅔ | 87 50 | 175 00 | 350 00 |
| 10000 | 1 94 | 13 61 | 29 17 | 58 33 | 175 00 | 350 00 | 700 00 |

## Discount and Premium.

When a person buys an article for $1,00—20 per cent off, (or discount,) and sells it again for $1,00, he makes a profit of 25 per cent on his investment. Thus He pays 80 cents and sells for $1,00—a gain of 20 cents, or 25 per cent of 80 cents And for any transaction where the sale or purchase of gold, silver, or currency is concerned, the following rules will apply in all cases

RULE 1st —To find premium when discount is given　Multiply 100 by rate of discount and divide by 100, less rate of discount

RULE 2d —To find discount when premium is given　Multiply the rate of interest by 100, and divide by 100, plus the rate of premium

Suppose A has $140 in currency, which he wishes to exchange for gold, when gold is 27 per cent premium, how much gold should he receive? In this case the premium is given, consequently we must find the discount on A's currency and subtract it from the $140, as per rule 2d, showing the discount to be a trific more than 21 per cent and that he should receive $110 60 in gold

| 5 pr ct Dis allows | †5½ pr ct Pre or profit |
|---|---|
| 10 " " " †11 " " " |
| 15 " " " †17½ " " " |
| 20 " " " 25 " " " |
| 25 " " " 33½ " " " |
| 30 " " " *43 " " " |
| 40 " " " 69¾ " " " |
| 50 " " " 100 " " " |

☞ A dagger (†) denotes the profits to be a fraction more than specified　A (*) denotes profits to be a fraction less than specified.

---

## Table of Weights of Grain, Seeds, &c.

ACCORDING TO THE LAWS OF NEW YORK

| Barley weighs | .... .. 48 lb per bushel |
|---|---|
| Beans " | .. 62 " " |
| Buckwheat " | . ..... 48 " " |
| Clover Seed | .. .. 60 " " |
| Corn　weighs | .. .. 88 " " |
| Flax Seed* " | .. 55 " " |
| Oats " | .. 32 " " |
| Peas " | . 60 " " |
| Potatoes " | .. ... 60 " " |
| Rye " | ... 56 " " |
| Timothy Seed | .. .... .. 44 " " |
| Wheat " | .. 60 " " |

*Flax Seed by cust'm weighs 56 lb. per bush.

---

## Facts on Advertising.

The advertisements in an ordinary number of the London Times exceed 2,500　The annual advertising bills of one London firm are said to amount to $200,000, and three others are mentioned who each annually expend for the purpose $50,000　The expense for advertising the eight editions of the "Encyclopædia Britannia" is said to have been $15,000

In large cities nothing is more common than to see large business establishments, which seem to have an immense advantage over all competitors, by the wealth, experience, and prestige they have acquired, drop gradually out of public view, and be succeeded by firms of a smaller capital, more energy, and more determined to have the fact that they sell such and such commodities known from one end of the land to the other　In other words, the establishments advertise, the old die of dignity — The former are ravenous to pass out of obscurity into publicity, the latter believe that their publicity is so obvious that it cannot be obscured　The first understand that they must thrust themselves upon public attention, or be disregarded; the second, having once obtained public attention, suppose they have arrested it permanently, while, in fact, nothing is more characteristic of the world than the ease with which it forgets

Stephen Girard, than whom no shrewder business man ever lived, used to say 'I have always considered advertising liberally and long to be the great medium of success in business, and the prelude to wealth　And I have made it an invariable rule too, to advertise in the dullest times as well as the busiest, long experience having taught me that money thus spent is well laid out; as by keeping my business continually before the public it has secured me many sales that I would otherwise have lost.

---

## Capacity of Cisterns or Wells.

Tabular view of the number of gallons contained in the clear, between the brick work for each ten inches of depth

| Diameter | | Gallons |
|---|---|---|
| 2 feet equals | | 19 |
| 2½ | " | 30 |
| 3 | " | 44 |
| 3½ | " | 60 |
| 4 | " | 78 |
| 4½ | " | 97 |
| 5 | " | 122 |
| 5½ | " | 148 |
| 6 | " | 176 |
| 6½ | " | 207 |
| 7 | " | 240 |
| 7½ | " | 275 |
| 8 | " | 313 |
| 8½ | " | 353 |
| 9 | " | 396 |
| 9½ | " | 451 |
| 10 | " | 489 |
| 11 | " | 592 |
| 12 | " | 705 |
| 13 | " | 827 |
| 14 | " | 959 |
| 15 | " | 1101 |
| 20 | " | 1958 |
| 25 | " | 3059 |

## Brilliant Whitewash.

Many have heard of the brilliant stucco whitewash on the east end of the President's house at Washington  The following is a recipe for it; it is gleaned from the National Intelligencer, with some additional improvements learned by experiments;  Take half a bushel of nice unslacked lime, slack it with boiling water, cover it during the process to keep in the steam  Strain the liquid through a fine sieve or strainer, and add to it a peck of salt, previously well dissolved in warm water ; three pounds of ground rice, boiled to a thin paste, and stirred in boiling hot, half a pound of powdered Spanish whiting, and a pound of clean glue, which has been previously dissolved by soaking it well, and then hanging it over a slow fire, in a small kettle within a large one filled with water  Add five gallons of hot water to the mixture, stir it well, and let it stand a few days covered from the dirt

It should be put on right hot, for this purpose it can be kept in a kettle on a portable furnace  It is said that about a pint of this mixture will cover a square yard upon the outside of a house if properly applied  Brushes more or less small may be used according to the neatness of the job required  It answers as well as oil paint for wood, brick or stone, and is cheaper  It retains its brilliancy for many years  There is nothing of the kind that will compare with it, either for inside or outside walls

Coloring matter may be put in and made of any shade you like  Spanish brown stirred in will make red pink, more or less deep according to the quantity  A delicate tinge of this is very pretty, for inside walls  Finely pulverized common clay, well mixed with Spanish brown, makes a reddish stone color.  Yellow-ochre stirred in makes yellow wash, but chrome goes further, and makes a color generally esteemed prettier  In all these cases the darkness of the shades of course is determined by the quantity of coloring used.  It is difficult to make rules, because tastes are different  It would be best to try experiments on a shingle and let it dry  We have been told that green must not be mixed with lime  The lime destroys the color, and the color has an effect on the whitewash, which makes it crack and peel  When walls have been badly smoked, and you wish to have them a clean white, it is well to squeeze indigo plentifully through a bag into the water you use, before it is stirred in the whole mixture  If a larger quantity than five gallons be wanted, the same proportion should be observed

## How to get a Horse out of a Fire.

The great difficulty of getting horses from a stable where surrounding buildings are in a state of conflagration, is well known —  The plan of covering their eyes with a blanket will not always succeed

A gentleman whose horses have been in great peril from such a cause, having tried in vain to save them, hit upon the expedient of having them harnessed as though going to their usual work, when, to his astonishment, they were led from the stable without difficulty.

---

## The Chemical Barometer.

Take a long narrow bottle, such as an old-fashioned Eau-de-Cologne bottle, and put into it two and a half drachms of camphor, and eleven drachms of spirits of wine, when the camphor is dissolved, which it will readily do by slight agitation, add the following mixture  Take water, nine drachms, nitrate of potash (saltpetre) thirty-eight grains, and murlate of ammonia (sal ammoniac) thirty-eight grains  Dissolve these salts in the water prior to mixing with the camphorated spirit ; then shake the whole well together  Cork the bottle well, and wax the top, but afterwards make a very small aperture in the cork with a red-hot needle  The bottle may then be hung up, or placed in any stationary position  By observing the different appearances which the materials assume, as the weather changes, it becomes an excellent prognosticator of a coming storm or of a sunny sky

---

## Leech Barometer.

Take an eight ounce phial, and put in it three gills of water, and place in it a healthy leech, changing the water in summer once a week, and in winter once in a fortnight, and it will most accurately prognosticate the weather  If the weather is to be fine, the leech lies motionless at the bottom of the glass and coiled together in a spiral form, if rain may be expected, it will creep up to the top of its lodgings and remain there till the weather is settled, if we are to have wind, it will move through its habitation with amazing swiftness, and seldom goes to rest till it begins to blow hard, if a remarkable storm of thunder and rain is to succeed, it will lodge for some days before almost continually out of the water, and discover great uneasiness in violent throes and convulsive-like motions, in frost as in clear summer-like weather it lies constantly at the bottom; and in snow as in rainy weather it pitches its dwelling in the very mouth of the phial  The top should be covered over with a piece of muslin

---

To MEASURE GRAIN IN A BIN.—Find the number of cubic feet, from which deduct *one-fifth*  The remainder is the number of bushels—allowing, however, one bushel extra to every 224.  Thus in a remainder of 224 there would be 225 bushels  In a remainder of  448 there would be 450 bushels, &c.

# VALUABLE RECIPES.

---

[The following recipes are vouched for by several who have tried them and proven their virtues  Many of them have been sold singly for more than the price of this book —Pub ]

## HORSES

RING BONE AND SPAVIN —2 oz  each of Spanish flies and Venice turpentine, 1 oz. each of aqua ammonia and euphorbium ;  ⅓ oz red precipitate; ⅓ oz  corrosive sublimate, 1½ lbs. lard   When thoroughly pulverized and mixed, heat carefully so as not to burn, and pour off free from sediment.

For ring-bone, rub in thoroughly, after removing hair, once in 48 hours   For spavin, once in 24 hours   Cleanse and press out the matter on each application

POLL-EVIL —Gum arabic ⅓ oz ; common potash ⅓ oz , extract of belladonna ⅓ dr. Put the gum in just enough water to dissolve it   Pulverize the potash and mix with the dissolved gum, and then put in the extract of belladonna, and it will be ready for use   Use with a syringe after having cleansed with soap suds, and repeat once in two days till a cure is affected.

SCOURS —Powdered tormentil root, given in milk, from 3 to 5 times daily till cured.

GREASE-HEEL AND SCRATCHES —Sweet oil 6 ozs , borax 2 ozs , sugar of lead 2 ozs   Wash off with dish water, and, after it is dry, apply the mixture twice a day

CHOLIC IN HORSES —To ⅓ pt of warm water add 1 oz  laudanum and 3 ozs  spirits of turpentine, and repeat the dose in about ⅓ of an hour, adding ⅓ oz powdered aloes, if not relieved.

BOTS.—Three doses  1st, 2 qts milk and 1 of molasses  2d  15 minutes after, 2 qts, warm sage tea  3d  After the expiration of 30 minutes, sufficient lard to physic.— Never fails

## MISCELLANEOUS

PILES—PERFECTLY CURED —Take flour of sulphur 1 oz , rosin 3 ozs , pulverize and mix well together   (Color with carmine or cochineal, if you like.)  *Dose*—What will lie on a five cent piece, night and morning, washing the parts freely in cold water once or twice a day.  This is a remedy of great value

The cure will be materially hastened by taking a table-spoon of sulphur in a half pint of milk, daily, until the cure is affected.

SURE CURE FOR CORNS, WARTS AND CHILBLAINS —Take of nitric and muriatic acids, blue vitriol and salts of tartar, 1 oz  each   Add the blue vitriol, pulverized, to either of the acids, add the salts of tartar in the same way ; when done foaming, add the other acid, and in a few days it will be ready for use.  For chilblains and corns apply it very lightly with a swab, and repeat in a day or two until cured  For warts, once a week, until they disappear

HOOF-AIL IN SHEEP —Mix 2 ozs. each of butter of antimony and muriatic acid with 1 oz. of pulverized white vitriol, and apply once or twice a week to the bottom of the foot.

COMMON RHEUMATISM —Kerosene oil 2 ozs ; neats-foot oil 1 oz ; oil of organum ⅓ oz   Shake when used, and rub and heat in twice daily.

VERY FINE SOAP, QUICKLY AND CHEAPLY MADE.—Fourteen pounds of bar soap in a half a boiler of hot water , cut up fine , add three pounds of sal-soda made fine, one ounce of pulverized rosin ; stir it often till all is dissolved , just as you take it off the fire, put in two table-spoonfuls of spirits of turpentine and one of ammonia ; pour it in a barrel, and fill up with cold soft water ; let it stand three or four days before using  It is an excellent soap for washing clothes, extracting the dirt readily, and not fading colored articles.

**WATER PROOF FOR LEATHER** —Take linseed oil 1 pint, yellow wax and white turpentine each ½ ozs Burgundy pitch 1 oz., melt and color with lampblack

**To KEEP CIDER SWEET** —Put into each barrel, immediately after making, ¼ lb ground mustard, 2 oz salt and 2 oz pulverized chalk Stir them in a little cider, pour them into the barrel, and shake up well

**AGUE CURE** –Procure 1¼ table-spoons of fresh mandrake root juice, (by pounding) and mix with the same quantity of molasses, and take in three equal doses, 2 hours a part, the whole to be taken 1 hour before the chill comes on Take a swallow of some good bitters before meals, for a couple of weeks after the chills are broken, and the cure will be permanent

**CURE FOR SALT RHEUM OR SCURVY** —Take of the pokeweed, any time in summer; pound it, press out the juice; strain it into a pewter dish, set it in the sun till it becomes a salve—then put it into an earthen mug, add to it fresh water and bees' wax sufficient to make an ointment of common consistency, simmer the whole over a fire till thoroughly mixed When cold, rub the part affected The patient will almost immediately experience its good effects, and the most obstinate cases will be cured in three or four months Tested — The juice of the ripe berries may be prepared in the same way

**SUPERIOR PAINT—FOR BRICK HOUSES** — To lime whitewash, add for a fastener, sulphate of zinc, and shade with any color you choose, as yellow ochre, Venetian red, etc It outlasts oil paint

**FELONS** —Stir 1 oz, of Venice turpentine with ¼ tea-spoonful of water, till it looks like caudled honey, and apply by spreading upon cloth and wrapping around the finger If not too long delayed will cure in 6 hours. A poke root poultice is also said to be a sure remedy.

**WATER PROOF BLACKING AND HARNESS POLISH** —Take two and a half ounces gum shellac and half a pint of alcohol, and set in a warm place until dissolved, then add two and a half ounces Venice turpentine to neutralize the alcohol; add a tablespoonful of lampblack Apply with a fine sponge It will give a good polish over oil or grease

**MOSQUITOS** —To get rid of these tormentors, take a few hot coals on a shovel, or a chafing dish, and burn upon them some brown sugar in your bed-rooms and parlors, and you effectually banish or destroy every mosquito for the night

**CHEAP OUTSIDE PAINT.**—Take two parts (in bulk) of water lime ground fine, one part (in bulk) of white lead ground in oil. Mix them thoroughly, by adding best boiled linseed oil, enough to prepare it to pass through a paint mill, after which temper with oil till it can be applied with a common paint brush Make any color to suit. It will last three times as long as lead paint, and cost not one fourth as much IT IS SUPERIOR

**CURE FOR A COUGH** —A strong decoction of the leaves of the pine, sweetened with loaf sugar Take a wine-glass warm on going to bed, and half an hour before eating, three times a day The above is sold as a cough syrup, and is doing wonderful cures, and it is sold at a great profit to the manufacturers.

---

## How to Judge a Horse.

A correspondent, contrary to old maxims, undertakes to judge the character of a horse by outward appearances, and offers the following suggestions, the result of his close observation and long experience·

If the color be light sorrell, or chestnut, his feet, legs and face white, these are marks of kindness If he is broad and full between the eyes, he may be depended on as a horse of good sense, and capable of being trained to anything

As respects such horses, the more kindly you treat them the better you will be treated in return Nor will a horse of this description stand a whip, if well fed.

If you want a safe horse, avoid one that is dish-faced He may be so far gentle as not to scare; but he will have too much go-ahead in him to be safe with everybody

If you want a fool, but a horse of great bottom, get a deep bay, with not a white hair about him If his face is a little dished, so much the worse Let no man ride such a horse that is not an adept in riding —they are always tricky and unsafe

If you want one that will never give out, never buy a large, overgrown one

A black horse cannot stand heat, nor a white one cold

If you want a gentle horse, get one with more or less white about the head, the more the better Many persons suppose the parti-colored horses belonging to the circuses, shows, &c , are selected for their oddity But the selections thus made are on account of their great docility and gentleness

## Measurement of Hay in the Mow or Stack.—It is often desirable, where conveniences for weighing are not at hand, to purchase and sell hay by measurement It is evident that no fixed rule will answer in all cases, as it would require more cubic feet at the top of a mow than at the bottom The general rule adopted by those who have tested it, is 7½ cubic feet of solid Timothy hay, as taken from mow or bottom of stack. The rule may be varied for upper part of mow or stack according to pressure

# Almanac or Calendar for 20 Years.

| CB | A | G | F | E D | C | B | A | G F | E |
|---|---|---|---|---|---|---|---|---|---|
| 1864 | 1865 | 1866 | 1867 | 1868 | 1869 | 1870 | 1871 | 1872 | 1873 |
| D | C | B A | G | F | E | D C | F | E | D |
| 1874 | 1875 | 1876 | 1877 | 1878 | 1879 | 1880 | 1881 | 1882 | 1883 |
| 1 8 15 22 29 | Sun. | Sat. | Frid'y. | Thurs. | Wed. | Tues. | Mon. |
| 2 9 16 23 30 | Mon. | Sun. | Sat. | Frid'y. | Thurs | Wed. | Tues. |
| 3 10 17 24 31 | Tues. | Mon. | Sun. | Sat. | Frid'y | Thurs. | Wed. |
| 4 11 18 25 .. | Wed. | Tues. | Mon | Sun. | Sat. | Frid'y | Thurs |
| 5 12 19 26 . | Thurs. | Wed | Tues | Mon. | Sun. | Sat. | Frid'y. |
| 6 13 20 27 .. | Frid'y. | Thurs | Wed. | Tues. | Mon. | Sun. | Sat. |
| 7 14 21 28 .. | Sat | Frid'y. | Thurs. | Wed. | Tues. | Mon. | Sun. |
| Jan. and Oct. | A | B | C | D | E | F | G |
| May. | B | C | D | E | F | G | A |
| August. | C | D | E | F | G | A | B |
| Feb., Mar., Nov. | D | E | F | G | A | B | C |
| June. | E | F | G | A | B | C | D |
| Sept & Dec. | F | G | A | B | C | D | E |
| April & July. | G | A | B | C | D | E | F |

EXPLANATION.—Find the Year and observe the Letter above it, then look for the Month, and in a line with it find the Letter of the Year, above the Letter find the Day, and the figures on the left, in the same line, are the days of the same name in the month.

Leap Years have two letters; the first is used till the end of February, the second during the remainder of the year.

# CORTLAND COUNTY.

---

*THIS COUNTY* was formed from Onondaga, April 8, 1808, and embraces the original townships of Virgil, Cincinnnatus, Homer, Solon, and the south half of Tully and Fabius, in the southeast corner of the "Military Tract." It was named in honor of Pierre Van Cortlandt, the first Lieutenant Governor of the State of New York, and an extensive owner of lands upon the Military Tract. It lies near the center of the State, upon the northern spurs of the Alleghany Mountains, and just south of the watershed between Susquehanna River and Lake Ontario. It contains an area of 485 square miles, and is centrally distant 120 miles from Albany. The surface is hilly and in some places broken, consisting chiefly of arable ridges with narrow valleys between them. The highlands are divided into three general ridges, extending in a northerly and southerly direction. The first of these ridges occupies the extreme eastern border of the County, and is bounded on the west by the valley of Otselic River; the second lies between the Otselic and Tioughnioga Rivers; and the third embraces all the highlands lying west of the Tioughnioga River. The highlands are all divided latterly by the valleys of small streams, and in some places they are little more than a collection of sharp ridges, separated by narrow ravines. The northern part of the County spreads out into a high plateau, broken by hills. This level has an average elevation of 1,100 to 1,200 feet above tide, and the ridges are from 200 to 500 feet higher. A broad plain occupies the center of the western part of the County, and into this most of the valleys of the tributaries of the Tioughnioga open. South of this the valleys contract until they become mere ravines. The highest points of the County are Mount Toppin, in Preble; the Truxton Hills and the Owego Hills, in Virgil and Harford; which attain an elevation of 1,600 to 2,100 feet above tide.

Tioughnioga River constitutes the principal drainage of the County, flowing as it does through near the center. It enters the County by two branches, the eastern entering Cuyler from Madison County, and the western taking its rise in the small lakes in the northern part of Preble and the southern part of Onondaga County. The principal branches of the Tioughnioga are the Otselic, Trout, Cheningo and Labrador Creeks, and Cold and Factory Brooks. Otselic flows through a deep valley in the eastern part of the County, from Chenango County. The Skaneateles Inlet drains the north-western part of the County, the branches of Fall Creek the extreme western, and Owego Creek the south-western parts Skaneateles Lake, bordering on the north-western corner, is the largest body of water in the County. There are several small lakes in the northern part of the Tioughnioga Valley.

The Hamilton group of rocks enters the northern portions of the County; and towards the south, successively above this, appear the Genesee slate and the Portage and Chemung groups The Hamilton rocks consist of calcareous shale, with limestone and slate intermixed. Quarries of sandstone and limestone, affording excellent building material, are worked in Scott, Homer, Cortlandville, and several other parts of the County. A short distance south-east from Cortlandville are several small lakes, containing deposits of marl, from which an excellent quality of lime is manufactured. The soil upon the hills is chiefly a sandy or gravelly loam, and that of the valleys is of similar character, with a large mixture of disintegrated slate, shale and limestone.

This County is more elevated above tide than the regions north and west, and as a consequence has a colder climate. The winters are longer, and the snow falls to a greater depth. Agriculture constitutes the chief occupation of the people. Spring grains are largely produced in the valleys, but the whole County is better adapted to pasturage than to tillage. Dairying and stock raising are carried on extensively. Considerable attention is being paid to the raising of wool. Fruits are produced to some extent, but are liable to injury from frosts in the fall and spring. There is but little manufacturing carried on in the County.

The Syracuse, Binghamton and New York Railroad extends through the County, along the valley of the Tioughnioga, connecting with the New York & Erie at Binghamton, and with the New York Central at Syracuse. It has stations at Preble, Little York, Homer, Cortland, Blodgetts Mills, State Bridge and Marathon. The completion of this road has given an additional impulse to every branch of business, and has greatly increased the value of farms by furnishing an easy, direct and rapid communication to the great markets of the country.

It was evident to the early settlers of this County that the Tioughnioga River, as a commercial highway, could never be made available to any great extent, and that other channels of communication must be provided to encourage enterprise and promote the best interests of the inhabitants. State roads had been laid out and were improved to some extent, and the various towns were connected only by the imperfect roads which had succeeded the bridle paths through the forest, with marked trees as the only indication that human footsteps had ever before pressed the soil. Previous to the construction of the Erie Canal, the heavy goods of the merchants were brought up the Hudson River to Albany, and conveyed by land to Schenectady; thence up the Mohawk and through the canal at Little Falls to Rome; thence to Wood Creek, Oneida Lake, Seneca River, &c., a very roundabout way, from New York to Cortland. Sometimes goods were transported by land from Albany or Utica. Cattle were usually driven to Philadelphia, and potash was carried to New York or Montreal, for a market Grain was shipped on arks down the Tioughnioga and Susquehanna to Baltimore. Though these modes of conveyance were very tedious they were the best available, and at an early day the people set about devising some more expeditious means of transportation. In 1826 the New York Legislature granted a charter for a railroad from Syracuse to Binghamton. This was the first charter ever granted by the Legislature of this State. The inhabitants of Cortland County were greatly elated at the prospect of direct and speedy communication with the Erie Canal, which was completed in 1825. Their hopes were destined to be disappointed, and for more than a quarter of a century were not realized. In the mean time the population of the County had greatly increased and the commercial products had surpassed in amount the wildest dreams of the most sanguine. The West was so rapidly increasing in population and resources that the Erie Canal was no longer deemed sufficient for the commercial interests of the east and west, and the New York and Erie Railroad was projected and fast approaching completion The coal fields of Pennsylvania and the Great Lakes must be connected by some easy and cheap mode of transportation, whose route would lie through this County and open to its inhabitants a great thoroughfare for the transfer of their products. Under these circumstances the project of a railroad to connect the sea-board with the Great Lakes was revived and a new charter obtained. Books were opened for subscription, and in 1850 a sufficient amount of stock had been obtained to warrant the necessary surveys to be made. Most of the active participants in this enterprise were residents of Homer and Cortland. The road from Binghamton to Syracuse was commenced in 1852 and completed in 1854. The formal opening took place on the 18th and 19th of

October, amidst bon-fires, illuminations and every demonstration of joy. The length of the road is eighty miles and its cost about one and a quarter millions of dollars. For some time the Directors of the Syracuse & Binghamton Road were unable to make any satisfactory arrangements with the Oswego & Syracuse Road, and a charter was granted for another broad gage road on the east side of Onondaga Lake, but on account of financial embarrassments the road was not constructed. Recently a third rail has been laid on the Oswego & Syracuse Road, and now freight from Oswego can be shipped direct to New York and all points on the New York & Erie Road without change of cars. The coal trade is of vast importance to this road, as will be evident to any casual observer of the coal yards of Syracuse and other places on the line.

The County Seat is located at the village of Cortland. The Court House is a substantial brick building, located upon the corner of Court and Church streets. The Jail is of hewn stone and stands in the rear of the Court House; and the Clerk's Office is a brick structure standing on the west side of Main street The County Courts were first held at the school house, on lot 45, in Homer. By an act of April 5, 1810, Joseph L. Richardson, of Auburn, Nathan Smith, of Herkimer, and Nathaniel Locke, of Chenango, were appointed commissioners to select a site for a Court House, and $2,000 were appropriated for the erection of the building. The first County Officers were John Keep, *First Judge*, William Mallory, *Sheriff;* and John McWhorter, *Surrogate*. The County Poor House is situated upon a farm about three miles north-east of Cortland Village.

The first newspaper published in Cortland County was

*The Cortland Courier*, established at Homer in 1810, by James and Samuel Percival. In 1812, H. R. Bender and R. Washburne became the proprietors, and changed its name to

*The Farmers Journal.* In 1813, Jesse Searl became its proprietor, and issued it as

*The Cortland Repository*, and continued it till 1825, when Milton A. Kinney became its proprietor and changed its name to

*The Cortland Observer.* In 1833 it passed into the hands of S. S. Bradford, and in 1836 into those of Mr. Holmes, by whom its name was changed to

*The Homer Eagle.* In 1837 it was united with the *Cortland Republican*, and issued by R. A. Reid as

*The Republican and Eagle*, and continued until 1852. C. B. Gould then became proprietor and changed it to

*The Cortland County Whig.* In 1856 J. R. Dixon became proprietor and issued it as

THE CORTLAND COUNTY REPUBLICAN, and has continued its publication to the present time.

*The Protestant Sentinel* was started at Homer in 1831, by John Maxon, and continued until 1833.

*The Cortland Republican* was started in 1815, at Cortland Village, by James Percival, and was continued by him, by Osborn & Campbell, and by Campbell Brothers, until 1821

*The Western Courier* was founded at Homer in 1821, by Roberts & Hull, and was soon after removed to Cortland Village. In 1824 it appeared as

*The Cortland Journal*, and in 1832 as

*The Cortland Advocate.* It was published successively by C. W. Gill, H. S. Randall and David Fairchild, and in 1845 it was styled

*The Cortland Democrat.* It was subsequently published by Seth Haight and H. G. Crouch, and by A. P. Cole, who changed it to

*The Cortland Gazette* in 1857.

*The Cortland Chronicle* was started in 1828 by Reed & Osborn. It was sold to R. A. Reed in 1832, and by him called

*The Anti-Masonic Republican.* In 1833 it was issued as

*The Cortland Republican*, and in 1837 it was united with *The Homer Eagle.*

*The Liberty Herald* (semi-monthly,) was published at Cortland Village in 1844 and 1845, by E. F. Graham.

*The True American and Religious Examiner* was started in 1845, at Cortland Village, by C B. Gould. The next year it passed into the hands of S. R. Ward, and was issued by him as

*The True American*, and continued until 1848.

*The Republican Banner* was started in 1858 by C. D. Van Slyck and P. H. Bateson.

*The South Cortland Luminary* was published in 1840, at South Cortland, by M. Reynolds.

*The Morning Star* was published at McGrawville in 1850, and *The Central Reformer* in 1858 *

The Military Tract, of which this County forms a part, consisted of twenty-six townships, granted by the Legislature of the State of New York to soldiers of the Revolutionary war. Each township was ten miles square and contained one hundred lots. Each non-commissioned officer and private was entitled to 500 acres, to be drawn by lot. Congress subsequently passed an act granting 100 acres to each soldier, the land appropriated for this purpose being located in Ohio. Arrangements were made allowing the soldiers from this State to draw the whole 600 acres here, on their relinquishing all claim to the Ohio lands; but if the soldier neglected to do this, one-sixth part of what his patent called for reverted to the State, and subsequently became known as the "State's Hundred." Certain lots in each township were set apart for the sup-

*For further history of the Press in Cortland County, see *Errata*, following the Introduction.

port of the Gospel and schools. Lots 69, 76 and 81, in the township of Tully, 55 and 58, in Fabius; 4, 34, 70, 85, 93, 98, in Homer; 22, 25, 30, 41, 64, 98, in Solon; 20, 36, 51, 86, 91, 99, in Virgil; and 1, 16, 37, 49, 53 and 62, in Cincinnatus, were set apart for the foregoing purpose.

The first settlements of the County were made at Homer in 1791, in Virgil and Cortlandville in 1794, and in other towns before the commencement of the present century. Being remote from the great routes of travel, its settlement advanced more slowly than the more distant Genesee Valley, whose fertility attracted the pioneers of this remote region. The early settlers were from the Eastern States, and their habits of industry and frugality, as well as their religious principles, have been impressed upon the present generation, and are seen in their schools, academies and churches, which form so prominent a feature in the County. The early settlers were not entirely free from fear of Indian massacres, which had so often desolated the homes of other settlers, and sent a thrill of horror through their hearts almost as great as if actual hostilities were being carried on. The wild beasts often robbed them of a portion of their flocks and herds as well as of their growing crops, and long weary journeys were made to mill and to market, over roads impassable to all except the most daring. But these difficulties have passed away, mills have sprung up in all parts, good roads intersect the County in all directions, and the Iron Horse has placed the citizens within a few hours ride of the great metropolis of the nation; all this has been accomplished within little more than half a century.

*The Cortland County Agricultural Society* was organized on the first day of October, 1838, with the following officers: William Berry, President; Jesse Ives, Vice President; Cephas Comstock, Vice President; C. P. Jacobs, Secretary; Henry S. Randall, Corresponding Secretary; Rufus Boies, Treasurer; Paris Barber, Joseph Reynolds, Chas. McKnight, Israel Boies, Morris Miller, Chester H. Harris, Executive Committee. The first Fair was held in Cortland Village on the first Wednesday of September, 1839.

The following table will exhibit the names of the Presidents, as they were elected from year to year, the receipts of the Society, expenditures, &c.:

| | | | | | |
|---|---|---|---|---|---|
| 1840, | John Miller.... | Receipts, | $ 65,00.. | Expend's | $ 75,00 |
| 1841, | Jesse Ives...... | " | 37,00.. | " | 104,00 |
| 1842, | Dann Hibbard.. | " | 128,00.. | " | 125,00 |
| 1843, | William Randall | " | 115,00.. | " | 137,00 |
| 1844, | J. Barber...... | " | 187,00.. | " | 140,00 |
| 1845, | Rufus Boies.... | " | 185,00. | " | 173,00 |
| 1846, | H. S. Randall.. | " | 160,00.. | " | 128,00 |
| 1847, | Amos Rice..... | " | 168,00 | " | 168,00 |

| | | | | | |
|---|---|---|---|---|---|
| 1848, | Jas. S. Leach... | " | 210,00.. | " | 172,00 |
| 1849, | Peter Walrod.. | " | 296,00.. | " | 214,00 |
| 1850, | Hiram Hopkins | " | 260,00.. | " | 207,00 |
| 1851, | N. Hitchcock, jr | " | 311,00.. | " | 263,00 |
| 1852, | Anthony Freer. | " | 445,00.. | " | 571,00 |
| 1853, | Paris Barber... | " | 574,00.. | " | 482,00 |
| 1854, | F. H. Hibbard. | " | 670,00.. | " | 779,00 |
| 1855, | G. J. J. Barber | " | 1455,00.. | " | 1029,00 |
| 1856, | Israel Boies.... | " | 1305,00.. | " | 762,00 |
| 1857, | A. Chamberlain | " | 1082,00 . | " | 1007,00 |
| 1858, | S. D. Freer.... | " | 2721,00.. | " | 2658,00 |
| 1859, | M. Hobert .... | " | 1678,00.. | " | 1586,00 |
| 1860, | W. P. Randall.. | " | 1938,00.. | " | 1583,00 |
| 1861, | W. E. Tallman. | " | 1010,00.. | " | 938,00 · |
| 1866, | H. Van Hoesen | " | 2387,00.. | " | 1724,42 |

*The Cortland County Medical Society* was organized August 10, 1808, at which time Dr. Lewis S Owen was chosen President; Dr John Miller, Vice President; Dr. Jesse Searl, Secretary; Dr Robert D. Taggart, Treasurer. Dr. Owen held the office of President from 1808 until 1822, having been elected annually up to that time. Dr. Searl held the office of Secretary until 1820. In 1820 Dr. Lewis Riggs was chosen Secretary, and held the office for three years. In 1823 Dr. Searl was again elected and held the office for two years. In 1825 Dr. George W. Bradford was elected and has held the office ever since. The following is a list of the Presidents of the Society, as they have been elected, up to the present time :

In 1822, John Lynde ; 1823, Lewis S. Owen ; 1824, Miles Goodyear ; 1825, Lewis Riggs ; 1827, Jesse Searl ; 1828, A. Blanchard; 1830, Levi Boies ; 1831, Miles Goodyear ; 1832, Horace Bronson ; 1833, Lewis Riggs ; 1834, Miles Goodyear ; 1841, A B. Shipman ; 1842, Miles Goodyear ; 1843, A. B. Smith ; 1845, Horace Bronson ; 1846, Lyman Eldridge ; 1847, Miles Goodyear ; 1848, P. H. Burdick ; 1849, Frederick Hyde ; 1851, P. H. Burdick ; 1852, Caleb Green ; 1853, C. M. Kingman ; 1854, Geo. W. Maxson ; 1855, L. J. Keean ; 1856, Geo. W. Bradford ; 1857, William Fitch ; 1858, John Miller ; 1859, Frederick Hyde ; 1860, Chas. M Kingman ; 1861, John H. Knapp ; 1862, Caleb Green ; 1863, William Fitch ; 1864, Seneca Beebe ; 1866, D. W. Warner ; 1867, John H. Knapp.

We are indebted to Geo. W. Bradford, the Secretary, for the statistics in relation to the Medical Society.

When the tocsin of war sounded in April, 1861, the inhabitants of Cortland County were engaged in the peaceful pursuits of agriculture. Like the great mass of American citizens, war had no charms for them. But when the Stars and Stripes, the emblem of our Na-

E

tion's freedom and glory, was stricken down by traitor hands, the descendants of Revolutionary sires "rallied around the Flag," and from every hill-top and every valley went forth the cry, "The Union, it must and shall be preserved." *The census reports about one thousand as having volunteered to leave the comforts of .home and the society of friends for the camp and the battle-field, that they might preserve to their posterity the blessings of civil and religious liberty bequeathed to us by our fathers.   Nearly one fourth of that number are reported as having been killed in battle or died from injuries received while in the service.   While shafts of marble and granite arise to commemorate the deeds of our fallen countrymen, let us who survive see to it that we do not allow the enemies of our country to gain at the ballot-box what they failed to gain upon the battle-field, but that "Union and Liberty, now and forever, one and inseparable," may ever be inscribed on our Nation's banner.

*From an examination of the census reports of many counties of the State, we have invariably found the number of enlistments reported to be far below the actual number enlisted.—[PUB

# GAZETTEER OF TOWNS.

*CINCINNATUS* was formed from Solon, April 3, 1804. It embraced the original township of Cincinnatus, or No. 25 of the Military Tract. The present town embraces one-fourth of the original township of 100 lots, or 64,000 acres, Freetown, Willett and Marathon having been taken from it in 1818. It is situated on the east border of the County, south of the center. The surface consists of the valley of the Otselic River and of the ridges which rise upon each side. Nearly the whole surface of the town is divided into steep ridges by the deep ravines, through which flow the tributaries of the Otselic, extending far into the interior. The soil is generally a gravelly loam, not as fertile as in some other sections, but well adapted to grazing. Lots 1, 16, 37, 49, 53 and 62, of this township, were set apart for the support of the Gospel and schools.

*Cincinnatus*, (p. v.,) situated on the Otselic Creek, contains three churches, viz., Congregational, Methodist and Baptist, an academy, two hotels, two tanneries, a foundry, a gristmill, a sawmill, and about 550 inhabitants. *Cincinnatus Academy* was built in 1856, and is under the Principalship of C. E. Babcock, A. M. It is now in a flourishing condition.

*Lower Cincinnatus* is a small village about a mile south of Cincinnatus Village, and contains a church, a hotel, several shops and about 200 inhabitants.

The first settlement of this town was commenced by Ezra and Thadeus Rockwell, from Lenox, Mass. Ezra settled on lot 19, in 1795, and Thadeus on lot 9, the same year. Zurial Raymond, from Williamstown, Mass, came in about the same time and settled on lot 29, on a revolutionary claim which he received through his wife. John Kingman was another of the early settlers, a native of Massachusetts. He came in and located on lot 19, in 1795, and

worked during the day clearing his land, and in the evening worked
at his trade, shoemaking.  Dr. John McWhorter, from  Oxford,
Chenango County, was also among the first settlers.  He married
Miss Katy Young, step-daughter of Mr. Raymond.  This was the
first wedding in the town, and as there was no one authorized to
marry in the town, a clergyman from Oxford was employed; but
on his arrival another difficulty arose; the clergyman was not authorized to marry outside of Chenango County.  To obviate this
difficulty the party started for Chenango County, and when they
supposed they were over the border, the ceremony was performed
in the open air, in the midst of the forest.  Samuel Vining was another early settler, as were also Phineas Sargent, Jesse Locke and
Ebenezer Crittenden.  Charles DeBille, from Berkshire County,
Mass., settled on lot 9, in 1797.

During the first few years after the settlement, the Indians were
accustomed to visit the Otselic Valley.  In 1796, forty of the
Oneidas camped upon the site of the village, and, during the fall
and winter, killed forty-two bears.  The oil preserved was used for
cooking purposes.  The Indians were uniformly peaceable and well
disposed towards the whites.

The first merchants were James Tanner and Elijah Bliss   Col.
John Kingman kept the first inn and erected the first store.  The
first frame house was erected by Dr. John McWhorter, about 1802;
and the first school was taught by Miss Hepsy Beebe.  The first
death was that of Daniel Hartshorn, in 1796.  The first birth was
that of Sally Rockwell, in 1796.  The first sermon preached within
the limits of the town was by Rev. Dr. Williston, in a log barn,
from the text, "Hear Ye."  The first church (Presbyterian) was
organized at a much later day by a union of the people of several of
the adjacent towns.  Previous to 1798 the citizens were compelled
to go to Chenango Forks, Ludlowville, or Manlius Square, to have
their grinding done, transporting their grists on drays drawn by
oxen.  These drays were made of the crotches of trees, with a few
pieces of board attached to them by wooden pins  They were
from six to eight feet in length, and eight or ten bushels made a
very respectable load for one pair of oxen.

The population of the town in 1810 was 1,525, but the town at
that time embraced about four times the amount of territory contained in it now.  The population in 1865 was 1,169, and its area
15,819 acres.

**CORTLANDVILLE** was formed from Homer, April 11,
1829, and embraces the south half of the original township of Homer and a small portion of the north-east corner of Virgil  The
name was applied to the town from its being the County Seat of
Cortland County.  It is situated on the west border of the County,

but extends east to the center. The east and west branches of the Tioughnioga River unite in this town. A considerable portion of the surface is level, but the eastern and southern parts are hilly An observer, standing upon an eminence a short distance west of Cortland Village, can see seven distinct valleys, separated by ranges of hills, radiating in different directions. The ridges rise from 200 to 400 feet above the valleys. The southern part of the town is a broken upland region, the hills being arable to their summits. The Tioughnioga River receives as tributaries in this town, Trout Brook from the east, and Dry and Otter Brooks from the west. A part of the western portion of the town is drained by streams flowing west to Cayuga Lake. In the south-west part of the town are three small ponds, fed by springs, and furnishing a large amount of marl, from which an excellent quality of lime is produced. The marl, as it comes from the ponds, is generally of an ash color, but whitens on exposure to the air. When partially dried it is moulded into the form of bricks, which are thoroughly dried and burned. In some places this marl is twenty feet thick. The soil along the Tioughnioga River is a rich alluvium ; on the higher lands it is a gravelly and argillaceous loam.

*Cortland Village*, (p. v.) incorporated in 1853, and special charter obtained in 1864, is the County Seat of Cortland County, and situated on the Syracuse, Binghamton and New York Railroad, about midway between Binghamton and Syracuse. The main street extends nearly north and south, and is about one mile in length. The streets and walks are wide and ornamented with shade trees, and the main street is well paved. There are many neat and beautiful residences in various parts of the village, with grounds ornamented with flowers and shrubbery, which add greatly to the appearance of the village. There are five churches, three printing offices, three banks, State Normal School building, four hotels, several stores, manufactories, &c., and about 3,500 inhabitants. The streets are lighted with gas.

*The State Normal School* is located on a beautiful site in this village. We are indebted to the Hon. Charles Foster for the following description of this magnificent structure :

The Legislature of 1866 authorized any county, city or village, to make propositions to a Commission composed of certain State Officers, to furnish buildings, sites, &c., for a Normal School, to be located in such county, city or village, and authorized the Commission to accept not to exceed four of such propositions. In November, 1866, the village of Cortland made a proposition which was accepted by the Commission, and in the spring of 1867 the village commenced the erection of the buildings proposed, and they will be completed by the first of October, 1868. The site is in the central part of the village and consists of nearly four acres  The school building is composed of a main or center building, 84x44 feet, with a wing 40x36 feet on either side, and at the end of each of these wings is a building, parallel with the main building, 36x72 feet. The basement extends under the whole, and rises five feet above the grade. The building is two stories above the basement, of brick, with a French or Mansard roof, furnishing a third story. The central or end buildings are each surmounted by a dome. The top of the center dome is about sixty-four feet above the grade. Two towers, one upon either side of the main building, rise ninety-six feet above the grade. The extreme length of the entire structure is two hundred and twenty-six feet. The basement contains kitchen, pantries, cellars, laundries, and steam heating apparatus and steam force pump. The first and second floors are occupied for school and recitation rooms, family rooms, &c. The third floor under the center dome is furnished for a gymnasium, and the remainder of this story is divided into smaller rooms, to be used as dormitories, bath rooms, &c., for the students who may board in the building. Steam is used for heating all rooms on the first and second floors. Water is carried through all the building by force pumps, and each story is supplied with hose to be used in case of fire. All the main rooms and the dormitories are carefully ventilated, and gas is supplied for lights. This school is to be managed by a local Board of citizens, the State furnishing them yearly $12,-000 for expenses, this Board being subject to the supervision of the State Superintendent of Public Instruction. The school will probably be divided into primary, intermediate, normal and academical departments, so that a child may commence its education within its walls and graduate as teacher from the normal department. Tuition in all the departments, except the academical, will be free. The building and site are furnished by the village of Cortland at a cost of about $90,000. The construction has been carried on under the supervision and control of the Village Trustees, as a corporate matter. The whole expense of this enterprise, to the completion of the building and its acceptance by the State, rests entirely upon this public spirited village.

*Cortlandville Academy.*—We are indebted to Hon. Horatio Ballard for the following article in relation to the *Cortlandville Academy:*

Public instruction commenced in this Institution on the 24th day of August, 1842. The first report to the Regents bears date the 3d day of January, 1843, and on the 31st day of January, of the same year, it was incorporated. It soon took rank among the best academies of the State, and its high standing has been maintained. Many of the most promising young men in the country have gone forth from this Institution. Three times the building has been enlarged to make room for the increasing number of students. The average attendance is over two hundred each term. Located at the County Seat, in a village unsurpassed in beauty, and in the midst of a population distinguished for enterprise and intelligence, it has exerted an extended and elevating influence in this and adjacent counties. Three members of the Board of Trustees formed in 1842, viz., Henry Stephens, Horatio Ballard and Jas. C. Pomeroy, are still members. The following is the present Faculty:

Prof. J. J. Pease..........................Principal.
   "        Harkness............. .Associate   "
Miss L. Porter.........................Preceptress.
   "   Hattie S. Curtis...........Associate      "
   "   Libbie D. Curtis.......Intermediate Department.
   "   Martha Roe...............Primary       "
—— Bates.... .................Teacher of Music.  .

Under the administration of these teachers the prospects of the school are unabated.

The site ultimately selected for the State Normal School joins the site on which the Academy is located. On the 13th of July, 1867, the Trustees of the Academy passed a resolution in favor of adding the Academy lot to the site of the Normal School building, upon the condition that an Academic Department be maintained in the Normal School building. It is expected that the Academy will thus be transferred to the Normal School building, and there be continued under the patronage and at the expense of the State.

*Messenger Hall.*—Akin to the institutions of learning in the village of Cortland, is the beautiful Hall in the Messenger Block, on the west side of Main street. This Hall is gorgeously decorated and fitted up with all the modern improvements. It is fifty-five feet square. The following remarks taken from an address delivered at its dedication, by Hon. Horatio Ballard, will give a good idea of its object and design.

" We are here to celebrate the completion of this magnificent Hall; and we do so because it is an event which illustrates the material growth and prosperity of this beautiful town. He saw the business of this town demanded more room, and he projected the erection of this block, which lifts its majestic proportions to the sight and embraces this splendid Hall. And for this edifice, grand in size, elegant in finish, useful in arrangement, durable in structure, we would here record our thanks and tender our gratitude to our noble citizen, Hiram J. Messenger. It is a monument of his genius, his taste and his liberality. He has connected his memory with the best specimens of architecture, and the most superb styles of internal finish, as the exquisite work on this lofty Hall fully attests And while it is now dedicated to the use of public assemblies, let us hope that its fair walls may hereafter be associated in the memory with all that is exalted in intellect and attractive in truth.  Free discussion in the public halls of the land is one of the most powerful agencies to purify, to strengthen and perpetuate our civil and religious liberties.  We will hold this place consecrated to these high purposes—to the cause of Liberty and Union."

*The Court House* is a substantial brick building, standing upon the corner of Church and Court streets.  The Jail is of hewn stone and stands in the rear of the Court House; and the Clerk's Office, of brick, stands on the west side of Main street.

The manufacturing establishments of the village consists of a foundry, machine cooperage, oil mill, grist mill, two planing mills, a sash, door and blind factory, a pottery, a woolen factory, two carriage factories, a saw mill and several mechanic shops.  The foundry is devoted chiefly to the manufacture of agricultural implements, and employs about twenty men.

Kinne's Machine Cooperage was commenced in 1843, and run with varied success until 1859, when Trapp's Patent Barrel Machinery was introduced.  The present owner, C. W. Kinne, came in possession in 1861.  In 1863 a new building was erected.  The motive power is water, with a 35 horse-power steam engine.  The Factory is turning out about 17,000 butter packages and $8,000 worth of churns annually.  The present year the proprietor has commenced the manufacture of cheese boxes and scale boards.  It is giving employment to 15 men constantly.  The Oil Mill has two hydraulic presses and is capable of running 100 bushels of seed per day.  The Planing Mills prepare lumber for any purpose for which it is used about a building.  The Mill is both a Grist and Flouring Mill, and capable of running from 300 to 400 bushels of grain per day.  There is also a very extensive Lumber Yard, near the depot, in the east part of the village.

Daily lines of stages run from this village to Groton, Ithaca, Norwich and Pitcher; and a tri-weekly line to Virgil.

*The Cortland Silver Cornet Band* is an organization of this village.

Cortland has an efficient Fire Department, consisting of three separate organizations, viz., Water Witch Co., Excelsior Hook and Ladder Co. No. 1, and Water Witch Hose Co. No. 1.  *The Water Witch Company* was organized June 14, 1854, and numbers about forty members.  *Excelsior Hook and Ladder* was organized December 10, 1864, and numbers about fifty members.  *Water Witch Hose Company No.* 1 was organized in 1863, and consisted of twenty members, the present number is twenty-five.

*The Young Men's Christian Association* was organized in 1868, for the development of Christian character and the promotion of Evangelical Religion, and especially for the improvement of the mental, moral and spiritual condition of young men.

The first settler of Cortlandville was John Miller, a native of New Jersey, but more recently from Binghamton. He located on lot 56, in 1792. In 1794 Jonathan Hubbard and Moses Hopkins came in, Mr. Hubbard locating on the site of Cortland Village and Mr. Hopkins settling on lot 64, one mile west. Thomas Wilcox, from Whitestown, located on lot 64, in 1795, and Reuben Doud on lot 75. James Scott, John Morse and Levi Lee, located upon the same lot; and Dr. Lewis S. Owen, from Albany, on lot 66. During the years 1796–97, Aaron Knapp settled on lot 55, and Enoch Hotchkiss on lot 76. Samuel Crittenden and Eber Stone, from Connecticut, located on lot 66. Mr. C. came with an ox team and was twenty-five days on the road. Samuel Ingles and his son Samuel came from Columbia county in 1798, and located on lot 75; and in 1800, Wilmot Sperry came from Woodbridge, Conn, and located on lot 73. Wm. Mallery, from Columbia county, came in 1802. Samuel McGraw, from whom McGrawville derived its name, came from New Haven, Conn., to Cortlandville, in 1803, and located on lot 87, purchasing 100 acres. In 1809 he removed to McGrawville and purchased 200 acres. He had a large family, eight sons and four daughters. David Merrick came from Massachusetts in 1800, and located on lot 44 In 1797 he went to Whitestown to purchase a tavern stand and one hundred acres of land, then valued at three hundred dollars. He left without making the purchase, but went to Whitestown the next year to close a trade, and learned that the property was then valued at ten thousand dollars.

The first inn was kept by Samuel Ingles, in 1810, on the site of the Barnard Block; and the first school, on the present site of the Eagle Hotel. The first grist mill was erected by Jonathan Hubbard, in 1779.

The first church (Baptist) was organized Oct. 3d, 1801. There has been some dispute as to this subject, but it appears from an old record by Judge Keep, dated Oct. 3d, 1801, that "a council convened at Homer, at the request of a number of Baptist brethren, for the purpose of organizing a Baptist Church." This was the first church organization in the County. Rev. Mr. Hotchkin, in his History of the Presbyterian Church in Western New York, says the first organization was Oct. 12th, 1801, and that it was a Congregational Church. This old record of Judge Keep appears to settle the question. The number of members at the time of the organization was sixteen, the present number is 312. The first church edifice of the First Baptist Church was erected in 1811; it stood between the villages of Cortland and Homer, and was occupied until 1833, when the present building was erected in Cortland Village.

The first Methodist meeting was held at the house of Jonathan Hubbard, in 1804. A sermon was preached by Rev. Samuel Hill, and subsequently a class was formed of ten members. This was the germ of the Centenary M. E. Church, which now numbers 400 members. Their first church edifice was erected in 1821 and was occupied until 1867, when their present building was erected. It is a substantial brick structure, ninety-seven feet by sixty, and one hundred and thirteen feet to the top of the spire. The cost was $25,000.

*Grace Church* (Episcopal) was organized in 1859, with fifteen members, and the church edifice was erected the same year. The present number forty.

*The Universalist Church* was organized in February, 1835, with 101 members. Their house of worship was erected in 1837, and is a substantial stone structure, the basement of which is owned by the town and used as a Town Hall.

At an early day the people of Cortland turned their attention to the subject of education, as the following record will show. It is given just as it was found in the Book of Records :

"Homer November 20—1806.
At a meeting of the inhabitants of the Second School District in Homer [now Cortland]

1 Voted Levi Lee Moderator

3 Voted to build A School house 20 by 26

4 Voted to Set the Said house on Lot No 65 Near the Crotch of the Road that A Summer School shall be Kept this this Summer in Said District. a womans "

At another meeting we find the following :

" November 4'1809
Agreeabel to Notification of the Second School District
P M                              Meeting opened at 6 o'clook

1 Voted to appoint a day to git up wood

3 Voted that all that Neglect to git longer than the first of January Shall pay for gitting their Share of wood.

4 Voted to Set up Gitting wood at Vandue. John Morse bid it of a 5s pr Cord and if he Neglects to Git Said wood he is to pay the expence for Such Days that the School must Lie Still
Dissolved the meeting "

At another meeting we find the following :

" 2 Voted the Committee be Instructed to hire Mr Bato [Barto] for Six months and that the price Does not exceed twelve Dollars Payabel Three fourths in grain and one fourth in Cash."

This old record is found in the same book in which the records are now kept.

From such small beginnings their march has been onward and upward until the youth of Cortland are now permitted to attend, within the shadow of their own homes, some of the best institutions of learning in the State.

The population of the town in 1865 was 5,008 and its area 31,119 acres.

Among the distinguished men who have at various times resided in this town is SAMUEL NELSON, Justice of the Supreme Court of the United States. He was born in Hebron, Washington County, Nov 10, 1792. He was sent to the district school at an early age, where he made commendable progress. He fitted for college in Salem and at the Granville Academy, then in charge of the distinguished Salem Town. He entered Middlebury College in 1811 and graduated in 1813, at the age of twenty-one He adopted the legal profession and studied law in Salem, and was admitted to the Bar in 1817, and soon after located in Cortland Village. His talents soon won for him an enviable position among his associates. In 1823 he was appointed one of the Circuit Judges, and in 1831 he was appointed to the Bench of the Supreme Court of the State. In 1837 he was appointed Chief Justice of the State of New York. He filled this position with distinguished ability until 1845, when he was appointed Associate Justice of the Supreme Court of the United States, a position which he still holds. His career upon the Bench has been characterized by honesty, firmness, discretion and liberal equity. His great learning, eloquence and genius, have secured for him a pre-eminence in his profession, affording an illustrious example for the ambitious youth of our country. His present residence is Cooperstown, N. Y.

IRA HARRIS was born in Charleston, Montgomery County, May 31, 1802. His parents removed to Cortland County in 1808, and located on Preble Flats. He remained with his father, alternately working upon the farm and attending the district school until he was seventeen years old, when he entered Cortland Academy at Homer, where he pursued the studies which enabled him to enter the Junior Class of Union College in September, 1822. He graduated with the highest honors in 1824, and immediately entered upon the study of law in Cortland Village, where he remained one year. He then directed his course to Albany and in two years was admitted to the Bar. During the succeeding twenty years he rose to an enviable position among the most distinguished of the Albany Bar. In 1847 he was appointed to the Bench of the Supreme Court, which position he held until 1861, when he was elected to the United States Senate for six years. He was elected to the Assembly of the State in 1844 and 1845. He was elected to the Constitutional Convention in 1846, and was also a member of the Convention in 1867. While in the United States Senate he served on several important committees, and was one of the National Committee appointed to accompany the remains of President Lincoln to Illinois.

*CUYLER* was formed from Truxton, November 18, 1858. It is the north-east corner town of the County. The surface is a broken and hilly upland. The east branch of the Tioughnioga River enters the town near the north-east corner and flows diagonally across, leaving near the center of the east line. The other streams are small brooks, and most of them tributaries of the Tioughnioga. Muncey Hill, near the center, is the highest land in the town, and is a wild, broken region, poorly adapted to cultivation. The soil is chiefly a sandy and gravelly loam.

*Cuyler*, (p. v.) situated a little north of the center of the town, contains a Methodist Church, a hotel, several mechanic shops and about 200 inhabitants.

*Keeney Settlement*, situate on the north line of the town, contains a Baptist Church and about a dozen houses.

The first settlement of this town was made in 1794, by Nathaniel Potter, who removed from Saratoga County with a wife and a daughter five weeks old. He settled on lot 96, paying one dollar and ten cents an acre for his land. He was killed in 1798 by the fall of a tree; his little boy about five years old was with him at the time. Mrs. Joseph Keeler was the first to find him, crushed beneath a large tree, but still alive. He asked for water and was supplied by Mrs. Keeler, taking his hat as the only substitute for a pail. He then requested her to pray with him, but this request was not granted. The daughter of Mr. Potter is the mother of Stephen Patrick, and now lives with Wesley Patrick, in this town. Mr Morse was a soldier of the Revolution and drew lot 87, upon which he located. He came from New Jersey. James Lockwood came with him from Pennsylvania. They came in a canoe up the Tioughnioga River, and then took an ox team to their place of destination. Joseph Keeler and brother settled on the same lot. Isaac Brown settled on lot 99, about the year 1806, and Zebadiah Gates on lot 88 in 1807. Charles Vincent settled on lot 78 in 1806, and James Vincent in 1800. Jesse Blanchard settled on lot 66 in 1798, and Benjamin Brown, from Connecticut, settled on lot 57 in 1795. Daniel Page settled on lot 79, where widow Hinds now lives. James Dorwood, from Rhinebeck, came into the town in 1806. He was an ingenious mechanic and is said to have built the first carding machine in the State. He was a native of Scotland, and left his native country when eighteen years of age to avoid being drafted into the army by King George III. Huldah Dorwood, now 97 years of age, lives in the town. Jacob Hollenbeck and John Brown settled on lot 77 in 1806–8. Thomas Fairbanks, from

Good Printing is an Article that People are beginning to appreciate more than formerly. And it is an abſurd Idea that the Newſpapers attempt to make the Public believe, that they alone can make beſt Work.

B. HARMON SMITH,
Job Printer,
4 West Fayette St.,
SYRACUSE, N. Y.

"Animis opibusque parati."

A .......... Office fitt.......... expreſſly for Job .......ing, in all its branches, can do its Work better and cheaper than any Newſpaper Concern in exiſtence. Such a One is mine. See next Page.

Syracuſe, January 1, 1869.

Theodore E. Hart kept the first store. The first school was taught by Miss Betsey Curran, in 1807. The first birth was that of Dr. Charles Barnes ; the first marriage that of Obed Graves and Alice Munroe; and the first death that of Mrs Dorastus DeWolf Nathan Heaton built the first grist-mill in 1814, and Lewis Moore kept the first inn. Rev. Seth Williston was the first preacher, and the first religious services were held in 1804. The first church (Baptist) was organized in 1815. The first post-office was established in 1825, the place being then called *Worthington*, but was subsequently changed to Harford.

The first church edifice erected in this town was a Union church, erected in 1832–3 by Methodists, Congregationalists and Universalists. It was dedicated in the fall of 1833. Organizations of these denominations had existed for several years previous to the erection of the church. In 1857 the Methodists erected a church for themselves, and this is now the only church used regularly for church purposes in the town. Rev. J. Lord is the present pastor.

The population in 1865 was 888, and its area 13,886 acres.

*HOMER* was formed March 5, 1794. Solon was taken off in 1798, Virgil in 1804 and Cortlandville in 1829. It lies upon the west border of the County, a little north of the center. The surface is uneven and consists of the valleys of the two branches of the Tioughnioga River and the ridges which border upon them The valley of the western branch is about a mile in width and elevated 1,096 feet above tide. The eastern valley is narrower. The two valleys are separated by a ridge of hills from 200 to 500 feet above the river, and another similar ridge occupies the south-eastern corner of the town. The western part of the town is a hilly upland, 1,500 to 1,600 feet above tide The Tioughnioga receives Cold and Factory Brooks from the west, which are its chief tributaries The valleys of these streams open into corresponding valleys to the northward, through which flow streams emptying into Otisco and Skaneateles Lakes. The soil upon the river flats is a deep, rich alluvial loam, well adapted to tillage ; upon the highlands it is a sandy and gravelly loam, better adapted to pasturage.

*Homer,* (p. v.) incorporated May 11, 1835, is finely situated on the Tioughnioga River and is a station on the Syracuse, Binghamton and New York Railroad. It contains four churches, an academy, a newspaper office, a bank, three hotels, several manufactories and about 2,000 inhabitants. The streets and walks are very broad and ornamented with beautiful shade trees, which add much to the general appearance of the village. There are many very pretty residences and some very fine business blocks. The main street extends nearly north and south, is about a mile in length and embraces most of the business part of the village. Near the center of

F

the village is a beautiful park, upon the west side of which stand the Baptist, Methodist, Congregational and Episcopal churches, and the Cortland Academy, all facing the park. The streets are lighted with gas.

*Cortland Academy* was incorporated February 4, 1819. The course of study includes all the branches usually taught in the common schools, in our best academies, and most of the studies pursued in our colleges. The library numbers over fifteen hundred volumes of choice works in the various departments of literature and science    The philosophical and chemical apparatus is ample for illustrating the principles of these sciences. The geological and mineralogical cabinet has been much enlarged by the liberality of the President of the Academy, and now includes a complete suit of rocks and minerals of this State, and many foreign specimens of great beauty and value. The library, apparatus and cabinet are arranged in a room which has been elegantly fitted up by the citizens of the village and is always open to visitors. A new edifice is in process of erection which will be an ornament to the village and an honor to its projectors. The new edifice occupies the site of the old one, is of brick, ninety-six feet long, and its greatest width seventy-two feet. The corners of the end projections and of the central tower are of hewn stone. The main entrance in the tower is finished in the same way and arched. The windows are all surmounted by cut stone. The lower story is for the heating apparatus and for chemical and lecture rooms. The second story is for the library, the cabinet, the mathematical and two large study rooms. The third story is for chapel and four study and recitation rooms A Mansard roof gives room in the fourth story for two ante-rooms and a large hall with a central height of twenty-six feet. There are two rear entrances with stair-cases communicating with every story. George Almy is the architect

The village contains two public halls.

*Barber's Hall* is seventy-five feet by eighty, finished in the most elaborate style and capable of seating 1,000 persons. It is one of the finest halls in Central New York.

*Wheadon Hall* is forty by fifty feet in size and capable of seating about 700 or 800 people.

*Homer Flouring and Gristmill* is situated on the west bank of the Tioughnioga River, near the center of the village. It is owned by Messrs. Darby & Son, and is capable of grinding about 300 bushels per day.

*An Oil Mill*, located in the south-west part of the village, is doing a good business.

*The Edge Tool Manufactory* of R. Blanshan & Co., upon the east bank of the river, is run by steam and manufactures all kinds of edge tools of an excellent quality.

*A Marble Factory*, near the depot, turns out very nice work.

*A Brewery*, upon "Brewery Hill," is doing a fair business.

*A Flax and Cordage Mill* is located a little outside of the corporation, owned by John L. Boorum. This mill produces about a tun of cotton cordage per day, and manufactures the flax from about 1,000 acres per year, valued at forty dollars per acre. There are fifteen tenart houses connected with the factory which employs about thirty-five hands.

*Glen Wood Cemetery* occupies an elevated position about half a mile west of the village. The grounds include about thirty acres, are laid out with much taste and overlook the villages of Homer and Cortland, and a large extent of surrounding country The Cemetery is under the control of an association organized February 21, 1862.

*Homer Mechanical Brass Band* was organized in 1865, and furnishes music for all occasions.

*East Homer*, (p. v.) situated in the east part of the town, near the Tioughnioga River, contains a church (M. E.,) a hotel, a blacksmith shop, a carpenter and wagon shop, a school house and about 150 inhabitants. The church was erected in 1841 and dedicated in 1842. Rev. H. Hawley was the first pastor.

*Hibbard's Butter and Cheese Factory* is situated about one-half mile north-east of East Homer. The building was erected in 1866 and is thirty feet by one hundred and twenty, and two stories high. The milk of from 300 to 500 cows is used, and from 20,000 to 37,-000 pounds of butter, and from 55,000 to 100,000 pounds of cheese are made annually. The heating of the vats and the churning are done by steam. Twenty churns can be run at a time and thirty cheeses pressed.

*Carpenterville*, situated on the east branch of the Tioughnioga River, about four miles from Cortland Village, contains a gristmill, a sawmill, a wagon shop, a blacksmith shop, two turning shops and about a dozen houses

Mr. V. Carpenter, on lot 47, has a fine trout pond, well stocked with fish of all sizes from the smallest size to two pounds in weight.

*Little York*, (p. v.) situated on the west branch of Tioughnioga River, in the north part of the town, contains a hotel, a store, a very fine school house, a gristmill, a sawmill, a peg factory, a wagon shop and about twenty dwellings.

*Homer Cheese Factory* is situated about one and a half miles from Homer Village, it was erected in 1864 and uses the milk of from 600 to 1200 cows. The building is 175 feet by 32, and two stories high. In 1865, 573,868 pounds of cheese were made; in 1866, 382,579 pounds; and in 1867, 233,571 pounds were made.

The first settlement of this town, and of Cortland County, was made in 1791, by Spencer Beebe and his brother-in-law, Amos

Todd. They emigrated from New Haven, Conn., in 1789, and located at Windsor, Broome County. In the fall of 1791 they settled a little north of Homer Village. Mrs. Beebe was the only female who accompanied them. Their first residence was composed of poles and was twelve by fifteen feet. Previous to its completion their team strayed away and Messrs. Beebe and Todd both went in pursuit, leaving Mrs B. alone for three days, with no protection but the four walls of their cabin, without roof or floor, and only a blanket fastened by forks for a door. Without, the howling wolf and screaming panther made night hideous. During the following winter the husband and the brother of Mrs. Beebe again left her to return to Windsor for their goods, and were snow-bound for six weeks, during which time she was the sole occupant of her lonely cabin and the only human being within a circuit of thirty miles. Their goods were brought up the river in a boat. At Binghamton they were joined by John Miller, who assisted them in removing obstructions and propelling the boat. Where the water was too shallow for the boat it was drawn across by the oxen. Mr. Todd located on lot 42 In the spring of 1792 John House, James Matthews, James Moore, Silas and Daniel Miller, came from Binghamton. Squire Miller located on lot 56 and Mr. Matthews on the same lot. Darius Kinney came from Brimfield, Mass., in 1793, and located on the east river. Thomas L and Jacob Bishop located on lot 25 in 1795, and Thomas Wilcox on lot 64 John Keep, Solomon and John Hubbard, came from Massachusetts and settled, Mr. Keep on lot 56, Solomon Hubbard on lot 25, and John on lot 26.

The first male child born in the town was Homer Moore, and the first female, Betsey House The first death was that of Mrs. Thomas Gould Alvord, in 1795, and the first marriage that of Zadoc Strong and Widow Russell. The first school house was built a little north of Homer village in 1798, and the first teacher was Joshua Ballard. Enos Stimson kept the first inn and John Coats the first store. Jedediah Barber was the first permanent and successful merchant. The first gristmill was built in 1798 by John Keep, Solomon Hubbard and Asa White. Luther Rice was the first physician and Townsend Ross was the first lawyer and postmaster. Prof. W. B. Beck was the first daguerreian artist and built the first daguerreian carriage in the State

In 1798 forty dollars and seventy-eight cents were appropriated for the common schools of the town. The annual town meeting was held at Mr. Miller's house, April 8, 1796. John Miller was elected supervisor and Peter Ingersoll town clerk. In 1796 it was voted 'that every man make his own pound. That hogs run at large without yokes or rings That fences be made four feet and a half high, and not to exceed four inches between logs or poles.' In 1797 it was agreed by a unanimous vote 'that every man in the town may provide his own pound for every creature that does him damage, and yet be entitled to damage the same as at the town pound, and that hogs be free commoners.' In 1798 a wolf's scalp commanded a premium of from five to ten dollars, according to size; that of a bear, five dollars; a panther ten dollars, and fox fifty cents. The population of Homer in 1797 was ninety-two.

In 1815 William Sherman came to Homer and erected a machine shop for the manufacture of nails, the machinery being so constructed as to feed, cut, head and stamp the letter S on the head of each nail, without any hand work. This was the first of the kind in the State of New York. Iron was very high at that time and fourpenny nails were worth twenty-five cents a pound. Mr Sherman also engaged in the manufacture of oil. In 1827 he erected the "Homer Exchange" store in which for nearly thirty years he conducted a heavy mercantile trade.

John Hubbard, the father of Simon Hubbard, was one of the early settlers; he located here in 1794. The first millstone ever used in Cortland County was taken from the farm now owned by Simon Hubbard The place from which it was taken is distinctly visible at this time. William Blashfield came from Hampden County, Mass., in 1802, and helped to clear the land upon which Homer village is located. Mr. Blashfield died in 1864, upon the farm where he had lived for forty-seven years. Mrs Electa Hobert came in 1800, and has lived sixty years upon the same farm, known as the Hobert farm. Mr. Gideon Hobart, whose name was formerly Hoar, came to this town in 1799, with an ox team, from Brimfield, Mass. Harvey Fairbanks, one of the early settlers, is still alive, and has lived for fifty three years on the same farm. The valley in which he now lives was a wilderness which he helped to clear. William Walter came from Litchfield, Conn, in 1808, and has since lived upon the farm upon which he first settled. On lot 13 is a small but finely situated cemetery, called the Atwater burying ground, the land having been given by Mr. Atwater. Some of the most distinguished of the early settlers are buried here, among them Thomas G., Ebenezer and Charles Alvord, and others.

Mr. Conrad Delong, the father of Mrs. Daniel Topping, who resides upon lot 8, is now living and retains his faculties to a remarkable degree for one of his age He was born March 4, 1772, in Dutchess County, and is of course a little more than four years older than our Republic. With one exception he has voted at every spring and fall election since he cast his first vote, and greatly regrets that he failed in one instance. He has voted at every Presidential election since, and at the last one he rode two miles and cast his vote for Ulysses S. Grant. His hearing is greatly impaired but his eyesight and his memory are good, and with the aid of a staff is able to walk half a mile and return without serious inconvenience.

The pioneers of Homer were religious people, and when six families had arrived they assembled together for religious worship on the Sabbath, and from that time (1793) to this there has been only one occasion on which the Sabbath service has been omitted. In 1794 or 1795 a number of families came from Massachusetts and Connecticut, and these formed the germ of the future church. Meetings were held in a log barn in the summer and in a dwelling house in the winter. In the fall of 1798 a grist mill was erected which served the people as a place of worship upon the Sabbath. The first sermon was preached by Elder Peter P. Roots, of the Baptist denomination, in Mr. Baker's barn, from the text, "Faith, Hope, Charity." The second was preached by Rev. Asa Hillyer, of New Jersey. Mr. H. was in the place on business and attended the raising of a building; when it became known that ne was a preacher he was invited to preach to the settlers, which he did in the open air under a beech tree. In 1799 an organization for sustaining public worship was formed under the title of "The First Religious Society of the town of Homer," which is the title of the society connected with the Congregational Church at the present time  In December of the same year a house of worship was erected on the north-east corner of the village green. Rev. Dr. Williston, one of the early preachers of this town, says, under date December 15, 1799: "This is almost the only house in all this western country which has been erected with a principal reference to the worship of God."

*The first Congregational Church* was organized October 12, 1801, by Rev. Hugh Willis, of Solon. It consisted of fourteen members. The first stated supply was by a Mr. Jones. The first settled pastor was Rev. Nathan B. Darrow, who was ordained and installed February 2, 1803. This was the first instance of ordination by the denomination in the Military Tract, and the third installation. By the terms of his settlement he was to receive a salary of $300 a year, one-half of which was to be paid in cash and one-half in wheat, and it was to be increased annually ten dollars until it should amount to $400. The ordination was performed by an Ecclesiastical Council, composed of ministers and delegates from churches in Aurelius, Geneva, Owasco, Lisle, Pompey, Clinton and Cazeno..a. Mr. Darrow, after serving the church about six years, was succeeded by Rev. Elnathan Walker, October 25, 1809. Mr. Walker continued until his death in 1820. Rev. John Keep was the next pastor, and Rev. Dennis Platt and Rev. Thomas K. Fessenden were successively pastors of this church. The church now numbers five hundred and fifty. Rev. J. C. Holbrook, D. D., is the present pastor. The present house of worship is an elegant brick structure with stone facings, stained glass windows, and a tower surmounted by a tall and graceful spire, furnished with a bell and clock.

*The First Baptist Church* was dedicated November 4th, 1827. The number of members at the date of its organization was 130 and the present number 384.

*The M. E. Church* was organized in 1833, with forty-five members, under the pastoral labors of Rev. Nelson Rounds. The present number is 124. Rev. A. M Lake is the present pastor.

*Calvary Protestant Episcopal Church* was organized in 1831, and the church edifice erected in 1832 The first rector was Rev Henry Gregory. The number of communicants at the date of organization was twenty; the present number is forty-five Rev. A. W. Cornell is the present rector.

Among the former residents of this town who have attained a national reputation is MR. FRANCIS B. CARPENTER, the artist who gave to the world the "First Reading of the Emancipation Proclamation." The history of that picture is told in his "Six Months at the White House" Mr. Carpenter was born in Homer, August 6, 1830, his father having settled here in 1800. His educational advantages were limited to the common school and one term at the academy in his native town. He early manifested a desire to become an artist and of course exhibited a strong aversion to the labors of the farm. The fences and out-buildings upon the farm were decorated by the ideal images formed in the brain of the young artist and executed with chalk, brick-dust, lamp-black and any other materials upon which he could lay his hands. The father opposed what he regarded the "boy's nonsense," but the mother sympathized with him and at length sat for her portrait, which was so accurate a likeness that the father gave up his opposition and became the second person to sit for a likeness. Soon after completing the portrait of his father he entered the studio of Sandford Thayer, of Syracuse, where he remained about five months, receiving assistance from that artist and making rapid progress in his chosen avocation. While here he made the acquaintance of the artist Elliott, recently deceased, who encouraged him and gave him such instruction as he thought would aid him in his work. In 1846, before he was sixteen years of age, he returned to his native town and opened a studio. Here he received little encouragement at first, the citizens distrusting his ability. As prejudice gradually wore away, he began to receive encouragement, and the field of his operations was gradually enlarged Hon. Henry S. Randall was one of the first to encourage the young artist by his patronage, having employed him to prepare some drawings for a work which he was about to publish, and subsequently sat for his portrait. In 1850 he located in New York and has been growing in favor ever since.

The population of Homer in 1865 was 3,856 and its area 29,321 acres

*LAPEER* was formed from Virgil, May 2, 1845, and embraces the south-east quarter of that township. It is situated upon the high ridges west of the Tioughnioga River, on the south border of the County, west of the center. The declivities of the hills bordering upon the river are precipitous. "Luce Hill," in the northwest part of the town, is the highest point and is 1,600 to 1,700 feet above tide. The streams are all small brooks. Hunt's Falls, upon Fall Creek, near the south border of the town, is a beautiful cascade about 70 feet high. The soil is a gravelly and sandy loam A large part of the town is still unsettled.

*Hunts Corners* (p o.) is a hamlet in the south part of the town; and

*Lapeer* (p o.) is near the center

The first settlement was made in this town in 1799, by Primus Grant, a colored man, on lot 594. He was a native of Guinea and the farm upon which he settled has since been called by that name. Aaron Jennings now occupies the place. Peter Gray, a native of Fishkill, Dutchess County, was the first white settler. He came from Ulster (now Sullivan County) in July, 1802, and settled on lot 70. In 1803 Seth Jennings, from Connecticut, settled on lot 597, where he resided until his death. Mason Jennings now resides on the same farm. Simeon Luce, from Massachusetts, settled on lot 57 in 1805. The farm is now occupied by his son, Ebenezer Luce. Mr. L died at an extreme old age, leaving a numerous posterity. At the time of his settlement he had no neighbors within four miles in one direction and five in the other. Captain Thomas Kingsbury, a Revolutionary soldier, settled in the southeast part of the town in 1802, on the farm now occupied by E. Evans. Timothy Robertson came into the town about 1803. He was a Revolutionary soldier and was with Montgomery at the storming of Quebec, in 1775. Zachariah Squires and Robert Smith came in 1806, and settled on lot 70. Mr. Smith was a soldier of the Revolution and held a commission under Washington. He was the father of Abram Smith, now living in town. John S. Squires from New Haven, Conn., settled on lot 68 in 1807 The place is now owned by Hon Dan C. Squires In 1813 a company of volunteers was organized for the war; Simeon West was Captain, John S. Squires, Lieutenant, and William Powers, Ensign. The members of the company were regarded as minute men, but their services were not required.

Simeon Luce and Rebecca Ayers were married in Virgil, in 1805, while on their way to their home on Luce Hill.

The first marriage in the town was that of James Parker and Lucy Wood, who settled where Alford Alvord now lives. The first birth was that of John Gray, son of Peter Gray, in 1803. The first death was that of Robert C Squires, May 9th, 1809.

Sixteen soldiers of the Revolution settled in Lapeer, all but one of whom died here. The following are the names of fourteen of them : Robert Smith, George Tatman, Thomas Kingsbury, Stephen Kelley, Oliver Hopkins, William Parker, David Crowell, Nathan Smith, Henry Turk, Nathan Walker, Timothy Robertson, Samuel Soule, Asa Parker, James Pollard.

Prince Freeman, from Queensbury, N. Y., settled on lot 67 in 1810, on the farm now occupied by Elijah Freeman Wolves were very numerous at this time and in one night killed twelve sheep for Mr. Freeman. Jabez Hazen, from Windham, Conn., came in 1809, and settled on lot 53, where Luke Hazen now lives

Simeon Luce erected the first grist mill, in 1827, and Samuel and John Gee the first saw mill, in 1825. Messrs. Nichols and Turpening were the first merchants, having commenced business in 1834 or 1835. The first postmaster was Royal Johnson, who still holds the office. Ebenezer Luce taught the first school, in 1814. Among the early clergymen of Lapeer were Rev. Mr. Harrison and Di. Williston, of the Presbyterian order, Rev. Mr. Sheopard, of the Baptist, and Rev. Mr Densmore, of the Methodist denomination.

A noted camping ground of the Indians was located a short distance north of the present residence of Jerome Squires. It was upon a bluff that overlooks Big Brook, and covered with an immense forest of elms, basswood, maple and other timber, in which roamed a multitude of wild animals. From the camping ground the Indians scoured the surrounding country in quest of game and returned at night loaded with the products of the chase. Bears, wolves, panthers, deer and other animals were very numerous.

This town, with a population of about 800, furnished fifty-two for the United States service during the late rebellion, many of whom became distinguished upon the battle-field and sealed their devotion to their country with their blood. We know of no town with the same population that showed a better record. The following are the names of those who died in the service of their country : David M. Turner, Francis E. Verran, Samuel D. Squires, William W. Jennison, Squires S. Barrows, Frederic Wilcox, David W. Parker, Linden Parker, Edgar Freeman, William H. Parker and John Flanley.

The population in 1865 was 762 and its area 14,147 acres

*MARATHON* was formed from Cincinnatus, April 21, 1818, as " Harrison," embracing the south-west quarter of the military township. Its name was changed in 1827 in consequence of there being another town in the State of the same name. It lies upon the southern border of the County, east of the center. It has a rugged and hilly surface, the ridges rising from 500 to 700 feet above the valleys. The Tioughnioga flows through the western part, in a deep, narrow valley, bordered by precipitous hillsides. Hunt Creek, in the north-west, flows through a narrow, deep valley, and Merrill Creek, in the east part, flows through a similar valley. The principal part of the arable land lies along the valleys; the uplands are broken and better adapted to pasturage. The soil is a sandy and gravelly loam.

*Marathon*, (p. v.) situated on both sides of the Tioughnioga, is a station on the Syracuse, Binghamton and New York Railroad, and contains three churches, an academy, a newspaper office, two hotels, a large grist and flouring mill, a number of sawmills, a large tannery, a number of stores and mechanic shops and about 1,000 inhabitants The main street extends east and west, and divides the village into two nearly equal parts.

*Marathon Grist and Flouring Mill* is capable of grinding 500 bushels per day, and gives employment to six or eight men. Deals largely in flour and feed, and has a capital of $40,000 invested

*Burgess' Mill* (circular saw) will cut 16,000 feet per day, and *Livingston's Mill* (circular saw) will cut about 20,000 feet in 24 hours

Cooperage business gives employment to eight or ten men and turns out about $10,000 worth of work annually.

*Marathon Tannery* employs eleven men and manufactures about 25,000 or 30,000 pounds annually. The capital invested is $50,000.

*Marathon Rural Cemetery* embraces about twelve acres, on a rise of ground about one fourth of a mile north-east of the village. It is under the control of an association of which Samuel M. Hunt is President.

*Marathon Academy* —This institution is situated on the west side of the river, about sixty rods from the railroad depot. It has a beautiful location on a good sized lot which slopes gradually to the east. It was chartered as an Academy by the Regents of the University in February, 1866. The building, as it then was, had been used and owned by E S. Weld, an enterprising young man, who, at the call of his country, left his "High School," as it was called, to engage in his country's defense, and who now fills an honored soldier's grave. Its dimensions were the same as now, but it required an expenditure of about $1,000 to bring it to its present condition. This was done by the stockholders the first season after they purchased it. There are forty shares of $100 each in the stock. The present value of the lot and buildings is set down at $4,800. M. L. Hawley, Esq., now editor of the *Binghamton Standard*, was engaged as Principal during the first two years of its existence as an academy. Mr. Hawley is an excellent teacher and well calculated to advance the interests of a school The school is

under the direction, for the present academic year, of Stephen Manchester, an experienced teacher and a good disciplinarian. The
officers of the Board of Trustees are: Hon. Dann C. Squires,
President, Sanford L. Baum, Secretary; Alanson Benjamin,
Treasurer.

An Iron Bridge is being erected across the river in this village,
which will cost about $14,000.

*Texas Valley*, (p. v.) in the north-east corner of the town, contains three churches and is quite a flourishing village.

The first settlement of this town was commenced in 1794, by
Dr. Japheth Hunt and his wife and two sons, James and William,
and three daughters. They entered the Tioughnioga Valley from
the south, in canoes, and located on lot 93, about a mile south of
the present village of Marathon. Dr. Hunt came from New England, and had served his country in the Revolutionary war as surgeon. He was too far advanced in life to commence a new settlement, but his children were of mature age and possessed vigorous
constitutions which fitted them for the laborious duties that de-
volved upon them. In 1796, John Hunt, the oldest son of the
Doctor came and settled on lot 72 Samuel M Hunt, his son, born
October 30, 1798, was the first child born in the town. John
Hunt was appointed a justice of the peace, about the commencement of the present century, and held the office until his death in
1815. His widow survived him a little more than half a century
and died May 7th, 1866, at the age of ninety-five years and seven
months. Abram Brink, with his family, moved into the town in
1800, and located on lot 82 He came up the river in a canoe,
opened an inn soon after his arrival, and kept it for more than
twenty years. Though he could neither read or write he was appointed the first postmaster in the town. A family by the name
of Alford and a man by the name of Lee were among the early
settlers Among the other early settlers were John S. Squires,
Ebenezer Carley and Patrick Mallory. The last named was a
brother of Esq. Hunt's wife, and settled one mile north of Marathon
village.

The first marriage in the town was that of Nicholas Brink and
Polly Alford; and the first death that of Dr. Hunt, in 1808, at the
age of 97. William Cowdrey taught the first school, in 1803;
John Hunt built the first sawmill; and Weed & Waldo, James
Burgess and David Munroe were early merchants.

In 1808 the father of THURLOW WEED removed to this town, and
here was laid the foundation of that career which made "T. W." a
power in the Empire State. Mr. Weed says, in a communication
to H. C. Goodwin, the Historian of Cortland County: "My first
employment was in attendance upon an ashery. The process of extracting lye from ashes, and of boiling the lye into black salts, was

common-place enough, but when the melting down into potash
came, all was bustle and excitement. This labor was succeeded,
when the spring had advanced far enough, by the duties of the 'sap-
bush.' This is a season to which the farmers' sons and daughters
look forward with agreeable anticipations. In that employment
toil is more than literally *sweetened*. The occupation and its asso-
ciations are healthful and beneficial. When your troughs are dug
out, (of basswood, for there were no buckets in those days,) your
trees tapped, your sap gathered, your wood cut, and your fires fed,
there is leisure for reading or 'sparking.' And what youthful den-
izens of the sap-bush will ever forget, while 'sugaring off,' their
share in the transparent and delicious streaks of candy congealed
and cooled on snow? Many a farmer's son has found his best opportunities for improvement in his intervals of leisure while 'tending sap-bush.' Such at any rate was my experience. At night
you had only to feed the kettles and keep up the fires, the sap having been gathered and the wood cut before dark During the day
we would also lay in a good stock of 'fat pine,' by the light of
which, blazing brightly in front of the sugar-house, in the posture
the serpent was condemned to assume as a penalty for tempting
our great first grandmother, I have passed many and many a de-
lightful night in reading. I remember in this way to have read a
history of the French Revolution, and to have obtained from it a
better and more enduring knowledge of its events and horrors, and
of the actors in that great national tragedy, than I have received
from all subsequent readings. I remember how happy I was in
being able to borrow the book of Mr. Keyes, after a two mile
tramp through the snow, shoeless, my feet swaddled in remnants
of a rag-carpet." He says he was large, healthy and strong, and
ambitious " to keep his row" in hoeing corn and potatoes. The
"logging bees" and other gatherings, accompanied by the indispensable gallon bottle of whisky, are duly noticed, as clearing the
land constituted the principal employment of the early settlers
He says: " Our first acquisition in the way of 'live stock' was a
rooster and four hens; and I remember with what a gush of glad-
ness I was awakened at break of day the next morning by the loud
defiant voice of chanticleer; and when, several days afterwards, I
found a real hen's nest in a brush-heap, with eggs in it, I cackled almost as boisterously as the feathered mother whom I had surprised
in the feat of parturition." The same writer gives the following
amusing account of an expedition to a new store and its results·
" I remember the stir which a new store, established in Lisle (some
seven or eight miles down the river) by the Rathbones, from Oxford, created in our neighborhood. It was 'all the talk' for several
weeks, and until a party of housewives, by clubbing with their products, fitted out an expedition. Vehicles and horses were scarce,

but it was finally arranged: A, furnishing a wagon; B, a horse; C, a mare, and D, a boy to drive. Six matrons, with a commodity of black salts, tow cloth, flax and maple sugar, went their way rejoicing, and returned triumphantly at sunset with fragrant Bohea for themselves, plug tobacco for their husbands, flashy calico for the children, gay ribbons for the girls, jack-knives for the boys, crockery for the cupboard, and snuff for granny." This expedition was a theme for much gossip. The wonders of the 'new store' were described to staring eyes and open mouths. The merchant and his clerk were criticised in their deportment, manners and dress. The former wore shiny boots and tassels, the latter a ruffle shirt, and both smelt of pomatum! I do not believe that the word 'dandy' had been invented, or it would have certainly come in play on that occasion. Thirty years afterwards I laughed over all this with my old friend, General Ransom Rathbone, the venerable proprietor of that 'new store.'" The same writer says: "There were neither churches nor 'stated preaching' in town. A Methodist minister came occasionally and held meetings in private houses or at the school house. In the winter there was a school on the river, and the master, who 'boarded round,' must have 'had a good time of it' on johnny-cake for breakfast, lean salt pork for dinner, and samp and milk for supper. There were few amusements in those days, and but little of leisure or disposition to indulge in them. Those that I remember as most pleasant and exciting were 'huskings' and 'coon hunts.' There was fun too in smoking woodchucks out of their holes."

*The First Presbyterian Church* was organized February 11, 1814, with ten members. The present edifice was erected in 1830. The church now numbers thirty-eight members.

*Marathon Baptist Church* was organized October 20, 1860, with twenty-five members; the present number is eighty-three. The church is in a flourishing condition with the prospect of a new building. J. H. Sage is the pastor.

*The Methodist Church* was organized by the formation of a class consisting of four members, in 1830; Orrin Carley was leader. Three members of the original class are still living, viz., Mrs. C. Newton, Orrin Carley and Mrs. Griffin. The church now numbers 170 members. Rev. A. C. Bowdish is the present pastor.

The population in 1865 was 1,485 and its area 15,945 acres.

THURLOW WEED was born in Cairo, Greene County, N. Y., November 15, 1797, and, at the age of eleven, removed with his parents to Cincinnatus, now embraced in the town of Marathon. In the summer of 1806 he was employed as cook and cabin boy on board the sloop *Ranger*, of Catskill, and on the sloop *Jefferson* in 1807. In the winter of 1808 his father removed to this County and young Thurlow found himself soon after in an ashery, engaged in making black salts. His parents were poor and unable to give him the advantages of a school education. Previous to his removal from Greene County, he had worked in the printing office of Macky Croswell, at Catskill, and had acquired the title of "Printer's Devil." In 1811 he was employed in the *Lynx* office, at Onondaga Hollow, and in 1812 he was employed in the office of Thomas Walker, of Utica, and worked on the *Columbian Gazette;* and in 1813 on the *Herkimer American.* From this time until 1815 he was employed at Auburn, Spring Mills, Sangerfield, Cazenovia and Cooperstown He worked at offices in Utica and Herkimer for a time, and then went to Albany and New York, working as a journeyman until 1819 At this time he established a weekly newspaper in Norwich, Chenango County, called *The Agriculturist.* In 1821 he removed to Manlius and established the *Onondaga County Republican.* From this place he went to Rochester, where, after working two years, he purchased the paper, *The Rochester Telegraph.* He subsequently published the *Anti-Masonic Inquirer,* which soon became the leading paper of his party in the State. In 1830 he removed to Albany and established the *Evening Journal,* which was conducted with great ability for more than a quarter of a century, during most of which time he probably exerted a greater influence upon the political affairs of the State than any other man. In 1843 he went to Europe and visited the British Islands and several countries upon the continent. His letters furnished for the *Journal* during his travels were exceedingly interesting and were extensively copied into other papers and subsequently published in book form. Since his retirement from the *Evening Journal* he has been connected with the Press of New York City.

DAVID R. LOCKE, known throughout the country as *Petroleum V. Nasby,* is a native of this town, and his father, Nathaniel Locke, still resides here.

*PREBLE,* named in honor of Commodore Edward Preble, was formed from Tully, upon the organization of Cortland County, April 8, 1808, and embraced the south half of that town. Its size was diminished in 1815 by taking off the town of Scott. It is situated upon the north border of the County, west of the center. The surface is somewhat broken and diversified, consisting of the valley of the western branch of the Tioughnioga River, which is about two miles wide, and the ridges which rise on the east and west. Mount Topping, situated south-west of the village, is 1,700 feet above tide. The declivities of the hills are steep, and their summits in some instances sharp ridges. A valley extending northward, opens into the valley of Otisco Inlet. Several small lakes are situated in the north part of the town, and others similar are situated in the south part, known as Little York Lakes. The soil is a fine quality of gravelly loam.

*Preble,* (p. v.) situated on the Syracuse, Binghamton and New York Railroad, contains two churches, a hotel, two general merchandise stores, one hardware and one drug store, one cooper shop, one school, employing two teachers; a harness shop, two blacksmith shops, one wagon shop and several other shops of various kinds, and about 400 inhabitants.

A Good Templar's Lodge was organized in July, 1868

*Preble Cheese Factory* is located about a mile south-east of the village. It was built in 1863–4 by Moses and William Palmer. The building is 100 feet by 35, and two stories high, with an engine room 12 by 16 feet. The vats are heated by steam, and the milk of from 500 to 600 cows is used annually.

*Baltimore* and *Preble Center* are hamlets.

The first settlement of this town was made in 1796 by James Cravat and John Gill. Mr. Cravat was a native of Connecticut, but removed from Pompey Hill and located on lot 68　In 1798 Harry Hill and Elijah Mason came in and settled on lots 87 and 78. During the next two years Seth Trowbridge, Minnah Hyatt and Samuel Orvis settled on lot 59　Augustus Thorp located on lot 78 in 1801, and Jabez B. Phelps, John Osgood, Silas Topping and Samuel C. Buckelow settled in various locations in the town in 1802. Judge Phelps located on lot 88, practiced medicine for a time but subsequently turned his attention to politics, and was elected to various responsible offices. Lytle Ferguson, Amos Skeel and Jason Comstock came into the town in 1802–3, and John Callyer, Dr. Robert D. Taggart and Edward Cummings in 1804. Mr. Cummings came from Peterboro, N. H., and settled on lot 59. He purchased one hundred acres and reared a family of thirteen children. Among the other early settlers were Garret Van Hoesen and his sons, Garret, Francis and Albert, William Vandenburgh, John C. Hollenbeck and Richard Egbertson, most of whom were from Greene County.

The first school in this town was taught by Miss Ruth Thorp, in 1801　Previous to the establishment of a post-office at Preble Corners, about 1812, the settlers received their mail from Pompey Hill. The first birth in the town was that of Nancy Gill, October 25, 1796 ; the first marriage was that of Amos Bull and Sally Mason, in 1799 ; and the first death that of John Patterson, in 1798 The first gristmill was erected in 1806 by Samuel C. Woolson. In 1827 the building was taken down and the main part of the present mill erected on the original site. Amos Skeel was the first supervisor and the first justice of the peace of the town; Garret Van Hoesen the first town clerk, and Samuel Taggert the first constable.

The first church was organized the 27th of August, 1804, consisting of eleven members. It was called the Congregational Church
of Tully, but has since been designated as the First Presbyterian
Church of Preble. It was formed chiefly through the instrumental-
ity of Rev. Theodore Hinsdale and Joel Hale, missionaries from
Connecticut. Rev. Matthew Harrison, the first pastor, commenced
his labors in 1812.

The Baptist denomination was organized at an early period with
fourteen members, under the labors of Elder Abbott.

The Methodist Church was organized in 1827 by Calvin Winslow; Rev. Mr. Sayers was the first regular preacher. Elder
Puffer, commonly called "Old Chapter and Verse," was at one
time the preacher at this place. It was said that if the Bible should
be destroyed he could re-write every chapter, verse and even word
in its proper place.

The population in 1865 was 1,267 and the area 16,114 acres.

*SCOTT* was formed from Preble, April 14, 1815, and named
in honor of General Winfield Scott   It lies in the north-west corner
of the County. Its surface is chiefly an upland, broken by two
deep and narrow valleys which extend north and south through
the town. The declivities of the hills are very steep and in some
places precipitous. Cold Brook flows through the eastern valley
and Factory Brook and Skaneateles Inlet through the western.
Skaneateles Lake touches the north-west corner   The soil is chiefly
a sandy and gravelly loam, better adapted to grazing than to tillage.

*Scott Center*, (Scott p. o.) situated near the center of the town,
contains three churches, viz., Presbyterian, Methodist and Seventh
Day Baptist, and about 300 inhabitants.

*East Scott*, (p. o.) in the north-east part, on Cold Brook, is a
hamlet.

The mills of J. L & L. H. Comstock are situated on Skaneateles
Inlet, about a mile from Scott. The gristmill is three stories high
and contains three runs of stones. The gristmill and shingle mill
of George Southwick is situated on Skaneateles Inlet. There are
several other mills in various parts of the town

The first permanent settlement was made in 1799 on lot 82, by
Peleg and Solomon Babcock and Asa Howard, from Leyden,
Mass., and George Dennison, from Vermont. Cornish Messenger
and Daniel Jakeway, from De Ruyter, settled on lot 92 in 1800,
and Maxon Babcock upon lot 82 in 1801. Gershom Richardson
and his two sons-in-law, by the name of Clark, came from Pompey
and settled on lot 71, and Henry Burdick, from Colraine, Mass., on
lot 72. John Gillet, from Connecticut, came here in 1805, and subsequently located on lot 84. Mr Gillett was a justice of the peace
for twenty years, associate judge for fifteen years, a member of the

# ALEX. MAHAN,

## NO. 1 MESSENGER HALL BLOCK,

### CORTLAND, N. Y.

At the above location the citizens of Cortland and adjoining counties, can always feel confident of finding a large and choice selection of

## MISCELLANEOUS BOOKS AND SCHOOL BOOKS,

#### And a large stock of

# STATIONERY,

Initial Paper, stamped to order. People may order by mail just as safely as if purchasing in person.

At the above named Store is always kept one of the most complete and varied stocks of

## WALL PAPER AND SHADES

in the State, outside of New York City. Dealers will find it profitable to call, as the wholesale rates in this department are unapproachable.

In addition to the above, the Proprietor of the Store has added a full line of

## Musical Instruments and Sheet Music,

Making this a separate branch, and an addition to his regular trade, it will be seen at once that his prices will be made to suit every one. Let no one go to a larger Town to purchase an Instrument, where expenses are high, and dealers depend entirely upon this branch for profits, when they can do better near home.

Any person, whether wishing to purchase or not, may pass a pleasant hour at this Store, admiring the large collection of beautiful Chromos and Paintings, Statuettes and Groups, collections of rare Shells, cases of Birds, and fine Gift Books. This stock consisting of

## FINE FANCY GOODS

of every description, is kept full the year round for the accommodation of persons desiring Wedding or Birthday Presents. All are invited.

Legislature and Presidential Elector, all of which offices he filled to the general satisfaction of the public and with credit to himself. Jacob Smith, from Delphi, located on lot 84, and Daniel Double-day on lot 85, where he spent a long and prosperous life. In 1805 Elisha Sabins and John Babcock cleared a road from Scott's corners to Babcock's corners They transported their goods to their new homes on sleds. The next year Isaac Hall passed over the road with a wagon and a load of lumber. Game was very abundant, bears were very troublesome to the farmers, destroying their corn and in other respects proving themselves very troublesome neighbors. Deer were also very numerous, and one of the early settlers relates that he went to the woods to cut a broom-stick, accompanied by a large dog. The snow was deep and the crust sufficiently hard to bear a man Before he had secured his broom-stick he had killed seven deer.

The first merchant in the town was Nathan Babcock; the first inn keeper, James Babcock, and the first postmaster, John Gillett. The first birth was that of Harriet Babcock; the first marriage that of Solomon Babcock and Amy Morgan, in 1802. There being no person near who was authorized to marry, the parties went to Homer on horseback, attended church and then called on Esquire Bishop, who performed the ceremony for them. The first death was that of an infant daughter of Peleg Babcock. The first school was taught by Amy Morgan. The first post-master at East Scott was Alvin Kellogg, of whom Ex-President Fillmore learned his trade, that of a clothier. The first ordained preacher was Elder Town.

The town of Scott was greatly harrassed by the depredations of bears, and in March, 1799, three persons started in pursuit One of the hunters soon gave out and the other two continued the trail leading towards Skaneateles Lake. The snow was deep and these two soon gave up the chase and returned by a circuitous route, hoping to meet with an old bear that had wintered in the neighborhood of the hunters' home. As they approached the den of the old depredator he was discovered and both hunters discharged their guns, but only wounded the bear He hastily left for other quarters and was pursued all day, and, after camping out near Skaneateles Lake, they drove the bear into a clearing some eight miles from home, where they killed him and took off his hide, out of which they made each of them a cap, which served to commemorate the event.

The population in 1865 was 1,149 and its area 12,928 acres.

**SOLON** was formed from Homer, March 9, 1798. It embraced the original military township, No. 20. Its original area was diminished April 4, 1811, by annexing a part to Truxton, and, in 1849, by the formation of Taylor. It is an interior town, lying

G

near the center of the County    The surface is broken and diversified by numerous narrow valleys of small streams which flow
through it.   The hills upon the east border are from 1,400 to 1,500
feet in height above tide.   Many of the highest summits are covered with forests and are too rough for cultivation.   Trout Brook
flows in a westerly direction through near the center of the town,
in a narrow, fertile valley.   The soil is a gravelly loam, better
adapted to grazing than to the raising of grain.

*Solon*, (p v ) situated in the central part of the town, contains
two churches, a hotel, a store, several shops and about 100 inhabitants.

The first permanent settlement was made in 1794 by Roderick
Beebe and Johnson Bingham   The former settled on lot 75 and
the latter on lot 62   Mr. Bingham purchased 550 acres, reared a
large family of children and died at the age of 79   Col Elijah
Wheeler, from New Haven, Conn , located on lot 100 in 1801.
Garret Pritchard, from Litchfield, Conn., located on lot 74 in 1807.
He came with a pack on his back, having only $16 50 in money.
His father came in the previous year under very embarrassing circumstances, but the son, with the nerve and energy which characterized many of the early settlers, determined to succeed.   After
earning and paying $500 for his father, he located on lot 75, where
he became a prosperous farmer.   Henry L. Randall came from
Sharon, Conn., in 1808, and located on lot 74   He came with a
two-horse team, bringing a few necessary articles for immediate
use.   He resided for more than fifty years on the same lot and
reared a large family, two of whom, William Randall and Eliza
Stephens, now reside in the town.   Jonathan Rundall also located
on lot 74, and Ebenezer Blake on 84   The latter was a soldier of
the Revolution and fought at the battle of Bunker Hill   Luke
Cass, from New Hampshire, settled on lot 51, where F. L. Boyce
now lives   Columbus Cass, son of Luke, came with his father and
now lives on lot 61.   In 1812 Eben Wilcox built the gristmill now
owned by Philo F Moses, it has two runs of stones and is a flouring and custom mill.   Stephen N. Peck, with his wife and two children, came from Dutchess County in 1805.   He located on lot 62,
and is still living at the age of ninety years and retains to a good
degree all his faculties.   Lyman Peck, E. Burlingham, Platt and
John Peck, now live in town.   Russell Warren settled on lot 51,
where M. O'Brien now lives, in 1817.   Four of his children, viz.,
Pierce, Ransom, Alfred and Polly Gilbert, now reside in town.
Samuel Gilbert and Stephen Pendleton, Revolutionary soldiers,
settled and died here   Josiah Bean, from New Hampshire, settled
on lot 72, where Quigley now lives.   Lydia Randall, his daughter,
now lives in town.   Luke Chapin, the father of Hiram Chapin, now
living in town, came from Massachusetts in 1805 and settled on

was organized in 1811, by Rev. Wm. J. Wilcox, assisted by Rev. John Davenport and Rev. Joseph Avery, missionaries from Massachusetts. Deacon John Severance is the oldest member now living, he having joined in 1812.

The population in 1865 was 1,689 and its area 27,780 acres.

*VIRGIL* was formed from Homer, April 3, 1804, and named in honor of the distinguished Roman poet. It was number 24 of the Military Townships. Harford and Lapeer were taken off in 1845. A small portion of the east part has been annexed to Cortlandville and Freetown. It lies upon the west border of the County, south of the center. The surface is a broken and hilly upland; greatly diversified, and exhibits a variety of picturesque scenery. The Owego Hills, in the south-west part, are about 600 feet above the valleys and about 1,700 feet above tide. The valleys are narrow and bordered by the steep declivities of the hills. The principal streams are Virgil and Gridley Creeks, the former flowing west, the latter east. The soil is a gravelly and sandy loam, best adapted to pasturage.

*Virgil,* (p. v.) situated a little west of the center of the town, on Virgil Creek, contains three churches, a hotel, a marble shop, several stores and mechanic shops, and between 200 and 300 inhabitants.

*East Virgil,* (p. v.) situated in the south-east part, contains a church, several mills and mechanic shops, and about 100 inhabitants.

*State Bridge* (Messengerville p. o.) is a station on the Syracuse, Binghamton and New York Railroad, in the south-east corner of the town.

*Frank's Corners,* in the south-west part, is a hamlet.

The first permanent settlement was made by Joseph Chaplin, on lot 50. He erected a log house here in 1792, while engaged in laying out the road from Oxford to Cayuga Lake, but did not move his family until 1794. This road, about sixty miles in length, was a very great improvement and was a general thoroughfare for emigrants. John M. Frank settled on lot 43 in 1795. John Gee, from Pennsylvania, settled on lot 21 in 1796. He was a soldier of the Revolution and had previously erected a log house, twelve by sixteen feet, for the reception of his family, which consisted of his wife and six children together with his father and mother.

John E. Roe, from Ulster County, moved into the town in the winter of 1797–8 The journey was made in a sleigh which contained also a few of the most valuable of their household effects. When they arrived at the river opposite the residence of Mr. Chaplin, there was no bridge, and in consequence of the rise of the water the canoe in which the passage was usually made had been carried away. The prospect was not very encouraging, for they must either cross the stream or remain where they were without shelter.

Mr. Chaplin's hog trough was procured and in it Mrs. R. was safely landed upon the opposite shore. The horses and the cow swam the stream in safety, and our pioneers put up for the night. The horses were tied to the sleigh, and for want of more nutritious feed ate the flag bottoms of the chairs. The next day they proceeded on their journey to their new home. Mr. Roe had erected a log house in the spring, split plank and laid the floor, and peeled bark for the roof which a man in Homer had agreed to put on, but on their arrival they found their cabin roofless and the snow as deep inside as out. The snow was shoveled away from one side and a fire built against the logs, some blankets drawn across the beams for a shelter, and thus they passed their first night in their new home.

In 1798, James Bright, James Knapp, Bailey, John and James Glenny, and Wait Ball, came in and settled in different parts of the town. The next year Enos Bouton, Dana Miles, John Lucas, Henry Wells, Jared Thorn and Primus Gault came in. The early settlers had to contend against wild beasts, and after all their precautions their flocks and herds sometimes fell a prey to the wolves. The first flock of sheep brought into the town by Mr. Frank were all destroyed. Fifteen wolves were killed in one year by Mr. Roe and Capt. Knapp. The following incident will show the dangers to which the children were exposed:

David Scofield, when but a lad, was once playing upon a brush-fence, and suddenly falling off was seized by a bear that hastened with him towards her den. Passing near his father's house his aged grandmother saw his perilous condition and snatched a warm loaf of bread and hastened to his rescue. Just as the bear was entering her den the old lady threw the bread in front of the bear, at which she dropped the boy, seized the bread and disappeared, leaving the boy to return to the arms of his doting grandmother.

During the year 1800 we find the names of several additional settlers; among them James Wright, John Calvert, James Sherwood, Peter Jones, Seth Larabee, John Ellis, Moses Rice, Abiel Brown, Oren Jones, Moses Stevens and Jason Crawford. The next year Daniel Edwards, Nathaniel Bouton, Prince Freeman and James Clark came in and settled in various parts of the town. During the next two or three years we find the names of Jonathan Edwards, Samuel Carson, Alex. Hunt, George Wright, Abner and Ezra Bruce, Wm. Lincoln, Peter Graw, Moses Olmsted, John I. Gee and others. Elisha Woods settled in this town in 1815, four years after which he removed to Freetown. June 17, 1815, snow fell in this town to the depth of two and a half inches.

Some of the early settlers are described as being destitute of all the luxuries and most of what would be considered the necessaries of life. One man had a cow, an ax and an auger, and his furniture consisted of a hewn slab, standing on four legs, for a table, square blocks for chairs and a corn husk rug for a carpet. Chips served for plates, and a bake kettle for dish kettle, water and milk pail, soup dish, frying pan and coffee pot, showing conclusively that the real necessaries of life are very few

Considerable interest was manifest at an early day in the cause of education. The "Virgil Library" was established in 1807, and another under the name of the "Virgil Union Library" in 1814.

The first birth in the town was that of a son of Mr Chaplin, and the first death that of a stranger, Charles Hoffman, in April, 1798. The first death of a resident was that of Mrs Derosel Gee, in March, 1802. The first marriage was that of Ruluff Whitney, of Dryden, and Susan Glenny, of Virgil, in 1800. The first school house was erected in 1799, and the first teacher was Charles Joyce. Daniel Sheldon was the first merchant, and Daniel Edwards built the first saw mill. Peter Vanderlyn and Nathaniel Knapp erected the first grist mill, in 1805. This was an important work, for previous to its erection the settlers were compelled to go to Chenango Point or Ludlowville. It was not uncommon for them to carry a grist upon their backs more than twenty miles. The first cider was made by Enos Bouton, in 1819, it was worth four dollars a barrel. The apples were mashed by a pestle hung to a spring sweep, and the juice extracted by a simple lever press. The first supervisor of the town was Moses Rice, and the first town clerk, Gideon Messenger.

The first religious meeting was held in 1802, and the first church (Congregational) was organized February 28, 1805, consisting of eight members, by Rev. Seth Williston. The Baptist Church was organized in 1807. The Methodist Church was organized in 1826 or 1827, and their house of worship erected in 1831.

An Agricultural Society was organized in 1853 and held its first annual Fair in 1854. In 1857 it was re-organized and a piece of ground was secured upon which to hold their Fairs, and buildings were erected upon it for the use of the society.

The population in 1865 was 2,009 and its area 28,751 acres.

**WILLETT,** named in honor of Colonel Marinus Willett, was formed from Cincinnatus, April 21, 1818. It lies in the south-east corner of the County. The surface consists of the narrow valley of Otselic River and of the high ridges which rise on either side. The uplands are broken by narrow ravines through which the small streams flow. Much of the surface is unsettled and too rough for profitable cultivation. Bloody Pond is a small sheet of water in the north-west part. The soil is a sandy and gravelly loam

*Willett,* (p. v.) situated a little north of the center of the town, contains three churches, two stores, a hotel, several mechanic shops and mills, and about twenty dwellings.

*Burlingame's Mills* is situated a short distance east of Willett and contains several mills, mechanic shops, stores, &c.

The first settler in this town was Ebenezer Crittenden, in 1797. He was from Barrington, Mass., but had married in Binghamton. Having embarked upon a rude boat, with his wife, child and goods, at Chenango Forks, he forced his way up the river by means of one paddle and a setting pole, to his place of settlement His first shelter was formed by means of some crotches and poles covered with bed clothes. He soon after built a log house which he covered with shingles of his own make. His gristmill was made by hollowing out the top of a stump and erecting a spring-pole for a pestle. His gun furnished his meat and the Otselic his drink. For nine years he was the only inhabitant of the town. In 1806 or 1807, Benjamin Wilson, from Westchester County, John Fisher, from England, John Gozlay, from Dutchess County, and Thomas Leach, from Madison County, settled here. Jabez Johnson, Phineas Sargent and Ebenezer Andrew came in in 1807–8. Other early settlers were Joseph Merritt, Solomon Smith, Daniel Roberts, John Coverts, William Greene, Ira Burlingame, Altitius Burlingame and Edward Nickerson, all of them settling in 1809. Arnold Thomas came here in 1810, and Solomon Dodge in 1811.

The first birth was that of a child of Ebenezer Crittenden; the first marriage was that of Solomon Smith, and the first death that of the wife of Solomon Smith. Benjamin Wilson built a grist mill, a saw mill and a clothing mill, in 1807–8 The first school house was built in 1814; the first post-office was established in 1823, and Samuel Dyer was appointed post-master. William Throop was the first supervisor and Samuel Dyer the first town clerk. The first church (Methodist) was organized in 1816. In 1818 Mr. Arnold Thomas and his wife were drowned in Otselic River, in attempting to cross on a raft The Baptist Church was organized in 1821, and the Congregational in 1852.

The population in 1865 was 982 and its area 15,664 acres.

# CORTLAND COUNTY
# BUSINESS DIRECTORY.

## EXPLANATIONS TO DIRECTORY.

Directory is arranged as follows 1 Name of individual or firm. 2 Post office address in parentheses 8 If a farmer, the lot number indicates his residence. 4. Business or occupation.

A Star (*) placed before a name, indicates an advertiser in this work For such advertisement see Index.

Figures placed after the occupation of *farmers*, indicate the number of acres of land owned or leased by the parties

Names set in CAPITALS indicate subscribers to this work.

**For additions and corrections see Errata following the Introduction.**

## CINCINNATUS.
### (Post Office Addresses in Parentheses.)

Adams, Benjamin L , (Cincinnatus,) lot 36, farmer 173

Andreas, James, (Cincinnatus,) lot 19, farmer 97

Babcock, J S , (Cincinnatus,) blacksmith

Bailey, William B., (Cincinnatus,) lot 50, farmer 207

Barnes, J M , (Cincinnatus,) (*Hitchcock & Barnes*)

BARNES, N ROUNDS, (Cincinnatus,) (*Holmes & Rounds,*) physician and postmaster

BASSETT, GEO , (Cincinnatus,) (*Bassett & White*)

BASSETT & WHITE, (Cincinnatus,) (*Geo Bassett and Lewis White,*) iron founders and machinists.

Beckwith, Samuel, (Cincinnatus,) mechanic and farmer 83

Beebe, Seneca, M. D., (Cincinnatus,) physician.

Beedle, A D , (Cincinnatus,) carpenter and joiner

Benjamin, F N , (Cincinnatus,) lawyer

BENNETT, ALFRED L , (Cincinnatus,) lot 10, farmer 107

BLAKSLEE, ALBERT S , (Cincinnatus,) lots 19 and 20, cattle broker and farmer 50

Blanchard, James, (Cincinnatus,) lot 10, farmer 100

Blanchard, John R , (Cincinnatus,) lot 10, farmer 73

Bourne, R W , (Cincinnatus,) lawyer

BOVEE, O. A., (Cincinnatus,) carpenter and joiner.

BOYD, JACOB B , (Cincinnatus,) lot 19, town assessor, cattle dealer and farmer 11

Bryan, R , (Cincinnatus,) lot 7, farmer 91¼

Bunnell, C. K., (Cincinnatus,) lot 20, farmer 157.

Burgett, Levi, (Cincinnatus,) lot 9, farmer leases of John Payne, 137

Cahill, M. J., (Cincinnatus,) blacksmith.

CANNISS, JANE MRS , (Cincinnatus,) lot 19, farmer 29

*CARRUTH, WM S , (Cincinnatus,) dentist

Clark, Richard H Rev , (Cincinnatus,) pastor M E Church

Cobb, Melvin, (Cincinnatus,) lot 18, farmer leases of Uriah Cobb, 100.

Cole, Ray G , (Cincinnatus,) lot 19, farmer 30

COLGROVE, E J. & E J , (Cincinnatus,) lot 19, farmers 217

Cooper, Charles, (Cincinnatus,) lots 40 and 50, farmer 125

Cooper, W , (Cincinnatus,) lot 17, farmer 91½

CORBIN, JOHN P , (Cincinnatus,) lot 48, farmer leases 140

Cornell, Jeremiah, (Cincinnatus,) lot 6, farmer 27

Cornell, Richard, (Cincinnatus,) lot 6, farmer 62.

CRITTENDEN, JULIUS, (Cincinnatus,) lot 48, farmer 480

Crittenden, Porter, (Cincinnatus,) lot 19, farmer 25.

Crosby, M S , (Cincinnatus,) lot 7, farmer 68

Dana, William H , (Cincinnatus,) harness maker

Delevan, Albert, (Cincinnatus,) lot 47, farmer 204

DWIGHT, G S., (Cincinnatus,) lot 80, farmer 240

Dwight, Horace, (Cincinnatus,) lot 20, farmer 63

Dwight, Sollom, (Cincinnatus,) lot 10, farmer 80

Edwards, Elijah, (Cincinnatus,) lot 46, farmer 135

Edwards, George, (Cincinnatus,) lot 36, farmer 107

Edwards, George, (Cincinnatus,) lot 8, farmer 99

Edwards, Simon, (Cincinnatus,) lot 8, farmer 150½

Fish, Charles, (Cincinnatus,) lot 6, farmer 60

Fish, E D , (Cincinnatus,) lot 16, farmer 170

FISH, ELIJAH, W , (Cincinnatus,) lot 7, farmer 133

Fish, George, (Cincinnatus,) lot 16, farmer 117

Fish, Isaac, (Cincinnatus,) lots 26 and 28, farmer 110

Fish, James D , (Cincinnatus,) lot 7, farmer 75½

Ford, Chauncy, (Cincinnatus,) lot 6, farmer 70

Ford, Oscar, (Cincinnatus,) lot 6, farmer 83½

Foster, Dwight M , (Cincinnatus,) lot 27, farmer 190

Fralic, Lysander, (Cincinnatus,) lot 47, farmer

Glover, Jacob, (Cincinnatus,) lot 47, farmer 28

Glover, John, (Cincinnatus,) lot 46, farmer 104

GREENE, A. C , (Marathon,) carpenter and joiner, contractor and builder

Harrington, George W , (Cincinnatus,) lot 49, farmer 800

HARRINGTON, PORTER C , (Cincinnatus,) lots 6 and 7, veterinary surgeon and farmer 235

HARRINGTON, WARNER, (Cincinnatus,) lot 38, farmer 450

Harrison, John, (Taylor,) lot 10, retired farmer 6

Harvey, James, (Texas Valley,) lot 26, farmer 196

Harvey, Solomon, (Cincinnatus,) lot 20, farmer 86

Harvey, Thomas, (Cincinnatus,) lot 16, farmer 100

Hayes, Samuel E , (Cincinnatus,) lot 19, farmer 7

Healhey, Paul B , (Cincinnatus,) lot 20, retired farmer 18

Herrington, Alden, (Cincinnatus,) lot 7, farmer 175

Higgins, Charles, (Cincinnatus,) harness maker.

Hitchcock & Barnes, (Cincinnatus,) (C B Hitchcock and J M Barnes,) undertakers and furniture dealers

Hitchcock, C B , (Cincinnatus,) (Hitchcock & Barnes )

HOLMES & BARNES, (Cincinnatus,) (Wilber Holmes and N Rounds Barnes,) drugs, medicines and groceries

Holmes, Peleg, (Cincinnatus,) lot 19, cattle dealer and farmer 100.

HOLMES, WILBER,(Cincinnatus,)(Holmes & Barnes )

Holroyd, Ebenezer Rev , (Cincinnatus,) Baptist minister

Hopkins, Dennis J , (Cincinnatus,) (with Samuel,) lot 8, farmer 143

Hopkins, Samuel, (Cincinnatus,) (with Dennis J,) lot 8, farmer 143

HOPPER, L MISS,(Cincinnatus,) milliner

Huntley, William, (Cincinnatus,) lot 30, farmer 86

Janson, Lewis, (Cincinnatus,) lot 30, farmer 6

Johnson, R N., (Cincinnatus,) boot and shoe maker.

Jones, Benjamin, (Cincinnatus,) lot 46, farmer 120

Jones, Erastus, (Cincinnatus,) lots 18 and 28, farmer 163

Jones, F M Miss, (Cincinnatus,) milliner

Joyner, John J , (Taylor,) carriage manufacturer

Kellogg, Stephen, (Cincinnatus,) lots 8 and 9, lawyer and farmer 60

Kellogg, Wilber, (Cincinnatus,) lot 30, farmer 80

Kingman, D F , (Cincinnatus,) hardware merchant

Kingman, H M , (Cincinnatus,) (Kingman & Sturtevant )

Kingman, Oliver, (Cincinnatus,) (Kingman & Sturtevant )

Kingman & Sturtevant, (Cincinnatus,) (H M Kingman, J W Sturtevant and Oliver Kingman,) general merchants

Knickerbocker, Henry, (Cincinnatus,) lot 8, farmer 85

LARRABEE, L. J., (Cincinnatus,) cutter manufacturer

Letts, Cornelius, (Cincinnatus,) lots 16 and 17, prop of cheese factory and farmer 400

Lock, E G , (Cincinnatus,) butcher and stock dealer

Lotridge, Orrin, (Cincinnatus,) lots 18 and 28, farmer 115

Lotriga, Malden, (Cincinnatus,) lot 19, farmer 14

Magunnis, William, (Cincinnatus,) lot 16, farmer 100

Maricle, John, (Cincinnatus,) lot 36, farmer 160

Maricle, Martin, (Cincinnatus,) lot 36, farmer 90

Maricle, Nicholas, (Texas Valley,) lot 26, farmer 150

Mathews, David, (Cincinnatus,) lot 17, farmer 117

Mathews, Judson C , (Cincinnatus,) lot 27, farmer 100

Mathews, Thomas, (Cincinnatus,) lot 7, farmer 40

McLoughlin, Fergus, (Taylor,) lot 10, farmer.

MEAD, NATHANIEL J , (Cincinnatus,) lot 8, farmer 70

MESSENGER, MENSON K , (Cincinnatus,) hotel proprietor

Miller, Seth M , (Cincinnatus,) (*Miller & Wood* )

Miller & Wood, (Cincinnatus,) (*Seth M Miller and Wallace W Wood,*) dealers in boots, shoes, groceries and provisions

Mooney, George A , (Cincinnatus,) lot 50, farmer

Mortimer, Thomas, (Cincinnatus,) lot 6, farmer 158¾

Nichols, Charles, (Cincinnatus,) lot 7, farmer 100

NICHOLS, HARRY S , (Cincinnatus,) lot 16, farmer

Nichols, Samuel, (Cincinnatus,) lot 16, farmer 100

Peck Nathan B , (Cincinnatus,) tailor

Pendleton, Albert, (Cincinnatus,) dealer in ready made clothing

PLACE, ELBERT, (Cincinnatus,) lot 47, farmer

Place, William R , (Cincinnatus,) lot 47, town assessor and farmer 166

Potter, John, (Cincinnatus,) lot 10, farmer 100

Preston, William H , (Cincinnatus,) lot 8, farmer 56

Prichard, C , (Cincinnatus,) lot 9, farmer 124¾

PRITCHARD, W L , (Cincinnatus )   .

Quivey, A , M. D , (Cincinnatus,) physician

Rathbun, J E , (Taylor,) lot 10, farmer 2

REED, MYRON D , (Cincinnatus,) photographer and dealer in silver and plated ware

Rice, Jason, (Cincinnatus,) lot 28, farmer 528

Richards, James, (Cincinnatus,) undertaker

Robbins, Horace, (Cincinnatus,) lot 10, farmer 10

Roberts, Henry, (Cincinnatus,) gunsmith

Rogers, Edson Rev , (Cincinnatus,) pastor of Presbyterian church

Roods, Enoch, (Cincinnatus,) lot 30, farmer 87

Root, James S , (Cincinnatus,) lot 29, farmer 40,

ROOT, S W , (Cincinnatus,) lot 29, farmer 125

Roripaugh, J , (Cincinnatus,) lot 19, farmer 15

SAMSON, I S , (Cincinnatus,) hardware merchant.

Seamans, Noel & Son, (Taylor,) lot 10, farmers 77

Seeber, C Mrs , (Cincinnatus,) lot 87, farmer 85

Seeber, George, (Cincinnatus,) lot 46, farmer 113.

SHATTUCK, DAVID T , (Cincinnatus,) jeweler.

Shufelt, George W , (Taylor,) lot 10, constable and farmer 88

Smith, A J & Sons, (Cincinnatus,) (*S W and J P ,*) leather manufacturers

SMITH, A L., (Cincinnatus,) lot 38, farmer 100

Smith, C W , (Cincinnatus,) leather manufacturer

Smith, Emerson, (Cincinnatus,) farmer 359

SMITH, HARRY C , (Cincinnatus,) lot 19, farmer 46

SMITH, HENRY A , (Cincinnatus,) lot 38, farmer 140.

SMITH, J G , (Cincinnatus,) hotel proprietor

SMITH, J P , (Cincinnatus,) (*A J Smith & Sons* )

SMITH, MARCELLUS R , M D., (Cincinnatus,) lot 19, physician

Smith, Monroe E , (Cincinnatus,) (*Wells & Smith,*) supervisor

Smith, S W , (Cincinnatus,) (*A J Smith & Sons* )

SPENCER, F L , (Cincinnatus,) farmer

Spencer, George W , (Cincinnatus,) lot 40, shoemaker and farmer 30

Spencer, Lafayette, (Cincinnatus,) lot 40, farmer 74

Spencer, Orange, (Cincinnatus,) lot 40, farmer 91

Spencer, Philemon, (Cincinnatus,) boot and shoe manufacturer

Sturtevant, J W , (Cincinnatus,) (*Kingman & Sturtevant* )

Sweet, E , (Cincinnatus,) lot 46, farmer 80

TILLINGHAST, BENJAMIN F , (Cincinnatus,) lot 19, assistant assessor, conveyancer, insurance agent and retired farmer

Tory, Tracy, (Cincinnatus,) lot 26, farmer 77

UFFORD, DAVID D , (Cincinnatus,) general merchant

Vanderwaker, Adam, (Cincinnatus,) lot 36, farmer 150

Wells, Harrison, (Cincinnatus,) (*Wells & Smith* )

Wells & Smith, (Cincinnatus,) (*Harrison Wells and Monroe E Smith,*) produce dealers

WHITBY, JOSEPH, (Cincinnatus,) lot 9, farmer 77

White, Augustus, (Texas Valley,) lot 26, farmer 107

White, Burel, (Cincinnatus,) lots 39 and 40, farmer 300.

White, David, (Cincinnatus,) lot 39, farmer 298

# CLIFTON W. WILES

## FREETOWN, N. Y.,

### DEALER IN

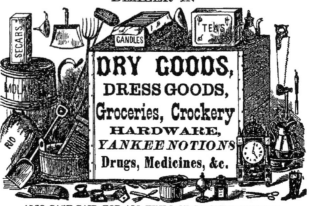

**DRY GOODS,**
**DRESS GOODS,**
Groceries, Crockery
**HARDWARE,**
*YANKEE NOTIONS*
Drugs, Medicines, &c.

ALSO CASH PAID FOR ALL KINDS OF COUNTRY PRODUCE

# PLANING MILL

## AND

# WOOL CARDING!

The subscriber having purchased the old CARDING MACHINE at

## BLODGETT'S MILLS,

Begs leave to announce to the public that he has entirely refitted and remodeled the same, and is now prepared to do all work entrusted to him with neatness and dispatch

He has also put into the building a new

## PLANING & MATCHING MACHINE,

And is prepared to execute all orders in that line to the entire satisfaction of the public He will keep constantly on hand

## Hoe Handles, Fork Stales, Neck Yokes,

and every variety of TURNED WARES, which will be sold at the lowest possible market price    BRACKET SAWING DONE TO ORDER

## ALLEN POTTER.

White, Isaac, (Cincinnatus,) lot 18, butcher and farmer 86
White, Israel, (Cincinnatus,) lot 28, farmer 119
WHITE, JEROME, (Cincinnatus,) lot 28, carpenter and joiner
White, John, (Cincinnatus,) lot 18, farmer 270
WHITE, LEWIS, (Cincinnatus,) (Bassett & White.)
White Stephen, (Cincinnatus,) lot 27, proprietor saw mill and farmer 300
WHITE, WILLIAM G , (Cincinnatus,) lot 29, dairyman and farmer 315

Wicks, Allen, (Cincinnatus,) lot 50, farmer 56
Wiles, Peter, (Cincinnatus,) lot 46, farmer 70
Williams, Daniel B , (Cincinnatus,) lot 38, farmer 120
Williams, James, (Cincinnatus,) lot 17, farmer leases of Patrick McMann, 115
Williams, Nelson, (Cincinnatus,) lot 38, farmer 110
Williams, Niles R., (Cincinnatus,) lot 38, farmer
Wood, A J , (Cincinnatus,) painter
Wood, Wallace W., (Cincinnatus,) (Miller & Wood )

---

# CORTLANDVILLE.

## (Post Office Addresses in Parentheses )

Alger, Charles O , (McGrawville,) lot 80, farmer 67½
Alger, J C , (McGrawville,) administrator of the estate of J W Alger, dealer in tin, hardware &c
ALGER, SILAS J , (McGrawville,) lot 67, farmer 110
ALGER, WM H , (McGrawville,) lot 58, farmer 96
Allen, Arnold, (Cortland Village,) lot 73, farmer 30
Allen, Elijah M., (Cortland Village,) lot 83, farmer 77
Alport, Thomas. (Cortland Village,) carpenter and builder
ALVORD, WILLIAM, (Cortland Village,) carpenter, master builder and farmer 13½
Angell, Sheldon H , (Blodget Mills,) lot 87, farmer 177
ANTISDEL, A , (Cortland Village,) lot 63, farmer 30
ANTISDEL, SIMON, (Cortland Village,) lot 63, farmer 110
Atkins, Lorenzo B , (McGrawville,) lot 90, farmer 100
BABCOCK, LUCIUS, (McGrawville,) lot 79, farmer 60
Bacon, Samuel F , (Cortland Village,) pastor First Presbyterian church
Baldwin, Charles E , (South Cortland,) lot 93, farmer 40
Baldwin, Eben R , (Cortland Village,) lot 51, peddler and farmer 8
Ball, Jay, (Cortland Village,) physician and surgeon.
BALLARD, HORATIO, (Cortland Village,) (Ballard & Warren.)
BALLARD & WARREN, (Cortland Village,) (Horatio Ballard and William H Warren,) attorneys and counselors at law

Ballard, Wm. P , (Homer,) lot 54, share of late A Ballard's undivided estate of 110 acres
Barber, John S , (Cortland Village,) attorney at law
Barker, A F , (McGrawville,) lot 79, farmer 28
Barker, Geo. L , (McGrawville,) lot 80, farmer 103.
Barnum, Delos, (Cortland Village,) photographer
Barnum, John, (Blodget Mills,) lot 98, minister and farmer 53
BARRON, E. M MRS , (Cortland Village,) prop boarding house, opposite Messenger House.
Bates, Henry, (Cortland Village,) paper hanger and painter
Bates, Lemuel, (Cortland Village,) lot 72, farmer 50
Bauder, Delos, (Cortland Village,) prop of Cortland House
Beach, Samuel D , (Cortland Village,)(S. D Beach & Co )
Beach, S D & Co , (Cortland Village,) (Samuel D Beach and J Dayton,) wholesale and retail grocers
BEAN, ALBERT, (McGrawville,) lot 78, farmer 307
Bean, Jacob, (McGrawville,) lot 80, farmer 8.
Beers, Joseph C , (Cortland Village,) lot 64, mason and farmer 24½.
Bell, R C , (Blodget Mills,) lot 88, farmer 2½
BENEDICT, ALBERT, (Cortland Village,) lot 51, farmer 184
Benedict, A. W , (Cortland Village,) lot 51, farmer 74
Benedict, Horace, (Cortland Village,) lot 51, farmer 69

Benedict, Lydia Mrs., (Cortland Village,) milliner

Benedict, Rensaelaer D , (Cortland Village,) lot 51, farmer 60.

Benjamin Brothers, (Cortland Village,) (*Stillwell M and John W*,) manufs and dealers in head stones, monuments, &c

Benjamin, John W , (Cortland Village,) (*Benjamin Brothers*)

Benjamin, Stillwell M , (Cortland Village,) (*Benjamin Brothers*)

BENTON, HENRY F , (Cortland Village,) (*Hopkins & Benton,*) (*H F Benton & Co,*) prop of lumber yard, 20 R R

BENTON, H F & CO , (Cortland Village,) (*Henry F Benton and Everett P Scutt,*) props of planing mill, sash, blind and door factory

BENNETT, SIDNEY, (McGrawville,) lot 59, farmer 58

BENNET, WILSON, (McGrawville,) lot 79, farmer 89.

Berggrew, Benjamin P , (Cortland Village,) blacksmithing and horse shoeing

Bervee, M Widow, (McGrawville,) lot 89, farmer 189

Bervee, Orlando, (McGrawville,) lots 89, 88 and 93 farmer 122

BIGSBEE, AARON, (Blodget Mills,) blacksmith

Bingham, Johnson, (McGrawville,) lot 80, retired farmer

Bingham, O , (McGrawville,) lot 80, farmer 103

BLACKMER, E N , (McGrawville,)(*Black mer & Tarble*)

BLACKMER & TARBLE, (McGrawville,) (*E N Blackmer and Wm H Tarble,*) grocers

Blackmer & Terrill, (McGrawville,) vinegar manufs

BLAIR, SAMUEL, (Cortland Village,) lot 73, farmer 82

Blanchard, J M , (Cortland Village,) lot 14, farmer 59¼

Blanchard, W T , (Cortland Village,) lot 74, farmer 20

Bliss, DeLoyd, (Cortland Village,) dealer in groceries and provisions

BLISS, HARLOW P , (Cortland Village,) lot 77, hop grower and farmer 74

BLODGETT, A D , (Cortland Village,) lots 66 68 and 55, farmer 180

Blodgett, Charles C., (Blodget Mills,) lot 96, farmer 57

Blodget, Geo , (Blodget Mills,) lots 96 and 97, farmer 155

Blodgett, Wm , (McGrawville,) lot 10, farmer 106

Bockins, K Mrs , (Cortland Village,) dress and cloak maker

BOIES, WM A , (Homer,) lot 54, farmer leases 100

Bond, Geo , (Cortland Village,) lot 72, farmer leases 40

Bonney, Levi, (McGrawville,) lot 57, farmer 40

Bouton, Lewis, (Cortland Village,) attorney and counselor at law

Boyce, L D , (Cortland Village,) lot 85, farmer 180

Boyle, John, (Cortland Village,) rector of Grace church

Boynton, Adna, (McGrawville,) lot 69, farmer 55

Boynton, A L , (McGrawville,) (*with C H Card,*) lot 58, farmer 110

Boynton, Morton, (McGrawville,) lot 69, farmer 25

Brabrook, Wm , (South Cortland,) lot 92, retired farmer 2¾

Bradford, Daniel, (Cortland Village,) druggist and grocer

Bradford, Gershom W , (Cortland Village,) druggist and bookseller

Bramas, James, (Cortland Village,) lot 81, farmer 65

BRAYTON, THOMAS, (Homer,) horse farmer

Brewer, Henry L , (Cortland Village,) (*Henry Brewer & Son.*)

Brewer, Henry & Son, (Cortland Village,) (*Henry L ,*) dealers in and manufs of harness, saddles, trunks, whips, &c

Brewer, Stephen, (Cortland Village,) claim agent and dealer in patent rights

Briggs, Jonathan, (Cortland Village,) lot 82, farmer 50

Briggs, Timothy, (South Cortland,) lot 92, farmer 50

Brooke Isaac, (Cortland Village,) lot 94, farmer 128

BROOKS, JAMES H , (McGrawville,) (*Brooks & Sons*)

Brooks, Jonathan H , (McGrawville,) lot 69, farmer 1

BROOKS, L A , (Cortland Village,) lot 77, farmer 94.

BROOKS, LUCIUS E , (McGrawville,) (*Brooks & Sons*)

Brooks, Ransom G , (Cortland Village,) lot 85, farmer 55

BROOKS, SETH D , (McGrawville,) (*Brooks & Sons,*) lot 80, farmer 25.

BROOKS & SONS, (McGrawville,) (*Seth D , James A. and Lucius E ,*) lot 80, manuf of cheese boxes, pump fixtures, &c

Brown, Alvin, (Cortland Village,) retired farmer

BROWN, C. W , (Blodget Mills,) cheese factory

Brown, Daniel, (Blodget Mills,) lot 9, farmer 50

BROWN, DANIEL S , (Cortland Village,) lot 94, farmer 24

BROWN, ELIZA MRS , (Cortland Village,) lot 95, farmer 14

Brown, Eugene, (Blodget Mills,) boot and shoe maker

Brown, George S., (Cortland Village,) (*G S Brown & Co*)

Brown, G S & Co , (Cortland Village,) (*George S and Isaac W ,*) props of livery stable

BROWN, G W , (Blodget Mills,) lot 9, stock dealer and farmer 240

BROWN, ISAAC W , (Cortland Village,) (*G S Brown & Co ,*) sheriff of Cortland Co

BROWN, JOHN, (Blodget Mills,) lot 97, farmer 165

Brown, Marcus, (Cortland Village,) lot 81, farmer leases 6

Brown, Rufus, (Blodget Mills,) lot 97, farmer 100

BROWN, T NEWTON, (Homer,) lots 63 and 64, farmer 116

Brown, William, (Cortland Village,) undertaker, carpenter and joiner

BROWN, WM W, (McGrawville,) harness manuf

BUCHANNAN, ELIZA MRS, (Cortland Village,) lot 52, farmer

Buchannan, Sandford, (Cortland Village,) lot 52, farmer 80

BUCHANNAN, WM W, (McGrawville,) lot 58, clock repairer and farmer 75

BUCK, ORSON S, (Cortland Village,) mover of buildings and farmer 73½

Buell, Horace H, (Cortland Village,) (Graham & Buell)

Bullman, Benoni, (Cortland Village,) lot 63, farmer 80

Bullman, Christopher, (Cortland Village,) lot 63, farmer 75.

Burlingham, Philip, (McGrawville,) lot 69, farmer 239

Barr, Daniel H, (Cortland Village,) (Burr & McGraw)

Burr & McGraw, (Cortland Village,) (Daniel H Burr and Dewitt C McGraw,) general insurance agents.

Butterfield, Parker, (Blodget Mills,) lot 98, farmer 160.

Cady, Henry, (McGrawville,) lot 80, Baptist minister and farmer 16

Caldwell, A S, (Cortland Village,) lot 77, farmer leases 194.

Calkings, George D., (Cortland Village,) lot 53, farmer 100

CALKINS, J D, (Cortland Village,) lot 81, farmer 140

Calkins, S. S., (McGrawville,) lot 90, farmer 17½

CALVERT, WILSON, (South Cortland,) lot 92, farmer 96¼.

Canington, Samuel P, (Cortland Village,) dealer in flour and feed.

Card, C H., (McGrawville,) (with A L Boynton,) lot 58, farmer 110

Carmichael, James C, (Cortland Village,) manuf and dealer in cabinet furniture.

CARR, A, W MRS, (McGrawville)

CARR, DAVID, (McGrawville,) lot 57, dairyman and farmer 103

*CARR, D. W., (McGrawville,) dry goods merchant

CARR, HIRAM H., (McGrawville,) lot 78, farmer 86

CARR, I Y, (Cortland Village,) lot 88, farmer 122

Carr, Peter C, (McGrawville,) lot 90, saw mill and farmer 70

Carr, Wm, (McGrawville,) lot 58, farmer 116½

Carson, H C Mrs, (Cortland Village,) lot 94, farmer 10

Chafy, Joseph D., (Cortland Village,) lot 62, farmer 69

Chafy, J M, (Cortland Village,) lot 72, farmer 50

CHAFY, THOMAS J, (McGrawville,) (Hamilton & Chafy)

CHAMBERLAIN, CHAS S, (Cortland Village,) (Chamberlain, Smith & Co)

CHAMBERLAIN, NORMAN, (Cortland Village,) (Chamberlain, Smith & Co)

H

CHAMBERLAIN, SMITH & CO, (Cortland Village,) (Norman and Chas S Chamberlain, Allen B and Henry C Smith,) props of agricultural warehouse, seed store, machine shop and general hardware.

Chapin, P. & M E, (McGrawville,) lot 76, farmer 100

Chatterton, Isaac, (Cortland Village,) lot 73, farmer 48

Chidester, Wm, (Blodget Mills,) lot 98, saw mill

Churchill, Morgan N, (Cortland Village,) lot 64, retired farmer 7.

Clark, Asel, (Cortland Village,) lot 94, farmer 9

Clark, Benj U, (Cortland Village,) lot 65, farmer 48

Clark, Elmer H, (Homer,) lot 56, farmer leases 67.

Cleary, M F, (Cortland Village,) (Holmes & Cleary)

Cloyes, W S, (Cortland Village,) lot 94, mason and farmer 76

*COLE, CHARLES P, (Cortland Village,) editor Gazette and Banner

Colegrove, J, (South Cortland,) carpenter

Collins, Charles W., (Cortland Village,) dealer in house furnishing goods, groceries, provisions and crockery

Collins, Halsey L, (Cortland Village,) justice of the peace

Collins, Jaber, (Cortland Village,) lot 56, farmer 67

Collins, J V, (Homer,) lot 54, farmer 5.

Collins, T D, (Cortland Village,) lot 56, farmer 18½

CONABLE, F. & G., (Cortland Village,) lot 76, farmers 370

Conger, Beemen S, (Cortland Village,) lot 56, farmer 10

Conger, Joseph, (McGrawville,) retired farmer 6.

Coon, ———, (Cortland Village,) (Sidman & Coon.)

Cooper, Gilbert, (Cortland Village,) lot 56, farmer 80

COPELAND, CHAS W, (Blodget Mills,) (Copeland & Tanner)

COPELAND & TANNER, (Blodget Mills,) (Chas W. Copeland and Peter R Tanner,) props of grist mill

Copeland, William S, (Cortland Village,) prop of Messenger House

Cory, Hiram D, (McGrawville,) proprietor of tannery

Corey, Philena, (Cortland Village,) lot 63, farmer 4.

Corkings, Chester W, (Cortland Village,) lot 2, farmer 100

CORNWELL, THEODORE, (Cortland Village,) (T. Cornwell & Co,) prop of meat market

Cornwell, T. & Co, (Cortland Village,) (Theodore Cornwell and Carl Aug Kohler,) ice dealers

Corp, John, (Cortland Village,) retired farmer 2½

*CORTLAND COUNTY STANDARD, (Cortland Village,) F. G. Kinney, editor

*CORTLAND DEMOCRAT, (Cortland Village,) Benton B. Jones, editor

Cortland Savings Bank, (Cortland Village,) William R Randall, president, Calvin P Walrad, secretary

Cortland Silver Cornet Band, (Cortland Village,) Henry C Johnson, leader

Corwin, C E , (McGrawville,) lot 79, farmer 26

Corwin, Ebenezer, (Blodget Mills,) lot 98, farmer 33

CORWIN, POLYDORE B Jr , (Cortland Village,) grocery and saloon.

Coach, John M , (Cortland Village,)(Shankland & Couch.)

COWAN, HECTOR, (Cortland Village,) lot 77, farmer

Cowan, James, (Cortland Village,) lot 77, farmer 225

CRAIN, JONATHAN G , (McLean, Tompkins Co ,) lot 81, farmer 83

CRANDALL, HIRAM, (Cortland Village,) attorney and counselor at law, and vice-president First National Bank

Crandall, H S , (Cortland Village,) lot 56, farmer 70

CRANE, PHILO J., (McGrawville,) lot 100, farmer 120

Crane, Wm H , (Cortland Village,) cashier 1st National Bank

Crisman, Nancy, (Cortland Village,) lot 83, farmer 4

CROSBY, J M ,(Marathon,) cabinet maker

Crowell, F C , (Cortland Village,) lot 67, farmer 100

CROWELL, Z P , (Cortland Village,) lot 67, farmer 110

Cudworth, John, (Cortland Village,) lot 57, farmer 56

Curtis, Edward C Rev , (Cortland Village,) pastor of Centenary M E church

Curtis, Wm R , (Cortland Village,) lot 82, farmer 78

Darby, Joseph, (Cortland Village,) lot 74, patent roofing and side walks, and farmer 51

DAVIS, P BACON, (Cortland Village,) attorney and counselor at law and secretary of Cortland Co Agricultural Society

Davis, Reuben, (Cortland Village,) lot 81, farmer 82.

Dayton, J., (Cortland Village,) (S D Beach & Co )

Dean, E B , (Homer,) lot 54, farmer 80

Delany, Michael, (Cortland Village,) lot 62, farmer 172

DEVINE, OLIVE M , (Cortland Village,) lot 94, farmer 12½.

DEXTER, LUCIAN, (Cortland Village,) prop hotel, restaurant and billiard saloon

DIBBLE, FORAN, (Cortland Village,) prop of woolen and cloth dressing manufactory

Dickinson, Dewitt C , (Cortland Village,) (Dickinson & McGraw,) farmer 15

Dickinson, James, (McGrawville,) lot 80, farmer 75.

Dickinson & McGraw, (Cortland Village,) (Dewitt C Dickinson and Marcus H McGraw,) manufs of and wholesale and retail dealers in boots, shoes and leather, tools, machinery and findings

DODD, JOHN, (Cortland Village,) lot 64, farmer 10

DODD, JOHN MRS , (Cortland Village )

DOUD, BERNARD, (Cortland Village,) (Doud & Gleeson )

Doud, E H., (Cortland Village,) (Sturtevant, Doud & Co )

DOUD & GLEESON, (Cortland Village,) (Bernard Doud and Timothy Gleeson,) bowling alley and saloon

Dond, Patrick, (Cortland Village,) lot 51, farmer leases 73

Dowd, Patrick, (Cortland Village,) lot 84, farmer 22

Downes, C S Mrs , (Cortland Village,) millinery and dressmaking

Duell & Foster, (Cortland Village,) (R Holland Duell and Chas Foster,) attorneys at law

DUELL R. HOLLAND, (Cortland Village,) (Duell & Foster )

Dunbar, H P , (Cortland Village,) (with Thomas S Vanhossen,) lot 71, farmer 167

Dutcher, D C , (Cortland Village,) lot 64, M E clergyman and farmer 15

Earl, Charles L , (South Cortland,) lot 92, farmer 150

Edgcomb, Isaac, (Cortland Village,) (I & M Edgcomb )

Edgcomb, I & M , (Cortland Village,) (Isaac and Martin,) harness, trunks, whips, &c

Edgcomb, Martin, (Cortland Village,) (I & M Edgcomb )

Edwards, Timothy, (Cortland Village,) photographer

EGGLESTON, ASAHEL, (Cortland Village,) lot 71, farmer 130

Eggleston, Francis, (Cortland Village,) brick maker and farmer 2

ELDRIDGE, FRANCIS, (Blodget Mills,) lot 96, farmer 80

ELDRIDGE, O & E , (Cortland Village,) lot 96, farmer 150

Ellsworth, Thomas Jr , (Cortland Village,) lot 64, carpenter and joiner and farmer 7

Ecker, Daniel D , (McGrawville,) lot 9, farmer 270

Evens, Joseph T , (McGrawville,) lot 80, farmer 6¾

FAIRCHILD, JAMES B , (Cortland Village,) lot 74, farmer 85

Finch, Calvin, (Cortland Village,) lot 56, retired farmer 9

First National Bank of Cortland, (Cortland Village,) Thomas Keator, president, Hiram Crandall, vice president , William H Crane, cashier

Fish, E A , (Cortland Village,) (Sturtsvant, Doud & Co )

Fisher, Cuthbert, (Homer,) lot 54, farmer 95

FITZGERALD, LAWRENCE, (Cortland Village,) (Fitzgerald & Rice,) carriage trimmer

FITZGERALD & RICE, (Cortland Village,) (Lawrence Fitzgerald and Melvin A Rice,) dealers in boots, shoes and rubbers

Fletcher, D Sheldon, (Homer,) miller

Fletcher, R B , (McGrawville,) cabinet maker

FORD, H C MISS, (Cortland Village,) lot 83, life insurance agent and school teacher

Forshee, Cornelius, (McGrawville,) lot 90, farmer 46

Forshee, I A., (McGrawville,) veterinary surgeon

Forshee, Isaac & Son, (McGrawville,) blacksmiths

Fosmer, Henry, (Cortland Village,) lot 72, millwright and farmer 30

Foster, Charles, (Cortland Village,) (*Duell & Foster*,) insurance agent

FOSTER, EMILY MRS , (Blodget Mills,) lot 9.

Foster, Wm J , (Blodget Mills,) lot 9, farmer 23

Fox, Warren Rev , (McGrawville,) pastor of M E church

Frederick, John D , (Cortland Village,) stone cutter

Frederick, Wm D , (South Cortland,) lot 93, cooper and farmer 15

Freer, Anthony, (Cortland Village,) farmer 5

FREER, JAMES, (Blodget Mills,) lot 87, farmer 70

FREER, JOHN J , (Blodget Mills,) lot 87, farmer

FREER, STEPHEN D , (Cortland Village,) prop of oil mill and farmer 25

FROST, FREDERICK, (Cortland Village,) lot 91, farmer 60

FULLER, E , (Blodget Mills,) head miller

Gager, D H , (Cortland Village,) lot 81, farmer 100

Gager, Edward W , (Cortland Village,) lot 81, farmer 51

Gager, Judson G , (Cortland Village,) lot 81, mason and farmer 33

Gallagher, Andrew, (South Cortland,) lot 93, farmer 214

Gallagher, Andrew Jr , (South Cortland,) lot 93, farmer

GALLAGHER, GEO , (South Cortland,) lot 93

Gallagher, John, (South Cortland,) lot 93, farmer 96

Gallusha, T B , (Homer,) lot 55, farmer 40

Galusha, Orman, (Homer,) lot 55, farmer 100

GARITY, JOHN, (Cortland Village,) stage proprietor, (daily,) Cortland to Ithaca

GARLICK, F A , (McGrawville,) (*Wood & Co* )

Garrison, Levitt D , (Cortland Village,) (*Garrison & Ogden* )

Garrison & Ogden, (Cortland Village,) (*Levitt D Garrison and Allis W Ogden*,) bakery and confectionery

Gates, Asa, (McGrawville,) lot 60, farmer 25

GATES, A W , (Cortland Village,) lot 57, keeper of Cortland Co poor house

GAYLORD, W S , (Cortland Village,) lot 63, farmer 138

*GAZETTE & BANNER, (Cortland Village,) Chas P Cole, editor

Gazlay, Henry C , M D , (Cortland Village,) eclectic physician and surgeon, over National Bank

Gee, Oliver C , (Cortland Village,) manuf of carriages of every description, West Court

Gibbens, Michael, (Cortland Village,) lot 62, farmer 38.

Gilbertson, J , (McGrawville,) dry goods dealer

Gilkerson, James, (Homer,) retired mechanic.

Gillen, John W , (South Cortland,) lot 91, farmer 25

Gillet, J L , (Cortland Village,) lot 82, manuf of marl lime and farmer 95

GILLETT, FRANK H , (Cortland Village,) lot 84, farmer 60

GIVENS, AMASA, (Cortland Village,) (*James S. Squires & Co* )

GLEASON, LUKE, (Cortland Village,) lot 77, sash and blind manuf and farmer 30

GLEESON, TIMOTHY, (Cortland Village,) (*Doud & Gleeson*.)

*GOLDSMITH, ISRAEL I , (Cortland Village,) dealer in clothing and furnishing goods

Goodell, Geo , (Blodget Mills,) lot 98, farmer 10½

Goodell, J , (McGrawville,) lot 69, farmer 90

Goodell, J. M , (McGrawville,) painter

Goodrich, Horace P , (Cortland Village,) (*Mills & Goodrich* )

Goodyear, Franklin, (Cortland Village,) allop physician and surgeon

Goodyear. Miles, (Cortland Village,) retired physician and farmer 26

Graham & Buell, (Cortland Village,) (*Ira Graham and Horace H Buell*,) dealers in silver-plated ware, clocks, watches and jewelry

Graham, Erastus, (Cortland Village,) lot 58, share in brick yard and farmer 110

Graham, Ira, (Cortland Village,) (*Graham & Buell* )

Green, James, (Cortland Village,) lot 52, farmer leases 106

GREENE, RANSOM, (Homer,) lot 55, farmer 107

Greenman, Chas D , (McGrawville,) builder and farmer 20

GREENWOOD, ISAAC K , (Cortland Village,) lot 77, farmer 125

Greenwood, James R , (Cortland Village,) lot 77, carpenter and joiner and farmer 6

Gross, Andrew, (McGrawville,) lot 69, farmer 27

Haight, Orville, (Homer,) wood turner,

Hakes, Deforest, (Cortland Village,) lot 67, farmer 10

HALE, LUCIEN, (Cortland Village,) (*W C Tisdale & Co* )

Hall, Wm A , (Cortland Village,) lot 57, farmer 14.

HAMILL, DAVID D , (Cortland Village,) ornamental painter

HAMILTON & CHAFY, (McGrawville,) (*Henry Hamilton and Thomas J Chafy*,) stone pump manufacturers

HAMILTON, HENRY, (McGrawville,) (*Hamilton & Chafy* )

HAMMOND, GEORGE R , (Cortland Village,) lot 88, farmer 200

Hammond, H C., (Cortland Village,) farmer leases 40.

HANNUM, LEWIS, (Cortland Village,) prop restaurant and billiard room.

Hardy, David, (Homer,) lot 56, apiarian

# Cortland County Republican.

## J. R. DIXON, Ed. and Prop'r,

## Homer, Cortland County, N. Y.

TERMS —The REPUBLICAN is issued every Thursday Morning, and furnished to Office and Mail Subscribers for **$2.00**, payable in advance    It is devoted to Literature, Temperance, the News of the Day, and the maintenance of sound Republican principles.

### RATES OF ADVERTISING.

TWELVE LINES OF NONPARIEL, OR LESS, MAKE A SQUARE

| | | | | | | | |
|---|---|---|---|---|---|---|---|
| 1 square | one year | $10 00 | 1 square | 3 months | $3 75 |
| 2 " | 6 months | 10 00 | 1 " | 2 " | 2 50 |
| 1 " | 9 " | 8.00 | 1 " | 4 weeks | 1 75 |
| 1 " | 6 " | 6 00 | 1 " | 3 " | 1 50 |
| 1 " | 5 " | 5 25 | 1 " | 2 " | 1 25 |
| 1 " | 4 " | 4 50 | 1 " | 1 " | 75. |

☞ One Column one year $100.   ☞ Legal advertising done at Legal Rates

## Cortland Co. Republican

### Plain & Fancy Book & Job Power Press

# PRINTING OFFICE,

## HOMER, N. Y.,

## Office in Mechanics' Hall, Main Street.

BOOK AND JOB PRINTING in all its branches executed in as good style as at any other establishment in this County.

Harmon, Curtis, (Cortland Village,) lot 83, farmer 68
HARMON, NORMAN G , (Cortland Village,) lot 78, farmer leases 48
Haskell, Harris, (McGrawville,) lot 59, farmer 10
Haskell, Seth, (McGrawville,) lot 59, farmer 80
Haswell, William J , (Cortland Village,) practical upholsterer
Hatch, Franklin, (Cortland Village,) lot 83, farmer 154.
HATFIELD, IRA, (Cortland Village,) lots 82 and 92, manuf of marl lime and farmer 109
HATFIELD, MASON, (South Cortland,) lot 83, farmer 105
HATFIELD, WM S , (Cortland Village,) lot 61, farmer 125
Heffron, Cordelia N Miss, (McGrawville,) preceptress of McGrawville Academy
Heffron, Lucius, (McGrawville,) (Jones & Heffron )
Hendrick, H. C., (McGrawville,) physician and surgeon
HIBBARD, F H , (Cortland Village,) lots 73, 72 and 62, farmer 145
Hicks, E W , (McGrawville,) lot 69, farmer 27
Hicks, Geo W , (McGrawville,) lot 69, farmer 88
Hicks, Huldah, (Cortland Village,) lot 67, farmer 25
HICKS, IRA V., (Cortland Village,) carriage manufacturing in all its branches
Hicks, Mary A., Mrs., (Cortland Village,) lot 95, farmer 74
Hicks, Orlando, (McGrawville,) lot 90, farmer 70
Higgins, Catharine, (Blodget Mills,) lot 98, farmer 48.
Hill, Robert E , (Cortland Village,) (J C Pomeroy & Co.)
Holden Geo L , (Cortland Village,) (Hyatt & Holden )
Holden, Stillman, (McGrawville,) lot 80, farmer 11
Holden, Wm , (McGrawville,) carpenter and farmer 12.
Holister, Francis H , (Cortland Village,) lot 61, farmer 88
HOLMES, ARTHUR, (Cortland Village,) (Holmes & Cleary,) attorney and counselor at law and farmer 253.
Holmes & Cleary, (Cortland Village,) (Arthur Holmes and M F Cleary,) props of nursery, 45.
Holmes, Julius P., (Cortland Village,) assistant revenue collector and insurance agent.
Hopkins & Benton, (Cortland Village,) (L D. C. Hopkins and H F Benton,) planing mill
HOPKINS, JOHN P , (Cortland Village,) wagon maker (with I. V Hicks )
Hopkins, L D C , (Cortland Village,) (Hopkins & Benton )
Hopkins, Wm H , (Cortland Village,) lot 52, general mechanic
HORTON, ISAAC, (Cortland Village,) lot 63, farmer 25
Hotchkiss, J J , (Cortland Village,) lot 64, farmer 30

HOWARD, THOMAS H , (Cortland Village,) prop livery stable
Hoxie, Wm S (Blodget Mills,) lot 9, millwright, prop of steam saw mill and farmer 30.
HUBBARD, HENRY B., (Cortland Village,) (James S Squires & Co )
HUBBARD, NORMAN, (Cortland Village,) lot 74, farmer 60
Hubbard, Samuel E , (Cortland Village,) (Rouse, Hubbard & Co )
Hughes, James W , (Cortland Village,) physician and surgeon
Hull, Geo W , (Cortland Village,) gold and silver plating and dentistry
Hunt, Patrick, (South Cortland,) lot 91, farmer 16.
HUNTER, STEPHEN R , (Cortland Village,) justice of the peace and attorney at law
Hyatt, F C., (Cortland Village,) (Hyatt & Holden )
Hyatt & Holden, (Cortland Village,) (F C Hyatt and Geo L Holden,) practical dentists, corner Main and Court
HYDE, FREDERICK, M D , (Cortland Village,) professor of surgery in Geneva Medical College
Hyde, Miss G , (Cortland Village,) allop physician
Ives, Frederick, (Cortland Village,) (Ives & Schermerhorn )
Ives & Schermerhorn, (Cortland Village,) (Frederick Ives and John E Schermerhorn,) produce dealers and farmers 40
Ives, William L , (Cortland Village,) (Owen & Ives )
JACOBS, H S , (McGrawville,) lot 90, farmer 56
Jacobs, Wm., (McGrawville,) lot 90, farmer 56
Jarvis, Albert J , (Cortland Village,) (Perkins, Jarvis & Co )
Jarvis, Horace A , (Cortland Village,) postmaster
Jewett, H C , (Cortland Village,) allop physician
Johnson, Billings, (Cortland Village,) lot 57, farmer 25
Johnson, Eardley N , (Cortland Village,) dealer in dry goods
JOHNSON, FRANKLIN, (McGrawville,) prop of saloon
Johnson, Henry C , (Cortland Village,) leader of Cortland Silver Cornet Band
Johnson, Joseph, (Cortland Village,) lot 67, farmer 93
Johnson, Nathan S , (McGrawville,) farmer 138
Johnson, Sanford, (McGrawville,) lot 90, farmer 54
Jones, Amasa, (McGrawville,) (Jones & Heffron )
*JONES, BENTON B , (Cortland Village,) editor of Cortland Democrat, published every Friday morning
Jones, Charles A , (McGrawville,) (Warren & Jones )
JONES, GEO B , (Cortland Village,) attorney and counselor at law, owns one-fifth of 80 acres on lot 75
Jones & Heffron, (McGrawville,) (Amasa Jones and Lucius Heffron,) lot 79, props of stone mill

JONES, HENRY S , (McGrawville,) miller

Jones, John W , (Cortland Village,) carpenter and builder

Judd, C. L , (Cortland Village,) lot 94, farmer 25

Katline, John M , (Cortland Village,) tailor

Keator, Thomas, (Cortland Village,) president 1st National Bank

KEENAN, JAMES, (Cortland Village,) lot 81, farmer 55

Kelsey, A (South Cortland,) lot 92, M E clergyman and farmer 10

KENNEDY, HENRY, (Cortland Village,) lot 86, farmer 225

Kent, Horace, (Cortland Village,) (Kent & Sperry )

Kent & Sperry, (Cortland Village,) (Horace Kent and Geo G Sperry,) clothing and furnishing goods.

*KINNE, CHAS W , (Cortland Village,) prop of machine cooperage, and owns 320 acres

KINNEY, CHAS D., (Cortland Village,) dealer in ladies' fancy goods, also agent for the Eliptic sewing machine

Kinney, Charles L , (McGrawville,) lot 60, farmer 100.

Kinney, Cornelius, (Cortland Village,) prop of tannery,

KINNEY, EDWIN, (Cortland Village,) lot 53, farmer 115

*KINNEY, F G., (Cortland Village,) editor Cortland Standard

Kinney, John, (Blodget Mills,) lot 97, farmer 60

KINNEY, JOSEPH, (Cortland Village,) lots 63 and 64, farmer 118

KINNEY, J L , (Cortland Village,) lot 62, prop of saw and cider mills and farmer

KINNEY, SYLVESTER, (Cortland Village,) lot 52, farmer 113,

KNIGHT, FREDERICK E , (Cortland Village,) civil engineer and surveyor

Knox, Philip, (McGrawville,) lot 100, farmer 100

Kohler, Carl A , (Cortland Village,) (T Cornwell & Co )

LAMONT, J B , (McGrawville,) grocer

Lamont, Stewart, (Cortland Village,) lot 83, farmer 100

Larabee, J. S , (Cortland Village,) lot 53, farmer 113

LATTING, R , (McGrawville,) photographer

Leach, Joseph, (McGrawville,) coopering.

Letts, Abram, (Cortland Village,) lot 51, farmer 96.

Lewis, Joel, (Blodget Mills,) lot 98, farmer 50.

Lindsay, Orrin, (Cortland Village,) lot 77, sawyer

Loope, John H., (Cortland Village,) lot 77, farmer 53

LOOMIS DAVID, (McGrawville,) blacksmithing

Loring, Asa, (Cortland Village,) lot 55, surveyor and farmer 140

LORING, MASON T , (Cortland Village,) lot 56, farmer 70

Loucks, Ozias, (Cortland Village,) lot 76, farmer 131

Lucas, Simeon, (Cortland Village,) lot 53, farmer 100

MAHAN, ALEX , (Cortland Village,) books, stationery and fancy goods

Mahan, Henry, (Cortland Village,) lot 94, farmer 40

Maritt, Stephen L , (Cortland Village,) manuf of boots and shoes

Marshall, L Mrs , (South Cortland,) lot 92, farmer 15

MATTESON, LOIS MRS , (Cortland Village,) lots 56 and 57, farmer 30

May, John S , (Cortland Village,) lot 74, wagon maker and farmer 27

May, Wilber C , (Cortland Village,) lot 84, farmer 37

Mayhury, Josiah J , (Blodget Mills,) lot 97, farmer 9

McCarthy, John, (Cortland Village,) sewing machine agent, 2nd floor, Moore Block

McELHENEY, BARNUM, (McGrawville,) lot 59, farmer 72½

McElheney, Geo , (McGrawville,) lot 57, farmer 109

McElheney, Ranson, (McGrawville,) lot 68, farmer 93

McGRAW, DEWITT C , (Cortland Village,) (McGraw & Rounsevell,) (Burr & McGraw )

McGraw, Hiram, (McGrawville,) retired merchant

McGraw, Marcus H , (Cortland Village,) (Dickinson & McGraw )

McGRAW, PERRIN H & D , (McGrawville,) produce dealers

McGRAW & ROUNSEVELL, (Cortland Village,) (Dewitt C McGraw and Alvin N Rounsevell,) attorneys and counselors at law

McGrawville Academy and Union Free School, (McGrawville,) principal, A M Smallie, preceptress, Miss Cordelia N Heffron, teacher in preparatory department, Miss Mary Palmer, teacher of music, Mrs P Smealie

McGnKin, John, (Cortland Village,) grocery store

McLoghlin, B F Rev , (Cortland Village,) Catholic pastor

McNish, James, (Cortland Village,) lot 82, farmer 102

McNish, Samuel, (South Cortland,) lot 93, thresher and farmer 30

McTigue, Catharine, (Cortland Village,) dress and cloak maker.

McUmber, A , (Blodget Mills,) farmer leases 220

McUmber, Henry, (McGrawville,) lot 90, farmer 44

McUmber, Martin, (McGrawville,) lot 80, farmer 85

McUmber, Moses, (McGrawville,) lot 90, farmer 66

McVean, John A , (Blodget Mills,) lot 97, farmer 8

MEDES, HENRY, (Cortland Village,) carpenter and builder

Merrick, Martin, (Cortland Village,) lot 66, farmer 10

MERRICK, MINER, (Blodget Mills,) lot 87, farmer 95

Merritt Edmond P , (Cortland Village,) painter

Messenger, Mrs D , (Cortland Village,) millinery store

Michelson, M , (Cortland Village,)dealer in clocks, watches, silver ware, &c

Miller, George, (Cortland Village,) lot 65, farmer 18

MILLER, NET, (Cortland Village,) cloak and dress maker

MILLER, RICHARD, (Cortland Village,) lot 61, farmer leases 26

Miller, Wm , (Cortland Village,) lot 55, farmer 10.

Mills, Amelia M Mrs , (Blodget Mills,) lot 87, farmer 211

Mills, Andrew V , (Cortland Village,) (Mills & Warren )

Mills & Goodrich, (Cortland Village,) (Myron H Mills and Horace P Goodrich,) dealers in hardware, stoves, gas fitting and plumbing, also dealers in wool

Mills, Myron H , (Cortland Village,) (Mills & Goodrich.)

Mills- & Warren, (Cortland Village,) (Andrew V Mills and Geo L Warren,) dry and fancy goods

Mills, Wm , (Blodget Mills,) lot 98, farmer leases 48

Monroe, Wm. B , (Cortland Village,) lot 77, farmer 21.

Montgomery, E , (South Cortland,) lot 92, boot and shoe maker and farmer 5

Moore, Rensselaer R , (Cortland Village,) gunsmith

More, Duncan G , (Cortland Village,) produce dealer

More, George, (Cortland Village,) (with Mitchell J Robinson,) lot 81, prop of saw, planing, lath and cider mill, also farmer 54

More, Thomas W , (McGrawville,) mason

MOREHOUSE, B B , (Cortland Village,) lot 82, farmer leases 92

Morey, l D , (McGrawville,) grist mill

MORGAN, JOHN W , (Cortland Village,) lot 71, farmer 40

MORRIS, JOHN, (Cortland Village,) tailor

Morris, Walter, (Cortland Village,) lot 72, farmer 44

Munson, Charles, (Cortland Village,) farmer leases 17

Marphy, Mahlon D , (Cortland Village,) general life insurance agent and speculator

Nason, John, Rev , (Blodget Mills,) pastor of Wesleyan church

Newkirk, William, (Cortland Village,) (Smith & Newkirk )

Niles, John, (Cortland Village,) lot 82, farmer 5

NILES, RILEY, (South Cortland,) lot 92, farmer 122

Niles, Wells, (South Cortland,) lot 93, peddler and farmer

NIXON, JAMES A , (Cortland Village,) dealer in coal, plaster, salt, water lime, &c

Nottingham, George, (Cortland Village,) carriage and sleigh maker

NOYES, E H , (Cortland Village,) lot 91, farmer 10

Odell, William A , (Cortland Village,) butcher

Ogden, Allis W , (Cortland Village,) (Garrison & Ogden )

O'Grady, Patrick, (Cortland Village,) lot 68, blacksmith and farmer 14

Olds, Amos, (McGrawville,) lot 78, farmer 29

Olds, Geo H , (McGrawville,) lot 68, farmer 68

Olds, Henry, (McGrawville,) lot 68, farmer 80

Olds, Wm , (McGrawville,) lot 60, farmer leases 110

Osborne, Noah H , (McGrawville,) justice of the peace.

Owen, E , (Cortland Village,) lot 74, supernumerary M E clergyman and farmer 10

Owen, Henry, (McGrawville,) farmer 60

Owen & Ives, (Cortland Village,) (O Darwin Owen and William L Ives,) dealers in all kinds of furniture and undertaking

Owen, Nelson, (McGrawville,) lot 80, farmer 75

Owen, O Darwin, (Cortland Village,) (Owen & Ives )

OWEN, WM N , (Blodget Mills,) grocer and depot agent.

PALMER, DANIEL D., (South Cortland,) blacksmith

Palmer, Irving H , (Cortland Village,) (Palmer & Pratt,) insurance agent

Palmer, L B , (McGrawville,) jeweler

Palmer, Mary Miss, (McGrawville,) teacher of McGrawville Academy

Palmer & Pratt, (Cortland Village,) (Irving H Palmer and John T Pratt,) attorneys and counselors at law

Palmer, Prosper, (Cortland Village,) lot 77, sash and blind maker and farmer 27

Park, John, (Cortland Village,) lot 86, farmer 217

PARK, JOHN S , (Cortland Village,) lot 86, farmer

Parker, Betsy Mrs , (Cortland Village,) lot 72, farmer 58

Parker, Hibbard, (Cortland Village,) lot 83, farmer 74

PARKER, J B , (Cortland Village,) lot 71, farmer 150

PATTERSON, ROBERT, (South Cortland,) farmer

Peck, John E , (Cortland Village,) (Peck & Pierce )

Peck & Pierce, (Cortland Village,) (John E Peck and Wilson A Pierce,) dealers in tobacco, snuff and cigars

Peck, Reed, (Cortland Village,) lot 66, farmer 10

PECK, T Z , (McGrawville,) dentist

Pendleton Clark, (Cortland Village,) lot 76, farmer 100

Perkins, Jarvis & Co , (Cortland Village,) (Theodore Perkins, Albert J Jarvis and James A. Schemerhorn,) groceries and provisions

Perkins, Theodore, (Cortland Village,) (Perkins, Jarvis & Co )

Perry, Daniel, (Cortland Village,) lot 62, farmer 155

Persons, Carmi, (McGrawville,) lot 50, farmer 96

Persons, C A , (Cortland Village,) lot 72, farmer 50

Persons, Reuben, (McGrawville,) lot 59, farmer 83.

Persons, Wm , (McGrawville,) lot 69, farmer 90.

PETRIE, REUBEN A , (Cortland Village,) lot 95, farmer 110½

PHELPS, BENJ C , (McGrawville,) lot 60, farmer 150

Phelps, Byron, (McGrawville,) lot 59, farmer 80

Phelps, Enon W , (McGrawville,) farmer

Phelps, Honry E , (McGrawville,) lot 60, farmer 51

Phelps, Myron R , (McGrawville,) lot 60, farmer 21½

Philips, Henry M , (Homer,) lot 56, share in brick-yard and farmer 80

PHILLIPS, LESTER A , (Homer,) lot 55, agent for Barnes & Co's, publishers, N Y , and farmer 68

PHILLIPS, WM , (Cortland Village,) lot 67, farmer 54.

Pierce, Levi, (McGrawvilla,) lot 80, farmer 33.

Pierce, N L , (McGrawville,) (*Totman & Pierce* )

Pierce, S S., (McGrawville,) (*Totman & Pierce* )

Pierce, Wilson A ,(Cortland Village,) (*Peck & Pierce* )

Pike, H J , (Cortland Village,) lot 72, farmer leases 44.

PLACE, FRANK, (Cortland Village,) county clerk of Cortland Co , surveyor and civil engineer, Main, opposite Masonic Hall

Pomeroy, J C & Co , (Cortland Village,) (*J C and James M Pomeroy and Robert E Hull,*) grocers and general produce dealers

Pomeroy, James M , (Cortland Village,) (*J C Pomeroy & Co* )

Pomeroy, Theodore C , M D , (Cortland Village,) druggist and physician.

*POTTER, ALLEN, (Blodget Mills,) wool carding, planing and turning mill

POTTER, DELOS, (Cortland Village,) life insurance agent

POULTON, WM , (South Cortland,) farmer 86

Pra't F , (Cortland Village,) lot 72, farmer 50

Pratt, John T , (Cortland Village,) (*Palmer & Pratt* )

Pratt, Sherman, (Cortland Village,) lot 82, farmer 71

PRATT, ZERAH, (Cortland Village,) lot 82 farmer 13

PRICE, ALBERT T , (Cortland Village,) lot 95, farmer

Price, Jacob D , (Cortland Village,) lot 95, farmer 85

PRICE, JOSEPH P , (Cortland Village,) lot 73, farmer 82

Primney C L & Son, (McGrawville,) general merchants

RANDALL ;BANK, (Cortland Village,) Wm R Randall, president

Randall, Charles P , (Cortland Village,) lot 81, farmer 2

Randall, Henry P , (Cortland Village,) lot 84 farmer leases 145

RANDALL, HENRY S , (Cortland Village ) farmer 560

Randall, Roswell S , (Cortland Village,) lot 84, farmer leases 221

Randall, William P , (Cortland Village,) prop of livery and sale stable, also farmer 150.

RANDALL, WILLIAM R , (Cortland Village,) president of Randall Bank and Cortland Savings Bank

Rankin, Alvin, (McGrawville,) lot 79, farmer 70

Raymond, Wm , (Blodget Mills,) lot 88, farmer 31

REED, AARON D , M D , (Cortland Village ) physician and surgeon.

Reed, Marvin, (Cortland Village,) lot 84, farmer 80

Reese, Philo, (South Cortland,) lot 91, farmer 47

Reynolds, Orrin H , (Cortland Village,) lot 96, farmer 100

RHODES, BENJAMIN T , (Cortland Village,) barber and hair dresser

RICE, MELVIN A , (Cortland Village,) (*Fitzgerald & Rice* )

Riley, William, (Cortland Village,) saloon keeper

Rindge, Clinton T , (Cortland Village,) lot 57, farmer 178

RINDGE, EDWIN C , (Cortland Village,) farmer.

Robbins, Jeremiah, (Cortland Village,) lot 95, farmer 100

ROBINSON, DAVID J , (Homer,) (*Tisdale & Robinson* )

ROBINSON, HENRY M , (Cortland Village,) lot 85, farmer 65

ROBINSON, MITCHELL J , (Cortland Village,) (*with George More,*) lot 81, prop of saw, planing, lath and cider mills, also farmer 54

Robinson, Smith, (Cortland Village,) (*Robinson & Snyder* )

Robinson & Snyder, (Cortland Village,) (*Smith Robinson and Henry S Snyder,*) meat market

ROCHE, PATRICK, (Cortland Village,) tailor

ROCKWELL, JOSEPH G., (Cortland Village,) lot 53, farmer 80

Roe, Sylvester M , (Cortland Village,) dealer in butter, cheese, wool, hides, &c

Rogers, Henry L , (Cortland Village,) ticket, station and express agent

Rood & Brother, (Cortland Village,) props of omnibus, carting, expressing, &c

Rood, Lorenzo L . (Homer,) lot 55, farmer 18 and leases 60

Rood, Reuben, (South Cortland,) lot 92, farmer 101½

ROSE, DANIEL, (Cortland Village,) prop of grist, flour and saw mills, and owns 40 acres

Rose, Joseph, (Cortland Village,) lots 56 and 66, brick manuf. and farmer 170

ROUNSEVELL, ALVIN N , (Cortland Village,) (*McGraw & Rounsevell* )

Rouse, Hilton R , (Cortland Village,) (*Rouse, Hubbard & Co.*)

Rouse Hubbard & Co , (Cortland Village,) (*Hilton R. Rouse, Samuel E Hubbard and Edward M Seacord,*) wholesale and retail grocers

Rowe, Elisha, (McGrawville,) lot 90, farmer 53

ROWE, JAMES R., (McGrawville,) farmer 2

Rowe, Laura Mrs , (McGrawville,) lot 79, farmer 25

ROWE, NELSON, (Homer,) lot 56, farmer 122

Rowe, Perry W , (McGrawville,) lot 89, farmer 57

Rowe, Riley, (McGrawville,) lot 89, farmer 50

ROWE, RUFUS & SON, (McGrawville,) lot 89, farmer 200

Rowley, Addison P , (South Cortland,) post master

Rowley, P C., (South Cortland,) lot 93, farmer 150

RUNDLES, JAMES B , (Cortland Village,) lot 63, farmer 90

Russell, Allen, (McGrawville,) builder

Russell, Zina, (McGrawville,) lot 88, farmer 100

Ryao, John, (Cortland Village,) billiard and eating saloon

SAGER, AARON, (Cortland Village,) druggist and apothecary, agent for Bassett's cement pipe. cor Main and Wall

Salisbury & Brother, (McGrawville,) (E A and E E ) druggists

SALISBURY, ELISHA, (Cortland Village,) teamster and farmer 10½

Salisbury, E A (McGrawville,) (Salisbury & Brother )

SALISBURY, E E , (McGrawville,) (Salisbury & Brother,) physician and surgeon

SALISBURY, NATHAN P , (Cortland Village,) lot 66, farmer 151

Sanders, Charles E , (South Cortland,) lot 92, farmer leases 80

SANDERS, DELOS, (Cortland Village,) dealer in clocks, watches, jewelry, &c

SANDERS, MARTIN, (Cortland Village,) lot 85, farmer 98

Schermerhorn, James A , (Cortland Village,) (Perkins, Jarvis & Co )

Schermerhorn, John E,, (Cortland Village,) (Ives & Schermerhorn )

SCOTT, THOMAS, (Homer,) lot 53, farmer 95.

SCRANTON, HIRAM, M D , (McGrawville,) eclectic physician

Scutt, Everett P , (Cortland Village,) (H F Benton & Co )

Seacord, Edward M , (Cortland Village,) (Rouse, Hubbard & Co )

Seacord, James, (Cortland Village,) lot 84, farmer 44½

Seaman, John F., (Cortland Village,) lot 81, dealer in patent rights and farmer 242

Sears, Albert, (Cortland Village,) lot 61, farmer 350.

SEARS, FRANKLIN H , (Cortland Village,) farmer

SEVERANCE, CALVIN, (Cortland Village,) lot 64, farmer 60

SEYMOUR, HENRY, (McGrawville,) wagon making

Shafer, Henry, (Cortland Village,) barber and hair dresser

Shankland & Couch, (Cortland Village,) (William H Shankland and John M Couch,) attorneys and counselors at law

Shankland, William H , (Cortland Village,) (Shankland & Couch.)

SHAW, ROBERT H , (South Cortland,) lot 93, painter and farmer 13½

Shaw, William H , (Cortland Village,) horse shoer

Shearer, Seth, (McGrawville,) lot 59, farmer 144

Shearrer, Reuben, (McGrawville,) lot 59, farmer 97

Shearrer, Wm , (McGrawville,) lot 59, farmer 78

SHEEROR, A A , (South Cortland,) foreman cheese factory

Sherman, Daniel, (McGrawville,) lot 10, farmer 82

Sherman, Lodema, Mrs ,(Cortland Village,) dress maker

*SHIRLEY, HENRY F , (Cortland Village,) painter, paper hanger and decorater

Shoales, Sherman, (Blodget Mills,) lot 8, farmer 120

Short, J H ,(McGrawville,) lot 60, farmer 65

SHORT, MANASSEH, (McGrawville,) lot 60, farmer 53½

Shuler, W C , (McGrawville,) lot 80, farmer 55

Sidman & Coon, (Cortland Village,) blacksmiths

Simms, Thomas, (Cortland Village,) (Simms & Van Buskirk.)

Simms & Van Buskirk, (Cortland Village,) (Thomas Simms and John Van Buskirk,) house and sign painting, decorating, &c

Sinton, Benjamin, (Cortland Village,) custom blacksmith

Slafter, Edwin P , (Cortland Village,) (Slafter & Sumner )

Slafter & Sumner, (Cortland Village,) (Edwin P Slafter and Peabody Sumner,) dry goods merchants

Smeallie, A M , (McGrawville,) principal of McGrawville Academy

Smeallie, P Mrs , (McGrawville,) teacher of music, McGrawville Academy

SMITH ABNER L , (Cortland Village,) druggist

SMITH, ABRAM P , (Cortland Village,) county judge, surrogate, attorney and counselor at law

SMITH, ALLEN B , (Cortland Village,) (Chamberlain, Smith & Co.)

Smith, Daniel E , (Cortland Village,) lot 73, farmer 109

Smith, Eli, (McGrawville,) tinner and dealer in stoves

SMITH, HENRY C , (Cortland Village,) (Chamberlain, Smith & Co )

Smith, John W , (McGrawville,) lot 100, farmer 50

Smith, Linus A , (Cortland Village,) lot 52, farmer 75

SMITH, MOSES G , (McGrawville,) merchant tailor and post master

Smith & Newkirk, (Cortland Village,) (Robert B. Smith and William Newkirk,) groceries and provisions

Smith, Robert B , (Cortland Village,) (Smith & Newkirk.)

SMITH, ROMANZO A , (Cortland Village,) (M Woodruff & Co )

Smith, Rufus, (Blodget Mills,) lot 98, farmer 11

SMITH, S. B , (Blodget Mills,) lot 98, blacksmith
SMITH, TIMOTHY, (Cortland Village,) lot 94, farmer 88
Smith, William H , (Cortland Village,) dealer in groceries, boots and shoes
Snyder, Henry S , (Cortland Village,) (*Robinson & Snyder.*)
Spencer, E K , (Blodget Mills,) lot 97, farmer 76
Spencer, Isaac, (Blodget Mills,) lot 88, farmer 15
Spencer, James L , (Cortland Village,) lot 95, farmer 75
*SPENDLEY, R H. & CO , (Cortland Village,) dealers in hats, caps and furs
Sperry, Burdett, (Blodget Mills,) lot 95, farmer leases 117¾
Sperry, Daniel J, (Cortland Village,) prop of Sperry's Hotel, owns 15 acres
Sperry, Geo G , (Cortland Village,) (*Kent & Sperry* )
SPERRY, JUDSON A , (Blodget Mills,) lot 88, dealer in patent rights
Sprague, Albert, (Blodget Mills,) lot 96, farmer 40
Sprague, James, (Cortland Village,) lot 81, farmer 76 and leases 49
SQUIRES, JAMES S , (Cortland Village,) (*James S Squires & Co* ,) farmer 20
SQUIRES, JAMES S & CO , (Cortland Village,) (*Amasa Givens and Henry B Hubbard*,) staple and fancy dry goods
STANTON, JOSHUA O., (Blodget Mills,) lot 97, farmer 121
STARKEY, JEREMIAH, (Blodget Mills,) lot 98, farmer 47
Stedman, A , (South Cortland,) lot 97, farmer 60
STEVENS, LUCIUS D., (Cortland Village,) lot 73, prop stage line (tri-weekly) from Cortland to Ithaca, leaving Cortland at 10 30 a m , and Ithaca at 8 a m , and also farmer 35
STEWART, ALEXANDER, (Cortland Village,) lot 51, farmer 200
STEWART, J S , (Homer,) manuf of furniture in the white and prop of saw mill
STILLMAN, LINUS, (Homer,) lot 54, farmer 117
Straat, Cyrus G , (Cortland Village,) builder and contractor
Strobeck, Peter, (Cortland Village,) lot 52, farmer 100
STROWBRIDGE, LYDIA A. MRS , (Cortland Village,) physician
Sturtevant, Doud & Co , (Cortland Village,) (*J W Sturtevant, E H. Doud and E. A Fish,*) dealers in foreign and domestic dry goods
Sturtevant, J W , (Cortland Village,) (*Sturtevant, Doud & Co* )
Sumner, Peabody, (Cortland Village,) (*Slafter & Sumner* )
SWEET, MICHAEL M , (McGrawville,) lot 70, farmer 64¾
Sweetlove, Nelson, (Cortland Village,) lot 91, farmer 100
Tanner, Abram T , (Cortland Village,) (*Tanner Brothers* )
Tanner, Adolphus F , (Cortland Village,) (*Tanner Brothers* )

Tanner Brothers, (Cortland Village,) (*Adolphus F and Abram T ,*) dealers in staple and fancy dry goods
*TANNER, J H , (Blodget Mills,) lot 98, general merchant
TANNER, PETER R , (Blodget Mills,) (*Copeland & Tanner,*) justice of the peace and postmaster
TARBLE, WM H , (McGrawville,) telegraph operator
TARBLE, WM H , (McGrawville,) (*Blackmer & Tarble* )
Taylor, Amasieh W , (Blodget Mills,) lot 88, farmer 45.
Taylor, J W. Col , (Cortland Village,) lot 53, retired farmer 2¼
Terill, —— , (McGrawville,) (*Blackner & Terill* )
TERRY, EDWIN N , (Cortland Village,) blacksmith
Terry, Nancy M Mrs , (Cortland Village,) lot 56, farmer 10
Thayer, Horace S , (McGrawville,) lot 100, farmer 108
Thompson, L L , (Blodget Mills,) lot 87, boot and shoe maker.
TISDALE, JAMES A , (Homer,) (*Tisdale & Robinson.*)
TISDALE & ROBINSON, (Homer,) (*Jas A Tisdale and David J Robinson,*) lot 55, props of grist mill,
TISDALE, WAYLAND D , (Cortland Village,) (*W D Tisdale & Co* )
TISDALE, W D & CO., (Cortland Village,) (*Wayland D. Tisdale and Lucien Hale,*) dealers in coal, lime, plaster, flour, feed &c
Todd, Jared A , (Cortland Village,) dentist
THOMPSON, ISAAC P , (Cortland Village,) lot 81, farmer 10½
Totman, H C & Pierce, (McGrawville,) livery and express
Totman, H D , (McGrawville,) (*Totman & Pierce* )
TOTMAN, JAMES F , (McGrawville,) lot 69, mason,
Totman, J L , (McGrawville,) (*Totman & Pierce* )
Totman & Pierce, (McGrawville,) (*J L, Totman and N L Pierce,*) manufs of boots and shoes
Totman & Pierce, (McGrawville,) (*H D Totman and S S Pierce,*) props of livery
TOWNLEY, H T , (Cortland Village,) lot 65, farmer 50
TRAVIS, CHARLES W , (McGrawville,) lot 78, farmer leases 67
TRIPP, LAFAYETTE, (McGrawville,) lot 89, farmer 200
TRIPP, R W , (Cortland Village,) lot 81, manuf of marl lime and farmer 51
Tripp, Wm , (McGrawville,) lot 89, farmer 110
Tyrrell, Garry, (Cortland Village,) lot 53, farmer 58
Vanaletine, Herman, (Cortland Village,) lot 56, farmer 1
VAN BERGEN, ANDREW, (Cortland Village,) produce dealer and farmer 120
Vanburen, Moses, (McLean, Tompkins Co ,) lot 81, farmer 22½

# J. H. TANNER,

### AT BLODGET MILLS,

### DEALER IN

## Dry Goods, Groceries, Crockery, Hardware, Boots & Shoes,

### Hats, Medicines,

And everything usually kept in a Country Store.   With good facilities and light expenses can sell goods at lowest prices

# Henry F. Shirley,

## PAINTER,

# PAPER HANGER & DECORATOR,

## CORTLAND, N. Y.

# House, Sign

### AND

# DECORATIVE   PAINTING.

All kinds of Paints and Varnishes for Sale.  Satisfaction guaranteed in all cases.

Van Buskirk, John, (Cortland Village,) (*Simms & Van Buskirk*.)
Vanderburgh, S A, (Cortland Village,) lot 66, farmer 35
VAN HOESEN, ISRAEL, (Cortland Village,) lot 64, farmer 27
Van Hoesen, Julia, (Cortland Village,) lot 63, farmer 40.
VANHOESEN, THOMAS S, (Cortland Village,) (*with H P. Dunbar*,) lot 71, farmer 167
Vanhusen, Daniel, (Cortland Village,) carpenter and joiner and farmer 10.
*VANSLYCK, WILLIAM H, (Cortland Village,) bill poster and paper hanger
Vanvaling, Oliver T, (Cortland Village,) gardener 4
WADSWORTH, E., (Cortland Village,) lot 64, farmer 28.
Wallace, Aaron H., (Blodget Mills,) lot 88, farmer 10
Walrad, Calvin P, (Cortland Village,) secretary of Cortland Savings Bank.
Walsworth, Nelson, (Cortland Village,) lot 72, farmer 50
Warfield, T, (Cortland Village,) lot 62, farmer 60.
Warner, I. D & L. C., (McGrawville,) physicians and surgeons
Warren, Charles B, (McGrawville,) (*Warren & Jones*)
Warren, Geo L, (Cortland Village,) (*Mills & Warren*)
Warren & Jones, (McGrawville,) (*Charles B Warren and Charles A Jones*,) dealers in drugs and medicines
WARREN, WILLIAM H., (Cortland Village,) (*Ballard & Warren*)
WARWICK, JOHN, (McGrawville,) lot 58, farmer 189
WATERS, ALVAH D, (Cortland Village,) (*Waters & Waters*)
Waters, Charles H, (McGrawville,) lot 69, carpenter, joiner and farmer 5
WATERS, HARVEY, (McGrawville,) sexton of the cemetery and farmer 3
WATERS, MORDARENT M., (Cortland Village,) (*Waters & Waters*)
WATERS & WATERS, (Cortland Village,) (*Mordarent M and Alvah D*,) attorneys and counselors at law
Watrons, Lyman, (Cortland Village,) lot 77, farmer 120
WEATHERWAX, BENJ F, (South Cortland,) lots 82, 83 and 92, farmer 180
WEBB, MORGAN L, (Cortland Village,) treasurer Cortland Co. Agricultural Society.
WEBSTER, MINER, (McGrawville,) dealer in boots and shoes
Webster, Willard, (Cortland Village,) lot 95, farmer 96
Welch, Benjamin, (McGrawville,) lot 78, lumberman, owns saw mill and farmer 100

Welch, Samuel E, (Cortland Village,) dealer in dry goods, groceries, hats and caps
Wellington, Alvin A, (McGrawville,) lot 87, farmer 60
Westcott, Geo N, (Homer,) wood turner.
Westcott, Owen, (Homer,) lot 55, farmer 8
Wheeler, Charles, (Cortland Village,) lot 85, farmer 100
White, James, (Cortland Village,) lot 71, farmer 85
WHITE, JOHN, (Cortland Village,) dealer in general produce
White, John, (Cortland Village,) lot 71, farmer 90
WHITMARSH, JOB, (Cortland Village,) lot 76, retired farmer 11
Wickwire, Chester F., (Cortland Village,) dealer in general hardware, manuf of Eureka sash, lock and saddle gate hinge
Wickwire, R, Mrs., (Cortland Village,) lot 176, farmer 175
Wilber, Jonathon, (Homer,) lot 58, farmer 87
Wilcox, Miss, (Blodget Mills,) tailoress
Wilkins, Andrew Rev., (Cortland Village,) pastor of First Baptist Church of Cortlandville.
Williams, Agar, (Cortland Village,) lot 73, farmer 180
Williams, Charles R, (Cortland Village,) boarding house
Wilson, Pliny A, (Cortland Village,) mason and farmer 7
WILSON, WM, (McGrawville,) lot 78, farmer 100½
WOOD & CO, (McGrawville,) (*William A Wood and F A Garlick*,) cooperage
Wood, Jonah, (Cortland Village,) lot 94, farmer 26
WOOD, WM A., (McGrawville,) (*Wood & Co.*)
Woodard, Ephraim, (McGrawville,) lot 10, farmer 116
Woodruff, Henry, (Cortland Village,) merchant tailor
WOODRUFF, MADISON, (Cortland Village,) (*M Woodruff & Co.*,) farmer 8
Woodruff, M & Co, (Cortland Village,) (*Madison Woodruff and Romanzo A Smith*,) props. of Tioughnioga pottery
Woodward, Alburtus N., (McGrawville,) butcher.
WOODWARD, WM C., (Homer,) lot 56, carpenter and joiner and farmer 34.
Woodworth, B B, (Cortland Village,) agent for Messenger Hall
WOOSTER, MYREN, (Homer,) lot 55, farmer 71.
Wright, J. W., (McGrawville,) lot 60, teacher and farmer 195
YAGER, HARVEY, (Cortland Village,) lot 95, farmer 80.
Yager, Wm, (McGrawville,) boot and shoe dealer.

# CUYLER.

(Post Office Addresses in Parentheses)

ACKLEY, DeWITT C, (Cuyler,) hotel proprietor

Albro, George W , (DeRuyter, Madison Co ,) lot 78, hop cultivator and farmer 105

Albro, James, (Truxton,) lot 6, dairy 25 cows and farmer 117

Albro, J J , (Cuyler,) lot 87, dairy 16 cows and farmer 103

ALBRO, JOHN M , (Cuyler,) lot 18, farmer 12½ and leases 38

ALBRO, SAMUEL, (Cuyler,) lot 97, dairy 10 cows and farmer 103.

Aldrich, F J., (Linklaen, Chenango Co ) lot 18, farmer 40

ALLEN, ALBERT, (Cuyler,) lot 88, dairy 35 cows, farmer 60 and leases 176

ALLEN, HARVEY B , (DeRuyter, Madison Co ,) lot 28, prop saw mill and farmer 101

Allen, Seymour, (DeRuyter, Madison Co ,) lot 79, farmer 40

ALLEN, TROBRIDGE, (DeRuyter, Madison Co ,) lot 80, dairy 14 cows and farmer 72

Andrews, Grant O , (DeRuyter, Madison Co ) lot 59, dairy 7 cows and farmer 56

ANDREWS, HARLAN P , (Keeney's Settlement,) lot 57, dairy 85 cows and farmer 260.

Angel, Pardon, (Linklaen, Chenango Co ,) lot 39, dairy 40 cows and farmer 540.

Angel, Z Y., (Linklaen, Chenango Co ,) lot 29, dairy 10 cows and farmer 154

ANNAS, ABIJAH N , (De Ruyter, Madison Co ,) lot 80, hop cultivator and farmer 290

BABBIT, REUBEN, (Linklaen, Chenango Co ,) lot 10, dairy 20 cows and farmer 310

Babcock, Dennis, (DeRuyter, Madison Co ,) lot 79, prop grist and saw mills and farmer 15

Babcock, Isaac C , (Keeney's Settlement,) lot 57, farmer 87

BABCOCK, NOBLE L , (Fabius, Onondaga Co ,) lot 59, horse dealer, dairy 17 cows, ½ prop in Cole Settlement cheese factory and farmer 228

Baker, Henry, (Keeney's Settlement,) lot 55, farmer 47

BAKER, RUSSELL, (Truxton,) lot 6, carpenter and joiner and farmer 54

Barker, Joseph, (DeRuyter, Madison Co ,) lot 79, dairy 9 cows and farmer 70

BEMISS, EDWARD, (Linklaen, Chenango Co ,) lot 40, dairy 32 cows and farmer 240

Benjamin, Alpheus, (Linklaen, Chenango Co ,) lot 80, dairy 15 cows and farmer 75

Benjamin, Emerson, (DeRuyter, Madison Co ,) lot 79, farmer 23

BENJAMIN, EZRA, (DeRuyter, Madison Co ,) lot 79, dairy 25 cows and farmer 125

BLANCHARD, MARSHALL, (Cuyler,) general merchant, prop of stage route from Fabius to DeRuyter, and postmaster

Blanchard, William, (Cuyler,) town clerk and blacksmith

BOGARDUS, GEORGE, (Cuyler,) lot 88, dairy 36 cows and farmer 190

BOGARDUS, MARTIN, (Cuyler,) lot 88, dairy 15 cows and farmer 117

Bogardus, William, (Cuyler,) lot 88, commissioner of highways and farmer 15

Bond, George W.,(DeRuyter, Madison Co ,) lot 9, farmer leases 55

BOURKE, JEREMIAH, (Keeney's Settlement )

Bowen, Amos, (Linklaen, Chenango Co ,) lot 33, farmer 50

BOYCE, HENRY T , (DeRuyter, Madison Co ,) lot 80, dairy 20 cows and farmer 126

Breed, James, (Cuyler,) lot 8, farmer 30

Breed, John W , (Linklaen, Chenango Co ,) lot 37, carpenter and farmer 8

Bronson, Asher, (DeRuyter, Madison Co ,) lot 79, farmer 28

BROWN, BENJAMIN, (Cuyler,) lot 87, dairy 45 cows and farmer 305

BROWN, CHARLES W , (DeRuyter, Madison Co ,) lot 100, assessor, hop cultivator, dairy 40 cows and farmer 293

Brown, David S , (Linklaen, Chenango Co ,) lot 20, farmer 57

Brown, George H , (DeRuyter, Madison Co ,) lot 79, farmer 22

BROWN, HEPSEY A , (DeRuyter, Madison Co ,) lot 90, dairy 16 cows and farmer 198

BROWN, ISAAC N , (Cuyler,) lot 99, dairy 13 cows and farmer 125

Brown, John W , (Cuyler,) lot 77, dairy 18 cows and farmer 122.

BROWN, NORMAN B , (Cuyler )

Brown, Shubal N , (DeRuyter, Madison Co ,) lot 60, dairy 27 cows and farmer 153

Buckley, John, (Truxton,) lot 17, dairyman and farmer 119

Burdick, Irving, (Cuyler,) lot 8, farmer 115

Burdick, James, (DeRuyter, Madison Co ,) lots 8 and 9, dairy 18 cows and farmer 190

BURDICK, JOSEPH L , (DeRuyter, Madison Co ,) lot 80, dairy 20 cows and farmer 182

Burdick, Phineas C , (DeRuyter, Madison Co.,) lot 9, dairy 15 cows and farmer 118

BURDICK, SYLVANUS, (DeRuyter, Madison Co ,) lot 90, hop cultivator, farmer 50 and leases 60.

BURKE, JOHN, (Keeney's Settlement,) lot 55, dairy 18 cows and farmer 125

Burlingame, Harriet, (DeRuyter, Madison Co ,) lot 79, farmer 57

BURT, HENRY, (Cuyler,) lot 100, dairy 15 cows and farmer 118.

Cardner, Amasa L , (DeRuyter, Madison Co ,) lot 9, dairy 20 cows and farmer 148.

Cardner, B B , (Linklaen, Chenango Co ,) lot 19, farmer 252

Cardner, Chauncy, (Linklaen, Chenango Co ,) lot 19, farmer 25

Church, Eli, (Keeney's Settlement,) lot 67 farmer 4½

Cole, David, (Cuyler,) shoemaker

COMERFORT, JOHN, (Keeney's Settlement,) lot 65, dairy 16 cows and farmer 160

CONNERS, THOMAS, (Truxton,) lot 17, dairy 35 cows and farmer 276

COON, BRADFORD C , (DeRuyter, Madison Co ,) lot 90, hop cultivator, dairy 15 cows and farmer 77

Coon, Dyar, (DeRuyter, Madison Co ,) lot 90, farmer 20

Coon, Ethan R , (DeRuyter, Madison Co ,) lot 69, dairy 6 cows and farmer 60

Coon, Ruth, (Fabius, Onondaga Co ,) lot 59, farmer 10

Coon, William M , (DeRuyter, Madison Co ,) lot 90, dairy 7 cows and farmer 52½

COREY, WANTON JR , (Cuyler,) lot 87, dairyman and farmer 66

Couch, Leonard, (Cuyler,) lot 78, dairyman ard farmer 50

COUCH, ORAL D , (Cuyler,) farmer (with L Couch.)

COUCH, SYLVESTER, (Cuyler,) farmer (with L Couch )

CRANDALL, ALONZO W , (DeRuyter, Madison Co ,) lot 70, dairy 25 cows and farmer 184

Crandall, Henry J , (DeRuyter, Madison Co ,) lot 69, hop cultivator, dairy 10 cows and farmer 90

CRANDALL, J CLARK, (DeRuyter, Madison Co ,) lot 60, stock and wool dealer, dairy 25 cows and farmer 191

Craw, Edwin, (Fabius, Onondaga Co ,) lot 59, dairy 15 cows and farmer 51 ½

Craw, Horace D , (Fabius, Onondaga Co ,) lot 59, dairy 30 cows and farmer 200

Craw, House & Babcock, (Fabius, Onondaga Co ,) proprietors Cole Settlement Cheese Factory which receives milk from 200 cows

Culver, Charles F , (DeRuyter Madison Co ,) lot 89, dairy 5 cows and farmer 30

Cuyler Hill Cheese Manufacturing Association, (DeRuyter, Madison Co ,) receives milk from 300 cows, J H Lyon, supt

Dager, David A , (Truxton,) lot 87, dairy 13 cows, carpenter and joiner and farmer 175

Darwood, Huldah, (DeRuyter, Madison Co ,) lot 79, dairyman and farmer 100

DEAN, JOHN, (Truxton,) lot 17, dairy 15 cows and farmer 136

DENNIS, GILLMAN, (DeRuyter, Madison Co ) lot 69, dairy 16 cows and farmer 110

Dennison, William, (Cuyler,) lot 86, farmer 2

Dewirs, John, (Truxton,) lot 75 dairyman and farmer 60

Dobbins, Almira, (Truxton,) lot 75, dairyman and farmer 132

Dorwood, Hulah, (DeRuyter, Madison Co ,) lot 69, farmer 100

DUNBAR, AARON W , SEN , (Cuyler,) resident,

DUNBAR, AARON W , JR., (Cuyler,) lot 88, dairy 15 cows and farmer 165

DUNCE, ALEXANDER, (Cuyler,) lot 87, supervisor and farmer 21

DUTTON, GORLETTE, (Keeney's Settlement,) lot 67, dairy 25 cows and farmer 107

EATON, MOSES D., (Keeney's Settlement,) lot 57, dairy 27 cows and farmer 147

FAIRBANK, GEORGE G., (Cuyler,) carpenter and joiner

Fairbank, Henry S , (DeRuyter, Madison Co ,) lot 70, dairy 10 cows and farmer 57

Fairbanks, Nahum, (Cuyler,) lot 87, prop saw mill and farmer 8½

Fairbanks, Wales, (DeRuyter, Madison Co ,) lot 70, farmer 57

Farrington, Edward, (DeRuyter, Madison Co ,) lot 69, dairy 21 cows and farmer 126

Fox, Wesley, (Keeney's Sattlement,) Methodist minister and postmaster

FULLER, ADELBERT, (Cuyler,) general merchant

GALVIN, LAWRENCE, (Keeney's Settlemant,) lot 65, dairy 30 cows and farmer 277

GARNER, JACOB, (DeRuyter, Madison Co ,) lot 9, dairy 16 cows and farmer 181

Gates, Elias, (Cuyler,) lot 88, dairy 15 cows and farmer 122

GATES, JOHN, (Cuyler,) lot 29, dairyman and farmer 173

GATES, STEPHEN, (Cuyler,) lot 88, overseer of the poor, dairy 10 cows and farmer 68

Gibson, Zachariah, (DeRuyter, Madison Co ,) lot 90, farmer 10

Gleason, Mary, (Keeney's Settlement,) lot 56, dairy 35 cows and farmer 234

GLEESON, PATRICK, (Keeney's Settlement,) lot 56, farmer

GRACE, PIERCE, (Keeney's Settlement,) lot 65, dairy 16 cows and farmer 235

Hammond, Frank, (Cuyler,) lot 100, farmer 10

Haneen, Edward, (Cuyler,) lot 7, farmer 60

Harris, Richard, (Cuyler,) lot 96, farmer 2

HASKINS, NELSON, (Keeney's Settlement,) lot 57, dairy 21 cows and farmer 128

HASKINS, SILAS, (Keeney's Settlement,) lot 57, dairyman and farmer 97

Hathaway, L F , (DeRuyter, Madison Co ,) lot 78, farmer 8.

Heart, Silas, (DeRuyter, Madison Co ,) lot 8 , cabinet maker

Heath, Luther, (Linklaen, Chenango Co ,) lot 27, farmer 95

HEATH, OLIVER, (Truxton,) lot 29, dairy 18 cows and farmer 170

Heith, Joseph, (Truxton,) lot 75, carpenter and joiner and farmer 25

HILLMAN, DANIEL D , (Cuyler,) lot 96, dairy 26 cows and farmer leases of Mrs Buel 158

Hills, Bernard S , (Cuyler,) lot 67, farmer 40

Hills, Clarissa, (DeRuyter, Madison Co ,) lot 59, farmer 10

HINDS, DEBORAH, (DeRuyter, Madison Co ,) lot 79, dairy 30 cows and farmer 188

# J. C. GRAY,

## MARATHON, N. Y.,

DEALER IN

# AMERICAN, ENGLISH & SWISS
# WATCHES!

EIGHT-DAY, CALENDAR AND ALL OTHER STYLES OF

# Clocks

**Coin Silver and Plated Ware, Spectacles,
Pocket Cutlery, Musical Instruments
and the very best quality of Italian
Strings, Bird Cages, Fish Tackle.**

Toys and Fancy Goods in Great Variety.

**REPAIRING IN ALL ITS BRANCHES.**

Also, PHOTOGRAPHING in all its branches, Copying, Engraving and Coloring in the highest Style of the Art and the best of satisfaction guaranteed.

HOLL, EDWARD, (Linklaen, Chenango Co,) lot 30, dairy 17 cows and farmer 270

HOLL, JOEL, (Linklaen, Chenango Co,) lot 28, dairy 15 cows and farmer 100

HOLL, WILLIAM R, (Linklaen, Chenango Co,) lot 30, dairy 20 cows and farmer 160

Hollenbeck, Caspar, (Cuyler,) lot 18, dairy 36 cows and farmer 247

Hollenbeck, George, (Cuyler,) lot 67, farmer 20

Hollenbeck, George, (Keeney's Settlement,) lot 67, farmer 20

House, Calvin P, (DeRuyter, Madison Co,,) lot 70, dairy 25 cows and farmer 140

House, Elisha, (DeRuyter, Madison Co,) lot 59, prop saw mill, dairy 7 cows and farmer 49

House, Morris, (DeRuyter, Madison Co.,) lot 59, hop cultivator and farmer 50

Hoyer, Jacob, (Cuyler,) lot 96, farmer 49

HUDSON, WARREN, (DeRuyter, Madison Co,) lot 59, dairy 15 cows and farmer 144

Hulbert, John, (Linklaen, Chenango Co.,) lot 38, farmer 50.

HURLBERT, MORRISON B., (Cuyler,) lot 96, dairy 10 cows and farmer 78½

HURLBURT, O W, (Keeney's Settlement,) lot 87, farmer 90.

HYER, BENJAMIN F., (Truxton,) lot 28, farmer 75

Irish, Elias B, (DeRuyter, Madison Co,) lots 98 and 99, dairy 26 cows and farmer 215

ISBELL, CEYLON, (Cuyler,) prop Cold Spring Cheese factory

James, John W, (DeRuyter, Madison Co,) lot 80, farmer 36

JENKS, ELMER D, (DeRuyter, Madison Co,) lots 28 and 29, dairy 26 cews and farmer 400

Johnson, David, (Cuyler,) lot 8, dairyman and farmer 96.

Jones, William D, (DeRuyter, Madison Co,) lot 90, dairyman and farmer 50

KEELER, NELSON, (Cuyler,) lot 95, justice of the peace, dairy 70 cows and farmer 370

Keeney, Reuben, (Truxton,) lot 17, farmer 47

Keeney Settlement Cheese Manufacturing Company, (Keeney's Settlement,) receives milk from 700 cows, J C Smith, superintendent

KEMP, RUFUS, (DeRuyter, Madison Co.,) lot 89, hop cultivator, dairy 13 cows and farmer 88½

Kenyon, Mary J., (DeRuyter, Madison Co,) lot 59, farmer 62

KIBBE, A. M, (DeRuyter, Madison Co)

KIBBE, JAIRUS, (Keeney's Settlement,) prop cheese factory which receives milk from 200 cows.

Kibbe, Russell, (Linklaen, Chenango Co,) lot 28, farmer 48.

Kibbie, Joel, (Linklaen, Chenango Co.,) lot 38, farmer 25

KILLEEN, THOMAS, (Cuyler,) blacksmith.

KING, ELISHA, (Keeney's Settlement,) lot 55, dairy 50 cows and farmer leases 365.

Knapp, Stephen, (Keeney's Settlement,) lot 65, farmer 22.

Large, George, (DeRuyter, Madison Co.,) lots 9 and 19, dairy farmer 150

Leach, Isaac B, (Cuyler,) lot 7, dairy 25 cows and farmer 239

LEE, ALBERT L, (Cuyler,) lot 86, dairy 40 cows and farmer 343½

LEE, BENJAMIN F, (Cuyler,) lot 77, dairy 17 cows and farmer 87.

LEE, DAVID, (Truxton,) lot 75, dairy 18 cows and farmer 170.

Lee, John W, (Cuyler,) lot 78, dairy 40 cows and farmer 205

Lee, Milton, (Cuyler,) lot 65, dairy 55 cows and farmer 560

LEWIS, PERRY D, (DeRuyter, Madison Co,) lot 60, dairy 30 cows and farmer leases of A. N Annis, 210

Lundergan, James, (Truxton,) lot 75, dairyman and farmer 120

LYON, JOSEPH H, (DeRuyter, Madison Co,) seperintendent Cuyler Hill Cheese Manufacturing Association's factory.

MATTESON, N B., (Cuyler,) lot 77, prop. saw mill and farmer 8.

MAXON, MATHEW R, (Cuyler,) lot 98, dairy 16 cows and farmer 177

McAllaster, Edson, (Cuyler,) lot 99, dairy 27 cows and farmer 228

McGowan, R Emmet, (Keeney's Settlement,) architect and builder

McGraw, Patrick, (Cuyler,) lot 100, dairy 12 cows and farmer 49.

McLEAN, JOHN, (Cuyler,) wagon maker and repairer

MERCHANT, CHARLES, (Cuyler,) lot 7, dairy 20 cows and farmer 180.

MERCHANT, E B, (Cuyler,) lot 8, dairy 25 cows and farmer 206

MERCHANT, WILLIAM S, (Cuyler,) lot 18, dairy 20 cows and farmer 163

Merrile, Ora, (Cuyler,) lot 98, farmer 26.

MUNROE, JOHN B, (DeRuyter, Madison Co) lot 28, farmer 50

MORSE, JOSEPH, (Cuyler,) lot 87, attorney and counselor at law, dairy 5 cows and farmer 20

MORSE, WILLIAM A., (Cuyler,) lot 87, dairy 27 cows and farmer 110

MUNCY, ARZA, (Cuyler,) lot 98, justice of the peace, dairy 20 cows and farmer 150

MUNCY, MYRON, (DeRuyter, Madison Co)

Neal, Darius, (DeRuyter, Madison Co,) lot 79, farmer 4

Neal, Norman, (DeRuyter, Madison Co,) lot 79, dairy 14 cows and farmer 85

Nott, John, (Cuyler,) lot 78, cooper

ORCUTT, CHAS. G., (Truxton,) (Palmer & Orcutt)

PALMER, EGBERT, (Truxton,) (Palmer & Orcutt)

PALMER & ORCUTT, (Truxton,) (Egbert Palmer and Chas. G Orcutt,) lot 7, lumber and shingle dealers and farmers 100

Parker, A D, (Cuyler,) lot 8, farmer 50

PARKER, GEORGE H, (Cuyler,) farm laborer.

Parker, Prentiss, (Truxton,) lot 18, farmer 43

Parker, Roger, (Truxton,) lot 18, farmer 5

PATRICK, ALVA T, (Truxton,) lot 86, dairy 60 cows and farmer 258.

PATRICK, DEWITT M, (Keeney's Settlement,) lot 67, dairy 27 cows and farmer 146.

PATRICK, JOHN W, (Cuyler,) lots 86 and 87, dairy 60 cows and farmer 435½

Patrick, Stephen, (Cuyler,) lot 96, dairyman and farmer 214

PEASE, ELIJAH, (Cuyler,) lot 8, dairy 20 cows and farmer 192

PETRIE, ADAM, (Cuyler,) lot 77, assessor, live stock dealer, dairy 40 cows and farmer 192.

PETRIE, WILLIAM, (Cuyler,) lot 97, dairy 20 cows and farmer 147

PHILLIPS, GEORGE W, (Cuyler,) lot 78, prop. saw mill, millwright and farmer 14

PHILLIPS, RODNEY, (Cuyler,) lot 28, dairy 15 cows and farmer 142

Phillips, Welcome R, (De Ruyter, Madison Co ),lot 9, dairy 18 cows and farmer 156

PHILLIPS, WILLIAM H, (Cuyler,) lot 86, prop of flouring and custom mill and farmer 8

Pomroy, James, (Cuyler,) cabinet maker.

PORTER, L W, (Keeney's Settlement,) (with S,) lot 57, dairy 41 cows and farmer 268

PORTER, S, (Keeney's Settlement,) (with L. W.,) lot 67, dairy 41 cows and farmer 268

Potter, Charles, (Linklaen, Chenango Co ,) lot 38, farmer 75.

Potter, J E C G, (Linklaen, Chenango Co ,) lot 38, farmer 50

Potter, W J, (Linklaen, Chenango Co ,) lot 38, prop saw mill and farmer 69

Powers, Polly, (De Royter, Madison Co ,) lot 90, farmer 100

Quigly, Thomas, (Truxton,) lot 75, dairy 16 cows and farmer 100

Rainbow, Preston, (Linklaen, Chenango Co ,) lot 20, farmer 33

RANDALL, ALBERT R, (Linklaen, Chenango Co ,) lot 29, dairy 12 cows and farmer 155

Randall, William N, (Linklaen, Chenango Co.,) lot 29, dairy 10 cows and farmer 154

RANDALL, ZEBULON C, (Linklaen, Chenango Co ,) lot 30, dairy 48 cows and farmer 400.

RIELY, DANIEL, (Keeney's Settlement,) lot 55, dairy 25 cows and farmer 200

Rodgers, Abram,(Linklaen, Chenango Co ,) lot 39, farmer leases of D Collins, 90

Rood, Joseph, (Linklaen, Chenango Co.,) lot 29, farmer 104

Rood, Joseph, (Cuyler,) lot 29, farmer 105

Rose, Lyman L, (Cuyler,) lot 58, farmer 51

RYAN, EDMUND M, (Truxton )

Ryan, Patrick, (Truxton,) lot 75, dairyman and farmer 45

RYON, ROGER, (Truxton,) lot 27, dairy 33 cows and farmer 285

RYON, ROGER JR, (Truxton,) dairy 18 cows and farmer leases 164.

SANDERS, EDWIN, (De Ruyter, Madison Co ,) prop De Ruyter Cheese Factory, which receives the milk of 1000 cows

Sanford, Philo N., (Linklaen, Chenango Co ,) lot 29, farmer 105

SAUNDERS, PERRY H, (Keeney's Settlement,) lot 57, dairy 34 cows and farmer 164

SCOTT, M BURT, (De Ruyter, Madison Co ,) lot 70, horse dealer and farmer 26½

SEAMANS, ORLANDO, (De Ruyter, Madison Co ,) lot 59, farmer 40

SEAMANS, WM H, (De Ruyter, Madison Co ,) lot 69, farmer 20

Sharp, Richard, (Cuyler,) shoemaker

Shaw, Melissa, (Cuyler,) lot 100, dairy 5 cows and farmer 27

Sheldon, Samuel, (Cuyler,) lot 99, farmer 15

Shields, John, (Keeney's Settlement,) lot 57, farmer 70

Smith, Alfred B, (Cuyler,) farmer

SMITH, CYRUS A, (Truxton,) lot 37, dairyman and farmer 100

SMITH, GEORGE W, (Truxton,) lot 37, dairy 12 cows and farmer 137

Smith, Henry, (Cuyler,) lot 19, dairy 16 cows and farmer 146

SMITH, J CRAIG, (Keeney's Settlement,) superintendent Keeney Settlement Cheese Manufacturing Company's Factory

Smith, William, (Linklaen, Chenango Co ,) lot 19, farmer 100

SMITH, WILLIS, (Cuyler,) lot 19, dairy 42 cows and farmer 394.

SPERRY, SOLOMON S, (DeRuyter, Madison Co ,) lot 70, dairyman and farmer 42

STEDMAN, DANIEL, (Cuyler,) lot 96, carpenter, joiner and farmer 35

Steele, Elias, (Truxton,) lot 37, farmer 50

Steele, George G., (Truxton,) lot 27, dairy 15 cows and farmer 156

STILLMAN, ORVILLE L, (DeRuyter, Madison Co ,) lot 99, dairy 15 cows and farmer 115

Swan, Samuel P, (Linklaen, Chenango Co ,) lot 10, wagon maker, dairy 13 cows and farmer 100

THOMPSON, WILLIAM W, (Cuyler,) prop Cuyler cheese factory which receives milk from 600 cows

Turner, Henry, (Truxton,) lot 17, dairy 7 cows and farmer 85

TWOMY, MICHAEL, (Cuyler,) lot 98, dairy 5 cows and farmer 137

Vedder, Deloss, (Truxton,) lot 17, dairy man and farmer 28

Vincent, Charles, (Cuyler,) lot 88, dairy 14 cows and farmer 118

Vincent, Sherwood, (Cuyler,) lot 68, Methodist clergyman and farmer 128

VINCENT, VOLNEY S, (Cuyler,) lots 68 and 78, dairy 33 cows and farmer 120

Wales, Wainwright, (DeRuyter, Madison Co ,) lot 89, shoemaker and farmer 43

WATERS, HENRY D, (Cuyler,) lot 86, justice peace, dairy 35 cows and farmer 238

WEBSTER, JOHN B, (Keeney's Settlement,) lot 57, dairy 81 cows and farmer 176

WHITE, SAMUEL, (Cuyler,) lot 68, hop cultivator, dairy 18 cows and farmer 162

WHITMARSH, HIRAM HON , (Keeney's Settlement,) lot 77, dairy 80 cows and farmer 400

WILCOX, STEPHEN S , (Linklaen, Chenango Co ,) lot 10, licensed auctioneer, dairy 10 cows and farmer 88.

WINNE, PHILIP, (Truxton,) lot 6, dairy 15 cows and farmer 100

Wright, Charles, (DeRuyter, Madison Co.,) lot 80, dairy 7 cows and farmer 28.

YORK, ANNA H , (DeRuyter, Madison Co ,) lot 9, dairy 15 cows and farmer 183

# FREETOWN.

## (Post Office Addresses in Parentheses.)

AURINGER, DANIEL, (Solon,) (*with Wm F ,*) lot 5, dairyman and farmer 228

AURINGER, WM F , (Solon,) (*with Daniel,*) lot 5, dairyman and farmer 228

Barry, Daniel, (Freetown Corners,) lot 11, dairyman and farmer 75.

Bates, Wm W , (Freetown Corners,) lot 22, farmer leases 106

Bean, Andrew, (Texas Valley,) lot 24, hop grower and farmer 80

Bean, Harvey, (Texas Valley,) (*with William H ,*) lot 24, hop grower and farmer 30

Bean, Wm , (Texas Valley,) lot 34, farmer 25 and leases 60.

Bean, Wm H , (Texas Valley,) (*with Harvey,*) lot 24, hop grower and farmer 30

Benjamin, Joshua, (Freetown Corners,) lot 22, dairyman and farmer 118.

Bennett, Alvin Rev , (Freetown Corners,) Baptist minister

BONNEY, STILLMAN, (Freetown Corners,) lot 12, farmer leases of Nelson Owen, 97½

BORTHWICK, ALONZO J , (Freetown Corners,) lot 11, dairyman and farmer 116

BORTHWICK, ANDREW, (Freetown Corners,) lot 42, farmer 50½

BORTHWICK, MARCUS, (Freetown Corners,) lot 31, dairy and farmer 74

Bowdish, Albertus, (Texas Valley,) lot 45, farmer 124

Bowdish, Emory, (Texas Valley,) lot 25, farmer 63

Bowdish, Hannah, (Texas Valley,) (*with Uriah and Margaret,*) lot 35, hop grower and farmer 160

BOWDISH, JOHN, (Texas Valley,) lot 24, hop grower, dairyman and farmer

Bowdish, Margaret, (Texas Valley,) (*with Uriah and Hannah,*) lot 35, hop grower and farmer 160

Bowdish, Stores, (Texas Valley,) lot 24, hop grower, dairyman and farmer 114

Bowdish, Uriah, (Texas Valley,) lot 35, farmer 157, and (*with Hannah and Margaret,*) hop grower and farmer 160

Brainard, Alanson, (Freetown Corners,) lot 32, dairyman and farmer 270

Brooks, Benjamin, (Texas Valley,) lot 25, hop grower and farmer 61

BROWN, A D , (Freetown Corners,) lot 22, stock dealer and farmer 5

Brown, Joseph, (Freetown Corners,) lot 2, farmer 140

CAFFREY, BERNARD, (Freetown Corners,) lot 33, dairyman and farmer 213

Cain, Sarah Mrs , (Texas Valley,) lot 25, farmer 57.

CALDWELL, GEO. A , (Freetown Corners,) lot 24, farmer 60

Caldwell, Geo W , (Freetown Corners,) lot 14, farmer 113

CALDWELL, WM H , (Freetown Corners,) lot 14, hop grower, dairyman and farmer 111

Carr, Solomon, (Freetown Corners,) lot 21, dairyman and farmer 85

Carr, Wm., (Freetown Corners,) lot 20, dairyman and farmer 135

CARSON, CYRUS, (Freetown Corners,) lot 14, farmer 33.

Clegg, Robert, (McGrawville,) lot 2, dairyman and farmer 207

Conger, Harmon S., (Freetown Corners,) lot 3, farmer leases 74

Conger, Melvin W , (Freetown Corners,) lot 22, horse dealer and farmer 106

Conklin, Catharine, (Freetown Corners,) lot 11, farmer 55

Conrad, James, (Freetown Corners,) lot 32, farmer 139

Copeland, Jacob, (Freetown Corners,) lot 22, farmer 18

Cornell, Lyman, (Cincinnatus,) lot 5, farmer 190 and (*with Richard,*) stock dealer

Courtney, Jesse, (Texas Valley,) lot 45, dairyman and farmer 111.

Curtis, Hiram A., (Freetown Corners,) lot 22, mechanic, dairyman and farmer 63

Dart, Richard L, (Freetown Corners,) lot 21, dairyman and farmer 96

Davern, Michael, (Texas Valley,) lot 15, farmer 100

DAVIS, ANDREW, (Messengerville,) lot 41, (*Davis Brothers*,) farmer 137½

DAVIS, BROTHERS, (Messengerville,) (*Andrew and Seth*,) lumber mannfs and dairymen

DAVIS, SETH, (Messengerville,) (*Davis Brothers*,) lot 41, farmer 137½

Dexter, Wm A, (Freetown Corners,) lot 32, dairyman and farmer 68

Dickinson, Austin, (Freetown Corners,) horse dealer

Dickinson, Wm, (Freetown Corners,) lot 20 farmer 87

Dickinson, Wm. D., (Freetown Corners,) lot 1, farmer 150

Dunbar, Ithemer O, (Cincinnatus,) lot 5, farmer 100

Eades, John, (Freetown Corners,) lot 11, farmer 200

EATON, CALVIN, (Freetown Corners,) lot 22, dairyman and farmer 110

Edes, Wm, (Freetown Corners,) lot 2, dairyman and farmer 119

EDWARDS, STEPHEN, (Texas Valley,) lot 24, dairyman and farmer 190½

ESMAY, WM, (Marathon,) lot 34, dairy and farmer 65

Falk, Daniel, (Freetown Corners,) lot 23, farmer 140

FEETER, JOHN M, (Freetown Corners,) lot 33, commissioner of highways, dairyman and farmer 195.

Fuller, Benj B, (Freetown Corners,) lot 21 farmer 135

Furber, John, (Marathon,) lot 43, dairy and farmer 108½

FURBER, THOMAS H, (Freetown Corners,) lot 33, dairyman and farmer 110

Gardner, Charles, (Texas Valley,) lot 35, farmer 86

Gardner, Hiram, (Texas Valley,) broom maker and farmer 6

Gardner, Joseph, (Texas Valley,) mason

Gardner, Perry, (Texas Valley,) lot 35, farmer 100

Gardner, Stephen, (Texas Valley,) lot 25, farmer 66

Grant, Daniel, (McGrawville,) lot 2, dairyman and farmer 208

GRANT, JOHN, (Freetown Corners,) lot 22, stock dealer, butcher, cooper and farmer 94½

GRANT, L R REV, (Freetown Corners,) pastor of M E church

Grant, Mioer M, (Freetown Corners,) lot 4, dairyman and farmer 100

Grant, Philander D, (Freetown Corners,) lot 5, carpenter and joiner and farmer 80

Grant, Vander M, (Freetown Corners,) lot 5, dairyman and farmer 290

Guernsey, Amasa O, (Marathon,) lot 43, farmer 170

Guy, James, (Messengerville,) lot 41, farmer 3

HALL, HIRAM, (Freetown Corners,) lot 32, supervisor, dairyman and farmer 120.

Hall, Lester, (Freetown Corners,) lot 21, dairyman and farmer 109.

Hammond, John, (Texas Valley,) lot 34, farmer leases 115

Hammond, Sidney S, (Freetown Corners,) wagon maker

Harty, James, (Texas Valley,) lot 35, dairyman and farmer 45

Hollenbeck, John W, (Freetown Corners,) lot 31, farmer 10

Hollenbeck, Washington, (Freetown Corners,) lot 31, farmer 75

Hovey, Thomas, (Freetown Corners,) lot 22, farmer 12

Hoxie, Jonathan J, (Freetown Corners,) postmaster

IVES, KILBURN, (Freetown Corners,) lot 12, dairyman and farmer 53

Jacobs, James Henry, (Blodget Mills,) lot 20, minister of the gospel, agent for Thayer's Iron Mower and farmer 2½

Jacobs, Joseph W, (Freetown Corners,) lot 20, carpenter, joiner and farmer 50

Jacobs, Marcus, (Freetown Corners,) lot 20, carpenter and farmer 38½

Johnson, Charles, (Texas Valley,) lot 35, basket maker

Johnson, John, (Freetown Corners,) lot 34, farmer 50

JONES, JAMES F, (Texas Valley,) lot 45, town assessor and farmer 325

KNIGHT, MOSELEY C, (Texas Valley,) lot 25, shoemaker and farmer 40

Lamberson, James, (Marathon,) lot 42, farmer 52

Lampher, Descom, (Freetown Corners,) lot 23, farmer 50

Lampher, Henry O, (Freetown Corners,) lot 32, carpenter and farmer 90

Lampher Leonard, (Freetown Corners,) lot 2, mason, dairyman and farmer 97½

Lee, William, (Marathon,) lot 43, farmer 110

Madison, Eri, (Freetown Corners,) lot 23, farmer 130

Manroe, Daniel, (Freetown Corners,) lot 32, dairyman and farmer 172

MANROE, DANIEL JR, (Freetown Corners,) mason

McAllister, Sarah, (Freetown Corners,) lot 21, farmer 52

McCumber, Wm, (Freetown Corners,) lot 1, farmer 40.

McHevitt, Hugh, (Freetown Corners,) lot 13, dairyman and farmer 155

McSweeny, John, (Texas Valley,) lot 45, hop grower, dairyman and farmer 102½

McVean, Chas P, (Texas Valley,) carpenter and justice of the peace

Merihew, Samuel, (Marathon,) lot 41, dairyman and farmer 234

Moon, Nelson R, (Freetown Corners,)(*with Reuben Shepard*,) lot 32, butcher and farmer 6.

Northrup, Chas. E, (Freetown Corners,) lot 20, hop grower and farmer 76.

NORTHRUP, REUBEN, (Freetown Corners,) lot 20, dairyman and farmer 125

O'Connell, John, (Marathon,) lot 48, dairy and farmer 83

O'CONNELL, JOHN JR., (Marathon,) lot 43, dairyman and farmer 100

Ogden, Almeron, (Texas Valley,) lot 24, hop grower and farmer 59

OWEN, WM A , (Freetown Corners,) lot 41, farmer 34.

Pease, Sydney, (Messengerville,) prop steam saw mill and farmer leases 2

Persons, Charles, (Texas Valley,) lot 34, farmer 67

Persons, Milo, (Solon,) lot 5, farmer 75

PICKERT, NORMAN, (Texas Valley,) lot 44, dairyman and farmer 200

Rice, Charles, (Texas Valley,) lot 44, farmer 88

Richardson, Elias, (Marathon,) lot 43, farmer 158

Ripley, John D , (Freetown Corners,) lot 13, prop saw mill, carpenter and farmer 45

Robertson, Chas W., (Freetown Corners,) grocer and provision dealer

Robertson, Polly, (Freetown Corners,) lot 1, farmer 50

ROBERTSON, SOLOMON F , (Freetown Corners,) cooper

Rooks, Robert, (Marathon,) lot 43, dairy and farmer 75

RUSSELL, NELSON S , (Messengerville,) lot 41, wagon maker and farmer 50

Schouten, Jesse, (Texas Valley,) lot 35, farmer leases 95

Seeber, Jacob, (Texas Valley,) lot 35, dairyman and farmer 104

SEEBER, JAMES H , (Texas Valley,) lot 44, dairyman and farmer 287

SHEPARD, JOHN, (Freetown Corners,) lot 41, dairyman and farmer 111

Shepard, Reuben, (Freetown Corners,) (*with Nelson E. Moon*,) lot 32, butcher and farmer 6

Sherman, Isaac, (Freetown Corners,) lot 20, tanner, dairyman and farmer 80

SITES, PETER, (Texas Valley,) (*with Charles Woodruff*,) lot 45, dairyman and farmer 124

Slocum, Henry, (Freetown Corners,) lot 22, farmer 1.

Slocum, Ransom, (Freetown Corners,) lot 33, dairyman and farmer 202.

Smith, Archibald T , (Messengerville,) lot 31, lumberman and farmer 89

Smith, Chauncey, (Freetown Corners,) lot 23, dairyman and farmer leases of D Smith, 200

SMITH, HAMOLTON D , (Marathon,) saw mill, grist mill, cider mill, and manuf of cheese boxes

Smith, Jarvis R , (Freetown Corners,) lot 31, farmer 60

Smith, Jesse E., (Freetown Corners,) retired farmer

Smith, Levi A , (Freetown Corners,) lot 31, carpenter and joiner and farmer 35

SMITH, SYLVENUS, (Freetown Corners,) lot 11, dairyman and farmer 191

STANTON, CLINTON D , (Freetown Corners,) boot and shoe dealer

Stanton, Levi, (Freetown Corners,) lot 21, farmer 20

Steadman, Edgar R , (Freetown Corners,) lot 13, farmer 130

STEVENS, WILBER, (Freetown Corners,) lot 33, dairyman and farmer 107

Stone, Harry D , (Freetown Corners,) lot 1, dairyman and farmer 230.

Tanner, George, (Freetown Corners,) lot 42, farmer 103.

Tanner, Lorenzo D , (Marathon,) lot 42, farmer 66

Tarbell, Daniel, (Freetown Corners,) retired farmer

Tarbell, Lorenzo, (Solon,) lot 5, mason and farmer 74.

Travis, Truman, (Freetown Corners,) mason

Tripp, Septimus, (Freetown Corners,) lot 22, farmer 180

Tuttle, Chauncey, (Freetown Corners,) lot 12, prop. cheese factory, dairyman and farmer 360

Underwood, Alanson, (McGrawville,) lot 3, farmer 180.

Underwood, Alanson Jr , (McGrawville,) lot 4, farmer 80

UNDERWOOD, ELIAB Jr , (Freetown Corners,) lot 14, dairyman and farmer 110

Underwood, Joseph, (Freetown Corners,) lot 4, grafter of fruit trees, dairyman and farmer 70

Underwood, Lewis, (McGrawville,) lot 3, farmer leases 130

Underwood, Lyman A., (Texas Valley,) lot 25, farmer 42½

Underwood, Philander, (Freetown Corners,) lot 1, farmer 188

Underwood, Vandel, (McGrawville,) dairyman and farmer 450

Vandewarker, A , (Texas Valley,) lot 45, farmer 160.

WARREN, EDWARD L , (Freetown Corners,) lot 32, farmer 48.

Warren, Willard, (Freetown Corners,) lot 31, farmer 35.

WATROUS, BENJ B , (Freetown Corners,) lot 32, dairyman and farmer 139, 250th farm since canvass,

Watrous, Gilbert M , (Freetown Corners,) lot 13, dairyman and farmer 230

Watrous, Ira B , (Freetown Corners,) lot 24, dairyman and farmer 363

Watrous, Leonard J , (Freetown Corners,) lot 3, farmer 125

Wavle, Gilbert, (Solon,) lot 5, farmer 126

Wavle, James, (Solon,) lot 4, farmer 300

West, Joseph V , (Freetown Corners,) blacksmith

Wildman, Joseph, (Texas Valley,) lot 15, farmer 100

Wildman, Marcus N , (Texas Valley,) lot 15, farmer 80

*WILES, CLIFTON W , (Freetown Corners,) dealer in dry goods, dress goods, groceries, crockery, hardware, yankee notions and general merchandise.

Williams, E C , (Freetown Corners,) lot 24, farmer 248

Withey, Eber N , (Cincinnatus,) lot 5, farmer 78

WOODRUFF, CHARLES, (Texas Valley,) (*with Peter Sites*,) lot 45, dairyman and farmer 124

Woods, Elisha, (Marathon,) lot 42, shoemaker, dairyman and farmer 26

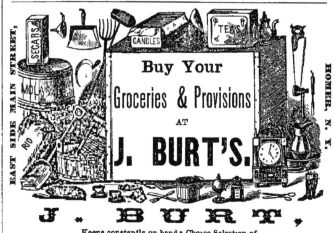

# HARFORD.

(Post Office Addresses in Parentheses.)

Adams, George B, (Harford,) lot 62, dairyman and farmer leases 130
ALLEN, SMITH, (Harford,) blacksmith
BAKER & BALL, (Harford Mills,) (*Wilber J Baker and L Clinton Ball*,) general merchants
BAKER, WILBER J, (Harford Mills,) (*Baker & Ball*,) telegraph operator
BALL, L CLINTON, (Harford Mills,) (*Baker & Ball*)
Ballard, Clark, (Harford,) lot 53, farmer 60
Ballard, Henry, (Harford,) lots 34 and 74, owns saw mill, dairyman and farmer 196
Banker, Abraham, (Harford,) carpenter and joiner, wagon and repair shop
Banker, Isaac W, (Harford,) mechanic, (*with A Banker*)
Barnes, George S, (Harford,) lot 63, dairyman and farmer 100
Barnes, John, (Virgil,) lot 55, farmer 63
Barr, John, (Lapeer,) lot 65, charcoal burner, dairyman and farmer 141½
Boice, William, (Harford Mills,) lot 590, farmer 90
Booth, Nathan, (Harford,) lot 565, farmer leases 48
Brown, A W., (Harford, Mills,) justice of the peace and wagon maker
Brown, Dexter, (Harford,) lots 71 and 81, dairyman and farmer 80
Brown, H J, (Harford,) farmer leases 80
Brown, J H, (Harford,) lots 71 and 61, dairyman and farmer 100
Brown, Morris, (Harford,) lots 81, 11, 72 and 584, dairyman and farmer 240
Brown, N L, (Harford,) lots 10, 11 and 12, dairyman and farmer 82
Bulman, C, (Harford,) lot 584, farmer 116
Bulman, Mattie E, (Harford,) school teacher
Burlingame, Peter M, (Harford Mills,) Christian minister, broom maker and farmer 22
Carpenter, Andrew J, (Harford,) lot 71, farmer 38¼
Carpenter, John, (Harford,) lot 51, farmer 60
Carpenter, Stephen, (Harford,) lot 51, dairyman and farmer 90
CATEN, HUGH, (Virgil,) lots 55 and 65, agent for Richardson's Little Washer, for Tompkins Co,, dairyman, farmer 324
Cheveler, Solomon, (Virgil,) lot 64, farmer 70
Clark, Asel, (Harford,) lot 52, farmer 20
Clark, Silas, (Harford,) lot 52, farmer leases of James Cole, Dryden, 105
Clark, Sterry, (Hunt's Corners,) lot 75, farmer 75
Cook, Martin M, (Harford,) lot 13, dairyman and farmer leases of A. Burlingame, Dryden, 140
Corbin, Joseph, (Harford,) lot 13, dairyman and farmer 70
Culver, Caroline J. Mrs, (Virgil,) lot 53, farmer 24

Culver, George, (Harford,) lots 52 and 62, dairyman and farmer 223
Culver, Simon B Rev, (Harford,) lot 51, Free Baptist minister and farmer 27
Day, Milo S, (Harford,) lot 585, dairyman and farmer 99 and 50 in Richford, Tioga Co
Decker, Benj H, (Harford,) farmer (*with P E N Decker*)
Decker, P E N, (Harford,) lots 22, 23, 584 and 587, dairyman and farmer 151
Delmater, Jacob H, (Harford,) lot 21, farmer 85
Dickinson, Lyman, (Harford,) lot 71, dairyman and farmer leases 54
Doty, William P, (Harford,) engineer
Edmons, Francis, (Harford,) lots 11 and 584, dairyman and farmer 95.
Elliott, Prentis, (Virgil,) lot 54, farmer 130
Elliott, Sylvester, (Virgil,) farmer (*with Prentis*)
Elliott, Warren, (Virgil,) lot 54, farmer 75
Ellis, Charles, (Harford,) constable, keeps stock horses
Ellis, John, (Harford Mills,) lot 587, shoemaker and farmer 6½
Field, B F, (Harford mills,) (*C & L Perrigo & Field*)
Forshee, William T, (Lapeer,) lot 75, dairyman and farmer 268
Foster, Amos, (Harford,) lot 64, farmer 45
Foster, John L, (Harford,) farmer 80
Foster, William, (Harford [...] and 587, farmer 62.
Frank, George, [...] leases of No[...]
Glazier, E B, (Vir[...] farmer 70
Griffin, S R, (Ha[...] general merchant
Hammon, William, (Harford,) lot 61, carpenter and farmer 27
Hammond, Samuel, (Harford,) lot 52, mason and farmer 20
Hammond, Thomas J, (Harford,) lot 52, mason and farmer 48
HARDENBERGH, PHILIP L, (Harford,) hotel keeper, merchant and farmer 16
Harrington, Charles, (Harford Mills,) harness maker
Haskell, Benj B, (Harford,) lot 52, grocer, basket maker and farmer 5
Haskell, D Mrs, (Harford,) lot 52, farmer 32
HEFFRON, J L, (Harford,) lot 75, farmer 112
HEMENWAY, MORRIS B, (Harford,) lots 73 and 585, dairyman and farmer 110
HEMINGWAY, A D & J D, (Harford,) lots 80, 32, 72 and 73, props steam saw mill, siding, planing and lath mills, dairymen and farmers 800
Hemmevay, Jacob, (Harford,) retired farmer
Hill, Osmer, (Dryden, Tompkins Co,) lot 51, farmer leases of Austen Hill, Dryden, 146
Hile, Thomas, (Harford,) lots 9, 21 and 71, farmer 100 and 60 in Dryden

HILE, THOMAS, 2ND., (Harford,) lot 9, wood sawyer, dairyman and farmer leases 180

Hoaldridge, E J , (Virgil,) lot 65, dairyman and farmer leases 214.

Holden, Benjamin, (Harford,) lots 71 and 72, dairyman and farmer 72

Holden, Samuel N , (Harford,) (*Tyler & Holden.*)

Holdridge, Thomas J , (Virgil,) lot 55, farmer 110

Howard, Richard, (Harford Mills,) lot 588, dairyman and farmer leases of S S Jackson, 80

Howard, William P , (Harford Mills,) house painter.

Hulslander, John, (Harford,) lot 9, farmer 103.

Hutchings, Leander S , (Virgil,) lot 53, farmer 30.

Jackson, S. S , (Harford,) lot 22, farmer 11.

Jennings, Ransom, (Harford Mills,) lots 74 and 75, stock dealer and farmer 540

Johnson, P, A , (Harford,) lots 11, 12 and 14, dairyman and farmer 108

Joiner, John, (Virgil,) lot 65, farmer 7.

Joiner, John, (Harford,) lot 63, farmer 48

Joiner, Nelson, (Harford,) lot 63, farmer 48

Jones, B F , (Harford,) lot 10, butter and produce dealer.

Jotes, A , (Harford,) lots 34 and 74, farmer 20

Keech, William O , (Virgil,) lot 54, farmer 47

Keeney, A. B. Rev , (Harford,) pastor M E Church

Kell, J , (Harford Mills,) farmer leases

Ketchum, John, (Harford,) lots 27 and 34,

Ketchum, A , (Harford,) lots 34 and 24, farmer

Ketchum, John, (Harford,) lots 27 and 34, farmer 146

KNAPP, JOHN H WILN, (Harford,) physician and surgeon

Lason, Nancy Mrs , (Harford,) lot 62, farmer 130

Lathrop, Denison, (Harford,) lot 535, dairyman and farmer 36 and 56 in Tompkins Co

Leonard, John, (Virgil,) lot 65, farmer leases 50

Lewis, Gile, (Dryden, Tompkins Co ,) lot 51, farmer 6.

Lindsay, George, (Dryden, Tompkins Co ,) lot 52, dairyman and farmer 88

Loomis, Dan C , (Virgil,) lot 54, stone mason and farmer 20

Loomis, Daniel W , (Harford,) lots 17 and 18, dairyman and farmer leases of Tyler & Burlingame, Dryden, 120

Mahan, Franklin, (Harford,) lot 22, dairyman and farmer 60.

Maricle, Frank, (Harford Mills,) blacksmith

MARICLE, JEROME, (Harford,) blacksmith

Marsh, Edward C , (Virgil,) lot 53, farmer 92.

Marsh, William, (Harford,) lot 71, cooper

Marshall, Guy, (Harford,) lot 61, carpenter and farmer 58

Marshall, Josiah, (Harford,) lot 61, dairyman and farmer 53.

MARTIN, WILLIAM H , (Harford,) lots 62, 71 and 72, dairyman and farmer 190

Mather, Ferrie Miss , (Hunt's Corners,) school teacher

MATHER, OGILVIE, (Hunt's Corners,) lot 74, dairyman and farmer leases 250

Mericle, Peter, (Harford Mills,) lots 64 and 65, farmer 60.

MILLEN, ANDREW D , (Harford Mills,) carpenter and joiner, millwright and foreman in C. & L. Perrigo & Field's steam mills

Miller, Charles, (Harford,) lot 62, dairyman and farmer 76

Miller, Damon, (Harford Mills,) blacksmith

Miller, D H , (Harford,) carpenter.

Miller, Erastus, (Harford,) lot 52, dairyman and farmer 100

MILLER, GEORGE W , (Harford,) lot 61, farmer leases of Guy Marshall, 68

Moore, Harriet S Mrs , (Harford,) lot 13, dairy and farmer 110.

Neff, Porter, (Virgil,) lot 53, farmer 37

Nelson, Samuel W , (Harford,) postmaster, justice of the peace and produce dealer.

Norwood, Philip G , (Harford,) lot 72, justice of the peace, dairyman and farmer 108

Okley, James M , (Virgil,) lot 54, dairyman, farmer 30 and leases 50

Okley, John, (Virgil,) lot 64, farmer 50

Parker, Andrew, (Harford,) lot 61, farmer leases of Mrs Parvis, Tompkins Co., 50

Parker, Benjamin, (Harford,) lot 62, farmer 55.

Perrigo, C & L & Field, (Harford Mills,) (*Chas and Lyman Perrigo and B F Field,*) lots 26, 28 and 29, props, steam saw mill, planing, matching and lath, farmers 190

Pierce, Martin, (Harford Mills,) lot 65, dairyman and farmer 100

Purvis, Robert, (Harford,) lots 71, 587, 25 and 63, dairyman and farmer 259, and 149 in Dryden, Tompkins Co

Rice, S. B , (Harford Mills,) lot 28, farmer 10.

Rockafeller, W H , (Harford Mills,) lot 590, farmer 143

Rood, Josiah W , (Harford,) lots 21, 23, 24 and 53, dairyman and farmer 293

Rood, L W , (Harford Mills,) lots 21, 22 and 23, dairyman and farmer leases of J W. Rood, 293

SEAMAN, SPENCER, (Harford,) lots 10 and 11, dairyman and farmer 90

Shevilear, John, (Harford,) lot 64, farmer 50

Shevilear, Richard, (Harford,) lot 64, farmer 50

Shevilear, Warren, (Harford,) lot 28, keeps a jack

Silsbee, B F , (Harford,) shoemaker

SMITH, ANDREW, (Harford Mills,) lot 588, dairyman and farmer 150.

Smith, D D , (Harford Mills,) farmer (*with A Smith* )

SMITH, JAMES W , (Harford,) lot 73, dairyman and farmer 50

Smith, Lyman M , (Virgil,) lot 53, dairyman and farmer leases of E W Smith, 73

Smith, Relyea, (Virgil,) lot 64, farmer 90

Stacy, William, (Harford,) lots 23, 24, 25 and 84, dairyman and farmer 115

Steele, Samuel H , (Harford,) lot 16, millwright, owns two saw mills in Richford, Tioga Co

Stowe, Elijah,(Virgil,) lot 53, farmer leases of C A. Keech, Dryden, 58.

Strong, C L , (Harford,) lots 71 and 72, dairyman and farmer leases of Daniel Phillips, Dryden, 163

Strong, Erastus, (Virgil,) lot 55, justice, assessor and farmer 60

Swart, George W , (Harford,) lot 20, dairyman and farmer leases of John Sothard, Dryden, 130

Taintor, Irving, (Harford,) lots 16, 19 and 33, dairyman and farmer 165

TANNER, LYMAN, (Harford,) town clerk, carpenter and joiner

Tanner, William, (Harford,) carpenter and builder

Tarbox, William H,, (Harford Mills,) lot 589, farmer 100

Tarbox, William N , (Harford Mills,) lot 597, farmer 27½

Tarbox, Worden, (Harford Mills,) farmer (*with Wm. N Tarbox*)

Teed, Jeffrey, (Virgil,) lot 55, dairyman and farmer 100.

Teed, Macvill, (Harford,) lot 586, dairyman and farmer 126

Terpenning, Arthur, (Dryden, Tompkins Co ,) lot 51, carpenter and farmer 30

Terpenning, Noah, (Dryden, Tompkins Co ,) lot 51, farmer 46.

Thomas, Michael 2nd, (Harford,) lot 61, farmer 79

Tillotson, Asel, (Lapeer,) lots 55 and 65, dairyman and farmer 114

Todman, L , (Harford Mills,) prop grist and saw mills

Tripp, Daniel A , (Harford,) lot 10, dairyman and farmer 54 and 78 in Dryden, Tompkins Co

Tucker, E H , (Dryden, Tompkins Co ,) lot 51, stock dealer and farmer 25

Tyler & Holden, (Harford,) (*Jno M Tyler and Samuel N. Holden,*) general merchants

Tyler, John M ,(Harford,) (*Tyler & Holden* )

Vunk, Gaylord, (Virgil,) lot 54, dairyman and farmer leases of Henry Vunk, Virgil, 195

Wagnor, William, (Harford,) lot 13, farmer leases 110

Weiler, Christian, (Virgil ) lots 54 and 55, dairyman and farmer 60

WEILER, GEORGE F , (Harford,) lot 585, dairyman and farmer 60

Wilcox, David Rev., (Harford Mills,) postmaster, Christian minister and farmer 22

Wilcox, Hiram, (Harford Mills,) lot 587, dairyman and farmer 100

Willcox, Gates, (Harford,) lots 18 and 636, dairyman and farmer 136

WILLCOX, GEORGE P , (Harford Mills,) lot 597, assessor, dairyman and farmer 103

Willcox, Wesley, (Harford,) lot 586, dairyman and farmer leases 86

Williamson, Amasa, (Harford,) lot 62, shingle maker and farmer 34

Williamson, James, (Harford,) lot 61, farmer 6

Yates, Benjamin, (Harford,) lot 61, assessor, owns saw mill, dairyman and farmer 91

Yates, C L , (Harford Mills,) lot 22, leases grist and saw mills of L Todman, farmer 61½

Yates, Daniel B, (Harford,) miller

# HOMER.

## (Post Office Addresses in Parentheses.)

Aaron & Doublin, (Homer,) (*Samuel Aaron and Pincus Doublin,*) props of Syracuse and Homer hoop skirt manufactory

Aaron, Samuel, (Homer,) (*Aaron & Doublin,*) lives in Syracuse

ABBOTT, ALFRED J , (Homer,) lot 34, drover, dairyman and farmer 100.

ABBOTT, FRANK, (Homer,) (*with Alfred Abbott,*) farmer

Abbott, George A , (Homer ) lots 47 and 7, dairy of 50 cows and farmer 230

Abbott, William O , (Homer,) lot 47, dairyman and farmer 77

Ackerman, Ebenezer, (East Homer,) lots 9 and 10, farmer 80

*ADAMS, GEO A Mrs , (Homer,) dress and cloak maker and dealer in hair work of all kinds

AKIN, GEORGE W , (Homer,) (*Rogers & Akin* )

ALEXANDER, IRVING, (East Homer,) lots 18 and 19, dairyman and farmer leases of Leonard Alexander, 118

Alexander, Leonard 2nd, (East Homer,) lot 19, dairyman and farmer 192

Alexander, Melvin L , (East Homer,) lot 8, dairyman and farmer 88

Almy, George W , (Homer,) architect and builder
Almy, Richard, (East Homer,) lot 20, farmer 4
ALVORD, C M , (Homer,) lot 13, dairyman, stock dealer and farmer 102
Alvord, Henry S , (Homer,) lots 2 and 13, farmer 160.
Alvord, Lucina, (Homer,) lot 1, dairyman and farmer 275
Andrews, Samuel, (Homer,) lot 22, carpenter and farmer 60
ANDRUS, WILLIAM, (Homer,) justice peace and general insurance agent.
Arnold, George, (East Homer,) lot 39, farmer leases of R Kenfield, 65
Arnold, J Albert, (East Homer,) lot 10, farmer 47
Arnold, Peleg, (Homer,) lot 15, farmer 106
Artchison, Martha Mrs , (Homer,) lot 7, dairy acd farmer 130
Atchison, George, (Homer,) lots 27 and 37, dairyman and farmer leases of Parker B Willson, 75
Atchison, James, (Homer,) lot 37, farmer 19¾
Atchison, Robert, (Homer,) lot 7, (with Mrs M Atchison,) farmer
Atkinson, George, (Homer,) lot 38, dairyman and farmer 160
BABCOCK, H. S & Co , (Homer,) (H H Brown,) merchant tailors, dealers in gents' furnishing goods and agents for Singer's sewing machines
BABCOCK, LEWIS G , (Homer,) lot 4, dairyman and farmer 80
Babcock & McDaniels, (Homer,) (Oscar A Babcock and George W McDaniels,) grocery and restaurant
Babcock, Oscar A , (Homer,) (Babcock & McDaniels)
Babcock, Wm , (Homer,) ticket, express and freight agent and telegraph operator
Bacon, Mrs , (Homer,) dress and cloak maker
Bagg, James H , (Homer,) prop. of photograph gallery
Baldwin, S R , (Homer,) lot 4, dairyman and farmer 147
BANKING HOUSE OF JEDEDIAH BARBER, (Homer,) Jedediah Barber, banker, Wm T Hicok, cashier
Barber, Geo J J , (Homer,) general merchant
BARBER, JEDEDIAH, (Homer,) banker of Barber's Banking House, prop of lumber yard and steam planing mill, coal, lime and plaster yard, president of the village corporation and farmer 90
Barber & Sherman, (Homer,) (Watts Barber and Caleb H Sherman,) produce and commission merchants
Barber, Watts, (Homer,) (Barber & Sherman.)
Barker, A , (Homer,) (with L E,) lot 25, dairyman and farmer 106
Barker, L E., (Homer,) (with A.,) lot 25, dairyman and farmer 106.
Barker, William C , (Homer,) lots 16 and 17, dairyman and farmer leases from D E Barker's estate, 100.

Barnes, J D Rev , (Homer,) pastor of First Baptist church of Homer
Bartlett, E. D., (Homer,) lots 44 and 45, farmer leases of Capt James' heirs, 10
Batchellor, L H Mrs , (Homer,) fancy goods, toys, &c.
Bates, Alexander, (Homer,) prop of carriage manufactory
Bates, C E , (Homer,) lot 35, speculator in farm produce
Bates, Lemnel, (Homer,) lot 35, dairyman and farmer 113½
BATES, STEPHENS S , (Homer,) lot 35, house, sign, carriage and ornamental painter and paper hanger
Beach, William B , (Homer,) lot 4, dairyman and farmer 220
Bean, William A , (Cortland Village,) lot 41, dairyman and farmer 103
Beattie, John, (East Homer,) lot 9, farmer 51
Bell, Robert, (East Homer,) lot 20, dairyman and farmer leases of S Klock, 192.
Benedict, Simon H,, (Cortland Village,) lot 41, (with Rensselaer Benedict, of Cortland,) dairyman and farmer
Bennett, Asa, (East Homer,) farmer (with David H Bennett)
Bennett, Augustus H , (Homer,) (Bennett & Corey)
Bennett, Benj F , (East Homer,) blacksmith
Bennett & Corey, (Homer,) (Augustus H Bennett and David B Corey,) manufacturers and dealers in boots and shoes, Wheadon Block.
Bennett, David H , (East Homer,) lot 19, farmer 59.
BENNETT, EDWIN, (East Homer,) lot 49, dairyman and farmer 100
Bennett, William, (East Homer,) lots 29 and 19, farmer 60
Berker, John, (Homer,) carpenter
Bierce & Fowler, (Homer,) undertakers and dealers in furniture.
Bigsby, Charles E , (Homer,) manufacturer of carriages and sleighs, and runs omnibus
Bishop, Osander, (Homer,) lot 45, carpenter and builder
BLANCHARD, SILAS, (Homer,) lot 44, dairyman and farmer 186
Blaney, William, (Homer,) lot 35, slaughter house and farmer 9.
BLANEY, WM H H , (Homer,) (Wilbur & Blaney)
BLANSHAW, RUSSEL, (Homer,) (R. Blanshaw & Co)
BLANSHAW, R & CO , (Homer,) (Russel Blanshaw and Darius W Stone,) manufacturers of axes and edge tools
BLASHFIELD, H W., (Little York,) lots 5 and 6, prop. of cider mill, saw mill and wood turning lathe, dairyman and farmer 150
Boice & Card, (Homer,) agents for the Cayuga Chief Mower and Reaper
Boice, Joshua, (Homer,) lot 31, owns cider mill, farmer 55 and leases of S Card, 55
Boland, Thomas, (Homer,) lot 45, partner in Starr's patent harrow and horse fork and farmer
*BONNER, WILLIAM J , (Homer,) dealer in hats, caps, satchels, umbrellas, &c

Bookhout, James, (Homer,) lot 12, dairyman and farmer leases of D H Hannum, 150

Boorum, John L , (Homer,) produce and commission merchant and prop ware house

*BOORUM, JOHN L , (Homer,) lots 22 and 23, prop of Homer Flax and Cordage Mill and farmer 213½, lives in village

Borrowdale, Thomas, (Homer,) lot 42, dairyman and farmer 87.

BOWEN, ANDREW, (Homer,) lot 5, farmer 20

Bozworth, Calvin, (Homer,) lots 87 and 38, farmer 25

BRADFORD, GEORGE W , M D, (Homer,) physician and surgeon

BRIGGS, ELLIS R , (Homer,) lot 38, masonry in all its branches and farmer 5

Briggs, William W , (East Homer,) lots 29 and 19, dairyman and farmer 208

Brockway, W N , (Homer,) undertaker and furniture dealer

Broomfield, William, (Homer,) lot 18, farmer 22

Brown, A, D , (Homer,) mason

Brown, A D Mrs , (Homer,) milliner

Brown, Charles S , (Homer,) lots 23 and 24, carpenter and builder and prop of saw mill

BROWN, H H , (Homer,) (*H S Babcock & Co*)

Brown, William R., M D , (Homer,) homeopathic physician and surgeon

Bunn, Abbie Miss, (Homer,) (*Miss F Knapp & Co*)

Bunn, Samuel, (Homer,) lots 32 and 43, dairyman and farmer 82.

Burnham, Eliza A Mrs , (Homer,) lot 35, dairy and farmer 118.

Burnham, Eugene A , (East Homer,) lot 29, dairyman and farmer leases of W W Haight, 50

Burnham, H M Mrs , (East Homer,) lots 29 and 30, dairyman and farmer 133

Burnham, Marvin, (East Homer,) lot 30, shoemaker, dairyman, dealer in bees and farmer 34.

BURRELL, NATHAN, (Homer,) wagon maker

*BURT, JOSEPH, (Homer,) dealer in groceries and provisions

Burvee, Harvey W , (East Homer,) farmer (*with Mrs S Burvee*)

Burvee, Serepta Mrs , (East Homer,) lot 40, dairy and farmer 110

Butler, Charles, (Homer,) painter

Butler, Leo Mrs , (Homer,) lot 32, dairyman and farmer 130

Butterfield, B M , (East Homer,) lot 29, musician

Button, Lewis W , (Homer,) lot 22, dairyman and farmer 120

Caldwell, A B , (Homer ) lot 21, farmer 150

Caldwell, J G , (Homer,) lot 21, dairyman and farmer leases of A B Caldwell, 150

Card, William, (Homer,) (*with Joshua Boice,*) farmer

Card, ———, (Homer,) (*Boice & Card* )

Carns, M E Mrs , (Homer,) dress maker

Carpenter, Asaph H., (Homer,) lots 16, 17 and 27, dairyman and farmer 175.

CARPENTER, HENRY L , (Homer,) lot 38, saw mill, turning shop and farmer 18.

Carpenter, Malvina Mrs , (Homer,) lot 38, colorist and taxidermist

Carpenter, Meriva Mrs , (Homer,) lot 38, farmer 5

Carpenter, Smith H , (Homer,) lot 25, dairyman and farmer leases of B H Sheffield, 76

Carpenter, V , (Homer,) lot 47, farmer 10

Carr, David Jr , (East Homer,) lot 28, dairyman and farmer 106

Carver, David W , (Little York,) lots 6, 7, 15 and 17, dairyman and farmer 111½

CARVER, SHUBAEL, (Homer,) school commissioner of the second district of Cortland Co , and pastor of the First Congregational Church at Union Valley

CHAMBERLIN, F. A., (Homer,) hair dresser, Main

Champlin, Jonathan, (Homer,) lot 44, farmer 5

Chapman, Harrison, (Homer,) lots 17 and 27, farmer 14

Chase, Ezra, (Cortland Village,) lot 31, carpenter and farmer 17.

Chollar, Isaac N , (Homer,) cartman

CHOLLAR, THOMAS D , (Homer,) dealer in boots, shoes and leather

Clark, Caldwell, (Little York,) lot 6, dairyman and farmer 50

Clark, Hiram, (Homer,) lots 16 and 17, dairyman and farmer 150

Coats, Hartley C , (East Homer,) lot 40, dairyman and farmer 60

Cobb, Calvin C , (Homer,) lot 3, dairyman and farmer 70

Cobb, W H , (Homer,) mason

Coggshall, William (Homer,) tannery

Collins, Chester A , (Homer,) (*Kinney & Collins* )

Combs, Carlos, (Homer,) hardware, stoves, tinware, &c

Conine, Philo, (Homer,) (*with P Jones,*) farmer

Cooke, M Louisa, M D , (Homer,) physician

Coon, E Harvey, (Homer,) carriage maker and blacksmith

Coon, Luke H , (Homer,) lot 46, dairyman and farmer 7, and leases of Samuel Coon, 144

Coon, Samuel, (Homer,) lot 36, farmer 144

Cooper, Giles B , (Homer,) supt flax mill

Corey, David B , (Homer,) (*Bennett & Corey* )

Corl, Giles, (Homer,) lots 27 and 37, dairyman and farmer 148

Corl, Harry, (Homer,) lot 27, dairyman and farmer 66

Corl, Jacob, (Homer,) lot 47, farmer 25.

Cornell, Augustine W , (Homer,) rector of Calvary Church

*CORTLAND COUNTY REPUBLICAN, (Homer,) published every Thursday, Joseph R. Dixon, editor.

Cortright, Moses, (Homer,) lot 1, dairyman and farmer 190

Cotterell, Geo. W., (Homer,) confectioner

Cowles, Parmenas S., (Homer,) lot 35, dairyman and farmer 45

CRAMPTON, E. H & S. H., (Homer,) lots 23 and 24, dairyman and farmer 120

Crampton, E. M., (Homer,) lots 23 and 24, dairyman and farmer 193

Crandall, De Ronda N., (Cortland Village,) lot 38, farmer 37 and leases of Mrs Harriet Abbott, 10

Crandall, Elias, (Homer,) lot 28, stock dealer and farmer 108

Crego, John H., (Homer,) (*Francis Sears & Co.*)

Crossman, Andrew J., (East Homer,) lot 18, farmer 86

Crossman, G. A., (East Homer,) machinist and farmer

CURTIS, SAMUEL, (Homer,) lots 31 and 32, painter, dairyman and farmer 34½

Cushing, Frederick A., (East Homer,) lot 18, dairyman and farmer 75

Cushing, James E., (Little York,) lot 6, postmaster, general merchant and farmer 8

Cushing, Thomas, (East Homer,) lot 80, dairyman and farmer 90

Daily, Patrick, (Homer,) lot 27, dairyman and farmer 87

Daly, John, (Homer,) lot 21, dairyman and farmer 60

DARBY, LYMAN, (Homer,) (*L. Darby & Son*)

DARBY, L. & SON, (Homer,) (*Lyman and William H.,*) grist and flouring mill

DARBY, WILLIAM H., (Homer,) (*L. Darby & Son*)

Dawson, William, (Homer,) lot 28, dairyman and farmer 100

Day, Samuel S. Rev., (Homer,) Baptist clergyman

Dayton, George W., (Little York,) lot 7, carpenter and joiner

DeBARR, THEODORE, (East Homer,) carpenter, joiner and millwright

DENISON, HENRY, (Homer,) lot 44, dairyman and farmer 150

Devoe, Abraham, (Homer,) lots 12, 13 and 22, dairyman and farmer 145

Devoe, Henry, (Homer,) lot 23, farmer 3

DEVOE, HENRY G., (Homer,) farmer (*with A. Devoe*)

DEVOE, JEREMIAH, (Homer,) lots 12, 13 and 22, dairyman and farmer 121

Devoe, William J., (Homer,) lot 13, nursery and hedging

Dick, Francis, (Little York,) lot 8, farmer 9

*DIXON, JOSEPH R., (Homer,) editor Cortland Co. *Republican*, published every Thursday

Dobbins, Edward, (Homer,) lot 31, farmer 114

Doubleday, Daniel H., (Homer,) lots 15 and 16, dairyman and farmer 50

Doublin, Pincus, (Homer,) (*Aaron & Doublin*)

Dowd, Harley, (Little York,) lot 6, farmer 90

Drew, Emily Mrs., (Homer,) lot 44, farmer 1½

Dunham, E. H., (Homer,) lot 45, dealer in wooden pumps, adjuster of tube wells and Rogers' patent cement roofing

Dunham, Miss Susan I., (Homer,) school teacher

EAST HOMER HOTEL, (East Homer,) Luther R. Rose, prop.

Eastmar, Benjamin F., (Homer,) lot 45, carpenter and builder

Eastman, James R., (East Homer,) lot 30, dairyman and farmer 74½

FAIRBANKS, CHARLES, (Homer,) lot 3, dairyman and farmer 108½

Finch, Daniel H., (Cortland Village,) lot 28, dairyman and farmer 51

FISHER, ALBERT, (Homer,) tobacconist and leader of Homer Mechanics' Brass Band

Fisher, Thomas, (Homer,) lot 44, dairyman and farmer 60

Fisher, Willet, (Little York,) lot 6, wagon maker

Ford, John, (Homer,) lot 22, dairyman and farmer 56

Foster, Isaac, (East Homer,) lot 39, dairyman and farmer 193

Foster, John, (Little York,) lot 7, dairyman and farmer 200.

Fowler, ———, (Homer,) (*Bierce & Fowler*)

Fox, David H., (Homer,) lot 24, farmer leases of Hermon Fox, 54

Fox, Hermon, (Homer,) lot 24, farmer 54

Fox, Ira, (Homer,) lot 35, dairyman and farmer 93

*FRALICK, LOUIS, (Homer,) tobacconist, No 2 Wall st

Frazier, Aaron, (Homer,) lot 36, dairyman and farmer 140

FREEMAN & BROTHER, (Homer,)(*Samuel and Lewis,*) merchant tailors.

FREEMAN, LEWIS, (Homer,) (*Freeman & Bro.*)

FREEMAN, SAMUEL, (Homer,) (*Freeman & Bro.*)

Gallup, Francis, (Homer,) lot 16, dairyman and farmer 132

GARDNER, W. H., (Homer,) lot 34, of firm of Carson & Gardner, publishers of *State League*, Syracuse, (*with Amasa Holmes,*) farmer

Gates, Henry M., (Homer,) lot 44, farmer 9½

Gates, Joel, (Little York,) lots 7 and 27, dairyman and farmer 123

GILES, CHARLES L., (Homer,) lot 34, machinist and moulder, and prop of cider mill, saw mill and wood turning machine

Giles, Gilbert, (Homer,) lot 34, prop. of saw mill and farmer 12

GILES, HENRY T., (Homer,) lot 34, prop of foundry and machine shop and manufacturer of portable circular saw mills

Gilkerson, George, (Homer,) lot 37, farmer 98

Gilkerson, John, (Homer,) lot 37, dairyman and farmer leases of Geo Gilkerson, 98

Gillett, Sylvanus H., (Little York,) machinist and millwright

GOODALE, FAYETTE, (Homer,) lot 31, dairyman and farmer 96.

Goodell, C. B., (Homer,) lot 26, dairyman and farmer 100

GOODELL, ERASTUS, JR., (Homer,) lot 26, dairyman and farmer 65.

Goodell, R. A., (Homer,) physician.

Goodwin, H C , (Homer,) lot 27, historian and farmer 18

Graham, Edward, (East Homer,) lot 9, dairyman and farmer 87

Graham, Mathew, (Preble,) *(with Wm )* farmer

GRAHAM, WILLIAM, (Preble,) lot 9, dairyman and farmer 183

GREEN, ALBERT, (Homer,) carpenter and builder

Green, Caleb, M D , (Homer,) physician and surgeon

Griffith, Abraham B , (East Homer,) lot 29, assessor, dairyman and farmer 100

Griffith, Joshua, (East Homer,) lots 29 and 9, farmer 110

Griner, John, (Homer,) lot 35, supt of cheese making at Homer cheese factory

GRISWOLD, ROBERT W , (Homer,) clock and watch maker and jeweler

GUTCHES, AMASA, (Homer,) lot 25, dairyman and farmer leases 99

Gutchens, Andrew, (East Homer,) lot 9, saw mill and farmer 88

GUTCHEUS, BEVERLY, (East Homer,) lots 38 and 19, dairyman and farmer 288

Gutchens, George A , (East Homer,) farmer *(with Andrew )*

Gutchens, Lorenzo D , (East Homer,) lot 29, carpenter dairyman and farmer 88

Gutcheus, Mekeel, (East Homer,) lot 19, dairyman and farmer 131

Haight, Charles, (East Homer,) honey dealer and farmer *(with Jabez Haight )*

Haight, Jabez, (East Homer,) lots 10 and 20, saw mill, dairyman and farmer 176

*HAIGHT, JAMES M , (East Homer,) planned the establishment of Haight's Museum, taxidermist

Haight, L A , (East Homer,) lot 29, carpenter and farmer 6.

Hakes, Marinons, (Homer,) lot 45, farmer 10

Hall, Hiram, (McGrawville,) lot 40, farmer leases of E W Learned, 100

Hallenbeck, Howard, (Homer,) lot 25, farmer leases of Walter Jones, 210.

Hammon, Charles, (Homer,) lot 14, dairyman and farmer 100

Hammon, David, (Homer,) lot 18, farmer 64

Hammon, William, (Homer,) lot 24, dairyman and farmer 127½

HAMMOND, JOHN, (Cortland Village,) l t 47, grist mill, saw mill, cheese box manufactory and farmer 2.

Hammond, Nathan, (Homer,) lot 11, dairyman and farmer leases of D. H. Hannum, 150

Hammond, Rufus, (East Homer,) lot 49, dairyman and farmer 100.

Hannum, D H , (Homer,) lives in village, dairyman and farmer 1,500.

Hare, Betsey, (Homer,) lot 31, farmer 30.

Harkness, David, (Homer,) lot 37, dairyman and farmer 48

Harrington, Daniel C , (Little York,) *(D. C Harrington & Co )*

Harrington, D C. & Co., (Little York,) *(Daniel C Harrington and Jay J Salsbury,)* lot 5, blacksmiths and wagon makers, props of saw mill and farmers 87

Harrington, Edgar, (Little York,) lot 6, blacksmith and carpenter

Hart, John, (Homer,) lot 11, dairyman and farmer 230

Hart, J Truman, (Homer,) farmer leases of Jno Hart, 230

Hatfield, Chas A , (Cortland Village,) lot 41, farmer 105

Hayes G W , (Homer,) lot 43, dairyman and farmer 114

HAYNES & KINGSBURY, (Homer,)( *Wm. H Haynes and Porter C Kingsbury,)* dealers in dry goods, groceries, crockery &c

HAYNES, WILLIAM H ,(Homer,) *(Haynes & Kingsbury )*

Head, A. L , M D , (Homer,) physician, surgeon and druggist.

Heberd, Ulysses, (Homer,) saw mill and farmer 140.

Henderson, John, (Homer,) lot 43, farmer leases of C Edgcomb, 33

Henry, Abraham, (East Homer,) lots 30 and 40, dairyman and farmer 150

Henry, Asa G , (East Homer,) superintendent cheese factory

Henry, O , (East Homer,) lot 9, farmer 32½

HIBBARD, MARQUIS M , (East Homer,) lot 30, justice peace, prop of butter and cheese factory , dairyman and farmer 175

Hicks, Jacob, (Homer,) lot 27, dairyman and farmer 60

Hicks, Z S , (Homer,) *(with Jacob,)* farmer

HICOK, JOHN H , (Homer,) in Barber's Bank.

HICOK, WM T , (Homer,) cashier of Jedediah Barber's Banking House and secretary and treasurer of Homer and Cortland Gas Light Co

Hinman, M, B , (Cortland Village,) lot 41, farmer 50

HINMAN, SHELDON REV ,(East Homer,) lot 29, Methodist clergyman, physician and farmer 19

Hitchcock, Noah, (Homer,) lot 25, dairyman and farmer 275

Hix, D B , (Homer,) lot 54, apiarian and farmer

Hoag, S. P , (East Homer,) lot 29, blacksmith

Hoag, William M , (Homer,) carpenter and master builder

Hoage, William, (Homer,) lot 38, shoemaker

Hobart, Alanson, (Homer,) lot 35, painter and farmer 16½

Hobart, D C , (Homer,) lot 13, supt of DeVoe Nursery

Hobart, Manley, (Homer,) lots 5, 15 and 35, assessor, dairyman and farmer 200

Hobert, Dicks, (East Homer,) lot 40, farmer 63

HOLBROOK, JOHN C REV , (Homer,) pastor First Congregational Church

Holenbeck, John, (Little York,) lot 6, mason and farmer 3

Hollister, Ezra, (Homer,) lots 31, 32, 41 and 42, dairyman and farmer 90

Hollister, Rossel L , (Homer,) livery stable.

Holmes, Amasa, (Homer,) lot 34, dairyman and farmer 80

Holmes, Samuel, (East Homer,) lot 10, farmer 60

Hulmes, Watson, (Homer,) lot 38, prop grist mill

Homer & Cortland Gas Light Company, (Homer,) James A Schermerhorn, president, Wm T Hicok, treasurer and secretary; Chas. H Parker, superintendent, J. H. Messenger, assistant superintendent

*HOMER FLAX AND CORDAGE MILL, (Homer,) John L Boorum, prop, Giles B Cooper, supt

Hopkins, Dan I , (Cortland,) lot 41, dairyryman and farmer 60

Hopkins, D S , (Cortland Village,) lot 41, dairyman and farmer 50

Hopkins, Melvin, (Cortland Village,) lot 31, dairyman and farmer 95

Hotchkiss, Ziba, (Homer,) lot 44, carpenter ar d joiner

HOUGH, WALTER, (East Homer,) lot 20, dairyman and farmer 150

Howard, Robert F , (Homer,) gardener and florist

Howe, Luman, (Homer,) lot 32, farmer 25

Hoys, Milo D , (Little York,) lot 6, carpenter and millwright

HOYT, HARRISON, (Homer,) (Hoyt & Smith,) deputy collector Internal Revenue and notary public

Hoyt, Joel, (Homer,) blacksmith

HOYT & SMITH, (Homer,) (Harrison Hoyt and Sam Tro Smith,) attorneys and counselors at law

HUBBARD, LYMAN, (Homer,) lots 25, 26, 35 and 36, dairyman and farmer 150

Hubbell, B B , (Homer,) lot 38, carpenter and joiner and farmer 18

Hulbert, Ira, (McGrawville,) dairyman and farmer with Lorin Hulbert

Hulbert, Lorin, (McGrawville,) lot 49, farmer 66

Hull, George N., (Homer,) lot 24, dairyman and farmer 84.

Hull, Harlom P , (Homer,) lot 13, dairyman and farmer 51½

Hull, Joel, (Homer,) lot 2, dairyman and farmer 103

Hull, J Dwight, (Homer,) lot 13, carpenter and joiner and farmer 7

Huntington, Winfield, (Homer,) lot 17, stock dealer and farmer 60

Huntley, Joseph, (Homer,) cooperage

Huntley, Silas C , (Homer,) lot 24, farmer 7

Hurlbut, Charles T., (Homer,) (with S S Hurlbut,) farmer

Hurlbut, Lesley L., (Homer,) lot 24, farmer leases 20

Hurlbut, Smith S , (Homer,) lots 23 and 24, dairyman and farmer 145

Huttleson, Lewis, (East Homer,) lot 29, carriage and wagon maker

HYNDS, A J., (Homer,) (Hynds & Northrup )

HYNDS & NORTHRUP, (Homer,) (A J Hynds and P S Northrup,) house, sign and ornamental painters and paper hangers

Ireland, John, (East Homer,) lot 39, dairyman and farmer 193

Ives, Edward, (Homer,) lot 16, dairyman and farmer 60

Ives, William M , (Homer,) lot 16, dairyman and farmer 58.

Jackson, Robert, (East Homer,) lot 40, dairyman and farmer leases of George Miller, 108

James, Capt , heirs of, (Homer,) lots 44 and 45, farmer 10.

Jebsom, Lewis R , (Homer,) telegraph operator and assistant freight agent

Janmars, James, (Homer,) lot 32, dairyman and farmer leases of Alva House, 181.

Jepson, Benjamin, (Homer,) prop. eating house, Homer depot

Johnson, Clara Mrs , (Little York,) lot 5, farmer 2½

JOHNSON, GEORGE, (Homer,) lot 46, dairyman and farmer 186

Johnson, Horace, (Homer,) lot 45, farmer 1

Jones, Amos, (Homer,) lot 14, dairyman and farmer 57

Jones, Erastus, (Homer,) lot 46, dairyman and farmer 100

JONES, NEWELL, (Homer,) (W T Smith & Co ) under sheriff

Jonas, Philo, (Homer,) lot 46, dairyman and farmer 119

Jones, Walter, (Homer,) lots 26 and 16, farmer 250

JOSLYN, CHARLES, (Homer,) lot 18, dairyman and farmer 106

JOSLYN, ORIN N , (Homer,) (with Wm A ) lot 18, dairyman and farmer 120

JOSLYN, WM. A , (Homer,) (with Orin N ,) lot 16, dairyman and farmer 120

Keeling, Henry D , (Homer,) lot 34, farmer 4

Keeling, Thomas, (Homer,) lot 45, carpenter and farmer

Kenney, E D & Co , (Homer,) props of Homer brewery and malt house

KEEP, TIMOTHY, (Homer,) lots 13 and 14, dairyman and farmer 190

Kenfield, Elijah, (East Homer,) lot 40, dairyman and farmer 104.

Kenfield, George, (East Homer,) lot 38, dairyman, thresher and farmer 50

Kenfield, John, (McGrawville,) lot 50, dairyman and farmer 72

KENNEDY, THOMAS H , (Homer,) lot 8, dairyman and farmer 243

Keys, John, (Homer,) lot 7, blacksmith

Kingsbury, Charles, (Cortland Village,) lot 47, dairyman and farmer 157.

KINGSBURY, PORTER C , (Homer,) (Haynes & Kingsbury )

Kinney & Collins, (Homer,) (Loammi Kinney and Chester A Collins,) merchant tailors

Kinney, Loammi, (Homer,) (Kinney & Collins )

Kinney, Maria W Miss, (Cortland Village,) school teacher

Kinney, Nathan, (Homer,) lot 13, farmer 6½

Klock, Stephen, (East Homer,) lots 39 and 20, dairyman and farmer 248.

Knapp, Miss F & Co , (Homer,) (Miss Abbie Bunn,) milliners.

KNAPP, JACOB S , (East Homer,) carpenter and builder

Knapp, John B , (East Homer,) lot 10, carpenter and farmer 49

Knapp, Levi, (East Homer,) lot 10, dairyman and farmer 50.

# R. H. SPENDLEY & CO.,

Wholesale and Retail Dealers in

# HATS, CAPS,

### AND

# FURS,

Corner Main and Court Streets, Cortland, N. Y.

---

## 3,000 Tons of Mowed and Pulled Flax Straw wanted at the

# HOMER FLAX & CORDAGE MILLS.

## JOHN L. BOORUM.

---

# W. H. VAN SLYCK,

## BILL POSTER,

# Circulator & Paper Hanger,

## CORTLAND, N. Y.

---

## ALFRED G. SMITH,

Manufacturer of and Dealer in

# BOOTS, SHOES & RUBBERS,

### Leather & Findings,

# MARATHON, N. Y.

A large assortment constantly on hand

# THE FLORENCE
# SEWING MACHINE,

## Is a Double Thread, Lock Stitch, Shuttle Machine.

It makes FOUR DIFFERENT KINDS OF STITCHES; it sews to the RIGHT or LEFT at option, by means of the

## Reversible Feed.    It Gathers a Ruffle,

AND

Sews it on at the Same Time,

There is no trouble with the TENSION, *it adjusts and arranges itself.* It is the

# BEST
# FAMILY
# SEWING
# MACHINE
# IN THE WORLD

And is giving everywhere it is shown, the best kind of **SATISFACTION.**

# W. C. ORCUTT,

General Agent for Central New York,

## No. 2 Yates' Block, E. Genesee Street,

**SYRACUSE, N. Y.**

Kocher, John J , (Homer,) tailor.

Lake, Reuben, (Homer,) lot 81, farmer 40

Lathrop, George M , (Homer,) lots 26 and 3b, farmer 83

Latimer, William, (Homer,) lot 42, dairyman and farmer 133

Lay, James, (Homer,) manufacturer and dealer in boots and shoes.

LEARNED, EDWARD W , (McGrawville,) lot 40, dairyman and farmer 100.

Linehan, Patrick, (East Homer,) lot 50, dairyman and farmer 102

Linehan, Timothy, (East Homer,) farmer (with Patrick Linehan )

LOCKE, BURREL B , (Homer,) lot 38, wagon and repair shop and farmer 4

Long, Patrick, (East Homer,) lot 38, farmer leases of Henry Musgrave, 35

Loomis, Ezra, M D , (Homer,) (E Loomis & Son,) physician and surgeon

Loomis, E. & Son, (Homer,) (Ezra and Geo W ,) druggists

Loomis, George W , (Homer,) (E Loomis & Son )

LORD, GEORGE W , (Homer,) lot 14, dairyman and farmer 98

Lord, Isaiah, (East Homer,) pastor of East Homer M E church

Lord, Richard, (Homer,) lot 45, gardener and farmer 14

Manchester, John, (Homer,) lot 12, dairyman and farmer leases of D H Hannum, 250

Marble, Martin, (Homer,) lot 42, farmer 20.

Martin, James, (Homer,) lot 37, dairyman and farmer leases of Joseph Corl, 86

Mason, E C , (Little York,) lot 6, prop Little York Hotel.

Mathews, Hiram, (Homer,) lot 34, farmer 23

Mathews, Willard E , (Homer,) lot 23, peddler and farmer 1

Maycumber, John, (Homer,) lots 45 and 46, farmer 15.

Maycumber, Mathew, (East Homer,) lot 8, dairyman and farmer 96

McDaniels, Geo. W , (Homer,) (Babcock & McDaniels )

McEvoy, Thomas, (East Homer,) lot 48, cooper, dairyman and farmer 131

McIntosh, James, (Homer,) surgeon dentist

MERRICK, MINER, (Homer,) lots 34 and 44, dairyman and farmer leases of D H Hannum, 185.

MERRILL, AUGUSTUS S , (Homer,) lot 2b, dairyman and farmer 100.

Miles, Joseph, (Homer,) lots 11 and 21, farmer leases of J Slover, of Summer Hill, 73,

MILES, PHILO, (Homer,) prop saw mill, dairyman and farmer

MILLER, ALFRED & SON, (Homer,) dealers in books, stationery, toys, yankee notions, &c , and agents for Grover & Baker's sewing machines

Miller, Geo P , (East Homer,) lots 30 and 20, saw mill and farmer 77

Miller, George W , (East Homer,) lot 40, farmer 108

Miller, Isaac, (Homer,) lot 39, dairyman and farmer 203

Miller, John K , (Homer,) lot 44, farmer leases of Mrs Pemelia Miller, 10.

Moran, Jane Mrs , (Homer,) lot 31, farmer 16

More, Charles W , (East Homer,) stone mason,

More, Nicholas, (East Homer,) lot 29, stone mason, carpenter and farmer leases 6

Morse, Daniel B , (Homer,) lot 47, farmer 10

Morse, Daniel D , (Homer,) lot 47, farmer 13,

MUDGE, POWERS C., (Little York,) lot 6, prop. of grist mill and grain dealer

Munger, J H., (Homer,) asst superintendent of Homer and Cortland Gaslight Co

Munger, J Hezekiah, (Homer,) dealer in drugs, medicines, hats, caps, stationery, toilet articles &c , also insurance agent

Murray, George,(Homer,) hardware, stoves, tinware &c.

Musgrave, Henry, (East Homer,) lots 48 and 39, farmer 50

MYNARD, JAMES E , (East Homer,) lot 19, dairyman and farmer 100

Nash, Lewis, (Homer,) lot 34, dairyman and farmer leases of I. M Sampson, 66

Newman, Elizabeth Mrs , (Homer,) lot 2, dairy and farmer 200

Newman, Peter, (Homer,) (with Mrs. E Newman,)

Newman, Rebecca Miss, (Homer,) school teacher

Newton, Alva, (Homer,) lot 27, farmer leases of Mrs Cornelia Gray of Cortland Village, 40

Niles, William B Dr , (Little York,) physician and farmer 2½.

NORTHRUP, P. S , (Homer,) (Hynds & Northrup )

Norton, William H , (Homer,) lot 35, dairyman and farmer 80.

Nye, Almareon T., (Homer,) dealer in butter.

O'Connor, Jeremiah, (Homer,) lot 36, farmer leases of Mrs Turner, 15

O'Conor, Patrick, (Homer,) lot 46, dairyman and farmer 150

Odell, Joshua, (Cortland Village,) lot 41, dairyman and farmer 158½

Ogden, David, (Homer,) lot 34, dairyman, mover of buildings and farmer 85.

Ormesby Daniel D , (Homer,) jewelry, watches &c

Out, Abraham, (Little York,) lot 7, dairyman and farmer leases of E P Stickney, 132

PALMER, GEORGE A , (Homer,) bookkeeper and secretary of Homer Lodge, No 852

Parker, Charles H , (Homer,) superintendent of Homer and Cortland Gaslight Co

PATTEN, JOHN, (Homer,) prop. of Patten's Hotel and billiard room

PAYNE, BARNEY W , (Homer,) lot 35, asst assessor internal revenue, insurance agent and farmer 25,

Peck, Lewis, (Homer,) lot 46, farmer 1

Pender, Joseph, (East Homer,) lot 29, farmer 24.

Perkins, Ebenezer, (Little York,) lot 6, farmer 5

J

Perkins, S D , (Little York,) lot 6, mason and farmer 88

Perry, E A , (Homer,) lots 12, 13 and 22, dairyman and farmer 150

Phelps, Darius B , (McGrawville,) lot 50, hop cultivator and farmer 55

Phelps, Francis, (McGrawville,) lot 50, farmer leases of E W Phelps, 218

Phillips, Cortland H , (East Homer,) lot 29, constable.

Phillips, Geo W , (Homer,) general merchant

Phillips, Levi, (East Homer,) lot 29, retired farmer

Phillips, Norman, (East Homer,) lots 28 and 18, farmer 96

Phillips, Orin, (Homer,) lots 16 and 17, farmer 75

Pickitt, William A , (Little York,) lot 5, farmer 85

Pierce, Justin M , (Homer,) justice of the peace

PIMM, GEORGE, (Homer,) (Pimm & Sidman )

PIMM & SIDMAN, (Homer,) (George Pimm and Peter Sidman,) custom blacksmiths

PINDAR, E B , (East Homer,) lot 29, carpenter, builder and wagon maker

PINDER, E B , (Homer,) lot 45, carpenter and builder

Plumb, Samuel, (Homer,) lot 35, farmer 27

Poppin, William, (Homer,) lot 42, dairyman and farmer leases of Mrs Amanda Reed, 140

Porter, Oliver, (Homer,) attorney at law

Pratt, Franklin F , (Little York,) lot 5, dairyman and farmer 50

Pratt, George T , (Little York,) (with John Pratt,) farmer

Pratt, John, (Little York,) lot 5, carpenter, dairyman and farmer 45

PRATT, JOSEPH D , (Homer,) carpenter and joiner, William st , Homer Village

Pratt, Melvin J , (Little York,) lot 15, (with S F Salisbury,) farmer

Preston, Ella Miss, (East Homer,) school teacher

Preston, E G & W W , (East Homer,) lot 20, manufacturers of solar salt vat rollers and farmers 46.

Preston, James, (East Homer,) lot 46, carpenter and repair shop and farmer 17

Price, Benjamin Dr , (Homer,) lots 23 and 24, allopathic physician and farmer 26

PRICE, JOAB H , (Homer,) lot 12, dairyman and farmer 110

QUINLAN, PATRICK, (Homer,) lot 33, dairyman and farmer 162.

Radway, M A , (Homer,) lot 24, dairyman and farmer 80.

Ranney, E G , (Homer,) lots 3 and 22, dairyman and farmer 190

Ransom, Adam G., (McGrawville,) lot 49, dairyman and farmer 100

REED, EDWARD C , (Homer,) attorney at law

Reed, Marvin, (Homer,) lot 42, (with Wadsworth,) dairyman and farmer 140

Reed, Wadtsworth, (Homer,) lot 42, (with Marvin,) dairyman and farmer 140.

REES, W D , (Homer,) treasurer of Homer Brass Band

RICE, ALBERT, (Homer,) lots 4 and 14, dairyman and farmer 250

Rice, R W , (Homer,) (with Albert Rice,) farmer

Riggs, Frederick L , (Homer,) (Riggs & Smith )

Riggs & Smith, (Homer,) (Frederick L Riggs and Philo F Smith,) grocers and provision dealers

Ripa, Thomas, (Homer,) lot 21, farmer 51½

Roark, Barton A., (Homer,) (Rockfellow & Roark )

Robins, Joseph H , (Homer,) lots 24 and 34, dairyman and farmer 71

Rockfellow, Levi, (Homer,) (Rockfellow & Roark )

Rockfellow & Roark, (Homer,) (Levi Rockfellow and Barton A Roark,) meat market

ROGERS & AKIN, (Homer,) (James A Rogers and George W Akin,) props of cider mill and vinegar factory and own 15 acres wine plant

Rogers, H N , (Homer,) lot 21, dairyman and farmer leases of Wm Rogers, 95½

ROGERS, JAMES A., (Homer,) (Rogers & Akin )

Rogers, William S , (Homer,) lot 21, dairyman and farmer 95½.

Rose, LaFayette, (East Homer,) lot 29, dairyman and farmer leases 200

ROSE, LUTHER R , (East Homer,) lot 29, prop of East Homer Hotel, postmaster and farmer 200.

Rose, Tobias L , (Homer,) lot 28, dairyman and farmer 100

Row, Sirenus, (Homer,) lots 18 and 28, dairyman and farmer 200

ROWLEY, DAVID R , (East Homer,) lot 80, dairyman and farmer 74

RUMSEY, HENRY D , (Homer,) photographer and portrait painter, Cortland st

Russell, Webster, (East Homer,) lot 19, dairyman and farmer leases of Beverly Gutchess, 80.

Salisbury, Burdett J , (Little York,) (with Milton L ,) lot 5, prop of peg factory, dairyman and farmer 295

Salisbury, Milton L , (Little York,) (with Burdett J ,) lot 6, prop of peg factory, dairyman and farmer 295

Salisbury, Stephen F , (Little York,) lots 5, 15 and 16 dairyman and farmer 112

Salisbury, William W , (Little York,) lot 5, lawyer, dairyman and farmer 114

Salisbury, Jay J , (Little York,) (D C. Harrington & Co )

Salisbury, Warren, (Homer,) lot 14, dairyman and farmer 160

Samson, Isaac M , (Homer,) prop of Temperance Hotel and farmer 55

Sanford, Heman H , (Homer,) principal of Cortland Academy

Schermerhorn, James A , (Homer,) president of Homer and Cortland Gas Light Company

SCHERMERHORN, SIMON, (East Homer,) lots 9 and 10, dairyman and farmer 120.

SCOTT, JOHN, (Homer,) (with Joseph,) lots 15 and 16, dairyman and farmer 218

SCOTT, JOSEPH, (Homer,) (*with John,*) lots 15 and 16, dairyman and farmer 218

Scudder, Anderson, (Little York,) lots 8 and 96, farmer 72

Scudder, John N , (Homer,) lot 18, carpenter and joiner, dairyman and farmer 82.

Scudder, Thomas C Jr , (Little York,) lot 6, farmer 28

Sears, Francis & Co , (Homer,) (*John H Crego,*) manufacturers of linseed oil and coal dealers

Sears, Odie M , (Homer,) dealer in flour, feed and groceries

Sessions, Charles C , (Homer,) lots 27 and 47, dairyman and farmer 61

Sessions, Henry, (Homer,) lots 17 and 27, dairyman and farmer 147

Share, L , (Homer,) lot 4, farmer leases of S R Baldwin, 25

Shearer, Reuben C , (Homer,) lot 36, dairyman and farmer 160

Sherman, Caleb H , (Homer,) (*Barber & Sherman*)

Sherman, James A , (Homer,) lot 47, retired farmer, owns 60 acres

Short, David, (East Homer,) lot 30, dairyman and farmer 51

SIDMAN, PETER, (Homer,) (*Pimm & Sidman*)

Simmons, Gideon H , (Homer,) lot 31, commissioner of highways, dairyman and farmer 212

SIMMONS, JOHN, (Homer,) lot 21, dairyman and farmer 105

Skeel, William W , (Little York,) lot 6, constable and conrt cryer

Slocomb, Calvin N , (Homer,) grocer

Smith, Giles, (Homer,) lots 26 and 25, wagon maker and farmer 16

Smith, Horace, (Homer,) lot 13, (*with H S Alvord,*) farmer

Smith, Leander, (Homer,) lot 35, dairyman and farmer 60

Smith, Philo F , (Homer ) (*Riggs & Smith*)

SMITH, SAM TRO, (Homer,) (*Hoyt & Smith* )

Smith, Solomon, (Little York,) lot 5, farmer 2.

SMITH, WILLIAM T , (Homer,) (*W. T. Smith & Co* )

SMITH, W. T & CO , (Homer,) (*Wm. T Smith and Newell Jones,*) carriage manufactory

Southworth, Leonard, (Homer,) lot 17, dairyman and farmer 118

Southworth, Norman, (Homer,) lot 17, dairyman and farmer 43

Spencer, Hiram H , (Homer,) lot 32, farmer 21

Spencer, Lydia Mrs , (Homer,) lot 31, farmer 11

Stafford, Henry, (Cortland Village,) lots 41 and 42, dairyman and farmer 135

Stafford, Leonard, (Cortland Village,) lot 41, dairyman and farmer 55

Starr, Nicholas, (East Homer,) lot 49, dairyman and farmer 188

Starr, Nicholas Jr., (East Homer,) inventor of Starr's chain horse power, horse fork, combined folding harrow and cultivator, and (*with N Storr Sen.,*) farmer

Stearns, Ephraim, (Homer,) lot 45, R R engineer and farmer 2

Stebbins, Aldana, (Homer,) lot 14, blacksmith, dairyman and farmer leases 100

Stebbins, Almua, (Homer,) lots 42 and 43, blacksmith shop and brewery, and (*with Lavoisure,*) dairy and farmer 191

Stebbins, Andrew, (Homer,) lot 43, dairyman and farmer 187

Stebbins, Franklin, (Homer,) lot 14, dairyman and farmer leases 160,

Stebbins, Joseph T , (Homer,) lot 43, dairyman and farmer 105.

Stebbins, Lavoisure, (Homer,) lots 42 and 43, (*with Almus,*) dairy and farmer 191

Stebins, Caleb V , (Homer,) lot 43, dairyman and farmer 166

Sticklin, Samuel J., (Homer,) lot 13, general book agent and farmer 65

Stickney, E P , (Homer,) retired farmer, owns 132 acres,

Stimson, Lucius, (Homer,) painter

Stoker, Benjamin, (Homer,) lot 43, dairyman and farmer 85

Stone, A , (Homer,) (*Stone Brothers* )

Stone Brothers, (Homer,) (*J A and W T ,*) foundrymen and machinists

STONE, DARIUS W , (Homer,) (*R. Blanshaw & Co* )

Stone, F. R , (Homer,) painter

Stone, J., (Homer,) (*Stone Brothers* )

Stone, W T , (Homer,) (*Stone Bros* )

Story, Daniel, (Homer,) lot 8, dairyman and farmer leases of John Hafey, of Syracuse, 170

Sumner, Henry D , (Little York,) lot 5, engineer and surveyor

Taft, L P , (Homer,) carpenter and joiner.

Taylor, A C , (Little York,) lot 6, carpenter and joiner

Taylor, E W , (East Homer,) lot 50, farmer 25

Terry, O E , (Homer,) photographer, cor. Main and James sts

Thomas, Catharine Mrs., (Homer,) lot 32, farmer 18

Thompson, Hammill, (Homer,) lots 45 and 46, farmer 115

Toppin, Martin, (Homer,) lot 32, painter

TOPPING, BENJAMIN N , (East Homer,) (*with Daniel D.,*) lot 8, dairyman and farmer 276

Topping, Daniel, (East Homer,) lot 8, farmer 47

TOPPING, DANIEL D , (East Homer,) (*with Benjamin N ,*) lot 8, dairyman and farmer 275

TOPPING, OLIVER H., (East Homer,) lot 29, mason and carpenter

Totman, David S , (Homer,) lots 15 and 16, dairyman and farmer 69

Townsend, Nicholas N , (Little York,) lot 6, dairyman and farmer 81

TRACY, LEANDER, (Homer,) lot 23, dairyman and farmer 73

TUBBS, IRA H., (Homer,) (*Wells & Tubbs* )

Turner, James, (Homer,) lot 37 farmer 4

Tuthill, Mrs E. H , (Homer,) milliner

Utley, Alfred, (East Homer,) farmer with Orin Utley.

UTLEY, C & B, J , (East Homer,) lot 29, prop'rs saw mill, cabinet shop and turning lathe

Utley, Orin, (East Homer,) lots 48 and 49, farmer 430

Van Denburg, Almeron H , (Homer,) (*with John R ,*) farmer

Van Denburg, John R , (Homer,) lots 25 and 26, dairyman and farmer 104

Wadtsworth, Enos, (Homer,) lot 31, dairyman and farmer 77

Wadtsworth, Manly, (Homer,) lot 44, farmer 25

Wagner, Amos B , (East Homer,) lot 10, farmer leases of Jabez Haight, 30

Wakefield, Henry, (Homer,) lots 1 and 11, dairyman and farmer 180

Walter, Hubbard M , (Homer,) lot 3, stock dealer and farmer 157½

Warn, George, (Little York,) lot 6, carpenter and builder and farmer 12

Warner, Theron R , (Little York,) lot 5, miller, cooper and farmer leases of W A Pickitt, 85.

Watson, Cyrus L , (Homer,) (*Jno Watson & Son*)

Watson, John & Son, (Homer,) (*Cyrus L ,*) druggists

*WATSON, JOSEPH, (Homer,) manufacturer of mantles, monuments, head stones, table tops, &c

Webb, Sumner C , (Homer,) physician

Welch, Vinson C , (Homer,) lot 34, farmer 76

Welch, William L , (Cortland Village,) lot 45, farmer 29

WELLS, FRANKLIN, (Homer,) (*Wells & Tubbs*)

WELLS & TUBBS, (Homer,) (*Franklin Wells and Ira H Tubbs,*) dealers in all kinds of harness, trunks, whips, blankets, &c

Wescott, Charles, (Homer,) carpenter and joiner

Wheadon, Charles H , (Homer,) harness maker and dealer in trunks, whips, &c

White, Thomas, (Homer,) prop of Homer Mansion House

White, Walter V , (Homer,) lots 34, 33 and 23, farmer 92

Whitney, James, (Homer,) lot 24, farmer leases 32

Wicks, John, (East Homer,) lot 10, farmer 40

WILBUR & BLANEY, (Homer,) (*John B Wilbur and William H H Blaney,*) meat market

WILBUR, JOHN B., (Homer,) (*Wilbur & Blaney*)

Willber, Thomas, (Little York,) lot 6, retired farmer

Williams, Mrs , (Homer,) lot 24, farmer 3

Williamson, Amasa, (Little York,) blacksmith

Willkins, Amos, (Homer,) lot 11, shoemaker and farmer 8

Willson, Parker B., (Homer,) lots 27 and 37, farmer 75

Winne, Mrs Ann, (East Homer,) lot 40, farmer 5

Wolsey, Henry R , (Homer,) prop of livery stable

Wood, Arlington, (Homer,) carpenter and joiner

Wood, Horace B , (East Homer,) lot 28, carpenter and joiner

Wood, Riley, (Homer,) lot 37, carpenter, cancer doctor and farmer 24

Wood, Scott, (Homer,) carpenter and joiner

Woodward, Alphena G , (Homer,) lot 38, dairyman and farmer 100

WOODWARD, CHARLES N , (Homer,) lots 37 and 47, dairyman and farmer 150

Woodward, Day E , (Homer,) lot 47, dairyman and farmer leases of Albert Sherman, 56

Woodward, Isaac D , (Homer,) lots 37 and 47, dairyman and farmer 95

Woodward, Otis B , (Homer,) lot 47, farmer 45

Wright, Egbert A , (Little York,) lots 5 and 7, dairyman and farmer 126

Young, John, (East Homer,) lots 20 and 30, dairyman and farmer 120

Zimmer, Philip, (Homer,) fashionable hair dresser

# LAPEER.

### (Post Office Addresses in Parentheses )

Allen, Mary Ann Mrs , (Lapeer,) lot 69, farmer

ALLEN, NATHAN A , (Marathon,) lot 57, dairy 15 cows and farmer 123½.

Alvord, Alfred, (Marathon,) lot 47, dairy 20 cows and farmer 224.

Atwood, Stephen, (Hunt's Corners,) lot 44, prop of upper leather tannery and farmer 50

Ayers, Franklin, (East Virgil,) lot 85, farmer

Ayers, Jesse, (Lapeer,) lot 58, dairyman and farmer 123

Ayres, Burden S , (East Virgil,) lot 60, farmer 15

Ayres, Darius, (East Virgil,) lot 59, dairy 10 cows and farmer 85.

Ayres, Rudolph, (East Virgil,) farmer.

AYRES, SARAH MRS , (East Virgil )

Baker, Jacob W , (Marathon,) lot 80, dairy 8 cows and farmer 49

Ballard, William, (Lapeer,) lot 66, dairy and farmer 50

Barrow, Isaac, (Hunt's Corners,) lot 37, dairy 9 cows and farmer 85

BAYS, JOHN, (Marathon,) lot 57, dairy 10 cows and farmer 100

Bell, Wallace, (Hunt's Corners,) blacksmith

BLISS, ISAAC, (Lapeer,) lot 38, dairy 6 cows and farmer 100.

Bliss, James W., (Hunt's Corners,) lot 38, dairy 7 cows and farmer 100

Bliss, Samuel S , (Lapeer,) lot 76, dairy 7 cows and farmer 60

BLODGET, WARREN, (Lapeer,) lot 76, inspector of elections, dairy 10 cows and farmer 163

Brazee, Eli, (Hunt's Corners,) lot 591, farmer 63

BROWN, ARNOLD, (Marathon,) lot 70, farmer

Brown, John, (Marathon,) lot 68, farmer 6

Brown, Margaret, (Lapeer,) lot 56, farmer 50

Burden, John, (Marathon,) lot 70, dairy 6 cows and farmer 100

Carrissa, Millious, (Hunt's Corners,) lot 591, farmer 160

Carter, Henry, (Marathon,) lot 80, dairy 11 cows and farmer 100

Chaplin, Benjamin F , (Messengerville,) lot 60, surveyor and engineer, dairy 6 cows and farmer 104

Chaplin, Walter L , (Messengerville,) lot 60, farmer 235

Clark, John, (Lapeer,) lots 76 and 86, dairy 24 cows and farmer 241½

CLEAVELAND, EUGENE, (Hunt's Corners,) lot 46, dairy 10 cows and farmer 96

CLEAVELAND, HENRY M , (Hunt's Corners,) lot 39, maker of spinning wheels

Cleveland, Nelson, (Hunt's Corners,) lot 39, farmer 100

Converse, Andrew M , (Lapeer,) lot 56, dairy 6 cows and farmer 100

COOK, ASAHEL, (Lapeer,) lot 56, dairy 10 cows and farmer 90

Darling, Sidney A., (Virgil,) lot 56, dairy and farmer 60

Davis, Peter H , (Hunt's Corners,) lot 46, carpenter and joiner, dairy 10 cows and farmer 109½

Day, Orrin S , (Hunt's Corners,) lots 543 and 595, dairy 14 cows and farmer 115

Delucia & Zeenah, (Marathon,) lot 79, custom weaving and farmer 62

ENSIGN, OZIAS W , (Hunt's Corners,) lot 594, farmer

Erskine, Smith, (Lapeer,) lot 66, farmer 100

EVANS, IRVIN W , (Hunt's Corners,) lot 54, dairy 12 cows and farmer leases 165

Forshee, John, (Hunt's Corner's,) lot 37, dairy 5 cows and farmer 60

FREEMAN, DELOS, (Lapeer,) lot 67, dairy and farmer 20

FREEMAN, DWIGHT, (Marathon,) lots 67 and 68, farmer 63

Freeman, Elijah, (Marathon,) lots 57 and 67, dairy 10 cows and farmer 110

Freeman, John W , (Marathon,) lots 56, 57 and 66, dairy 16 cows and farmer 135

Freeman, Orrin, (Hunt's Corners,) lot 42, carpenter and joiner and farmer 6

GLAZIER, CALVIN L , (Lapeer,) lot 76, carpenter and joiner, inspector of elections and farmer 46.

GOODALE, ASHER B , (Lapeer,) lot 77, dairy 5 cows and farmer 50.

GOODALE, GEORGE W , (Marathon,) lot 69, dairy 22 cows and farmer 177

Gray, Haley, (Marathon,) lots 69 and 70, dairy 18 cows and farmer 130.

GRAY, OGDEN, (Marathon,) lot 70, dairy 12 cows and farmer 125

Gray, Peter, (Marathon,) lot 70, dairy 12 cows and farmer 100

GRAY, WILLIAM E , (Marathon,) lots 69 and 70, dairy 14 cows and farmer 140

GROSS, PERRY D., (Marathon,) dealer in agricultural implements, selling town and county rights, also farmer 22¼.

HACKETT, ERON, (Hunt's Corners,) lot 42, blacksmith and farmer 8

Hall, Calsina, (Marathon,) lot 80, dairyman and farmer 36.

HAMMOND, JOHN H , (Hunt's Corners,) lot 42, boot and shoe dealer and grocer

Harvey, Dennis, (Lapeer,) lot 67, dairy 6 cows and farmer 70

Haskell, Benjamin, (Lapeer,) lot 56, dairy and farmer 61.

Haskell, Nelson, (Lapeer,) lot 56, dairy 8 cows and farmer 80

Hay, Lansing, (Lapeer,) lots 31, 32 and 86, prop of saw mill and farmer 371

Hay, Var Recssellaer, (Lapeer,) lot 76, dairy 10 cows and farmer 80

Hay, William H , (Hunt's Corners,) lot 33, dairy 10 cows and farmer 139

Hazen, Luke, (Marathon,) lots 55 and 55, dairy 11 cows and farmer 190.

Heffron, Dennis, (Marathon,) lot 76, shoemaker and farmer leases 29

Homer, Artemus G , (Lapeer,) lot 77, farmer 17½

HOPKINS, ARNOLD, (Hunt's Corners,) lot 42, dairy 12 cows and farmer 129.

Hopkins, Orlando, (Marathon,) lot 79, dairy 6 cows and farmer 50

HOPKINS, SAMUEL, (Lapeer,) lot 67, dairy 11 cows and farmer 101

Hopkins, Sheffield, (Lapeer,) lot 80, carpenter and joiner

Hudson, John, (Hunt's Corners,) physician and surgeon

Hunt, Asa, (Marathon,) lot 43, farmer 254½

HUNT, WILLIAM E , (Hunt's Corners,) lot 41, post master, dairy 20 cows and farmer 196

Janes, Henry, (Marathon,) lot 57, dairy 6 cows and farmer 100

JENNINGS, AARON B , (Virgil,) lot 597, dairy 16 cows and farmer 206

Jennings, Mason W , (Marathon,) lot 597, dairy 25 cows and farmer 216

JENNINGS, ORLANDO, (Hunt's Corners,) lot 40, dairy 11 cows and farmer 121

Jennison, Lucy, (Marathon,) lot 57, dairy 12 cows and farmer 148

JENNISON, SMITH B , (Marathon,) lot 57, dairy 9 cows and farmer 102.

Johnson, Abner, (Lapeer,) lot 67, dairy 10 cows and farmer 82½

Johnson, Abram B , (Marathon,) lot 80, dealer in sheep, dairy and farmer 80.

Johnson, Harvey, (Lapeer,) lot 78, dairy 6 cows and farmer 62

JOHNSON, HIRAM D., (Marathon,) lot 70, cattle dealer and farmer 119

Johnson, Horace, (Marathon,) lot 90, dairy 10 cows and farmer leases 70

Johnson, Horace B , (Marathon,) lot 80, dairy 10 cows and farmer 108

JOHNSON, JOHN, (Lapeer,) lot 78, dairy 7 cows and farmer 87

Johnson, Lee, (Hunt's Corners,) lot 42, dairy 18 cows and farmer leases 187½

Johnson, Lucion, (Marathon,) lot 79, dairy 7 cows and farmer 96,

JOHNSON, ROYAL, (Lapeer,) lot 78, post master and farmer 100

Johnson, Royal L., (Lapeer,) lot 78, dairy, farmer 50 and leases 100

Johnson, William, (Marathon,) lot 79, dairy 27 cows and farmer 240

Kloney, Sterry C., (Marathon,) lot 57, farmer 20.

LAIRD, CLINTON, (East Virgil,) lot 49, farmer

LATHROP, ERASTUS, (Lapeer,) lot 68, dairy 8 cows and farmer 92.

Luce, Ebenezer, (Lapeer,) lots 57 and 67, farmer 150

LUCE, WARREN, (Lapeer,) lots 67 and 37, dairy 11 cows and farmer leases 150

Mateon, Lyman, (East Virgil,) lot 56, dairy 12 cows and farmer 180

Matt, Alva, (Virgil,) lot 56, dairy and farmer 85

Ogden, John L , (Virgil,) lot 56, dairy 7 cows and farmer 90.

OGDEN, LORETTA L , (Marathon )

Ogden, Merrick, (Marathon,) lot 59?, dairy 11 cows and farmer 118½

PARKER, DARIUS, (Lapeer,) lot 58, dairy 15 cows and farmer 118

PARKER, ISAAC, (Lapeer,) lot 76, dairy 12 cows and farmer 188

Parker, James, (Lapeer,) lot 58, dairy 8 cows and farmer 77.

PARKER, MORTIMER W , (Lapeer,) lot 58, dairy 11 cows and farmer 108

Parker, Obadiah S , (Lapeer,) lot 58, town assessor, dairy 8 cows and farmer 68

Parker, Thomas, (Lapeer,) lot 67, dairy 16 cows and farmer 241¼

Parker, Wallace, (Hunt's Corners,) lot 32, dairy 15 cows and farmer 100

Pollard, Miles, (Hunt's Corners,) lot 59?, farmer

POTTER, ORRIN, (Lapeer,) lots 77 and 78, farmer 46 and leases 308

Quail, John, (Lapeer,) lot 56, dairy and farmer 112

QUAIL, ROBERT, (Lapeer,) farmer with W. B Quail

Quail, William B , (Lapeer,) lot 68, dairy 9 cows and farmer 123

Robinson, Eliphalet, (Marathon,) lot 59, dairy 15 cows and farmer 400.

ROBINSON, ELIPHALET Jr ,(Marathon,) lot 78, dairy 25 cows and farmer 220.

ROBINSON, JAMES, (Marathon )

Robinson, Lester, (Marathon,) lots 59 and 68, dairy 10 cows and farmer 83

Robinson, Simeon, (Marathon,) lot 60, dairy 18 cows and farmer 200

ROLINSON, ALANSON, (Marathon,) lot 59, dairy 10 cows and farmer 125

Runyan, David B , (Hunt's Corners,) lot 41, wagon maker and farmer 78

Seelye, William, (Lapeer,) lot 77, farmer 50

Sessions, John P , (Lapeer,) lot 79, dairy 15 cows and farmer 15

Seth, Parker, (Lapeer,) lots 67 and 68, farmer 50

Sexton, Erl, (Lapeer,) lots 78 and 77, dairy 14 cows and farmer 124

Shevalier, Jeremiah, (Marathon,) lot 79, dairy 8 cows and farmer 67

SMITH, CHARLES, (Marathon,) lot 80, dairy 8 cows and farmer 50

SMITH, LEROY, (Marathon,) lot 80, cattle dealer, dairy 12 cows and farmer 117.

SQUIRES, DANN C , (Lapeer,) lots 68, 69 and 78, justice of the peace, supervisor attorney, conveyancer, dairy 23 cows and farmer 383

SQUIRES, JEROME, (Lapeer,) lot 79, constable and farmer leases 150

STANLEY, RANSOM, (Marathon,) lots 68, 57, 58 and 59, dairy 18 cows and farmer 265.

STOCKWELL, WILLARD E., (Hunt's Corners,) lot 42, justice of the peace, prop of wagon and blacksmiths' shops

Sullivan, William, (Marathon,) lot 58, farmer 98

Snyder, Daniel O , (Hunt's Corners,) lot 84, dairy 13 cows and farmer 176

TALBUT, ALMERON, (Hunt's Corners,) lot 40, farmer

Talbut, Jacob, (Hunt's Corners,) lot 59?, farmer 4

Tarble, John, (Hunt's Corners,) lot 46, farmer 163 and leases 160

Terry, Oreon, (Lapeer,) lot 77, dairy 6 cows and farmer 71

Torry, Orrin L , (Lapeer,) lot 78, Methodist preacher, dairy 6 cows and farmer 80

Tryon, Freeman, (Lapeer,) lot 59?, farmer 47

Turner, David, (Lapeer,) lot 68, farmer 130

Tyler, Merrett, (Marathon,) lot 76, carpenter, joiner and farmer 10

Valentine, Geo N , (Lapeer,) lot 68, farmer

VALENTINE, JOHN A., (Lapeer,) lot 68, dairy 23 cows and farmer 197

VERRAU, CHARLES J , (Lapeer,) lot 79, custom boot and shoe maker and town clerk

Verran, Francis, (Lapeer,) lot 68, boot and shoe maker and farmer 8

Walker, Henry, (Lapeer,) lot 56, dairy 10 cows and farmer 120

Waters, Lyman, (Hunt's Corners,) lots 35 and 36, dairy 12 cows and farmer 193½.

Wauvle, Henry, (Marathon,) lot 79, dairy 27 cows and farmer leases 240,

Wheeler, Augustus, (Lapeer,) lot 67, dairy 6 cows and farmer

Willett, Jacob, (Marathon,) lot 52, boot and shoe maker.

Young, David, (Hunt's Corners,) lots 35 and 86, carpenter and joiner.

# MARATHON.

## (Post Office Addresses in Parentheses.)

ADAMS, CHARLES C , (Marathon,) real estate dealer and farmer 90

Adams, Lyman, (Marathon,) (*Tripp & Adams*)

Adams, Moses, (Marathon,) farmer 17

Albro, Archibald, (Marathon,) lot 82, farmer 65

Allen, Prentice S , (Marathon,) lot 75, farmer 160

Allen, William, (Marathon,) lot 73, farmer leases of Ruth Pierce, 27

Albee, Lizzie Mrs , (Marathon,) dress maker

Bacon, Ansel, (Marathon,) lot 81, farmer 170

Bacon, Solomon, (Marathon,) lot 81, carpenter, joiner and farmer

Baker, Austin, (Marathon,) (*Baker & Bro*)

Baker & Brother, (Marathon,) (*Austin E and Leonard T ,*) manufacturers and dealers in boots and shoes

BAKER, E D , (Marathon,) carriage manufacturer in all branches

BAKER, ELLIS L , M D , (Marathon,) eclectic physician

Baker, Joseph, (Marathon,) lot 81, farmer 18

Baker, Leonard T , (Marathon,) (*Baker & Bro*)

BARBER, ALBEM H , (Marathon,) station agent and foreman fire department

Barnes, E H , M D , (Marathon,) allop physician and surgeon

Bates, Otis L , (Marathon,) lot 82, farmer leases of Chas Simmons, 50

Baum, James N , (Marathon,) general merchant and agent for Florence sewing machine

Baum, Oliver, (Marathon,) lot 92, assessor and farmer 73

Beach, Philena, (Texas Valley,) lot 55, farmer 3

Bentley, W A , (Marathon,) (*Phillips & Bentley,*) farmer 16

Bhvio, Henry, (Upper Lisle, Broome Co ,) lot 95, farmer

Booth, Abram, (Marathon,) lot 75, farmer 86

BOURTHWICK, HARLOW , (Marathon,) (*Tanner & Bourthwick*)

Bouton, Charles H., (Marathon,) painter and farmer 8

BOUTON, NATHANIEL, (Marathon,) painter, general insurance agent, justice peace and farmer 5.

Bowdish, A C Rev , (Marathon,) pastor of M E Church

BOWEN, CHARLES D , (Marathon,) feather renovator

Bradford, William J , (Marathon,) pastor of Texas Presbyterian Church and farmer 6

Bradt, John H , (Marathon,) lot 61, farmer leases of Jabez Johnson, 100

BRINK, CHARLES, (Marathon,) carpenter and joiner and farmer 16½

*BRINK, CHAS G , (Marathon,) manufacturer and wholesale dealer in cigars

Brink, Chester, (Marathon,) farmer 279.

Brooks, James, (Marathon,) farmer 101

Brooks, L S & Co , (Marathon,) (*William J Holmes,*) props of Marathon Brewery

Bryant, Horace F., (Marathon,) surgeon and mechanical dentist

Bunn, Joseph D , (Marathon,) lot 85, millwright and prop steam saw mill

Burch, Levi S , (Marathon,) (*Carley & Burch*)

Burgess, Augustine, (Marathon,) (*Burgess Bros*)

Burgess Brothers, (Marathon,) (*George R. and Augustine,*) props meat market

Burgess, George R , (Marathon,) (*Burgess Bros*)

BURGESS, JAMES S , (Marathon,) (*L A Burgess & Son*)

BURGESS, LEWIS A , (Marathon,) (*L. A Burgess & Son,*) attorney, commissioner of excise, notary public and farmer 45

BURGESS, L A & SON, (Marathon,) (*Lewis A and James S ,*) props circular saw mill and planing machine

BURGESS, MOREAU, (Marathon,) carpenter and joiner and farmer 87

Campbell, Alvin, (Marathon,) lot 74, farmer

CARD, TRUMAN G , (Marathon,) undertaker and manufacturer and dealer in cabinet ware

CARLEY, ALANSON, (Marathon,) (*A. Carley & Son*)

CARLEY, ALBERTUS A , (Marathon,) (*A Carley & Son*)

*CARLEY, A & SON, (Marathon,) (*Alanson and Albertus A ,*) props Marathon Mills

Carley & Burch, (Marathon,) (*E Clark Carley and Levi S Burch,*) general merchants

Carley, E. Clark, (Marathon,) (*Carley & Burch,*) farmer 160

CARTER, CHARLES, (Marathon,) lot 54, farmer 160

Carter, Charles H , (Marathon,) lot 54, farmer 150

CARTER, GEORGE, (Marathon,) undertaker, manufacturer and dealer in cabinet ware and farmer 3

Casler, Henry, (Marathon,) lot 67, cheese box manufacturer

CHASE, ELISHA S & SON, (Marathon,) (*John L ,*) master builders

CHASE, JOHN L , (Marathon,) (*Elisha S Chase & Son,*) designer

Comstock, James, (Marathon,) justice of the peace and secretary of Marathon Cemetery

*CONE, HIRAM S., (Marathon,) manufacturer of window shades

Conger, Samuel, (Marathon,) produce dealer and farmer 102

Conradt, Jerome, (Texas Valley,) lot 55, farmer

Conradt, William, (Marathon,) lot 53, farmer 150

Coonradt, David, (Marathon,) lot 78, farmer leases of James Comstock, 20.

Coonradt, Nicholas, (Marathon,) lot 63, farmer 7

Corwin, Theo L , (Marathon,) dealer in harness, trunks &c

CRAIN, HANNAH B Mrs., (Killawog, Broome Co.,) lot 93

Crain, Lucien E , (Killawog, Broome Co ,) lot 93, farmer 230

CROSBY, J M , (Marathon,) framing pictures and hanging looking glasses

Davidson, Thomas, (Texas Valley,) lot 55, farmer

Davis, Adam W , (Marathon,) lot 63, carpenter and joiner and farmer 3

DAVIS, J M , (Marathon,) leader of Marathon Brass Band

DAVIS, ORSON, (Marathon,) lot 63, farmer 117

Dawn, P G Mrs , (Marathon,) milliner.

Dickinson, Horace, (Marathon,) prop of tannery and farmer 59

Dickinson, Jonathan, (Marathon,) lot 72, farmer

Dietrich, John, (Marathon,) lot 74, farmer 240

DORR, GEORGE N , (Marathon,) (*Griffith & Dorr*)

Draper, John, (Marathon,) lot 51, farmer

Durham, Fisher, (Marathon,) lot 73, farmer

Edwards R E , (Marathon,) general merchant

Feora, Patrick,(Texas Valley,) blacksmith

Ford, William H , (Marathon,) lot 84, farmer 85

Fralick, Elias, (Upper Lisle, Broome Co ,) lot 85, farmer 72

Fralick, Lysander P , (Marathon,) lot 75, farmer

Fralick, Walter, (Marathon,) lot 84, farmer 140

French, Calvin, (Texas Valley,) farmer 75.

GARDNER, NELSON, (Marathon,) lot 51, farmer 75

Gardner, William, (Marathon,) lot 51, farmer 155

Glover, Jacob 2nd, (Texas Valley,) lot 55, farmer 231

GOWDY, WILLIAM M , (Killawog, Broome Co ,) carpenter and builder, Lisle, Broome Co

*GRAY, J C , (Marathon,) jeweler and photograph artist

GRIFFITH & DORR, (Marathon,) (*William Griffith and George N Dorr,*) general merchants

GRIFFITH, WILLIAM, (Marathon,) (*Griffith & Dorr*)

Guernsey, Theron C , (Marathon,) lot 53, farmer 100

Hallock, Charles, (Marathon,) lot 52, farmer 100

Halsted, Joseph B , (Marathon,) lot 52, farmer 51

Hammond, C S , (Texas Valley,) lot 52, farmer 124

Hammond, Delos C ,(Texas Valley,) blacksmith and farmer 27

Hammond, George W., (Marathon,) lot 52, farmer 50

HAMMOND, SAMUEL, (Marathon,) lot 61, farmer 185

Hammond, Thomas L , (Texas Valley,) shoemaker

Harvey, Leonard W , (Marathon,) lot 62, farmer 95

HASBROUCK, GEORGE, (Upper Lisle, Broome Co ,) lot 95, farmer 80.

Hasbrouck, Levi, (Upper Lisle, Broome Co ,) lot 95, farmer 40

Hawley, Alexander F , (Marathon,) lot 93, farmer

Hawley, Sylvester, (Marathon,) lot 62, carpenter and farmer 2

HAWLEY, ZINA A , (Marathon,) lot 93, prop of brick yard and farmer 252

Hayes, Edward W , (Marathon,) lot 71, farmer leases of Burgess Squires, 117

Hazen, Lucian L , (Marathon,) prop of billiard room, dealer in horses, wool and lumber and farmer 14

Hillsinger, David, (Marathon,) prop saw mill

Hilsinger, Coonradt, (Marathon,) lot 72, mechanic and farmer 26.

Hilsinger, Peter, (Marathon,) lot 74, farmer

Hiltsinger, Albertus, (Marathon,) (*L P & A Hiltsinger,*) carpenter and joiner

Hiltsinger, Chauncey B ,(Marathon,) lot 73, farmer 116

Hiltsinger, David, (Marathon,) lot 74, farmer 220

Hiltsinger, Linden P , (Marathon,) (*L P & A Hiltsinger,*) millwright

Hiltsinger, L P & A , (Marathon,) (*Linden P and Albertus,*) props saw mill and farmer 105

Hiltsinger, William, (Marathon,) lot 52, farmer 6

Hinman, Seth V , (Marathon,) lot 84, farmer 121

Hinman, William, (Upper Lisle, Broome Co ,) lot 94, farmer 70

Holmes, Emma, (Marathon,) milliner and dress maker

Holmes, William J , (Marathon,) (*L S Brooks & Co*)

Hopkins, C B , (Marathon,) carpenter and joiner, mover of buildings and farmer 4

Hulbert, George A , (Marathon,) (*J Hulbert & Bro*)

Hulbert, Jerome, (Marathon,) (*J Hulbert & Bro*)

Hulbert, J & Brother, (Marathon,) (*Jerome and Geo. A ,*) produce dealers

Hulsinger, Barnabas, (Marathon,) lot 62, farmer 25

Hulslander, Wm, S , (Marathon,)lot 72, farmer leases of Nicholas Winters, 190

Hunt, Asa, (Marathon,)(*Hunt, Swift & Co ,*) farmer 200

Hunt, Burnham, (Marathon,) (*Hunt, Swift & Co* )

HUNT, CHARLES, (Marathon,) fashionable hair dresser, over post office

Hunt, Daniel D , (Marathon,) groceries, provisions, drugs and medicines, and farmer 45

HUNT, DeFOREST, M D , (Marathon,) allopathic physician and surgeon

Hunt, D M , (Marathon,) oyster saloon and grocery

HUNT, SAMUEL M , M D , (Marathon,) retired physician and farmer 100

Hunt, Swift & Co , (Marathon,) (*Asa and Burnham Hunt and Lewis Swift,*) hardware merchants

Husted, Ell B , (Marathon,) (*Husted & Lynde,*) farmer 215

Husted & Lynde, (Marathon,) (*Ell B Husted and Dewitt Lynde,*) clothiers

Isaaca, John J , (Texas Valley,) grocer and prop of U S Hotel

Jennings, Rufus H., (Killawog, Broome Co ,) lot 91, farmer 174

Johnson, Abner H , (Marathon,) farmer 105

Johnson, Alfred, (Marathon,) lot 71, farmer 20

Johnson, Jabez Jr , (Marathon,) lot 51, farmer 100

Johnson, Justus B., (Marathon,) lot 71, farmer 80

Johnson, Stephen S , (Marathon,) lot 61, farmer 175

Johnson, Washington G , (Marathon,) lot 71, farmer 85.

JONES, EDGAR, (Texas Valley,) lot 65, farmer 300.

Jones, Thomas, (Marathon,) lot 75, farmer 140

LA GRANGE, JOHN, (Marathon,) book and drug store

Lake, Henry M , (Marathon,) lot 71, cattle broker

Lathrop, Ezra H , (Killawog, Broome Co ,) lot 91, 223¼

LATHROP, JAMES H , (Marathon,) book store

Leach, Alfred, (Marathon,) lot 92, farmer 48.

Leach, Christopher W., (Texas Valley,) lot 65, harness maker and farmer 160

Lee, Simon, (Texas Valley,) lot 55, farmer 125

LITTLE, IRA L., (Marathon,) attorney and counselor at law

LIVINGSTON, CORNELIUS J , (Marathon,) lot 73, wagon maker and farmer 53

Livingston, Frank, (Marathon,) practical gunsmith

Livingston, James,(Marathon,) blacksmith

LIVINGSTON, JAMES JR , (Marathon,) prop Livingston saw mill and millwright

Livingston, Margaret L Mrs , (Marathon,) lot 73, tailoress

Locke, Nathaniel R , (Marathon,) (father of Petroleum V Nasby, P M , (which is postmaster,) Confederate X Roads, which is in the State ov Kentucky,) shoemaker

LOVELL, RANSOM M , (Marathon,) lot 73, farmer 80

Lombard, Nathan, (Marathon,) lot 52, farmer 36

Lyman, Huntington Rev., (Marathon,) pastor of Presbyterian church

Lynde, Dewitt, (Marathon,) (*Husted & Lynde* )

Lynde, Ira, (Marathon,) lot 83, farmer 120

Mack, William S., (Marathon,) cartman and farmer 4

Mallery, John H , (Marathon,) corporation collector and constable and farmer 213.

MALLERY, PATRICK, (Marathon,) farmer 315

MANCHESTER, MARY F MISS, (Marathon,) preceptress of Marathon Academy

MANCHESTER, STEPHEN, (Marathon,) principal Marathon Academy

MARATHON ACADEMY, (Marathon,) Stephen Manchester, principal, Miss Mary F Manchester, preceptress.

MARATHON MILLS, (Marathon,) A. Carley & Son, prop'rs, manufacturers and dealers in flour, meal, feed, grain, &c

*MARATHON WEEKLY NEWS, (Marathon,) published every Thursday, C Dwight Smith, Editor

MARICLE, SYLVESTER, (Marathon,) lot 73, carpenter and joiner and farmer

Marikle, Michael, (Marathon,) farmer 15

Marybew, Stephen, (Marathon,) lot 83, farmer

MAYBURY, F I , (Marathon,)(*R R Maybury & Co* )

MAYBURY, R R & CO ,(Marathon,)(*F I Maybury,*) manufacturers and dealers in harness, trunks and whips.

MAYNARD, ALTON B , (Marathon,) (*Tompkins & Maynard,*) homeopathic physician and surgeon and farmer 10

McCoy, Fanny, (Texas Valley,) tailoress and dressmaker

McDOWELL, CHARLES M , (Marathon,) lot 98, farmer

McMahon, Michael, (Marathon,) lot 62, farmer 50.

Meacham, Chancy, (Marathon,) lot 54, farmer 100

MEACHAM, EDGAR N , (Marathon,) prop of Meacham's Cheese Factory

Meacham, Eleazer D , (Marathon,) lot 52, farmer leases of E H Meacham

Meacham, Eleazer H , (Marathon,) lot 52, farmer 196

Miller, Catharine Mrs , (Marathon,) lot 71, farmer 1

Miller, Josiah L , (Marathon,) lot 81, blacksmith and farmer 1¾

Montgomery, Dubois, (Marathon,) lot 64, farmer 200

Moon, John C , (Marathon,) farmer 95.

Moore, George, (Marathon,) lot 92, farmer 50.

Moore, John, (Marathon,) lot 93, farmer leases of Patrick Malory, 310

Moore, William, (Marathon,) lot 84, farmer 100.

NICHOLS, CHESTER F , (Marathon,) carpenter and builder and prop of planing mill

Nichols, John D , (Marathon,) general tool maker

OAKLEY, GABRIEL L , (Marathon,) post master

OGDEN, GEORGE R , (Texas Valley,) lot 65, mason and stone cutter

Ogden, Oremenaz, (Marathon,) groceries and provisions, wall paper and notions

Parsons, Nelson W , (Marathon,) lot 64, farmer 50

Peck, Anson, (Marathon,) farmer 14

Peebles, Jonas B , (Upper Lisle, Broome Co ,) lot 85, farmer 50

PEEBLES, JOSEPH O , (Marathon,) lot 85, farmer 262

Penoyer, Garritt, (Marathon,) farmer 117.

Phettsplace, Thomas B , (Killawog, Broome Co ,) lot 91, farmer 169

Phillips & Bentley, (Marathon,)(*L S Phillips and W A Bentley,*) prop'rs of Marathon Tannery

Phillips, L. S , (Marathon,)(*Phillips & Bentley* )

Pickard, Morgan, (Marathon,) lot 64, farmer 150

Pierce, Albert, (Marathon,) farmer 220

PIERCE, DANIEL A , (Marathon,) lot 81, farmer 67.

Pollard, Richard, (Marathon,) lot 81, cooper and farmer 1

POLLARD, WALLACE R , (Marathon,) blacksmith

Potts, Charlotte, (Texas Valley,) lot 55

Potts, Cornelius M , (Marathon,) lot 53, farmer 129.

Powers, Wm W , (Marathon,) merchant tailor

Quinn, Alonzo, (Texas Valley,) lot 55, prop saw mill and farmer 5

Richardson, Chas M , (Marathon,) lot 82, farmer

Richardson, Isaac M , (Marathon,) lot 52, farmer 25

Richardson, John L ,(Upper Lisle, Broome Co ,) lot 95, farmer 94

Robertson, John M , (Marathon,) lot 53, farmer 26 and (*with Mary A and Martha J* ,) 87

Robertson, Martha J , (Marathon,) (*with John M and Mary A* ,) lot 53, farmer 87

Robertson, Mary A , (Marathon,) (*with Jno M. and Martha J* ,) lot 53, farmer 87

Robinson, John, (Texas Valley,) lot 55, farmer 50

Robinson, Lovell W , (Marathon,) lot 92, carpenter, joiner and farmer 37

Roe, John M , (Marathon,) produce dealer

Rogers, Moses, (Marathon,) prop Carley House, also Rogers House, Whitney's Point, and farmer 68.

Ryan, Patrick, (Texas Valley,) lot 55, farmer 141

Sage, J H Rev , (Marathon,) pastor of Marathon Village Baptist Church

Schouten, Jesse, (Marathon,) (*J W & J Schouten,*) farmer 97

Schouten, J W & J , (Marathon,) (*Jesse,*) grocers

Seber, Henry, (Texas Valley,) lot 55, carpenter, joiner and farmer 46

Sherwood, Clark, (Marathon,) lot 84, farmer 150

Sherwood, John, (Upper Lisle, Broome Co ,) lot 94, farmer 102.

Sherwood, Norman, (Marathon,) lot 84, wood mill and farmer 100

SHEVALIER, NICHOLAS, (Marathon,) lot 51, farmer 170

Shopley, Orswin, (Marathon,) lot 79, farmer leases of Mrs S L Pierce, 238

Shouls, Clinton, (Marathon,) prop Marathon House

Shueltz, L R , (Marathon,) hair dresser

*SMITH, ALFRED G , (Marathon,) manufacturer and dealer in boots and shoes

*SMITH, C DWIGHT, (Marathon,) editor of the Marathon Weekly News, published every Thursday.

Smith, Elbert B , (Upper Lisle, Broome Co ,) lot 94, farmer 75 and leases 95

Smith, Giles M , (Texas Valley,) pastor of the Presbyterian church

Smith, Jessie, (Marathon,) lot 61, farmer

SMITH, ORSON H , (Marathon,) horse shoer and jobber

Smith, Russell N , (Upper Lisle, Broome Co ,) lot 94, prop saw mill and farmer 210

Smith, Thomas Jr , (Marathon,) lot 81, carpenter and joiner and farmer 47

Squires, Burgess, (Marathon,)farmer 145½

Squires, George P , (Marathon,) lot 82, farmer 310

Stanley, Davison H., (Marathon,) lot 92, farmer 54

Stanley, Harris, (Marathon ) farmer 136

SWIFT EDWIN B , (Marathon,) (*George L. Swift & Co* )

SWIFT, GEORGE L , (Marathon,) (*Geo L Swift & Co* )

SWIFT, G.L & CO , (Marathon,) (*Geo L and Edwin B Swift,*) drugs and hardware

Swift, Lewis, (Marathon,) (*Hunt, Swift & Co* )

TANNER & BOURTHWICK, (Marathon,) (*Wallace Tanner and Harlow G Bourthwick,*) prop'rs livery stable

Tanner, Charles R , (Marathon,) lot 53, farmer 104¾.

TANNER, WALLACE, (Marathon,) (*Tanner & Bourthwick* )

Tarble, William L , (Marathon,) lot 71, farmer 159

Taylor, Ambrose S , (Marathon,) grocer and farmer 53.

Taylor, Francis M , (Marathon,) carriage manufacturer.

Taylor, Valentine, (Upper Lisle, Broome Co ,) lot 95, farmer

Terpenning, Marenus, (Marathon,) lot 71, farmer 140

Tillinghast, Thomas, (Marathon,) lot 93, farmer 200

Todd, Hiram, (Marathon,) (*with Samuel,*) farmer 30

Todd, Samuel, (Marathon,) lot 64, mason and farmer 45 and (*with Hiram,*) 30

TOMPKINS, FRANCIS F , (Marathon,) (*Tompkins & Maynard* )

TOMPKINS & MAYNARD, (Marathon,) (*Francis F Tompkins and Alton B Maynard,*)coopering in all its branches.

Tripp & Adams, (Marathon,) (*Jas H Tripp and Lyman Adams,*) general merchants

Tripp, James H , (Marathon,) (*Tripp & Adams* )

TURNER, JAY E , (Marathon,) lot 61, farmer 14 and leases of Russell Turner, 100

Turner, Russell, (Marathon,) lot 61, farmer 100

Upham, Thomas D , (Marathon,) lot 52, farmer 100

UPTEGROVE, LEWIS W , (Marathon,) lot 71, farmer 25

Valentine, Hiram K , (Marathon,) lot 54, farmer 105.

Valentine, William, (Marathon,) lot 63, farmer 82

VANVOST, WILLIAM S , (Marathon,) lot 64, farmer leases of Wm H Ford, 85

VOLZE, GEORGE, (Marathon,) prop bar ber shop and saloon, (sold to L. R Shueltz since our canvass )

Vunk, Alonzo H , (Marathon,) lot 75, farmer 50 and leases of Wm H Vunk, 165

Wakeman, David, (Marathon,) saloon keeper

Waller, Leonard S , (Marathon,) lot 93, farmer 172

WARD, LEWIS F., (Marathon,) fashionable tailor

Welch, Morris, (Texas Valley,) lot 55, farmer leases of C, S Hammond, 94

Welch, Richard, (Marathon,) lot 58, farmer leases of Michael McMahon, 80

WESTON, JOHN H , (Marathon,) blacksmith

Wheaton, Albert, (Marathon,) cartman

Whitmore, Daniel E , (Marathon ) school commissioner, insurance agent and farmer 26½

Wightman, Daniel, (Texas Valley,) lot 55, farmer 30

Wightman, Homer, (Marathon,) lot 64, prop of cheese factory and farmer 160

WILCOX, THURSTON, (Marathon,) farmer 126

*WILDEY, OSCAR, (Marathon,) dealer in dry goods.

Winters, Nicholas, (Marathon,) lot 72, farmer 192

WITTY, WILLIAM, (Marathon,) lot 91, farmer 123

Weed, Sherman L , (Texas Valley,) lot 65, farmer leases of Robert Davidson, 118

Weeds, Sylvester R , (Texas Valley,) lot 55, cattle broker and farmer 12

Weester, Milton A , (Marathon,) lot 51, farmer 180

Wright, Benjamin T , (Marathon,) attorney and counselor at law, solicitor of patents and general insurance agent

Young, Abram, (Marathon,) lot 62, farmer 150.

Young, James, (Marathon,) lot 62, farmer 36½

Youngs, Jedediah, (Marathon,) lot 63, farmer 85

YOUNGS, JOHN G , (Marathon,) lot 63, farmer

Youngs, Joseph, (Marathon,) lot 63, farmer 113.

---

# PREBLE.

## (Post Office Addresses in Parentheses )

Aldrich, Amasa G , (Preble,) lot 85, carpenter, joiner and farmer 77

Aldrich, George, (Tully, Onondaga Co ,) lot 59, dairyman, farmer 50 and leases 150

Aldrich, George, (Prable,) lot 59, dairyman, farmer 50 and leases 150

Aldrich, Stephen, (Preble,) lot 100, farmer 108

Avery, Martha Mrs , (Preble,) lot 99, farmer 17

Baldwin, Henry, (Preble,) lot 57, dairyman and farmer 47½

BALDWIN, SILAS, (Preble,) lot 57, dairyman and farmer 114

Ballard, Thomas, (Preble,) lot 97, farmer leases 24

Banks, Alanson, (Preble,) lot 65, farmer 28 and leases of Jno Briggs, 54

Beeman, David, (Preble,) lot 73, farmer 3

Beeman, James, (Preble,) farmer (with Nathaniel Beeman )

Beeman, Nathaniel, (Preble,) lots 68 and 78, farmer 110

BENNETT, JAMES E , (Preble,) lot 55, farmer 85

Bishop, George A , (Preble,) dentist

Blacklock, Fester, (Preble,) lot 100, dairyman and farmer 100.

Bradley, Thomas, (Preble,) lot 10, dairyman and farmer 50

Breed, James A , (Preble,) lot 56, farmer 10¾

Breed, James Mrs , (Preble,) weaver of rag carpets and woolen and linen cloths

Briggs, John, (Preble,) lot 55, farmer 54

Briggs, John B , (Preble,) lot 76, dairyman and farmer 60

Briggs, Wm B , (Preble,) lot 55, dairyman and farmer 50

Bugby, Rufus, (Preble,) lot 67, farmer 50 and leases of Mrs M Egbertson, 50

BURDICK, D W DR , (Preble,) physician and surgeon

BURDICK, P. H. DR , (Preble,) physician and surgeon and farmer 13

Burlingham, E F Mrs , (Preble,) lots 65 and 77, farmer 27

Burtis, John B , (Preble,) lot 66, dairyman and farmer 77

Burtis, S Arthur, (Preble,) (with John B ,) farmer

BUTLER, ADELBERT, (Tully, Onondaga Co ,) lots 70 and 80, assessor, dairyman and farmer 180

Butler, Roscoe, (Preble,) lots 79 and 80, farmer 110

Callen, D C , (Preble,) lot 97, prop threshing machine and farmer 50
Carhele, J C Mrs , (Preble,) lot 77, farmer
8
Carver, William, (Tully, Onondaga Co ,)
lot 60, dairyman and farmer 111
Churchill, Oliver, (Preble,) lot 65, dairyman
and farmer 80
COLLIER, CASPER, (Preble,) lots 77 and
78, farmer 50
Collier, Franklin J , (Preble,) lot 78, car-
penter and builder
Collier, Nicholas, (Preble,) lot 78, carpenter
and farmer leases 50
Collins, Joseph, (Preble,) lot 77, dairyman,
farmer 21 and leases 103
Conine, L M , (Preble,) lot 77, hardware
and tinware
Conine, Robert, (Preble,) lot 77, constable
and boot and shoe maker
Cornue, Annie Mrs , (Preble,) lot 77, mil-
liner
Cornue, Eugena, (Preble,) farmer (with H
S Cornue )
Cornue, Henry S , (Preble,) lots 79 and 89,
dairyman and farmer 171
Cornue, Job S , (Preble,) lot 77, mason,
blacksmith and wagon repairer
Cornue, Oscar, (Preble,) farmer (with H
S Cornue )
Crandall, Harrison, (Preble,) lot 100, far-
mer 25.
Crofoot, Annie Miss, (Preble,) school
teacher
Crofoot, D O , (Preble,) lot 97, dairyman
and farmer leases 203
Crofoot, David O , (Preble,) lot 66, (with
Wellington,) farmer 76
Crofoot, O E , (Preble,) shoemaker.
Crofoot, Wellington (Preble,) lot 66, (with
David O ,) farmer 78
Cummings, Adeen, (Tully, Onondaga Co.,)
lot 59, dairyman, hop cultivator and
farmer 100
Cummings, Chester, (Tully, Onondaga
Co ,) lot 59, farmer 150
Cummings, Chester, (Preble,) lot 59, far-
mer 150.
Cummings, Daniel M , (Preble,) lots 68 and
69, dairyman and farmer leases 95
Cummings, Harlan P , (Tully, Onondaga
Co ,) lot 59, dairyman and farmer leases
100.
Cummings, Harvey, (Preble,) lot 67, dairy-
man and farmer 143.
Cummings, James, (Preble,) lot 69, dairy-
man and farmer 105
Cummings, John B , (Tully, Onondaga
Co ,) lots 58 and 67, dairyman and far
mer 188
Cummings, Marvin, (Preble,) lots 68 and
79, dairyman and farmer leases 200
Cummings, Orlando J , (Preble,) farmer
with Harvey Cummings
Cumming, Silas, (Tully, Onondaga Co.,)
lots 59, 68 and 69, dairyman and farmer
195
Currie, John H , (Preble,) lot 90, dairyman
and farmer 60.
Dager, Peter, (Tully, Onondaga Co ,) lots
68 and 69, farmer 185
Dalley, C , (Preble,) lot 80, farmer 140.
Daley, Chester, (Preble,) lot 77, dairyman
and farmer 165

DALEY, EBEN, (Preble,) lot 77, stock
dealer, dairyman and farmer 210
Devraulx, Stephen, (Preble,) lot 78, dairy-
man and farmer 86
Dixon, John, (Preble ) lot 90, farmer 5
Dobins, John, (Preble,) lot 90, dairyman
and farmer 96
DUNBAR, ELAM, (Preble,) lot 77, farmer
42
Durkee, Erastus, (Preble,) lots 76 and 88,
dairyman and farmer 175
Egbertson, Alexander, (Tully, Onondaga
Co ,) lots 58 and 59, dairyman and far-
mer 130,
Egbertson, Andrew,(Preble,) lot 57, farmer
60
Egbertson, Barnet, (Preble,) lots 68 and
69, dairyman and farmer 200,
Egbertson, Henry W , (Preble,) lots 68 and
69, dairyman and farmer 175
Egbertson, Richard, (Preble,) lot 76,
dairyman and farmer 62½
ELLIOTT, T S , (Preble,) lot 77, carpen-
ter and joiner
Elliott, William, (Preble,) lot 99, dairyman
and farmer 110
Ellis, Robert, (Preble,) lot 90, dairyman
and farmer 94
ELSON, FREDERICK, (Preble,) lot 98,
dairyman and farmer 200
Etz, William N , (Preble,) lots 58 and 78,
prop hotel and farmer 80
Faning, Tim, (Preble,) lot 79, farmer 47
Ferguson, A H , (Preble,) lot 77, carpen-
ter and builder
Ferguson, John L , (Preble,) lot 77, consta-
ble and shoemaker
Folts, Peter, (Preble,) lot 70, dairyman and
farmer 216
Fox, Charles A , (Preble,) lot 75, dairyman
and farmer 87¾.
Fox, Joseph, (Preble,) lots 98 and 99, dairy-
man and farmer 102
Francisco, Anderson, (Preble,) lots 66 and
77, dairyman and farmer 125
Gay John, (Preble,) lots 65 and 66, dairy-
man and farmer 63.
Gay, John H , (Preble,) lot 75, dairyman
and farmer 70
Gay, William, (Preble,) lot 65, farmer 63.
Gitman, Jeff, (Preble,) lot 88, carpenter and
joiner
Gorman, John, (Tully, Onondaga Co ,) lot
56, farmer 100
Gorman, Philip, (Tully, Onondaga Co ,)
lot 69, dairyman and farmer 100
GRAHAM, JOHN B., (Preble,) (Graham &
Wellington )
GRAHAM & WELLINGTON, (Preble,)
(J B Graham and Harrison Welling-
ton,) lot 76, blacksmiths
Gray, John, (Preble,) lot 65, farmer 75
Gutsell, James, (Preble,) lot 77, pastor M
E. Church
Guy, Gurden, (Preble,) lot 65, carpenter
and joiner
Hall, Frank Miles, (Preble,) school teacher
Harris, C H , (Preble,) lots 88 and 97, far-
mer 250.
Harter, Henry F., (Tully, Onondaga Co ,)
lot 70, dairyman and farmer 286
Harter, W M., (Preble,) lot 97, cabinet
maker.

Hartman, Peter, (Preble,) lot 79, dairyman and farmer 147

Hasbrouck, Stephen, (Preble,) lots 77 and 87, carpenter, builder and farmer 7

Haviland, Henry, (Preble,) lot 88, dairyman and farmer 55

Haviland, John L , (Preble) lots 77 and 87, assessor and farmer 40

Haynes, A & Son, (Preble,) (Hiram,) lot 97, props saw, planing and cider mills, and turning lathe

Haynes, Calvin H., (Preble,) lot 67, stock broker

Haynes, Hiram, (Preble,) (A  Haynes & Son )

Haynes, J  D , (Preble,) lot 76, dairyman and farmer 140

Haynes, W  & P , (Preble,) lot 76, produce dealers

Helmer, Wm  J , (Preble,) carpenter, dairyman and farmer 65

Henry, Alexander, (Preble,) lot 75, dairyman and farmer 87½

Hey, George, (Preble,) lot 80, farmer 758

Highmoar, John, (Tully, Onondaga Co ,) lot 60, dairyman and farmer 111

Hilligne, John, (Preble,) lot 88, shingle maker

*HOAG, A  H , (Preble,) lot 77, wholesale dealer in butter, cheese and all kinds of farm produce

Hoag, Mary Mrs , (Preble,) milliner

HOAG, WILLIAM M , (Preble,) lot 77, carpenter, builder and contractor

Hobart, Jeremiah, (Preble,) lot 55, farmer

HOBART, SETH, (Preble,) lot 56, dairyman and farmer 120

Hoffman, Abner, (Preble,) lot 66, dairyman and larmer leases of A. Francisco, 121

Hollenbeck, Adelbert, (Tully, Onondaga Co.,) lot 58, farmer 1½

Hollenbeck, A H , (Preble,) lot 58, dairyman and farmer 101

Hollenbeck, Casper, (Tully, Onondaga Co ,) lots 57 and 58, dairyman and farmer 81

Hellenbeck, G , (Tully, Onondaga Co ,) lot 58, dairyman and farmer 108.

HOLLENBECK, HENRY, (Preble,) lot 57, dairyman and farmer 109

Hollenbeck, John G , (Preble,) lot 67, dairyman and farmer 105

Hollenbeck, Matthias, (Preble,) lot 87, farmer 5

Houghtaling, John, (Preble,) lot 88, farmer 10

Howard, Chester K., (Preble,) lot 77, farmer 10

Howard, Fredus, (Preble,) lot 77, justice of the peace and farmer 8.

Howard, Moses R , (Preble,) lot 77, resident

Hubbard, R B , (Preble,) lots 96 and 97, dairyman and farmer 125

Hunt, H D , (Preble,) lots 79 and 89, dairyman and farmer leases 207

Huntington, Reuben, (Preble,) lot 98, dairyman and farmer 100

Huntington, R  F , (Preble,) farmer (with Reuben Huntington )

JOHNSTON, RICHARD, (Preble,) lot 100, (with Wm ,) dairyman and farmer 100.

JOHNSTON, WILLIAM, (Preble,) lot 100, (with Richard,) dairyman and farmer 100

Kiff, William, (Preble,) blacksmith

King, Uri, (Preble,) (lives at Whitney's Point, Broome Co ,) lot 90, prop stave factory and farmer 375

KINGSLEY, TRUMAN, (Preble,) lots 79 and 89, prop stone quarry and farmer 55.

KINNER, C D , (Preble,) lot 77, general merchant

KLOCK, THERON H , (Preble,) lot 76, dairyman and farmer 150

Knapp, E H , (Preble,) lot 77, house and sign painter.

Knowlton, Chas J , (Preble,) lot 55, dairyman and farmer 66

Knowlton, Lafayette, (Preble,) lot 88, dairyman and farmer 130

Leverson, Abram, (Preble,) lot 77, dairyman and farmer 61

Leverson, Elliott, (Preble,) farmer (with Abram Leverson )

Long, John, (Preble,) lot 55, farmer 13 and leases 200.

Manchester, A , (Preble,) lot 55, dairyman and farmer 56

Manchester, Anthony, (Preble,) lots 57 and 58, farmer 53

MANCHESTER, JAMES, (Preble,) (with R H Van Buskirk,) lots 66 and 67, dairyman and farmer 280.

MARKHAM, CHESTER, (Preble,) lot 77, postmaster, boot and shoe maker and farmer 11

Maycumber, G W , (Preble,) lot 65, dairyman and farmer 109

McCue, Patrick, (Preble,) lots 56 and 57, farmer 140

McCumber, George, (Preble,) lot 77, resident

McCumber, Harriet Miss, (Preble,) dress maker and school teacher

McCumber, Martha Miss, (Preble,) school teacher

McCumber, R K , (Preble,) lot 86, dairyman and farmer leases 77

MERRY, BENJAMIN, (Preble,) lot 76, dairyman and farmer 104.

Mitchell, Robert, (Preble,) lot 79, farmer 100

Mitchell, R T , (Preble,) dairyman and farmer (with Robert Mitchell )

MOORE, EMORY, (Preble,) lot 86, dairyman and farmer 40

Morse, J B Rev , (Preble,) pastor of Presbyterian church

Murphy, Michael (Preble,) lot 75, farmer 21

Norton, L  P , (Preble,) lot 89, dairyman and farmer leases 156¾

O'Donell, Patrick, (Preble,) lot 100, dairyman and farmer 50

Orton, Henry, (Preble,) lot 96, dairyman and farmer 96

Out, J J (Preble,) lot 77, harness maker

Out, M  M , (Preble,) lot 77, depot and ticket agent for S  D R R., agent for U  S Express Co , telegraph operator, grain dealer and farmer 14

Pierce, Seril, (Preble,) lot 73, tanner and currier

Poor, Frederick, (Preble,) lot 67, farmer 25

PRATT, ORIN, (Preble,) lots 56, 67, 76, 77, 86 and 87, dairyman and farmer 76

PREBLE HOTEL, (Preble,) D  B  Van Auken, proprietor.

Rada, John, (Preble,) lot 90, farmer 100

RAYMOND, A B , (Preble,) lot 97, prop cheese factory

Ready, Morris, (Preble,) lot 80, farmer 135

REYNOLDS, JOHN, (Preble,) lot 75, dairyman and farmer 173.

Roe, John W , (Preble,) lots 55 and 65, dairyman and farmer 105

ROFE, BENJAMIN S , (Preble,) lots 98 and 99, dairyman, farmer 100 and leases of Lewis Frederick, Homer, 180

Rowe, Morris, (Preble,) lot 99, dairyman and farmer 135

Salisbury, William, (Preble,) lot 77, justice of the peace and farmer 8

SEARS, HENRY, (Preble,) lots 86 and 87, dairyman and farmer 116

Seedy, James, (Tully, Onondaga Co ,) lot 60, dairyman and farmer 130

Shea, J T , (Preble,) lot 59, farmer leases of Henry Monroe, Tully, Onondaga Co , 100

Shell, Henry, (Tully, Onondaga Co ,) lot 60, dairyman and farmer 140

Shoemaker, Adam, (Preble,) lot 80, dairyman and farmer 80

Shuler, Daniel W , (Preble,) lot 97, dairyman and farmer 130

Spaulding, Day, (Preble,) lot 99, prop stave mill and farmer 71

Sphan, L L , (Preble,) lot 78, carpenter and joiner.

SPORE, A. C & CO , (Preble,) (H M Spore,) drugs, liquors and groceries

SPORE, H M , (Preble,) (A C. Spore & Co )

Spore, Morris F , (Preble,) lot 77, prop and inventor of Spore's mechanical power improvement for pumping and churning

Squire, Charles, (Preble,) farmer (with Mrs Susan Square )

Squire, Susan Mrs , (Preble,) lots 86 and 87, dairyman and farmer 110

STANTON, ELIJAH, (Preble,) lot 87, prop of grist and saw mills, dairyman and farmer 250

Steele, James, (Preble,) lot 89, farmer 156½

Tallman, Chas P , (Preble,) farmer (with M T Tallman.)

TALLMAN, M T , (Preble,) lot 97, dairyman and farmer 203

Taylor, George D , (Preble,) lots 88 and 89, dairyman and farmer 166

TERWILLIGER, ABRAM, (Preble,) lot 66, dairyman and farmer 200

THOMAS, JEFFERSON, (Preble,) lot 87, miller, leases grist mill of E Stanton

Tully, H J B , (Preble,) lot 78, justice of the peace, dairyman and farmer 180

Tully, Newton G., (Preble,) lot 68, farmer

Tully, Wesley H , (Preble,) farmer (with H J B Tully )

Turner, Alanson, (Preble,) lot 86, dairyman and farmer 32

VAN AUKIN, D B , (Preble,) proprietor Preble Hotel

Van Buskirk, A H , (Preble,) lot 76, dairyman and farmer 102½

Van Buskirk, Charles L , (Preble,) farmer (with Leonard )

Van Buskirk, H M , (Preble,) lot 77, stock and produce dealer

Vanbuskirk, Isaac, (Preble,) lot 69, farmer 1.

Van Buskirk, John L , (Preble,) lot 77, farmer 102

Van Buskirk, Leonard, (Preble,) lots 55 and 56, dairyman and farmer 112

VAN BUSKIRK, R H , (Preble,) (with James Manchester,) lots 66 and 67, dairyman and farmer 230

Van Camp, S C., (Preble,) lot 77, teacher.

Van Denburg, Cornelius, (Preble,) lots 65, 66 and 7b, dairyman and farmer 54

VANDENBURG, RICHARD A , (Preble,) lot 86, dairyman and farmer 52¾.

Van Dinburg, D W , (Preble,) lot 77, carpenter and farmer leases 40

Van Hoesan, Caroline S Mrs , (Preble,) lot 67, farmer 12.

Van Hoesan, G S , (Preble,) lots 77 and 87, cooper and farmer 3.

Vanhoesan, Henry M , (Preble,) lot 77, cooper and dealer in bees and honey

Van Hoesan Platt, (Preble,) lot 67, dairyman and farmer 59

Van Hoesen, Albert, (Preble,) lot 87, resident

Van Hoesen, Albert M., (Preble,) lot 79, dairyman and farmer 147

Van Hoesen, Albert H , (Preble,) lot 88, dairyman and farmer leases 195

Van Hoesen, B F , (Preble,) lot 68, cooper and propagator of bees

Van Hoesen, Clark, (Preble,) farmer (with Nicholas )

*VAN HOESEN, E M & BRO , (Preble,) (Fred T.,) general merchants.

VAN HOESEN, FRED T , (Preble,) (E M Van Hoesen & Bro )

Van Hoesen, J S. Mrs , (Preble,) lot 68, dress maker

Van Hoesen, L. Mrs , (Preble,) lot 68, farmer 200

Van Hoesen, Loiss Mrs , (Preble,) lot 68, dairy and farmer 210

VAN HOESEN, MATTHIAS, (Preble,) lots 77 and 87, supervisor, lawyer and farmer 15

VanHoesen, Nicholas, (Preble,) lot 68, dairyman and farmer 100

VAN HOESEN, RICHARD S ,(Preble,)lot 88, dairyman and farmer 350

VanPatten, John R , (Preble,) lot 66, dairyman and farmer 225

VanPatten, Ryer, (Preble,) lot 56, farmer 70

WEEKS, H , (Preble,) lot 66, farmer 15

WELLINGTON, HARRISON, (Preble,) (Graham & Wellington )

Wells, Ezra,t(Preble,) lot 69, dairyman and farmer 90

White, John, (Preble,) lot 87, carpenter and joiner.

Wilber, Daniel W , (Preble,) lot 96, dairyman and farmer 118

Wilber, Edwin, (Preble,) lots 87 and 97, dairyman and farmer leases 60

Wilber, John, (Preble,) lots 87 and 97, dairyman and farmer 60

Willber, Isaac, (Preble,) lot 65, dairyman and farmer 72

Wood, Hiram, (Preble,) lot 100, farmer 50

Woolston, Joseph, (Preble,) lots 87 and 88, farmer 175

WOOLSTON, J D F , (Preble,) lots 87 and 88, surveyor, dairyman and farmer leases of Joseph Woolston, 175

# SCOTT.

(Post Office Addresses in Parentheses)

ALVORD, FENN G , (Scott,) farmer 81
ALVORD, JEREMIAH G , (Scott,) farmer 153
ALVORD, SHUBELL L , (Scott,) farmer 3
Alvord, William, (Scott,) farmer leases 3
Ames, Samuel, (East Scott,) farmer 115
Anthony, Comer, (Scott,) farmer 40.
Anthony, Harvey, (East Scott,) farmer 59
Anthony, Perrin, (Scott,) farmer 218½
Anthony, Rufus, (Scott,) farmer 10.
Babcock, Andrew J , (Scott,) farmer 75
Babcock, Burdett, (Scott,) farmer 10.
Babcock, Daniel, (Scott,) farmer 20
BABCOCK, D AUSTIN, (Scott,) tin and hardware merchant
BABCOCK, EZRA, (Scott,) mechanic
Babcock, Henry O , (Scott,) mechanic
Babcock, Henry W , (Scott,) merchant
Babcock, Hiram, (Scott,) blacksmith
BABCOCK, JARED E , (Scott,) farmer 25
BABCOCK, LEANDER H , (Scott,) merchant and justice of the peace
Babcock, Luke C., (Scott,) carpenter and joiner
Babcock, Thomas H , (Scott,) farmer 100
Babcock, William N , (Scott,) farmer leases 56
Bailey, Gordon, (Scott,) farmer 102
BARBER, A S., (Scott,) physician and house painter
BARBER, BYRON L., (Scott,) (Potter & Barber )
Barber, Clark J , (Scott,) farmer 20
Barber, George F , (Scott,) farmer
Barber, Henry, (Scott,) farmer 35.
BARBER, HENRY B , (Scott,) gunsmith, clock and watch repairer
Barber, John, (Scott,) shoemaker
BARBER, SILAS M , (Scott,) farmer 20
Barber, Welcome E , (Scott,) farmer 49
Barber, William W , (Scott,) farmer 123
Bedell, Wilford, (Scott,) farmer 30
BELLOWS, ISAAC N , (Scott,) grocer
BLACK, NORMAN C , (Scott,) (with Watson J ,) farmer 143
Black, Watson J., (Scott,) (with Norman C ,) farmer 143
Bockes, Smith, (Scott,) farmer 100
Brown, Amos, (Scott,) farmer 208
Brown, Dennison, (Scott,) farmer 75.
Brown, Jesse, (Scott,) farmer 285
Brown, John, (Scott,) farmer 107
Brown, Porter O , (Scott,) farmer 118½,
BROWN, SAMUEL C , (Scott,) prop livery.
Brown, Stephen S , (Scott,) farmer 148
Brown, William F , (East Scott,) farmer 102
Brown, Wm H , (Scott,) farmer 20.
Burdick, Amos R , (Scott,) farmer 5.
Burdick, D D L , (Scott,) house painter, paper hanger and undertaker.
Burdick, Edwin, (Scott,) painter
Burdick, Emerson I., (Scott,) (with Henry L ,) farmer 90
Burdick, Henry L , (Scott,) (with Emerson,) farmer 90.
Burdick, Hiram, (Scott,) farmer 90

K

BURDICK, JOSEPH T , (Scott,) constable and farmer 12
Burke, James, (East Scott,) farmer 64
Butts, Elias H , (Scott,) farmer 19
Butts, Reuben, (Scott,) farmer 100
Champlin, Jonathan, (Scott,) farmer 100
CHILDS, SAMUEL A , (Scott,) farmer 90
Churchill, Chauncy, (East Scott,) farmer 164.
Churchill, Lafayette M , (East Scott,) farmer 60.
CHURCHILL, SYLVENUS A ,(East Scott,) farmer 120
Churchill, Sylvester, (East Scott,)farmer 87
CLARK, ALEXANDER W , (Scott,) carpenter and joiner
Clark, Dwight, (Scott,) (with Salmon,) farmer leases 267
Clark, Elam, (Scott,) farmer 267
Clark, Elisha, (Scott,) carpenter and joiner and mason
CLARK, GERSHAM, (Scott,) farmer 45
CLARK, SALMON, (Scott,) (with Dwight,) farmer leases 267
Colwell, George, (East Scott,) farmer 67
COMSTOCK, JOHN L., (Scott,) (J L & L H Comstock )
COMSTOCK, J L & L H., (Scott,) (John L and Levi H ,) props. grist and saw mills and farmers 28.
COMSTOCK, LEVI H., (Scott,) (J. L. & L H Comstock )
Cook, W H , (Scott,) farmer 60
Cottrell, John B , (Scott,) farmer 135
Coventry, Hamilton, (Scott,) farmer 140
Crosley, Edmund D , (East Scott,) (with James A ,) farmer 223
Crosley, James A , (East Scott,) (with Edmund,) farmer 223.
Curtin, John, (Scott,) farmer 150.
Cutler, Almon, (Scott,) farmer 75
DALTON, JOHN , (Scott,) farmer 90
DANIELS, HENRY , (Homer,) farmer 110.
Davis, Martin L , (Scott,) farmer 115.
Dye, Annie, (Scott,) farmer 8.
Elston, William M , (Scott,) farmer 50
Fenton, James, (Scott,) prop saw mill.
Fish, John W , (Scott,) farmer 104
Fisk, Leonard, (Scott,) farmer 140
Frink, Jonas, (Scott,) carpenter and joiner
Frink, Martin, (Scott,) carpenter and joiner.
Frink, Martin M., (Scott,) carpenter and joiner
Frisbie, Elias T., (Scott,) (with George M and Mills G.,) farmer 200
Frisbie, George M , (Scott,) (with Elias T and Mills G ,) farmer 200
Frisbie, Mills G., (Scott,) (with George M, and Elias T.,) farmer 200
Fuller, Josiah P , (Scott,) farmer 100
Gay, Cornelius A , (East Scott,) farmer 62.
GERE, ABEL, (Scott,) farmer 81
Gillett, Charles H ,(Homer,) farmer 212
Gillett, John, (Homer,) lot 95, saw mill and carpenter
Gillett, John, (Homer,) farmer 245
GILLETT, JOHN H , (Homer,) farmer leases 245.

Gillett, John Jr , (Homer,) farmer
GOODALL, DAVID, (Scott,) farmer 47
Green, George S , (Scott,) farmer 150
Green, Wilmoth, (Scott,) farmer
Grout, Sylvenus, (Scott,) farmer 67
Gutchens, Theron, (Homer,) farmer 114
Hart, Jude, (Scott,) stone mason
Hazard, Francis, (Scott,) carpenter and joiner
HAZARD, GEORGE, (Scott,) blacksmith
Hazard, Henry, (Scott,) farmer 50
Hazard, Lewis S , (Scott,) carpenter and joiner
Herrington, Mortimer, (Scott,) (*with Whipples,*) farmer 58
Herrington, Whipples, (Scott,) (*with Mortimer,*) farmer 58
HOLKINGS, JAMES, (Scott,) (*Holkings & Snell*)
HOLKINGS & SNELL, (Scott,) (*James Holkings and John W Snell,*) carriage and sleigh makers
Hull, Martin, (Scott,) lot 2, farmer 65.
Hunt, George W , (Scott,) lot 2, stock dealer and farmer leases 126½
Hunt, G W . (Scott,) farmer 51
Hunt, Sarah Y Mrs , (Scott,) (*with Miss Mary Picket,*) lot 2, farmer 162¾
Hunt, William D , (Scott,) farmer
HUTCHENS, PHINEAS JR., (Scott,) salt manuf
HUTCHINSON, EDWIN D , (Scott,) shoemaker
Jenks, Rensselaer, (Scott,) farmer 150
Jones, George, (Scott,) farmer 24.
KELLOGG, CYRUS S , (East Scott,) farmer 220
Kent, Joseph, (Scott,) farmer 10.
Kenyon, Charles W , (Scott,) farmer 180
Kinney, Nathan A P , (Scott,) farmer 200
KLOCK, JOHN H , (Scott,) prop, Scott Hotel
Knapp, Martin E , (Scott,) farmer 12
Knight, Philander,(Little York,) farmer 240
Larison, Peter B., (Scott,) stone mason
Littlefield, William, (Little York,) farmer 45
MABIE, AARON, (Scott,) carpenter and joiner
Mahony, Dennis, (Scott,) farmer 34
Mahony, Timothy, (Scott,) farmer 30
MATHER, JOHN, (Scott,) millwright
Maxson, Albertus, (Scott,) cooper
Maxson, Amos R , (Scott,) stone mason and farmer 42
MAXSON, E U MRS , (Scott )
Maxson, George W , (Scott,) farmer 90
Maxson, George W., (Scott,) physician and surgeon
Maxson, Henry J , (Scott,) shoemaker
Maxson, Ira, (Scott,) farmer 80
Maxson, Morgan, (Scott,) carpenter and joiner and farmer 50
Maxson, Wilber, (Scott,) cooper
MEEKER, HENRY REV , (Scott,) Methodist clergyman
Melvin, James, (Scott,) telegraph operator.
Miller, Zenos, (Homer,) farmer 60
MONROE, JOSEPH, (Scott )
Moon, Benjamin, (East Scott,)(*with Wesley,*) farmer 96
Moon, Wesley, (East Scott,) (*with Benjamin,*) farmer 66

MORGAN, WILLIAM H , (Scott,) harness maker
Mott, Edward P , (Scott,) farmer leases 120.
Mott, Rodman, (Scott,) farmer 120
Mowry, George L , (Scott,) butcher
Niver, Elijah, (Scott,) farmer 127
NIVER, HENRY A , (Scott,) grocer and druggist
Northway, Jared H , (Scott,) farmer 143
Norton, Arthur M , (Sc tt,) farmer 185
Naman, Timothy, (Scott,) farmer 150
O'Brien, John, (Little York,) farmer 70.
Peck, Augustus D , (Scott,) farmer 140
Pickett, Erl, (Scott,) farmer 180
Pickett, E Franklin, (Scott,) farmer 180
Pickett, Mary Mrs , (Scott,) (*with Mrs Sarah Y Hunt,*) lot 2, farmer 162½
POTTER & BARBER, (Scott,) (*E H P. Potter and Byron L Barber,*) props of cheese factory
POTTER, E. H P , (Scott,) (*Potter & Barber* )
Potter, Thomas, (Scott,) farmer 70
PRATT, EDWIN W , (Scott,) farmer 107
Randall, Hosea, (Scott,) fisherman
Rice, Merick, (East Scott,) farmer leases 32.
ROE, VOLNEY C., (East Scott,) farmer 85
SALISBURY, ARTEMAS, (Scott,) farmer 130.
Salisbury, Nathan, (Little York,) farmer 150
Sargeant, Russell, (Scott,) farmer 18
SCOTT, OSCAR W , (Scott,) merchant
SCOTT, SAMUEL, (Scott,) farmer 50
Scott, Samuel J , (Scott,) lumberman
Share, James, (Scott,) farmer
Share, William (Scott,) farmer 22
Skelly, James, (Scott,) dealer in horses
SMITH, DAVID, (East Scott,) farmer 127
Smith, Erastus B , (Scott,) farmer 100
Smith, Frank, (Scott,) farmer leases 75
SNELL, JOHN W , (Scott,) (*Holkings & Snell* )
Southwick, Geo W , (Scott,) prop grist mill and shingle mill.
Spencer, Edwin D , (Scott,) dealer in patent rights
Spencer, Oliver, (Scott,) carpenter and joiner
SPRINGER, ALONZO B , (Scott,) farmer 125
Stanton, Carlos B , (Scott,) dealer in patent rights and farmer 40
Stevens, Elisha, (East Scott,) farmer 160
Stevens, Elisha B., (East Scott,) farmer leases 160
Stevens, George F , (East Scott,) farmer 155
Stevens, Horace B , (East Scott ) farmer 16
Stoker, Samuel, (Scott,) farmer 92
Stowe, Gardiner H , (Scott,) shoe maker
Sweeny, James, (Scott,) farmer 89
SWEET, CHARLES H , (Scott,) farmer 50
Sweet, Stephen, (Scott,) farmer 50
Truman, Irving P , (Scott,) homeo physician
Underwood, Harlow E , (East Scott,) farmer 105
Underwood, Timothy W , (East Scott,) farmer 120
Underwood, William, (East Scott,) farmer 80

VANDENBURGH, CHAPMAN L., (Homer,) farmer 30
Vandenburgh, Richard, (Homer,) farmer 145
Vanefer, Elias, (Scott,) farmer 1.
Vanhoozen, George, (Scott,) blacksmith.
Vincent, John L , (Scott,) farmer 160
Wakefield, George, (Scott,) farmer 98
Wakefield, James, (Scott,) farmer 100
Wakefield, Richard, (Scott,) farmer 43.
WATERS, DAVID C , (Scott,) allopathic physician
Weeks, Arnold P , (Scott,) lot 9, farmer 93

West, James K., (Scott,) farmer 45 and leases 55
West, Levi L., (Scott,) prop. of flax mill and farmer 60
Wheeler, Mary, (East Scott,) farmer 37
Whitcomb, Eugene F , (Scott,) farmer leases 130
Whiting, Anson L , (Scott,) dealer in flax and farmer 70
WHITING, HAMILTON I., (Scott,) dealer in flax
Williams, Benjamin, (Scott,) farmer 140
Williamson, John, (Scott,) farmer 23

---

# SOLON.

## (Post Office Addresses in Parentheses.)

Ackerman, Nelson, (McGrawville,) lot 51, farmer
ADAMS, ELI, (McGrawville,) lot 82, justice of the peace and farmer 110
Allen, Lorenzo, (Solon,) lot 95, farmer 50
Atkins, Albert H., (McGrawville,) lot 92, farmer 253
Atkins, Alfred, (McGrawville,) lot 92, farmer 50
Atkins, Jacob, (McGrawville,) lot 92, farmer 66
Atwood, Wm L , (McGrawville,) lot 81, carpenter and farmer 18½
BABCOCK, ISAAC S., (Solon,) lot 73, blacksmith.
Barnes, Patrick, (Solon,) lot 55, farmer 18
Bean, Cyrus, (McGrawville,) lot 62, farmer 210
Beher, Peter, (McGrawville,) lot 61, farmer 90.
Benjamin, Willard J , (McGrawville,) lot 81, farmer 180
BINGHAM, HENRY G , (Solon,) lot 63, dairy 10 cows, farmer 96.
BINGHAM, HORACE, (McGrawville,) lots 51 and 52, dairy 14 cows, farmer 105
BINGHAM, SAMUEL, (McGrawville,) lot 62, dairy 14 cows, farmer 130.
Blake, Jason, (Solon,) lot 64, dairy and farmer 80
Brooks, J L , (McGrawville,) (with Samuel A ) lot 71, prop saw mill
Brooks, Samuel A , (McGrawville,) (with J L ) lot 71, prop saw mill
Brown, John, (Solon,) lot 75, farmer leases 75
Brownell, David I Jr , (McGrawville,) lot 43, justice of the peace, dairy 12 cows, farmer 126
Brownell, David I. Sen , (McGrawville,) lot 43, farmer 10.
Burges, Gershom, (Solon,) lot 54, dairy 8 cows, farmer 82
BURKE, WILLIAM, (Solon,) lot 73, blacksmith

Burlingham, Emily Mrs , (Solon,) lot 73, farmer 25
Burlingham, George R , (Solon,) lot 73, mason
Burlingham, James, (Solon,) lot 64, dairy 13 cows, farmer 110
Burlingham, Johanna, (McGrawville,) lot 62, farmer 104
BURLINGHAM, MELDRIM, (Solon,) lot 54, carpenter and joiner and farmer 50.
BURNS, AARON, (McGrawville,) lot 71, dairy 14 cows, farmer 106
Barnes, Edward, (Solon,) lot 73, mason
Butman, John T , (Solon,) lot 94, farmer 65.
Caffrey, Patrick, (Solon,) lot 55, dairy 15 cows, farmer 110
Caruthus, John, (McGrawville,) lot 81, farmer 130.
CASS, COLUMBUS C , (McGrawville,) lot 61, dairy 27 cows and farmer 425
CHAPIN, ARZA, (McGrawville,) lot 42, dairy 15 cows, farmer 122.
CHAPIN, CHARLES B , (McGrawville,) lot 42, dairy, farmer 45
Chapin, Geo W , (McGrawville,) lot 42, farmer (with Hiram )
CHAPIN, HIRAM, (McGrawville,) lots 42 and 43, dairy 16 cows, farmer 130.
Coburn, Emery, (McGrawville,) lot 61, farmer 4
Daffy, Daniel, (McGrawville,) lot 51, farmer
Davis, Samuel, (McGrawville,) lot 83, farmer 245.
Davis, Walter, (McGrawville,) lot 61, farmer 3
Diper, Edward, (McGrawville,) lot 93, farmer 75
Dolan, Mary, (Solon,) lot 54, farmer 83
DONOGHUE, WILLIAM H , (Solon,) lot 74, carpenter and joiner
Doran, James, (Solon,) lot 95, farmer leases 109
DORTHEY, MICHAEL, (Solon,) lot 54, dairy 16 cows, farmer leases 184.

Dowd, Bernard S., (Solon,) lot 54, tanner and currier and farmer 98
Edwards, Elijah, (Solon,) lot 75, farmer 211
Edwards, Elijah, (Solon,) lot 75, farmer 170
Elwood, George W., (Solon,) lot 76, farmer 11
Elwood, Washington, (Solon,) lot 75, farmer 11
Emerson, Betsey, (Solon,) lot 74, farmer 50
Emerson, Elizabeth, (Solon,) lot 74, farmer 50.
Faint, George, (Solon,) lot 55, dairy 5 cows, farmer leases 112
Finn, James, (Solon,) lot 85, farmer 78
Finn, Thomas, (Solon,) lot 85, farmer 105
FISH, ROBERT B., (Solon,) lot 64, dairy 10 cows, farmer 125
Fox, George W., (Solon,) lot 74, shoemaker and farmer 5
Frazier, Henry, (Solon,) lot 93, farmer 123
Gardiner, George, (McGrawville,) lot 92, hop grower and farmer 73
Gardner, Aaron, (Solon,) lot 93, farmer 60
Gates, Martin, (McGrawville,) lot 43, farmer 7½
Gates, Henry, (McGrawville,) lot 52, farmer 121
Gilbert, David, (McGrawville,) lot 41, farmer 12
Gilbert, Moses, (McGrawville,) lot 41, farmer 25
Graves, Furman, (McGrawville,) lot 71, farmer 20
Graves, Polly, (McGrawville,) lot 81, farmer 24½
Gray, Thomas, (McGrawville,) lot 53, farmer 65
GREENMAN, HENRY B., (McGrawville,) lot 81, farmer leases 120
Greenman, Lora W., (McGrawville,) lot 82, farmer 62
Greenman, Wm L., (McGrawville,) lot 81, farmer 200.
Haley, Rodger, (McGrawville,) lot 52, dairy 13 cows, farmer 115
Hammond, Henry, (McGrawville,) lot 42, dairy 26 cows, farmer leases 172
HAMMOND, JASON D., (Solon,) (with Jas C Thompson,) lot 44, dairy 20 cows, farmer 124
Hanley, Henry, (Solon,) lot 55, dairy 24 cows, farmer 172.
Harden, William, (Solon,) lot 54, dairy 11 cows, farmer 112
Harvey, Chilus, (Solon,) lot 95, farmer 60.
Hatch, John, (Solon,) lot 82, farmer 50
Hatch, John, (McGrawville,) lot 91, farmer 118
HATHAWAY, CALVIN L., (Solon,) lot 73, administrator of the late Samuel G Hathaway's estate, 2,600 acres
Haughton, John, (McGrawville,) lot 61, farmer 75
Haye, Philip, (Solon,) lot 73, farmer
Haynes, Martin, (Solon,) lot 73, retired farmer.
Healey, Thomas, (McGrawville,) lot 41, farmer 30
Healy, Patrick, (McGrawville,) lot 41, farmer 40.
Hernon, Thomas, (Solon,) lot 64, farmer 112
Hickey, John, (Solon,) lot 73, carpenter and joiner and farmer 6½

Hobart, John P., (McGrawville,) lot 52, dairy 10 cows, farmer 66
Holden, Adelbert, (Solon,) lot 74, farmer 82½
HOLDEN, EDWARD C., (McGrawville,) lot 61, breeder and dealer in Ayrshire cattle, dairy 15 cows and farmer 122
Horton, John, (McGrawville,) lot 51, farmer 80
Hoyt, I Jerome, (Solon,) lot 85, farmer 117
Johnson, George, (Solon,) lot 41, farmer 51
Kelly, Patrick, (Solon,) farmer leases 100
Kelly, William, (Solon,) lot 55, dairy 18 cows, farmer 172
KERRIGAN, PATRICK, (Solon,) lot 73, farmer
Knap, E., (Solon,) lot 93, farmer 28.
Knapp, Ethmar, (McGrawville,) lot 93, farmer 80
Lannigan, Patrick, (Solon,) lot 54, farmer 15
Leek, Lyman, (Solon,) lot 84, farmer 210
Livingston, Abel, (Solon,) lot 85, farmer 100
Loomis, Jane Mrs., (McGrawville,) lot 92, farmer 55
Loop, John F., (Solon,) lot 95, farmer 50
Madden, William, (Solon,) lot 55, dairy 17 cows, farmer 92
MAIN, DANIEL, (McGrawville,) lot 42, dairy 12 cows, farmer 125
Manchester, Whitcomb, (Solon,) lot 64, dairy 12, farmer 178
Marks, Christopher, (Solon,) lot 44, farmer 20
Martin, Giles, (McGrawville,) lot 62, farmer 210
Martin, Simmons, (McGrawville,) lot 82, farmer 30
Martin, Simmons, (Solon,) lot 82, farmer 257
Matteson, Cyrus, (McGrawville,) lot 82, carpenter and farmer 30
MAYBURY, EUGENE B., (McGrawville,) lot 43, dairy 12, farmer 106
Maybury, Jerome, (McGrawville,) lots 51 and 41, dairy 8 cows, farmer 105
Maybury, John R., (Solon,) lot 63, dairy 8 cows, farmer 55
MAYBURY, LUCIEN, (Solon,) lot 64, mason and farmer 40
McGUYRE, SAMUEL, (Solon,) lot 73, attorney and justice of the peace
McKENDRICK, JOHN, (Solon,) lots 44, 54 and 55, assessor, dairy 27 cows, farmer 250
McKendrick, Peter, (Solon,) lot 72, farmer 15.
Miller, Paul S., (McGrawville,) lot 81, farmer leases 120
Miller, Samuel, (Solon,) lot 84, farmer (with P McGraw.)
MORRIS, JOHN, (Solon.)
MORRIS, WILLIAM, (Solon,) lot 65, dairy 22 cows, farmer 238
MOSES, PHILO F., (McGrawville,) lot 71, prop of flouring and custom grist mill, farmer 17
Moses, Philander P., (McGrawville,) lot 71, miller and millwright
Nickelson, Amy, (McGrawville,) lot 61, carpenter and joiner and farmer 9
O'Brien, Michael, (McGrawville,) lot 51, dairy 25 cows, farmer 170

O'Brien, Michael, (McGrawville,) lot 51, farmer 163
O'Donnell, Margaret Mrs., (McGrawville,) lot 41, dairy 50 cows, farmer 330.
O'DONNELL, PATRICK, (McGrawville,) lot 50, farmer 75
O'Donohue, Ann, (McGrawville,) lot 43, farmer 300.
Palmer, Earl, (McGrawville,) lot 71, dairy 8 cows, farmer 60
Parmer, Eli, (Solon,) lot 72, carpenter and joiner.
Peck, Hiram, (Solon,) (*with Nancy,*) lot 94, farmer 173.
Peck, Hiram, (McGrawville,) lot 94, farmer 173
Peck, John, (McGrawville,) (*with Platt,*) lots 61, 62 and 72, dairy 14 cows, farmer 307
PECK, LYMAN JR., (Solon,) (*R T Peck & Brother*)
Peck, Nancy, (Solon,) (*with Hiram,*) lot 94, farmer 173.
Peck, Platt, (McGrawville,) (*with John,*) lots 61, 62 and 72, dairy 14 cows, farmer 307
PECK, RUFUS T, (Solon,) (*R T Peck & Brother,*) postmaster
PECK, R T & BROTHER, (Solon,) (*Rufus T and Lyman Jr,*) merchants and produce buyers
Perry, Eliza, (McGrawville,) lot 41, farmer 24
PERRY, OLIVER D, (McGrawville,) lot 52, dairy 10 cows, farmer 75
Perry, Orrin O, (McGrawville,) lot 61, farmer leases 21½
Phelps, Henry, (Solon,) lot 95, farmer 147
Phelps, John, (Solon,) lot 85, farmer 85½
PHELPS, RUSSELL, (Solon,) lot 44, farmer 84
Phelps, William H, (Solon,) lot 85, farmer 85
PIERCE, A SMITH MRS, (Solon,) lot 73, prop of hotel and farmer 47½
PIKE, EZRA O, (McGrawville,) lot 42, carpenter and joiner
Prichard, Amos, (Solon,) lot 73, farmer 70
Prichard, Garret, (Solon,) lot 75, farmer 850½
Pritchard, Joel, (Solon,) lot 64, farmer 35 and leases 70.
Quigley, Mickel, (Solon,) lot 71, farmer leases 110
Randall, Orin,(Solon,) lot 74, town assessor, dairy 15 cows and farmer 114
RANDALL, WILLIAM, (McGrawville,) lot 71, shoe maker and farmer 20
Rawley, James H, (McGrawville,) lot 63, farmer 225
Reeves, Careline, (Solon,) lot 93, farmer 44
Rice, Rufus, (McGrawville,) lot 52, farmer 25
Ripley, Thomas L, (Solon,) lot 95, farmer 75
Roby, Jefferson, (McGrawville,) lot 81, farmer 21
Roden, Andrew, (McGrawville,) lot 92, farmer 86
Royce, Frank L, (McGrawville,) lot 51, farmer 191
Ryan, James, (Solon,) lot 95, farmer 62
Ryan, Mathew, (Solon,) lot 44, dairy 10 cows, farmer 75

Shattuck, DeWitt C., (McGrawville,) lot 82, dairy 7 cows, farmer 66.
Shular, Ransom, (McGrawville,) lot 51, dairy 16 cows, farmer 71.
Smith, Alfred, (Solon,) lot 85, farmer 180½.
SMITH, EPHRAIM Z, (Solon,) lot 63, farmer leases 57
Smith, Robert, (Solon,) lot 65, dairy 12 cows, farmer 95
Steele, James, (Solon,) lot 73, carpenter and joiner and farmer
Stephens, Ira, (Solon,) lot 58, farmer 81
Stephens, John, (Solon,) lot 78, farmer 20.
Stephens, John, (Solon,) lot 63, mason and farmer 20
Stevene, Amos, (Solon,) lot 53, farmer 114.
STEVENS, JACOB, (McGrawville,) lot 72, farmer 100
Stevens, Joseph, (McGrawville,) lots 52 and 62, dairy 18 cows, farmer 175.
Stevens, Septimus, (McGrawville,) lot 52, dairy 12 cows, farmer 96
Stevens, Silas, (Solon,) lot 53, farmer 75
STONE, HARVEY J, (Solon,) blacksmith, town clerk and constable, farmer leases 70.
Stone, Nathan, (Solon,) lot 55, farmer leases 205.
Stone, Nelson, (Solon,) lot 72, farmer leases 111
Taylor, Daniel B, (McGrawville,) lot 52, dairy 15 cows, farmer 123
Thayer, Edward E, (McGrawville,) lot 91, farmer 50 and leases 80
THOMPSON, JAS C, (Solon,) (*with Jason D Hammond,*) lot 44, dairy 20 cows, farmer 124
Thornton, Gideon, (Solon,) lot 45, dairy and farmer 42.
THORNTON, WILLIAM H, (Solon,) lots 44, 45 and 55, dairy 11 cows, farmer 180
TOTMAN, M L, (McGrawville,) lot 61, town collector, dairy 10 cows, farmer 97
Traverse, Gilbert, (McGrawville,) lot 71, dairy 24 cows, farmer leases 206
Tydiogs, Daniel, (Solon,) lot 63, farmer 195
Underwood, Eliah, (McGrawville,) lot 91, farmer 515
UNDERWOOD, ELIAS, (McGrawville,) farmer leases 200
Underwood, Uriah, (McGrawville,) lot 93, farmer 100
Walker, Samuel, (McGrawville,) lot 83, farmer 92.
Walworth, Rodolphus, (Solon,) lot 65, farmer 131
Warren, Alfred, (McGrawville,) lot 41, dairy 8 cows, farmer 100
Warren, Nicench, (McGrawville,) lot 51, farmer 87½
Warren, Percs, (McGrawville,) lot 51, dairy 12 cows, farmer 100.
WARREN, RANSOM, (McGrawville,) lot 42, dairy 26 cows, farmer 200
Welsh, Thomas, (Solon,) lot 94, farmer 114.
WHEELER, JOHNSON, (Solon,) lot 72, supervisor of the town and farmer 65
White, Asa, (Solon,) lot 84, farmer 204
Widger, Elkanah, (McGrawville,) lot 45, farmer 122.
Widger, Harvey, (McGrawville,) lot 45, farmer 400.

Wilcox, David, (McGrawville,) lot 61, farmer 89

Wilcox, David, (McGrawville,) lot 61, dairy 10 cows, farmer 130

Wilhey, Rufus, (Solon,) lot 74, farmer 60.

Woolsay, Lewis, (McGrawville,) lot 61, farmer leasee 63

WORDEN, JAMES, (Solon,) lot 73, hotel proprietor,

Wovle, Andrew, (Solon,) lot 74, farmer 70

---

# TAYLOR.

### (Post Office Addresses in Parentheses )

Allen, Alonzo C , (Solon,) *(with Leonard D ,)* lot 66, prop of saw mill and farmer 150.

Allen, Amanzo W , (Taylor,) lot 57, farmer 50.

Allen, Ambrose W , (Taylor,) lot 68, farmer 56

Allen, Arwin B , (Taylor,) lot 56, blacksmith and farmer 51

Allen, Leonard D , (Solon,) *(with Alonzo C ,)* lot 86, prop of saw mill and farmer 150

ALLIS, ALBERT, (Union Valley )

Allis, Israel, (Union Valley,) lot 48, farmer 88

Andrews, Clarinda, (Taylor,) lot 99, farmer 80.

Angel, Almon W , (Union Valley,) lot 60, justice and farmer 100

Angel, Jerome W., (Union Valley,) lot 60, allo physician

Angel, William C., (Union Valley,) lot 60, farmer 20

BAKER, P L , (Union Valley,) lot 60, farmer 60

BARBER, ALBERT D , (Union Valley,) lot 48, farmer 95

Barber, Calvin M , (Taylor,) lot 58, carpenter and farmer 43½

Barber, Orin C , (Taylor,) lot 58, farmer 40

Barker, Austin N , (Taylor,) lot 76, farmer 285

Beator, Daniel E , (Taylor,) lot 77, farmer 62½

Belden, Luman, (Union Valley,) lot 59, farmer 20

Bennett, Almon D., (Union Valley,) lot 49, farmer 53

Bowen, Asahel, (Union Valley,) lot 48, farmer 5

Boyd, Henry T , (Cincinnatus,) lot 88, farmer 225

Boyd, Orrin R Mrs , (Cincinnatus,) lot 98, farmer 106

Breed, William, (Union Valley,) lot 60, farmer 39

Brooks, Alfred, (Union Valley,) lot 60, farmer 56

Brooks, Asahel S , (Union Valley,) lot 70, farmer 165

Brooks, Nelson L , (Union Valley,) lot 60, postmaster and farmer 76

Brooks, Ransom, (Union Valley,) lot 50, farmer 54,

Brooks, Russall, (Taylor,) lot 75, farmer 125

Brooks, Thomas J , (Union Valley,) lot 60, farmer 92

BROOKS, WALTER S , (Taylor,) lot 68, farmer 139

Brown, Isaac P , (Taylor,) lot 79, farmer leases 72

Brown, Lorenzo W , (Pitcher, Chenango Co ,) lot 80, carpenter and farmer 12

Brown, Miles, (Taylor,) lot 69, farmer 78½

Burlingham, James E , (Truxton,) lot 46, farmer leases 50

BUSH, JAMES, (Taylor,) lot 46, farmer 160

BUSH, JAMES, (Taylor,) lot 67, farmer 88.

Cass, Joseph S , (Taylor,) lot 88, farmer 99

Cass, Ruggles A , (Taylor,) lot 77, farmer 130

Cass, Seth H , (Taylor,) lot 90, farmer 75

Chatfield, Curtis, (Taylor,) lot 100, constable, collector and farmer 1½

Clement, Daniel R , (Taylor,) lot 99, farmer 4.

Clowe, William, (Union Valley,) lot 60, eclectic physician

Converse, Adolphus, (Union Valley,) lot 60, farmer 5

CORNING, BENJAMIN L , (Union Valley,) lot 59, farmer 112½

Cotton, Henry S , (Taylor,) lot 57, farmer 50

COYE, JAMES R , (Union Valley,) lot 60, shoemaker

Craft, Eleazur, (Taylor,) lot 69, farmer 129.

Craft, Horace, (Taylor,) lot 58, farmer 201

Crane, Thomas, (Taylor,) lot 89, farmer 280

DAVIS, KELSEY, (Union Valley,) lot 48, farmer 100

Debell, John, (Taylor,) lot 89, farmer 33

DEBELL, TRUMAN, (Taylor,) lot 89, farmer 61

Elwood, Wilson M , (Taylor,) lot 69, farmer 12¾

Faint, George, (Taylor,) lot 57, farmer 168

FINN, LEROY D , (Solon,) lot 75, farmer 60

Fisk, Solomon, (Taylor,) lot 68, farmer 142

Forbes, Oramel F , (Taylor,) lot 99, farmer leases 100

Forrey, Esther, (Union Valley,) lot 60, farmer 22

Foster, Charles, (Taylor,) lot 58, farmer 52.

Fox, Arthur B , (Union Valley,) lot 60, farmer 92

Fox, Ira, (Taylor,) lot 58, farmer 42.

FRENCH, ALONZO H , (Taylor,) lot 58, farmer 45

Fuller, Bardett, (Union Valley,) lot 70, farmer 72

Fuller, Sullivan, (Union Valley,) lot 70, farmer 137

Gage, George W , (Taylor,) shoemaker

Garity, Mary, (Solon,) lot 90, farmer 64½

Gay, Sumner H , (Truxton,) lot 66, farmer 303.

Godard, Alonzo R , (Taylor,) lot 77, carpenter and farmer 2

Godard, Charles E , (Taylor,) lot 67, farmer 102

Goraline, William, (Pitcher, Chenango Co.,) lot 80, prop of cheese factory and farmer 396.

Green, Harriet, (Union Valley,) lot 60, farmer 60

Halbert, Enos, (Taylor,) (with Seth,) lot 79, farmer 242

Halbert, Ransom, (Taylor,) lot 76, farmer 123.

Halbert, Seth, (Taylor,) (with Enos,) lot 79, farmer 242.

HAWLEY, FRANCIS, (Taylor,) lot 77, justice and farmer 388.

HAWLEY, O. F , (Taylor )

Hawyer, Wallace, (Union Valley,) lot 48, farmer 100

Heath Chandler B , (Taylor,) lot 69, farmer 268.

Henry, Hiram, (Taylor,) lot 87, farmer 25

Hill, Jefferson O , (Truxton,) lot 66, farmer 214.

Holmes, Benjamin, (Truxton,) lot 46, farmer 14

Holmes, Leonard, (Taylor,) lot 88, farmer 182.

Holmes, Morris, (Truxton,) lot 46, farmer 243.

Hopkins, Jonathan, (Cincinnatus,) lot 96, farmer 25.

Hutchinson, Andrew, (Taylor,) lot 99, farmer 106

Jaquins, George E., (Taylor,) lot 78, farmer 260

JIPSON, DANIEL, (Union Valley,) lot 80, farmer 125

Jipson, Elijah, (Union Valley,) lot 80, merchant and farmer 25.

JIPSON, JAMES, (Union Valley,)

JIPSON, MICAHAL, (Union Valley,) lot 50, farmer 160

JOHNSON, ALBERT J., (Taylor,) lot 89, farmer 210.

Jordan, Albert H , (Taylor,) lot 78, farmer 126

JORDAN, PETER, (Taylor,) lot 68, farmer 52

JOSLIN, CLARK JR., (Taylor,) lot 59, farmer 120.

Kingsbury, Philander, (Union Valley,) hotel keeper and blacksmith

Lewis, Isaac, (Taylor,) miller

Lidell, Eugene, (Taylor,) lot 66, farmer 11

LIDELL, LERANCE H., (Taylor,) lot 66, farmer 50¼

Lidell, Levarna, (Taylor,) (with Allen,) lot 66, farmer 286.

Lieber, William, (Taylor,) farmer 88

Liever, Henry, (Taylor,) lot 78, farmer 154.

Livingston, John D , (Cincinnatus,) lot 86, farmer leases 212

Loop, Charles, (Taylor,) lot 47, farmer 70

LOOP, JOHN, (Taylor,) lot 48, farmer 50

Lord, Jared, (Taylor,) lot 67, farmer 175.

Lyon, Pardon H , (Union Valley,) lot 50, farmer leases 111.

Maine, Lewis J , (Taylor,) lot 79, farmer 150

MALLORY, FRANK L., (Taylor.)

MALLORY, LEVI, (Taylor,) lot 93, farmer 94

Manchester, William A., (Solon,) lot 47, farmer 58.

McDonald, George W , (Cincinnatus,) (with James L ,) farmer 150

McDonald, James L , (Cincinnatus,) (with George W ,) farmer 150

Miner, George W , (Union Valley,) lot 59, farmer 100

Mudg, Perry C , (Cincinnatus,) lot 87, farmer 118

Mudge, Martin K., (Cincinnatus,) lot 86, farmer 49.

Murray, William, (Cincinnatus,) lot 97, farmer leases 155

Neff, Benjamin, (Union Valley,) lot 47, farmer 80

NEFF, BENJAMIN L , (Union Valley,) lot 47, farmer 34

Neff, Luther, (Union Valley,) lot 47, farmer 22

Newell, Horace, (Taylor,) lot 87, farmer 200

Oliver, Orlando, (Union Valley,) lot 68, farmer 25.

Oliver, William H , (Taylor,) lot 47, farmer 26

Osborne, Ransom, (Taylor,) pastor of Wesleyan church.

Parker, Charles H., (Cincinnatus,) lot 93, farmer 198

Parks, Calvin E , (Pitcher, Chenango Co ,) lot 70, farmer 160

PERRY, HIRAM, (Truxton,) lot 56, prop of saw mill and farmer 108.

Perry, Mervin O., (Truxton,) lot 56, farmer 116

PERRY, NAHUM, (Truxton )

PHILLIPS, JOHN M., (Union Valley,) lot 49, farmer 58¼

Porter, Asenath, (Union Valley,) lot 59, farmer 4

POTTER, CHAUNCY D , (Taylor,) painter.

Potter, Edmund, (Taylor,) blacksmith, justice and postmaster

Potter, Harriet N , (Taylor,) lot 100, farmer 68.

Potter, Joel, (Union Valley,) lot 49, farmer 53

Potter, John I V , (Union Valley,) lot 48, prop of saw mill, grocer and farmer 140

Potter, Paris, (Union Valley,) lot 49, farmer 53

Potter, Philander, (Union Valley,) lot 58, farmer 64.

POTTER, SYRA, (Union Valley,) lot 59, farmer 59

Pudney, George S , (Taylor,) lot 57, carpenter and farmer 50.

Pudney, Hiram, (Taylor,) lot 57, farmer 88

Pudney, John A , (Taylor,) lot 57, farmer 80

Pudney, Mervin L , (Cincinnatus,) lot 97, farmer leases 3

Raymond, Dyer, (Taylor,) hotel keeper.

Reagan, Thomas, (Taylor,) lot 66, farmer 50

Reater, Cornelius, (Cincinnatus,) lot 97, farmer 104

Ripley, Samuel, (Taylor,) lot 79, farmer 72

Rockwell, Ira, (Taylor,) lot 100, farmer 240

Rogers, John C , (Taylor,) lot 69, carpenter and farmer 93

Ross, Allen, (Pitcher, Chenango Co.,) lot 90, farmer 261

SANDERS, GEORGE E , (Union Valley,) lot 49, farmer 285

SERGENT, LEWIS H , (Union Valley,) lot 59, farmer 90

Shufelt, Daniel, (Taylor,) lot 68, justice and farmer leases 130

Shufelt, Norman D , (Taylor,) lot 69, farmer 91

Skinner, George N , (Taylor,) lot 66, farmer 150

Skinner, Horace C , (Taylor,) lot 77, farmer 140

Skinner, William G , (Taylor,) lot 87, assessor and farmer 190

Smith, Abel B , (Taylor,) lot 88, farmer 140

Smith, Cortis, (Taylor,) lot 68, owns grist mill and saw mill, constable and farmer 50

Smith, Edward L , (Cincinnatus,) lot 86, farmer 190

Smith, Isaac H , (Taylor,) lot 68, grocer and farmer 220

Smith, Sterling A , (Taylor,) lot 47, farmer 73

Stevens, Alvin L , (Truxton,) lot 46, farmer 75

Tanner, Hiel, (Taylor,) carpenter and prop of gristmill, saw mill and cider mill

Taylor, Jesse, (Cincinnatus,) lot 86, farmer 51

Thompson, Samuel, (Taylor,) lots 77, 76 and 66, farmer 306

Thorington, Lorenzo, (Taylor,) lot 47, farmer 43.

Thorington, Solomon, (Taylor,) lot 47, farmer 75

TORREY, DANIEL B , (Union Valley,) lot 59, farmer 200

Torrey, James M., (Pitcher, Chenango Co ,) lot 80, farmer 1

Vansiclen, Cornelius, (Cincinnatus,) lot 97, farmer 133

Warner, Calvin P , (Pitcher, Chenango Co ,) lot 80, farmer 130

Watson, Benjamin L , (Taylor,) lot 68, farmer 100

Wavle, Festus, (Solon,) lot 96, farmer 123

Wavle, Joseph, (Cincinnatus,) lot 96, farmer 116

Wavle, Melvin, (Solon,) lot 96, farmer 41½

Weaver, Albert, (Taylor,) lot 88, farmer 93

Weeks, Clement, (Taylor,) lot 56, farmer 113

Weeks, Lora, (Taylor,) lot 79, farmer 50

Weeks, Thomas, (Taylor,) lot 79, farmer 35½

Wells, Randolph, (Taylor,) lot 99, farmer 102

Wentworth, Thomas C , (Union Valley,) lot 49, farmer 161

West, Albert, (Taylor,) merchant

Whitney, Thaddeus S , (Taylor,) lot 99, farmer 60

Wight, Charles, (Cincinnatus,) lot 97, farmer 118

Wire, Augustus, (Taylor,) lot 100, farmer 144

Wire, Ballard, (Taylor,) lot 90, farmer 69½

Wire, Dew L , (Taylor,) lot 99, farmer 93¾

Wire, Edwin, (Taylor,) lot 90, farmer 125

Wire, Elbert M , (Taylor,) lot 100, farmer

WIRE, MANSON, (Taylor,) lot 90, farmer 129

Wire, Martin C., (Taylor,) lot 110, farmer 101

---

# TRUXTON.

### (Post Office Addresses in Parentheses)

Ackerman, Charles, (Truxton,) lot 68, farmer

Ackles, Shelden, (Truxton,) lot 83, farmer

Albro, Andrew J , (Truxton,) lot 85, farmer.

Albro, Truman B , (Truxton,) lot 16, saw mill and farmer 108.

Aldrich, Francis J , (Truxton,) lot 6, farmer 16.

Andrews, David W , (Truxton,) lot 83, farmer 200.

Arnold, George H., (Truxton,) (*K. C Arnold & Brother*,) postmaster

Arnold, Kirtland C., (Truxton,) (*K C Arnold & Brother*)

Arnold, K C. & Brother, (Truxton,) (*Kirtland C. and George H ,*) druggists

Babcock, John R , (Truxton,) lot 69, farmer.

Barnes, Sylvester, (Truxton,) lot 5, farmer 1½

BARNES, OLIVER, (Truxton,) lot 5, farmer 50

Beattie, George, (Truxton,) lot 91, farmer 80.

Beattie, Thomas, (Truxton,) lot 22, farmer

BEATTIE, WILLIAM, (Truxton,) lot 12, prop of two cheese factories, manuf of English cheddar cheese and farmer 255

Ball, James, (Truxton,) lot 22, farmer 120

Bell, John, (Truxton,) lot 21, farmer 66.

Bell, Thomas, (Truxton,) lot 21, farmer leases 150

Bemis, Henry H , (Truxton,) lot 95, carpenter and joiner,

Bemis, Irena M Mrs , (Truxton,) lot 95, tailoress

Bemis, John, (Truxton,) lot 95, carpenter and joiner,

Bemiss, Solomon, (Truxton,) lot 23, farmer 874

Bennett, Jennings J , (Truxton,) lot 34, farmer 412

Bishop, William, (Truxton,) retired farmer

Bliss, George W., (Truxton,) (*Bliss & Maycumber* )

Bliss & Maycumber, (Truxton,) (*George W Bliss and William S Maycumber*,) general merchants

BLOW, HARVEY, (Truxton,) lot 4, hide and stock dealer and farmer 114

BOSWORTH, HIRAM J , (Truxton,) (*H J Bosworth & Co* )

BOSWORTH, H J & CO , (Truxton,) (*Hiram J Bosworth and Eden Corey*,) dealers in groceries and provisions, flour and feed, butter and cheese, also wholesale dealers in maple sugar

Bosworth, Jesse, (Truxton,) retired farmer.

Bosworth, Judson J , (Truxton,) lot 35, farmer 100

BOSWORTH, ROMANZO S , (Truxton,) lot 21, farmer 136.

Boutwell, Elijah S , (Truxton,) farmer 3

Brown, Abiather R., (Truxton,) lot 36, mason

BROWN, STEPHEN B , (Truxton,) lot 23, farmer 400

BROWN, SYLVESTER, (Truxton,) lot 36, mason and farmer 9

Bryant, Edmund W , (Truxton,) farmer

Bryant, Isaac S , (Truxton,) farmer 15

Buckley, John, (Truxton,) lot 62, farmer 100

Buckley, Thomas, (Truxton,) lot 62, farmer 30 and leases 78

Buell, Franklin M , (Truxton,) patentee of plastic ground sand roofing, also patentee of ground slate plastic for preserving wood and farmer 5

Buell, Howard F , (Truxton,) lot 94, farmer 75

Buell, Thomas, (Truxton,) lot 94, farmer 9.

Burke, Thomas, (Truxton,) farmer

Burke, Thomas T , (Truxton,) shoemaker

Burrow, James, (Truxton,) lot 91, farmer

Bushby, Joseph, (Truxton,) lot 22, farmer 71.

Bushby, Robert, (Truxton,) lot 61, farmer leases 145

Call, Joel, (Truxton,) supervisor and farmer 360

Card, John, (Tully, Onondaga Co ,) lot 51, farmer 70

Card, John W , (Tully, Onondaga Co ,) lot 61, farmer

Card, Richard, (Truxton,) lot 34, farmer, Chenango

Carr, Delevan W , (Truxton,) retired hardware merchant

Carr, Dennis, (Truxton,) lot 14, farmer 150.

CARROLL, JEREMIAH, (Truxton,) lot 34, farmer 282½

Christman, Wolcott, (Tully, Onondaga Co ,) lot 51, farmer 100.

Collius, Dennis, (Truxton,) blacksmith

COREY, EDEN, (Truxton,) (*H. J Bosworth & Co* ,) farmer 40

Courtney, John, (Truxton,) lot 4, farmer 70

CRAIN, ALMIRON W , (Truxton,) (*A W Crain & Son* )

CRAIN, A W & SON, (Truxton,) (*Almiron W and Perry P* ,) manufs of the celebrated farmers' woolen cloths and trimmings.

CRAIN, PERRY P , (Truxton,) (*A W Crain & Son* )

Crandall, Ira J , (Truxton,) lot 22, farmer 220

Crandall, Jason W , (Truxton,) lot 82, carriage maker &c

Crandall, Norman S , (Truxton,) lot 21, farmer 140

Cumming, Patrick, (Truxton,) lot 81, farmer 147

Daniels, Mary Mrs , (Truxton,) lot 16, farmer 158

Davis, Ambrose, (Truxton,) lot 94, carder and farmer 10½, Stileaville

Dickinson, Lewis, (Truxton ) boot and shoemaker

DODD, EDWARD, (Truxton,) lot 82, farmer 54

DODD, EDWARD, (Truxton,) lot 2, farmer

Dodd, John J , (Truxton,) lot 32, farmer 70

DODD, THOMAS, (Truxton,) (*Dodd & Webster* )

DODD & WEBSTER, (Truxton,) (*Thomas Dodd and Chauncey Webster*,) blacksmiths

DODD, WILLIAM, (Truxton,) carpenter and joiner

DONAHUE, GENEVA MRS , (Truxton,) lot 73

DOWD, THOMAS, (Truxton,) lot 71, farmer 96

Dwyer, John, (Truxton,) lot 61, farmer 200 and leases 65

Dwyer, John, (Apulia, Onondaga Co ,) lot 53, farmer 50

Dwyer, Michael, (Truxton,) lot 84, farmer 100

Dwyer, Richard, (Truxton,) lot 3, farmer

Dwyer, William, (Truxton,) lot 82, farmer leases 60.

Dwyre, Mary Mrs , (Truxton,) lot 74, farmer 240

EASTMAN, DANIEL T , (McGrawville,) lot 31, farmer 141

Eaton, Joseph, (Truxton,) lot 16, farmer

Eaton, Lucian E , (Truxton,) lot 16, farmer

FITZGERALD, WILLIAM, (Truxton,) lot 81, farmer 99

FLAHERTY, PATRICK, (Truxton,) lot 62, farmer 70

Flinn, Henry, (Truxton,) lot 26, farmer leases 104

Flood, John, (Truxton,) lot 63, farmer.

Foster, John, (Summit Station, Onondaga Co ,) lot 52, farmer 30

Freeman, Allen B , (Truxton,) lot 11, farmer 122

Freeman, James W , (Truxton,) lot 36, farmer

Freeman, Martin, (Truxton,) lot 4, farmer 160 and (*with Martin R* ,) 139

Freeman, Martin R , (Truxton,) (*with Martin*,) lot 34, farmer 139

Freeman, Rufus, (Truxton,) lot 4, carpenter and joiner and farmer 107

Freeman, Zenas, (Truxton,) lot 24, farmer leases 412

Fry, John, (Truxton,) lot 32, farmer 108

Galvin, John, (Truxton,) lot 84, farmer

Galvin, Lawrence, (Truxton,) (*with Michael*,) lot 64, farmer 277

Galvin, Michael, (Truxton,) (*with Lawrence*,) lot 64, farmer 277

Garner, Frederick, (Truxton,) lot 5, farmer 2½

Gates, Irving, (Truxton,) lot 32, farmer leases

Gates, Martin, (Truxton,) lot 21, farmer 212

Geweye, Ahram, (Truxton,) lot 94, shoemaker.

Ginader, George, (Truxton,) lot 15, farmer 100

Gleason, Francis, (Truxton,) dealer in groceries and provisions

Godard, James, (Truxton,) lot 34, farmer 188

GODDARD, DAVIS S , (Truxton,) lot 11, farmer 257

Goddard, Solomon, (Truxton,) retired carr age manuf and dealer in notes of exchange, &c

GRADY, JAMES, (Truxton,) lot 72, farmer leases 60

GRAHAM, WILLIAM, (Truxton,) lot 73, farmer leases 340

Green, Sarah, (Truxton,) lot 36, farmer 22

Greenman, Lyman S , (Truxton,) lot 5, farmer 40

GREENMAN, NORMAN L , (Truxton,) lot 5, farmer 80

GRIFFIN, JAMES, (Truxton,) lot 25, farmer 255½

Griffin, James Jr , (Truxton,) lot 25, farmer

Gutchia, Henry J , (Truxton,) lot 91, farmer leases 115.

Hackett, Alonzo, (Truxton,) harness maker

Hakins, Milo P , (Truxton,) lot 95, farmer leases 800

Haley, Patrick, (McGrawville,) lot 31, farmer 163¾

Haley, Thomas, (Truxton,) lot 15, farmer 50

Hall, Wesley, (Truxton,) lot 36, farmer

HARTNETT, DANIEL, (Truxton,) lot 82, farmer 78¾ and leases 85

HASKIN, WILLIAM, (Truxton,) lot 5, trapper, mason and farmer 42

Haskins, Ray, (Truxton,) lot 71, farmer 200

Hawkins, John, (Truxton,) lot 18, farmer 109

Haxton, John, (Truxton,) blacksmith

Hayes, James, (Tully, Onondaga Co ,) lot 51, mason and farmer

HENNISY, PATRICK, (Truxton,) lot 32, farmer 6

Henry, Edmund W , (Truxton,) lots 34 and 35, farmer, Cheningo

Herne, John, (Truxton,) lot 1, boot and shoe maker and farmer

Hibbard, Ashley M , (Truxton,) harness maker and farmer 2

Hickey, Philip, (Truxton,) lot 15, farmer leases 140

Hicks, Edward, (Truxton,) teamster

Hicks, Lodema, (Truxton,) dress maker

Hicks, Zadoc, (Truxton,) farmer

Hilent, J , (Truxton,) lot 2, farmer 14

HIDRETH, RICHARD, (Truxton,) carpenter and joiner

Hilts, John, (Truxton,) lot 35, farmer 10

Hobart, Martin J , (Truxton,) lot 82, farmer leases 112

Hodgson, John B , (Truxton,) blacksmith

Hogan, John, (Truxton,) lot 15, farmer 88.

HOLAHAN, JOHN B , (Truxton,) lot 35, justice of the peace and farmer 197

Hollister, Harvey D , (Truxton,) lot 34, painter and school teacher

Hollister, Theron N , (Truxton,) lot 34, farmer 340, Cheningo

Holly, Eraston, (Truxton,) lot 82, farmer 94

Holmes, Dr , (Truxton,) allop physician and surgeon.

HOLMES, RODOLPHUS, (Truxton,) lot 26, farmer 102

HOPE, JAMES, (Truxton,) lot 91, farmer 22

HORIN, TIMOTHY, (Truxton,) lot 81, farmer 200

Horsewell, Ezeriah, (Truxton,) lot 63, farmer

Hulbert, Shelden, (Truxton,) lot 5, farmer leases 100

HUNTINGTON, CHARLES E , (Truxton,) lot 21, farmer 98.

Hurlburt, Dudley, (Truxton,) lot 25, farmer

Hurlbart, Sylvester, (Truxton,) lot 24, farmer leases 82

JONES, SIMEON G , (Tully, Onondaga Co ,) lot 51, farmer 50

Jones, William, (Truxton,) carriage maker and farmer 900

KELLEY, PATRICK, (Truxton,) lot 31, farmer 110

Kenney, Alonzo I., (Truxton,) retired farmer

Kenney, H M , (Truxton,) (*Knapp & Kenney*,) farmer 150.

Kenney, James, (Truxton,) farmer 140

KENNEY, MOSES, (Truxton,) lot 93, prop of Truxton cheese factory, farmer 400 and leases 4

Kenney, Oscar J , (Truxton,) lot 2, farmer leases 400

Kenny, Amos L , (Truxton,) lawyer, town clerk and insurance agent

Kenny, Hosea, (Truxton,) farmer 5¼

Killean, Thomas Jr , (Truxton,) tailor

Knapp, C. N.,(Truxton,)(*Knapp & Kenney* )

Knapp & Kenney, (Truxton,) (*C. N Knapp and H M Kenney*,) dealers in hardware and stoves, manufs of and dealers in tin, copper and sheet iron ware.

Lansing, Alexander, (Truxton,) cooper

LANSING, ALVORADO L , (Truxton,) (*Meldrim & Lansing*,) cooper

Lansing, William Col , (Truxton,) wagon maker, has charge of U S Armory

LARABEE, ALVIN, (Truxton,) (*Larabee & Son* )

LARABEE, HAMILTON R , (Truxton,) (*Larabee & Son* )

LARABEE & SON, (Truxton,) (*Alvin and Hamilton R ,*) props of saw mill and farmers 3, Stilesville.

Laribee, Stephen, (Truxton ) constable

Letts, Henry, (Truxton,) lot 61, farmer

Lewis, Albert S , (Truxton,) (*with George W ,*) lot 35, prop of saw mill and farmer 125

Lewis, Francis Mrs , (Truxton,) tailoress

Lewis, George W , (Truxton,) (*with Albert S ,*) lot 35, prop of saw mill and farmer 125

Lillis, James, (Tully, Onondaga Co ,) lot 51, farmer 100

Lillis, Patrick, (Truxton,) (*with Richard,*) lot 72, farmer 216

Lillis, Richard, (Truxton,) (*with Patrick,*) lot 72, farmer 216

Lockwood, Lewiston, (Truxton,) lot 25, farmer 77

Lockwood, Thaxter, (Truxton,) lot 85, farmer 100

Long, James, (Truxton,) lot 62, farmer 200

MAASON, JOHN C , (Tully, Onondaga Co ,) lot 51, farmer 100

MALTBEE, HIRAM, (Truxton,) lot 35, prop of saw mill and cider mill, and farmer 4

Mark, Joseph, (Truxton,) lot 32, farmer 163

Mark, Joseph Jr , (Truxton,) lot 54, farmer

Maycumber, William S , (Truxton,) (*Blue & Maycumber* )

McAllister, Jerome, (Truxton,) manuf of firkins and tubs, also prop of planing mill

McAuliffe, Michael, (Truxton,) lot 26, farmer 60

McCarty, John, (Truxton,) lot 15, farmer 219

McChoulef, John, (Truxton,) lot 71, farmer

McDiarmid, Hugh, (Truxton,) lot 16, farmer 200

McDonald, Patrick, (Truxton,) retired farmer

McDONALD, PATRICK JR , (Truxton,) lot 71, farmer 355,

McGRAW, EDMUND, (Tully, Onondaga Co ,) (*E McGraw & Sons,*) farmer 58

McGRAW, E & SONS, (Tully, Onondaga Co ,) (*Edmund, Michael and John,*) lot 51, farmer 262

McGRAW, JOHN, (Truxton,) (*E McGraw & Sons* )

McGRAW, MICHAEL, (Truxton,) (*E. McGraw & Sons* )

McKevitt, Henry, (Truxton,) lot 4, farmer 36

McLean, William, (Truxton,) lot 93, sawyer and farmer

MELDRIM & LANSING, (Truxton,) (*Thomas Meldrim and Alvorado L Lansing,*) props of planing mill and cheese box manuf.

MELDRIM, THOMAS, (Truxton,) (*Meldrim & Lansing,*) farmer 12

Melody, Patrick, (Truxton,) lot 14, farmer leases 250

Miller, Daniel, (Truxton,) lot 94, dyer and clock and watch repairer, Stilesville

MILLER, GEORGE 2nd, (Truxton,) lot 22, farmer 178

Miller, George 3rd , (Truxton,) lot 94, farmer 156, Stilesville.

MILLER, JOHN, (Truxton,) lot 83, farmer 205.

Miller, Joseph, (Truxton,) lot 74, farmer 140

Miller, Richard, (Truxton,) retired farmer.

Miller, Thomas, (Truxton,) lot 4, farmer 11.

Miller, Thomas, (Truxton,) teamster.

MOORE, WILLIAM, (Truxton,) lot 26, farmer leases 108

MORRIS, ANTHONY, (Truxton,) lot 2, farmer 362

Morton, Edmund, (Truxton,) farmer 18.

MORTON, LAWRENCE, (Truxton,) lot 93, farmer 274.

Murdent, Henry, (Truxton,) lot 85, farmer leases 130

Neff, Charles L , (Truxton,) lot 83, farmer

Nelson, Judson C , (Truxton,) allop physician and surgeon

Negus, Edward, (Truxton,) lot 73, farmer 370

NIX, ANTHONY, (Truxton,) lot 74, farmer 210

Nix, John, (Truxton,) lot 12, farmer

Nix, Thomas, (Truxton,) lot 12, farmer

Nix, William, (Truxton,) lot 85, farmer 80.

Nodine, Downs, (Truxton,) lot 94, farmer

NORRIS, MICHAEL, (Truxton,) lot 72, farmer 129.

Nye, Ansel, (Truxton,) lot 63, farmer leases 4

O'CONNOR, CORNELIUS, (Truxton,) lot 83, farmer 209

O'Conor, Daniel, (Truxton,) lot 72, farmer

O'Grady, Charles, (Truxton,) shoemaker

O'GREADY, CORNELIUS, (Truxton,) lot 91, farmer leases 125

O'NEIL, BERNARD, (Truxton,) wagon maker

O'NEIL, MARY MRS , (Tully, Onondaga Co ,) lot 51, farmer 107.

Osback, Antony, (Truxton,) lot 2, farmer 10

Osterhout, Moses, (Truxton,) lot 95, farmer 62.

Parker, Lorina A Miss, (Truxton,) milliner

Parker, Obadiah, (Truxton,) lot 73, shingle maker, basket maker, trapper and farmer

Patrick, Stephen, (Truxton,) lot 5, farmer 873

Peck, Jacob H , (Truxton,) lot 26, farmer 104

Peck, John L , (Truxton,) (*with William H* ) lot 26, farmer 93

Peck, William H , (Truxton,) (*with John L* ) lot 26, farmer 93

Perry, Llewellyn, (Truxton,) lot 13, farmer

Perry, Stephen, (Truxton,) lot 13, farmer 390

Phelan, Thomas, (Truxton,) lot 13, farmer

Pierce, Albert, (Truxton,) lot 92, prop. of saw mill and farmer 2

PIERCE, CHARLES A , (Truxton,) lot 12, farmer 250

PIERCE, DEXTER, (Truxton,) lot 94, farmer 250

PIERCE, ETHAN A., (Truxton,) lot 12, farmer 475.

PIERCE, JOHN JR , (Truxton,) lot 2, carpenter and joiner

Pierce, Judah Col , (Truxton,) retired farmer

Pierce, Maria Mrs , (Truxton,) lot 4, farmer 55

Pierce, Milo, (Truxton,) lot 86, farmer 100

Pierce, Richard, (Truxton,) lot 4, farmer 138

Pierce, Sabin S , (Truxton,) lots 11 and 12, farmer 172

Pierce, Spencer S , (Truxton,) lot 4, farmer 65

Pierce, Thurlow, (Truxton,) lot 2, farmer 228

Pierce, Wilder E., (Truxton,) lot 2, carpenter and joiner

Pierce, Willard, (Truxton,) retired farmer

Pierce, William, (Truxton,) lot 13, farmer 418

Pierce, William 2d, (Truxton,) lot 13, farmer 20

Pierce, William T , (Truxton,) lot 13, farmer.

PINDER, JULIA, (Truxton,) lot 16, farmer 74

Pomeroy, Austin L , (Truxton,) justice of the peace, cabinet maker, undertaker, auctioneer and farmer 5

Potter, Aaron B , (Tully, Onondaga Co ,) lot 61, farmer 28

Potter, Hezekiah, (Truxton,) lot 91, farmer 38

POTTER, SAMUEL C , (Truxton,) lot 36, farmer 50

Preston, Alanson, (Apulia, Onondaga Co ,) lot 53, farmer 50

PULFORD, SAMUEL, (Truxton,) lot 95, prop of Manchester grist mill, saw mill and farmer 17

PUTNAM, WILLIAM W , (Truxton,) lot 34, farmer 116.

Quinlan, John, (Truxton,) lot 63, farmer leases 304

Radcliffe, Henry, (Truxton,) lot 91, farmer.

RADCLIFFE, J A. MISS , (Truxton,) lot 91, farmer 100

Radway, Orin K , (Truxton,) lot 3, farmer 50

Ransford, Randolph, (Truxton,) painter

Rice, Frank, (Truxton,) carpenter and joiner

Richardson, Erl, (Truxton,) lot 15, painter and farmer 60

RILEY, JEREMIAH, (Tully, Onondaga Co ,) lot 52, farmer 132.

Riley, Jerry, (Truxton,) lot 1, farmer 183

Rindy, Lucina, (Truxton,) prop of stage from Truxton to Apulia

Ripley, John, (Truxton,) lot 34, farmer, Cheningo

Risley, Alva, (Truxton,) lot 95, justice of the peace and farmer 300

Roach, William, (Truxton,) lot 14, farmer 63.

Robbins, John W , (Truxton,) lot 83, carpenter and joiner, and farmer 24

Rounds, Hezekiah, (Truxton,) lot 11, farmer 200.

Rowley, Daniel, (Truxton,) lot 63, farmer 500

Rowley, Levi, (Truxton,) lot 53, farmer 63

Rowley, Levi H , (Truxton,) lot 53, farmer 230

Ryan, Anthony, (Truxton,) lot 36, farmer leases 100

Ryan, Jerry, (Truxton,) lot 25, farmer leases 120

Ryan, Roger Jr , (Truxton,) lot 86, farmer leases 160

Ryan, Timothy, (Truxton,) lot 85, farmer 150

SCHELLINGER, LEVI, (Truxton,) (with Lewis,) lot 95, farmer 630

SCHELLINGER, LEWIS, (Truxton,) (with Levi,) lot 95, farmer 630

Schellinger, Rial, (Truxton,) prop of Schellinger House and farmer 10

SCHERMERHORN, FREEMAN, (Truxton,) lot 88, farmer 255

Schermerhorn, Henry, (Truxton,) lot 93, book agent and shoemaker

SEACORD, DANIEL, (Truxton,) lot 36, farmer 58.

SEACORD, DAVID H , (Truxton,) lot 35, farmer 120

Seacord, William R , (Truxton,) lot 36, carpenter and joiner and farmer 85

Severance, David S , (Truxton,) lot 3, farmer 170

Severance, John, (Truxton,) lot 8, farmer 20

Shaw, Appleton, (Truxton,) lot 35, blacksmith, Cheningo

SHAW, CHANCY L , (Truxton,) lot 35, blacksmith and collector of taxes, Cheningo

Shaw, Cornelius A , (Truxton,) lot 36, shingle maker and farmer

Sheehin, David, (Truxton,) lot 72, farmer

Sherman, Levi, (Truxton,) lot 54, carpenter and joiner, prop of saw mill and farmer 1½

Short, Joseph, (Truxton,) lot 91, farmer 20

SHUFELT, LORENZO, (Truxton,) lot 34, grocer, Cheningo

Skeele, Melvin C , (Truxton,) lot 94, school teacher and farmer 130

SLEITH, SAMUEL, (Truxton,) lot 36, saw mill and farmer 3

Smith, Boardman Mrs , (Truxton,) music teacher

Smith, David C , (Truxton,) lot 93, farmer

SMITH, EMELINE MRS , (Truxton,) lot 16, farmer 82

Smith, Lewis, (Truxton,) lot 3, farmer 126

Smith, Lewis. (Truxton,) farmer 6

Smith, Seneca P , (Truxton,) farmer 5½

Soules, Orren, (Truxton,) lot 26, farmer 10 and leases 8.

Steele, George W., (Truxton,) lot 26, farmer 96

STEVENS, ALBERT, (Truxton,) lot 93, prop of Willow Grove grist mill

STEVENS, BERDET, (Truxton )

Stevens, Chauncey, (Truxton,) justice of the peace

Stevens, Ervin, (Truxton,) ready made clothing, hats, caps, boots and shoes, &c

Stevens, William R , (Truxton,) lot 36, farmer 100

Stewart, Helen A , (Truxton,) lot 93, farmer 208

Stewart, John G., (Truxton,) harness maker

Stone, Chauncey, (Truxton,) lot 1, farmer

Swift, Lucius L , (Tully, Onondaga Co ,) lot 51, farmer 68

Talt, John, (Truxton,) lot 91, farmer 100

Taylor, Charles F., (Truxton,) lot 34, farmer 204

Taylor, D Rev , (Truxton,) pastor of Baptist Church

TAYLOR, LEROY D , (Truxton,) lot 33, farmer 286

Terry, Edward P , (Truxton,) lot 22, farmer 70

Thompson, Frank A., (Truxton,) lot 8, farmer

Thompson, Walter, (Truxton,) lot 95, farmer 90

Todhunter, William, (Truxton,) lot 91, farmer 103

Towle, George H , (Truxton,) boot and shoe maker

Twentyman, John, (Truxton,) lot 73, farmer 230

TWENTYMAN, JOSEPH, (Truxton,) lot 83, farmer 290

TWOGOOD, HENRY G , (Truxton,) prop of Truxton House

Vincent, A Murray, (Truxton,) wagon maker

Vincent, Pulaski J , (Truxton,) cabinet maker and constable

WALLACE, DAVID, (Truxton,) lot 72, farmer 139

WARE, NICHOLAS W , (Truxton,) lot 81, cooper and farmer 30.

Warfield, Henry M , (Truxton,) blacksmith

WEBSTER, CHAUNCEY,(Truxton,)(*Dodd & Webster* )

Welch, James, (Truxton,) lot 64, farmer leases 336

WELLS, JOHN, (Tully, Onondaga Co ,) lot 61, farmer.

Wells, John Jr , (Tully, Onondaga Co ,) lot 61, farmer 100.

WELSH, JAMES JR., (Truxton,) lot 54, farmer 330

Western, James, (Truxton,) lot 62, farmer leases

Whalon, Thomas, (Truxton,) farmer

WICKS, JOHN O , (Truxton,) lot 13, farmer 160.

Wicks, Zaphar, (Truxton,) farmer

Wigand, Charles T , (Truxton,) lot 92, farmer 140

Wiggins, John, (Truxton ) lot 94, spinner and farmer 10, Stillesville.

Willson, Horace 2d., (East Homer,) lot 31, farmer 60

Winne, William D , (Truxton,) lot 34, farmer, Cheningo.

Worfield, Henry M Mrs , (Truxton,) dressmaker

---

# VIRGIL.

## (Post Office Addresses in Parentheses.)

Abel, Stephen S , (Dryden, Tompkins Co ,) lot 41, farmer leases of Geo Hill, Dryden, 106½

Allen, George, (Dryden, Tompkins Co ,) lot 31, farmer 30

ANDREWS, CHAS W , (McLean, Tompkins Co ,) lot 1, farmer 35

Angell, Erasmus D , (East Virgil,) lots 48, 49 and 59, grocer, hotel prop and farmer 200

Atwood, Timothy, (Blodget Mills,) lot 18, farmer 57

Bailey, James K , (Virgil,) harness maker

Bailey, John, (Virgil,) lot 32, farmer

Bailey, Jonas, (Virgil,) lot 22, farmer 74

Bailey, Joseph, (Virgil,) lot 32, farmer

Bailey, Lemun, (Virgil,) lot 12, farmer 80

Bailey, Lyman, (Virgil,) lot 21, farmer 30

Baker, Abner A , (Virgil,) lot 37, mason and farmer 12

Baker, Barnabas, (Virgil,) lot 44, farmer 6

Baker, Hiram, (East Virgil,) lot 37, farmer 30

Baker, Salem, (Virgil,) lot 44, farmer 112

Ball, Lewis B , (Virgil,) lot 12, farmer 90

Ball, Shubel G , (Virgil,) cabinet maker

BALLOU, MYRON, (Blodget Mills,) lot 17, farmer 160

Barto, Benjamin B , (Virgil,) lot 42, farmer 6

Bays, William, (Cortland Village,) lot 15, farmer leases of Mrs Elizabeth Bays,40.

Bayaly, George, (Virgil,) lot 26, farmer leases 100

BEAM, CHAS. L , (Dryden, Tompkins Co ,) laborer.

Bell, Charles C., (Virgil,) lot 42, blacksmith and farmer 9

Bell, Lewis, (Virgil,) lot 26, farmer leases of Jerome B Rounds, 200.

Bell, William, (Virgil,) blacksmith and justice of the peace

Biggar, William R , (Blodget Mills,) lot 8, farmer 44

Blodget, George, (Virgil,) lot 24, farmer 21

Blodget, Josiah, (East Virgil,) lot 49, farmer 3

Bloomer, Isaac B , (Virgil,) lot 25, farmer 100

Bloomer, William, (Virgil,) lot 44, farmer 98

Blue, Levi H , (Dryden, Tompkins Co ,) lot 31, carpenter and farmer 40

Booth, Smith, (Virgil,) lot 36, farmer 50.

Bouton, John, (Virgil,) lot 32, farmer 70

Bouton, Joseph, (Virgil,) lot 42, prop of saw mill and farmer 55

Bouton, Lyman H , (Virgil,) butcher

BOUTON, NATHAN, (Virgil,) lot 42, farmer 115

Branch, Enoch D , (Virgil,) lots 2, 11 and 12, farmer 223

Branch, Harley H , (Virgil,) lot 12, harness maker and farmer 50

Branch, Jepthar M , (Virgil,) farmer leases 120

Branch, Sanford B , (Virgil,) lot 12, farmer 53.

Bristol, Benjamin F , (Virgil,) lot 3, farmer 107
Bronson, Horace, M D , (Virgil,) physician and surgeon
Brown, Lyman E , (Virgil,) lot 44, farmer leases 60.
Burchill, Keziah Mrs , (Dryden, Tompkins Co ,) lot 21, farmer 1½
Burdick, Benjamin J , (East Virgil,) farmer 2.
Burgess, Seth Rev:, (Blodget Mills,) lot 7, Wesleyan Methodist clergyman and farmer 36
Burlingame. Charles C , (Virgil,) lots 35 and 36, farmer 65
Burt, Thomas, (Blodget Mills,) lot 8, farmer 80
BYRAM, SAMUEL M , (Virgil ) lot 33, prop of grist and flouring mill and farmer 22
Calvert, John A , (South Cortland,) lot 1, farmer 80
Cargon, John P., (East Virgil,) let 37, blacksmith and farmer 16
Carson, Abraham, (Virgil,) lot 42, farmer 115
Chaplin, George H., (Messengerville,) lot 50, farmer 80.
Chatterton, George, (Cortland Village,) lot 6, farmer 136
Chatterton, Jacob, (Virgil,) lot 4, farmer 73½
Chrisman, Josiah, (Virgil,) lot 15, farmer 130
Clark, Albert, (Virgil,) lot 42, farmer 4
Clark, Uri H , (Virgil,) lot 33, farmer 93
Clow, Richard, (Virgil,) lot 4, farmer 123
Cole, John, (Virgil,) lot 32, farmer 58
Colligan, Arthur, (Cortland Village,) lot 6, farmer 112
Collings, Abraham, (Virgil,) cutter and tailor
Collins, Dennis, (Blodget Mills,) lot 9, farmer 23
Colwell, Harvey, (Virgil,) lot 24, farmer 100
Conrad, Hiram G , (Virgil,) lot 45, farmer 75.
Conrad, Nicholas, (Virgil,) lot 45, farmer 30
Conrad, Peter, (Virgil,) lot 45, farmer 25½
Crain, Edward A , (Virgil,) wagon and carriage maker
Crain, Sylvester, (Virgil,) wagon and carriage maker
CRANDALL, JOHN M Rev , (Virgil,) Free Will Baptist clergyman.
Croneo, William, (Blodget Mills,) lot 17, farmer 108.
CRONKRITE, SOLOMON, (East Virgil) mason
Curtis, Salmon, (Virgil,) lot 23, farmer 86,
Dann, Amariah, (Virgil,) lot 36, farmer 83
Dann, Darius, (Virgil,) lot 46, farmer 60
DANN, GEORGE P , (Virgil,) lots 26 and 16, farmer 142
Darling, Artemus, (East Virgil,) carpenter
DARLING, DARIUS, (East Virgil,) lot 48, farmer 91½
DARLING, DAVID, (East Virgil,) farmer
Darling, Lafayette, (East Virgil,) lot 47, farmer 56
Darling, Sidney A., (Virgil,) lot 46, farmer 60
L

Davern, James, (Virgil,) lot 36, farmer 179
Davis, Caleb K., (Messengerville,) lot 50, owns cider mill and lath mill and farmer 34.
Davis, Hammond, (Messengerville,) lot 50, farmer
Dearman, George W , (Cortland Village,) lot 5, farmer 95.
Demander, Henry, (Virgil,) painter
Dickinson, Alfred T., (Messengerville,)produce dealer
Dickinson, James A , (Messengerville,) dry goods and groceries
Dickinson, John O., (Messengerville,) (*Sherman & Dickinson* )
Dickinson, Wm , (Virgil,) lot 28, farmer 85
Driscoll, John, (Messengerville,) blacksmith.
DURKEE, NATHAN, (Blodget Mills,) farmer (*with E F Willett & Son* )
Ellison, Lorenzo,(McLean, Tompkins Co ,) lot 11, farmer 30
Ellison, William Jr , (McLean, Tompkins Co ,) lots 11, 20 and 21, farmer 80
Elster, George W , (Virgil,) lot 24, farmer 148
Elster, Gideon G , (Virgil,) lot 24, farmer 67
Elster, Orlando, (Virgil,) lot 15, farmer 149½
Evans, Mordica, (Blodget Mills,) lot 17, farmer 49½
Fitzhugh, Charles, (McLean, Tompkins Co ,) lot 11, farmer 18
Fortner, Elliot E , (Virgil,) lot 22, farmer 160
Francis, Richard, (South Cortland,) lot 2, farmer 112
Francis, Roswell, (Virgil,) lot 3, farmer 69
FRANK, JOHN M , (Virgil,) lot 43, farmer 62
FRENCH, FRANCIS M., (Virgil,) hotel prop
Frize, Thass W , (Cortland Village,) lot 6, shoe maker and farmer 173½
Fuller, Roswell D , (Virgil,) lot 13, farmer leases of Mrs Jas B Hewe, 106½
Gardner, Nathan, (Virgil,) lot 24, farmer 64
Gee, Emery, (Virgil,) lot 6, farmer 100
Gee, Parker, (McLean, Tompkins Co ,) lot 21, farmer 97
Gillem, Crosby, (Cortland Village,) mason
Gillen, Thomas E , (Virgil,) lot 11, carpenter and farmer 3
Givens, Charles, 2nd, (McLean, Tompkins Co ,) lot 21, farmer 50,
Givens, Cortland, (Virgil,) lot 21, farmer 104
Givens, William, (McLean, Tompkins Co ,) lot 11, farmer 86
Gleason, Sophia Mrs , (Virgil,) lot 14, farmer 83
Gray, Jesse, (Messengerville,) lot 50, farmer 2½
Green, Page, (Virgil,) lot 26, loan commissioner, lawyer and farmer 70
Greene, H Cooley, (Virgil,) school teacher and cheese maker
Gridley, Albert, (Blodget Mills,) lot 29, farmer leases 12½
Gridley, Luin, (Blodget Mills,) lot 40, farmer 125

Griswold, Oliver T., (Virgil,) lot 3, farmer 50

Grover, Charles A , (Virgil,) lot 12, farmer 50

Hall, Abner, (Virgil,) lot 17, farmer 106½

Hall, Garden, (Blodget Mills,) lots 16 and 17, farmer 70.

Hall, Sylvester, (Virgil,) lot 17, farmer 165

Hammond Adelbert, (Virgil,) lot 16, mason and farmer leases 70

Hammond, John, (Virgil,) lot 26, mason and farmer 66

Hammond, Riley, (Virgil,) lot 13, mason and farmer 123

Hammond, Thomas, (Virgil,) lot 42, farmer 76

Hard, John S , (South Cortland,) lot 2, farmer 95

Haskins, Alanson, (McLean, Tompkins Co ,) lot 1, farmer 90

Heffron, George, (Dryden, Tompkins Co ,) lot 41, farmer leases of Thos Lonnor, Dryden, 100

Henyan, Horace M , (Messengerville,) lot 50, farmer 26

Hicks, James, (Blodget Mills,) lot 8, farmer 20

Hill, John T , (Dryden, Tompkins Co ,) lot 41, prop of saw mill and farmer 90

Hoagland, Warren, (McLean, Tompkins Co ,) lot 1, farmer 68

Hobart, Dix, (Messengerville,) lot 39, farmer 101

Holdbrook, Phineas, (Virgil,) lot 46, farmer 39

Hollenbeck, Frederick, (McLean, Tompkins Co ,) lot 11, farmer 86

Holton, Rufus E , (Virgil,) lot 23, farmer 50

Homer, Henry, (Virgil,) lot 23, farmer 164

Homer, Lyman S , (Blodget Mills,) lot 27, carpenter and farmer 39

Hooker, Culver, (McLean, Tompkins Co ,) lot 11, farmer 71½

Hopkins, Adolphus, (East Virgil,) lot 48, farmer 69

Hopkins, Josiah, (East Virgil,) cooper

Hotchkiss, Chas A , (Virgil,) lot 43, farmer 100

Hotchkiss, Enoch D , (Virgil,) lot 43, farmer 70

House, Bradley M , (Messengerville,) post master, shoe maker, prop saw mill and agent for S B & N Y R R

House, Conrad, (Virgil,) lot 42, farmer 87

House, George, (Virgil,) lot 3, farmer 45

House, John C , (Virgil,) lot 32, farmer 60

Howe, James P , (Virgil,) carpenter and joiner

HUBBARD, HOWARD M ,(Virgil,) general merchant

Hull, Amos P , (Virgil,) lot 18, carpenter and farmer 50

Holslander, Lawrence T , (Virgil,) lot 36, carpenter and farmer 10

Humiston, Henry J , (East Virgil,) lot 49, farmer 1½

HUSON, RICHARD L , (Virgil,) carriage maker

Hutchings, Aaron, (Virgil,) lot 32, farmer 56

Hutchings, Abram L , (Virgil,) lot 23, farmer

Hutchings, Andrew, (Virgil,) lot 33, farmer 124

Hutchings, John B , (Virgil,) lot 33, farmer leases of Andrew Hutchings, 106

HUTCHINGS, MILES H , (Dryden, Tompkins Co ,) lot 41, farmer 57

Hutchins, Chas W , (Virgil,) lot 43, farmer 78

Hutchins, David, (Virgil,) lots 23 and 24, farmer 20

Hutchins, Rufus E , (Dryden, Tompkins Co ,) lots 42 and 52, carpenter and joiner and farmer 55

Hutchins, Samuel, (Virgil,) lots 43 and 44, farmer 175

HUTCHINS, WESLEY, (Virgil,) lot 22, carpenter and joiner and farmer 15

Hyde, Henry, (East Virgil,) lot 48, farmer leases 4.

Jameson, Alexander, (McLean, Tompkins Co ,) lot 21, farmer 55

Jameson, Gilbert, (Dryden, Tompkins Co ,) lot 21, farmer 100.

Jenkins, Warren F , (Virgil,) physician and surgeon

JOHNSON, CHARLES H , (McLean, Tompkins Co ,) lot 11, farmer 75

Johnson, Eli M , (Virgil,) lot 25, farmer 127

Johnson, Vivus, (Virgil,) lot 34, farmer leases 98

Joiner, Orrin, (Virgil,) lot 44, farmer 79

Jones, Benjamin J , (Virgil,) lots 23 and 24, broker, patent right dealer and farmer 40

Jones, Lyman, (Virgil,) lot 43, farmer 107

KENNEDY, THOMAS, (Messengerville,) (with John R Ragan,) lot 19, dairy and farmer 125

Keyes, Sylvester, (Virgil,) lot 18, farmer leases of Henry Homer, 2

Kincade, Charles, (Virgil,) shoe maker

Ladd, Augustus E H , (Virgil,) boot and shoe maker

Ladd, George H , (Virgil,) boot and shoe maker

Lamont, Peter, (Dryden, Tompkins Co ,) lot 31, farmer 100

Lane, John H , (Virgil,) lot 44 farmer (with Mrs Cynthia Sager,)

Lang, Robert, (Virgil,) lot 15, farmer 105

Lang, Thomas, (Cortland Village,) lot 5, farmer 80

Lathrop, Jared R , (Virgil,) lot 34, farmer 30

Leahy, Wilham, (Blodget Mills,) lot 8, farmer 20

Lee, John, (Blodget Mills,) lot 18, farmer 55

Leech, Rebecca Mrs , (Virgil,) lot 18, farmer 62

Leroy, Jacob, (Virgil,) lot 37, farmer 1

Leroy, Joseph, (Messengerville,) blacksmith

Lewis, Gilbert, (Dryden, Tompkins Co ,) lot 41, carpenter and farmer 6

Lewis, Isaac, (Virgil,) constable, carpenter and joiner

Lewis, Josiah, (Virgil,) lots 13 and 23, assessor and farmer 66

Lewis, Nathaniel, (Virgil,) lot 33, mail carrier and farmer 100

Lewis, Thomas G , (Virgil,) lot 42, carpenter and joiner and farmer 9

Low, Garrison H , (Virgil,) lot 26, farmer 98.
Low, Peter D , (Virgil,) (*Peter D Low & Son,*) lot 27, farmer 88
Low, Peter D & Son, (Virgil,) (*Zachariah,*) agents for Farmers' Joint Stock Insurance Co,
Low, Zachariah, (Virgil,) (*Peter D. Low & Son* )
Low, Zachariah, (Virgil,) lot 24, farmer 2½
Luce, Albert, (Virgil,) carpenter and joiner
Luce, John A , (Virgil,) lot 37, prop of saw mill and farmer 30
Marsh, Seymour, (Virgil,) cooper
Marshall, William, (Cortland Village,) lot 5, farmer 40
McCoy, David, (Virgil,) lot 44, farmer 41
McKinney, John, (Virgil,) lot 23, farmer 106
McLEAN, WARREN, (Dryden, Tompkins Co ,) lot 21, cooper and farmer 60
McVean, Alexander, (East Virgil,) justice peace and post master
Messenger, Johial, (Virgil,) lot 37, farmer 120
Miller, Ambrose, (Messengerville,) lot 39, farmer 38
Miller, Enos, (Virgil,) lots 27 and 28, farmer 140
Miller, George, (Messengerville,) lot 39, farmer 109
Miller, Horatio N , (East Virgil,) lot 49, farmer 50
Miller, Irene Mrs , (Virgil,) lot 24, farmer 25
Miller, John B , (Messengerville,) lots 28 and 29, farmer 166
Minard, Mirancy P , (Virgil,) lot 11, farmer 4½
Moorhead, Thomas, (Virgil,) lot 2, farmer leases of C Griswold, Dryden, 100
Morgan, Rodney S , (Dryden, Tompkins Co ,) lot 31, farmer 50
Mosher, John, (Blodget Mills,) lot 18, farmer 115
Mott, Alva S , (Virgil,) lot 46, farmer 85
Mott, Emelinda Mrs , (Virgil,) lot 45, farmer 90
Mott, Joshua, (Virgil,) lot 43, farmer 18
Mott, Samuel, (Virgil,) lot 23, drover and farmer 38.
Munson, Jerry L , (Virgil,) lot 4, farmer 100
Mynard, Perry W , (Dryden, Tompkins Co ,) lot 31, farmer leases 40
Northop, John H , (Dryden, Tompkins Co ) lot 41, farmer 100
Nye, George W , (McLean, Tompkins Co ,) lot 1, farmer leases 60
Nye, Warren, (South Cortland,) lot 1, farmer 40
Oaks, James H , (Virgil,) traveling agent for Agricultural Insurance Co , Watertown
Oaks, Maria Mrs , (Virgil,) lot 5, farmer 130
Oaks, Sylvester, (Virgil,) lot 4, farmer leases 100
Oaks, William, (Virgil,) lot 15, farmer 121½
Ogden, John L . (Virgil,) lot 46, farmer 92
Olmstead, Jackson, (Dryden, Tompkins Co ,) lot 31, farmer 92 ·
Olmstead, John Rev , (Virgil,) lot 22, Wesleyan Methodist clergyman and farmer 40½

Olmstad, Lurinda Mrs., (Virgil,) lot 24, farmer 18
Olmstead, William S , (Virgil,) lot 8, farmer 175.
Otis, Charles, (Virgil,) lot 14, farmer leases of Jno Hammond, 70,
Otis, James H , (Virgil,) lot 22, farmer 120
Overton, David, (Virgil,) lot 46, farmer 184
Owens, Harmonus, (Virgil,) lot 21, farmer 16
Palmer, Ebenezer, (Blodget Mills,) lot 29, farmer
Palmer, Isaac C , (Messengerville,) lots 30 and 40, farmer 278,
Palmer, Robert H , (Messengerville,) lots 50 and 60, farmer 185
Parker, Henry, (Messengerville,) lot 60, farmer leases 150
Parker, Hiram C , (Blodget Mills,) lot 19, (*with Thos A Wescott* )
Parker, William C , (Blodget Mills,) lots 19 and 29, farmer 96
Patten, John S , (Virgil,) lot 38, farmer 150.
Perkins, Ebenezer, (Virgil,) carriage maker and undertaker
Perkins, Horace, (Virgil,) lot 14, farmer leases of Prentis Allen, Marathon, 68
Pond, Timothy, (Virgil,) lot 42, farmer 60
Potter, James M , (Blodget Mills,) lot 29, farmer leases 4
Poulten, William, (South Cortland,) lot 3, farmer 86½
Price, Daniel, (Virgil,) lot 53, farmer 75
Price, David R., (Cortland Village,) lot 5, farmer 196.
Price, John B , (Virgil,) lot 25, farmer 124
Price, Sally Mrs , (Virgil,) lot 36, farmer 40
Price, Sanford B , (Virgil,) lot 25, farmer 100
Pulling, Daniel P , (McLean, Tompkins Co ,) lot 2, farmer 48
Pulling, Nathan H , (Cortland Village,) lot 2, farmer 31¾
RAGAN, JOHN R , (Messengerville,) (*with Thomas Kennedy,*) lot 19, dairy and farmer 132
Raymond, John, (Virgil,) lot 4, farmer leases 7
Reas, Jerome B , (Virgil,) lot 34, farmer 97
Reas, William H , (Virgil,) lot 34, farmer 93
Regan, Patrick, (Messengerville,) lot 39, farmer 100
Rice, Enos B , (Virgil,) lot 45, farmer 31
Rice, Jonathan, (Virgil,) lot 35, farmer 97
Richards, John, (Virgil,) lot 37, carpenter and farmer 80
Robinson, Norman, (Virgil,) lot 26, bricklayer and farmer 1
Robison, Horace, (Virgil,) lot 23, farmer 111¾
Rock, Adam, (Virgil,) lot 16, farmer 67
Rohrabacker, Joseph, (Blodget Mills,) lots 29 and 28, farmer 60
Rooke, James, (Cortland Village,)lot 6, farmer 45
Rooke, William, (Cortland Village,) lot 6, farmer 45
Rounds, Jerome B , (Virgil,) lot 26, farmer 200
Rounds, Samuel N , (Virgil,) lot 37, shoemaker and farmer 53¾
Rudd, Gains S , (East Virgil,) miller.

# PUBLISHER'S NOTICES.

**J. & F. B. Garrett,** Wholesale and Retail dealers in Printing, Writing, Wrapping, Tissue, Roll and Fancy Papers, Printers' Supplies, Shipping Cards, Blank Books, &c , at No 3 West Fayette street, Syracuse, have built up a heavy trade in their line, extending from Harrisburgh, in Pennsylvania, to the Canadian border   We have dealt considerably with this establishment, and have invariably been gratified in having our orders promptly filled, and always with just the article required.  See card, page 162

**Syracuse Marble Works.— Francis & Duffy,** Successors to G W M Lewis, West Onondaga St., opposite Binghamton R R Depot , also successors to Robert Spaulding, No 6 West Jefferson St , are the proprietors, and they are a firm that we can cordially recommend to all who want fair dealing   Their works are among the largest and most extensive in Central New York,  A large assortment of Monuments, Head Stones and Mantles constantly on hand, from which to select   It is to the interest of every one wanting Granite Monuments, or Granite Work, to give them a call, as their facilities for obtaining it are second to none   They are the only agents in the city for the sale of Freestone, which is so rapidly gaining favor for monumental work   Our patrons should bear in mind that this firm will not be undersold, and that all of their work is warranted as represented   See advertisement, page 162

**Warren Wight,** Propagator and dealer in the celebrated *Seneca Black Cap* and Davison's Thornless Raspberries, Grape Vines, Strawberries, and other small fruits, at Waterloo, Seneca Co , publishes a card on page 146   His experience in the business is large, and his soil is excellent, probably no better can be found in the State for the purpose he uses it   We advise our friends to peruse his advertisement and purchase their supplies of him   He uses great care in packing for shipment, and sends out none but first-class plants   It would do no harm to address him for a circular, and might be the means of affording you an abundance of his delicious fruits

**H. S. Cone,** manufacturer and dealer in Improved Slat Window Shades, Marathon, N Y , publishes a card on page 194   These shades are superior to any others now before the public, and have only to be seen to be appreciated   They have an advantage over every other shade in the following particulars   They are the most durable and will last a life time if used carefully   They are made of wood and can be cleaned like any other wood work.  They are the most convenient and can be made to suit a window of any size   For stores, offices, public buildings and private dwellings, they have no equal   Those in want of a superior shade can be supplied by sending the length and breadth of their windows to Mr Cone

**Mothers, Read This!—**So says Dr G T Taft & Co , of Seneca Falls   In their advertisement on page 20, they desire to inform you of the wonderful qualities of their "Oriental Syrup," for children   We have heard of many cases where this valuable medicine has given great relief   They are also proprietors of "Rosenberger's Balm of Gilead Ointment," for old sores, ulcers, rheumatism, burns, chilblains, piles, &c , and for galls, or wounds on horses, it is unsurpassed

**Important Knowledge.—**As music is now an indispensable necessity in every household, any reliable information is valuable as to the best place to buy musical instruments   We have been acquainted for years personally with the firm of Redington & Howe, and have known of their business facilities   *We know* that no House between New York and Chicago can compete with them successfully, as their facilities are unequaled   In addition to the immense capital at their control, they have *special contracts* with several leading first-class manufacturers, whereby they buy cheaper than any other dealers in the United States *anywhere*   Their immense trade requires only a small profit on each one of their many transactions to ensure them a handsome income   Their terms are most highly liberal   And another important consideration is that their treatment of their customers is perfectly honorable, a very important matter in the purchase of such a complicated affair as a musical instrument   Their recommendation of instruments can be *depended on* implicitly—This we know from an extensive acquaintance among hundreds to whom they have sold instruments   We advise our readers to give them a call, or certainly to write to them before deciding on the purchase of a Piano Forte, Organ or Melodeon, or any musical merchandise   See the Addenda to this volume, which contains a portion of their catalogue   Also see card on Co Map

**W. C. Orcutt,** General Agent for Central New York for the celebrated *Florence Sewing Machine,* prints a well displayed advertisement on page 152   The Florence Machine makes a beautiful piece of furniture, and as a Sewing Machine, is capable of taking a greater number of stitches than any other   Its work is equal to other first class machines, and its price as low   During the few years that the Florence has been in the market its sales have been very large   It is a general favorite   Call and see it when you visit Syracuse   Mr Orcutt may be found at No 2 Yates Block

**G. W. Silcox,** Engraver, Lithographer and Letter Press Printer, whose card appears on page 192, is prepared to execute with neatness and dispatch, all work entrusted to his care   Those wishing anything in his line cannot do better than to call at 67 South Salina street, and examine specimens of his work

Ryan, Caroline Mrs , (Virgil,) lot 46, farmer 100

Ryan, Elishup H , (Virgil,) lot 38, farmer 50

Ryan, John, (Virgil,) lot 35, farmer 100

Ryan, John Jr , (Virgil,) lot 4, farmer 140

Ryan, Jonathan, (Virgil,) lot 4, speculator and farmer 68

Ryan, William, (Virgil,) lot 46, farmer 90

Sager, Abram, (Virgil,) lots 23 and 38, farmer 136

Sager, Cynthia Mrs , (Virgil,) lot 44, farmer 50

Sager, Lisedel,(Virgil,) lot 21, farmer leases 60

Saltsman, John, (Virgil,) lot 42, farmer 149

Sands, Timothy W , (Virgil,) lot 32, farmer 74

Saxton, Nelson, (Virgil,) lot 36, farmer 50

Scofield, David, (Virgil,) cooper

Seager, Samuel, (Virgil,) lot 35, farmer 163

Seaman, Simon B , (Dryden, Tompkins Co ,) lot 41, farmer 67

Seamans, Charles H , (Virgil,) carriage ironer

Seamans, Isaac M , (Virgil,) blacksmith

Seamans, Julian C , (Virgil,) drover

Seamans, Samuel M , (Virgil,) blacksmith

Sheerar, John, (Virgil,) lots 36 and 37, farmer 150

Shepard, Hallet,(Virgil,)lot 45, farmer (*with Riley Shepard*)

SHEPARD RILEY, (Virgil,) lot 45, farmer 70

Sheridan, Thomas, (South Cortland,) lot 13, farmer 80

Sherman, Ann Mrs , (Virgil,) lot 13, farmer 50

Sherman & Dickinson,(Messengerville,)(*Hiram Sherman and John O Dickinson,*) wagon and carriage makers

Sherman, Eleazer, (Virgil,) (*with Washington,*) lot 21, farmer 60

Sherman, Hiram, (Messengerville,) (*Sherman & Dickinson* )

Sherman, Washington, (Virgil,) (*with Eleazer,*) lot 21, farmer 50

Shevalier, Briggs, (East Virgil,) lot 48, farmer

Shevalier, Christian, (East Virgil,) lots 48 and 49, farmer 118

Shevalier, DePuy, (Messengerville,) lot 49, farmer 100

Shevalier, Isaac, (Messengerville,) lot 39, farmer 170

SHEVALIER, JAMES B , (Messengerville,) lot 38, inspector of elections and farmer 95

SHEVALIER, JOHN, (Messengerville,) lot 49, assessor and farmer 130

Shults, David, (Virgil,) lot 45, cabinet maker and farmer 147½

Shults, Nathan, (Virgil,) resident

Shults, Theophilus, (Virgil,) lot 14, farmer 160

Simonds, Chester, (Virgil,) lot 43, blacksmith and farmer 32

Simonds, Eber, (Virgil,) lot 33, carpenter and joiner and farmer 5

Skeel, Albert, (Blodget Mills,) leases steam saw mill of Wm Skeel, Homer

Skeel, William, (Blodget Mills,) residence at Homer, prop of steam saw mill

Sly, Alanson M , (Virgil,) lot 27, farmer 66

Small, Melvin, (South Cortland,) lot 13, farmer 60

Smith, Amanda W Mrs , (Dryden, Tompkins Co ,) lot 41, farmer 1½

Smith, Harrison, (Virgil,) lots 14 and 15, farmer 106

Smith, Henry A , (Virgil,) lot 4, farmer 90

Smith, Nathan, (Messengerville,) lots 39, 49 and 50, farmer 112

Spencer, Amos C , (Blodget Mills,) lot 7, farmer

Spencer, Isaac Jr , (Blodget Mills,) lots 6, 16 and 17, farmer 350

SPENCER, NATHAN, (Virgil,) lot 26, drover and farmer 212

Sprague, Charity Mrs , (Virgil,) lot 27, farmer 25

Sprague, Charles, (Blodget Mills,) lot 7,farmer 106

Stafford, Hopkin, (Blodget Mills,) lots 8, 9, 18 and 19, farmer 234

Stafford, Josiah, (Blodget Mills,) lots 6 and 18, farmer 76

Stafford, Miles, (Cortland Village,) lots 19 and 20, farmer 85

Stanbro, Rebecca Mrs , (Virgil,) lot 3, farmer 60

Stillman, John, (Virgil,) lot 27, farmer leases

Stowell, Alvah, (Blodget Mills,) lot 8, farmer 100

Stowell, Jehial, (Blodget Mills,) lot 8, farmer 22

Stowell, John, (Blodget Mills,) lot 8, school collector and farmer 86

Suits, Henry P , (East Virgil,) lot 37, farmer 50

SWEET, ALBERT, (Virgil,) farmer (*with Nathaniel Lewis* )

Sweet, David R , (Virgil,) lot 38, farmer 100

SWEET, EBER, (Virgil,) owns right of Dr Eli Sweet's horse power elevator

Sweet, George H , (Virgil,) tanner

Tanner, Salem, (Blodget Mills,) lot 19, farmer 60

Terpenning, Abraham, (Virgil,) lot 35, farmer 24

Terpenning, Arthur, (Dryden, Tompkins Co ,) lot 41, farmer 23

Terpenning, Ceguismer, (Blodget Mills,) lot 15, farmer 140

Terpening, James T , (Virgil,) lot 24, carpenter and farmer 7

Terpening, Levi V , (Virgil,) lot 23, farmer 84½

Terpenning, William, (Virgil,) lot 16, farmer 102

Thomas, Ham, (Virgil,) lot 45, farmer 95.

Trapp, David R , (Virgil,) lot 11, farmer 180

Trapp, Jesse R , (Dryden, Tompkins Co ,) lot 21, farmer 48½

Tripp, John D , (Virgil,) physician and surgeon

Trapp, George M , (Virgil,) blacksmith

Tucker, Esek H , (Dryden, Tompkins Co ,) lots 41 and 51, farmer 25

Tyler, Allen W , (Virgil,) (*with D. F Wallace* )

Tyler, George, (Virgil,) lot 33, farmer 58.

Tyler, Jeremiah G , (Virgil,) lot 33, farmer 117

Tyler, John, (Virgil,) lot 42, farmer leases 70

## SOMETHING NEW!
# Hair Jewelry.

Any lady having cut off her Hair and wishing to sell
it, can do so by calling on

## Mrs. Geo. A. Adams, Pine Street,
# Homer Village,

*First Door East of J H Munger's Drug Store.*

Ladies wishing an elegant SWITCH can procure one by
saving all the hair combed from their head, laying it loose-
ly in a box, (don't waste a hair,) and taking it to Mrs Adams  She will straighten it out
and weave it into a beautiful switch  If you want a *Nice Set of Hair Jewelry*, call on Mrs
Adams  Any one wishing to learn Hair Jewelry or Hair Flowers will also please call
on Mrs Adams  **Cloak and Dress Making and Stitching** also done to order
at the same place  Please give her a call  Homer, N Y,

---

**S**ILCOX gets up the most **Elegant Wedding and Invita-
tion Outfits** in the country, from the fact that he has assistance
of GIMBREDE, of New York, and his mammoth establishment, to
supply all the LATEST NOVELTIES, both of his own and foreign
importations.  If you wish tasty

## JOB PRINTING,

SILCOX'S is the place.  He has the largest and best stock to select
from, and the only place in the city where can be found Fancy Cards,
Papers, &c  Call, or send, and get SILCOX's CIRCULAR upon CARD ETI-
QUETTE, and get posted upon the styles, forms, &c , for Visiting Cards, Weddings,
Monograms, Invitations, &c  He also manufactures to order any style of Envelope,
Billet and Note Papers, out of French, Persian or English Papers, does stamping in
gold and silver, embossed and colors  His visiting card engraving, executed by Gim-
brede, cannot be excelled  Remember and call before ordering  GEO W. SILCOX,
Engraver and Printer, 67 South Salina Street, Syracuse, N Y.

---

**Dr. Kingsley,** of Rome, justly celebrated for the many cures he has effected of
that most distressing disease, Cancer, publishes a notice on page 1  He is prepared
to treat all scrofulous diseases, and others
of long standing, and assures his patients
that they will not be charged a heavy bill
and dismissed without receiving any benefit.  Persons who cannot conveniently call
upon him in person, can address him by
letter, and will receive prompt attention
Dr K is a graduate, with an experience of
over fourteen years in the practice of medicine  Let the afflicted give him a call

**Jacob Miller,** Book Binder and Blank
Book manufacturer, in the Journal Building, Syracuse, carries on the most exten
sive business in his line, in Central New
York  He is provided with first class
machinery and a number of excellent workmen, who understand their business  See
card, page 173

**J. H. Tanner,** dealer in Dry Goods,
Groceries, Crockery, Hardware, and everything usually kept in a country store,
Blodget's Mills, publishes a card on page
128  He has been in the mercantile business eighteen years at the same place, and
from small beginnings has built up a flourishing trade  His effort to deal fairly with
all is appreciated, as is seen from his constantly increasing business in this and adjoining towns.

**R. H. Spendley & Co.,** Wholesale
and Retail dealers in Hats, Caps and Furs,
corner of Main and Cortland streets, Cortland, N Y , publishes a card on page 150
Those in want of furs of the best quality or
of the cheaper kinds will find Messrs
Spendley ready to supply them at reasonable rates  Their stock is large and their
qualities and prices to suit the times

**John L. Boorum,** advertises on
page 150 that he wants 3,000 tons of Flax
straw at the Homer Flax and Cordage
Mills, and though that is a large amount
we can assure the farmers in that region
that he is prepared to buy all that is offered
Flax is one of the most profitable crops
that can be raised, as those farmers knew
who have tried the experiment.  Mr. Boorum has Flax seed for sale and to let and
will give any information upon the subject
to all who may call at the mills

**The Cortland County Demo-
crat,** published by Benton B Jones, at
Cortland Village, has recently been enlarged and improved, and as it is the only
Democratic paper in the County, our
friends of that persuasion will do well to
give it a liberal patronage  As an advertising medium it has few equals in the
County. See card, page 184.

Tyler, Richard C , (Dryden, Tompkins Co ,) lot 41, farmer 510

Tyler, Samuel P , (Dryden, Tompkins Co ,) lot 31, farmer 70

Tyler, William, (Virgil,) lot 83, farmer 124.

Veeder, Cornelius, (Virgil,) lot 12, farmer 187

Vunk, David M , (Virgil,) lot 85, farmer 116½

Vunk, Henry, (Virgil,) lot 24, farmer 183½

WALLACE, DAVID F , (Virgil,) dry goods and groceries.

Waters, Benjamin F , (Virgil,) lot 47, farmer 214

Waters, Morris E , (Virgil,) lot 43, drover, patent right dealer and farmer 35

WATKINS, IRA W , (Virgil,) lots 24 and 34, drover and farmer 100

WATROS, NELSON, (Virgil,) lot 24, justice peace and farmer 40.

WATROS, NELSON M , (Virgil,) lot 23, farmer 73

Webber Rodner, (Virgil,) lot 45, farmer 66½

Webster, Stephen, (Virgil,) lot 24, farmer 37

WESCOTT, THOMAS A , (Blodget Mills,) lot 19, farmer 140

West, Punderson, (Virgil,) lot 42, farmer leases of Richard Tyler, Dryden, 70

White, William, (Virgil,) lot 22, farmer leases 100

Wilcox, Harry. (Virgil,) lot 15, farmer 14

Wilcox, John B , (East Virgil,) lot 48, farmer

Wilcox, Manley, (Cortland Village,) lot 3, farmer 50

Wilcox, Salem, (Virgil,) lot 15, farmer 83.

WILLETT, CHARLES A , (Blodget Mills,) (*with Enoch F* ,) lot 7, farmer 165

Willett Enoch F ,) (Cortland Village,) (*with Chas A* ,) lot 7, farmer 165

Williams, Charles D , (Virgil,) dealer in marble and grave stones

Williams, Marvin B , (Virgil,) wagon make

Williamson, Clark,(Dryden, Tompkins Co ,) lot 41, farmer 27

Winslow, Elisha, (Virgil,) post master and general merchant

Winslow, John E., (Virgil,) (*with E. Winslow* )

Winter, John S., (Messengerville,) lot 19, commissioner of highways and farmer 180

Winters, Henry, (East Virgil,) lot 88, farmer 280

Wood, Andrew J Rev., (Dryden, Tompkins Co ,) lot 21, Free Will Baptist clergyman and farmer 70

Wood, Edmund B , (Virgil,) lot 35, farmer leases 29

WOOD, JOHN, (Cortland Village,) lots 15 and 16, farmer 159

WOOD, MARVIN R , (South Cortland,) lot 2, farmer 126

Wood, Warren A , (Virgil,) lot 12, mason and farmer 6

Woodard, Archibald, (Messengerville,) lots 28 and 33, farmer 234

Woodard, Elijah, (Blodget Mills,) lots 18 and 19, farmer 64

Woodard, Lydia Mrs , (Messengerville,) lot 28, farmer 42½

Woodard, Peter, (Messengerville,) lot 28, farmer 78.

Woodden, Orrin, (East Virgil,) lots 29 and 33, farmer 175

Wooden, Isaac C & Orren Jr , (Blodget Mills,) lot 7, farmer 108

Wooden, John F., (Cortland Village,) lot 6, farmer 21

Wright, James, (Virgil,) lot 46, carpenter and farmer 116

Young, Josiah, (Blodget Mills,) lot 29, farmer leases 27

---

# WILLETT.

### (Post Office Addresses in Parentheses.)

Adams, Stephen J , (Willet,) farmer 368

Allen, Alford, (Willet,) farmer 89

Babcock, Andrew, (Upper Lisle, Broome Co ,) (*with Marvin*,) farmer 188

Babcock, Marvin, (Upper Lisle, Broome Co ,) (*with Andrew*,) farmer 188

Bancroft, Mercy, (Upper Lisle, Broome Co ,) farmer 10

Barnard, George, (Willet,) cooper

Barnes, Samuel L , (Willet,) farmer 90

Parry, David, (Texas Valley,) farmer 200

Barry, Thomas M , (Marathon,) farmer 179

Beardsley, Belah, (Willet,) surveyor and physician

Beardsley, Joseph, (Willet,) farmer 50

Bennett, William G., (Upper Lisle, Broome Co ,) farmer 95

Bliss, Joshua, (Upper Lisle, Broome Co ,) farmer 123

Bowen, George, (Willet,) farmer 90

Boyden, Francis, (Willet,) farmer 180

Boyden, Luther, (Texas Valley,) farmer 100

Brigham, Esther, (Marathon,) farmer 183.

Brown, Albert F. Rev., (Willet,) M E clergyman

Burgett, John, (Willet,) farmer leases 156

Burlingame, Miles E , (Willet,) lawyer

Burlingame, W , (Willet,) prop of flour mill

Campbell, Andrew, (Texas Valley,) farmer 42

Canfield, George R , (Upper Lisle, Broome Co ,) farmer 83½

Canfield, John, (Upper Lisle, Broome Co.,) farmer 33½
Canfield, Samuel, (Upper Lisle, Broome Co ,) farmer 33½, residence Erie city, Pa.
Clinton, Elias D , (Upper Lisle, Broome Co ,) farmer 100
CLINTON, JOHN D , (Upper Lisle, Broome Co ,) broom maker
Cole, Philip, (Willet,) farmer 4
Coonrad, William, (Texas Valley,) farmer 75
Covey, Charles H , (Smithville Flats, Chenango Co ,) farmer 65
Covey, Edward Jr , (Willet,) farmer 70
Covey, Edward W , (Smithville Flats, Chenango Co ,) farmer 165
Covey, Joseph, (Upper Lisle, Broome Co ,) farmer 103.
Crittenden, Riley, (Willet,) drover
Curewell, Nathan, (Willet,) farmer 40
Daremus, Andrew, (Texas Valley,) farmer leases 40
Davis, John, (Willet,) farmer 200
DAY, CHARLES, (Willet,) tanner
DAY, IRA, (Willet,) prop of tannery.
Decker, David, (Smithville Flats, Chenango Co ,) farmer leases
Delavan, Charles, (Willet,) farmer 314
Delevan, Charles H , (Willet,) farmer 100
DELLOW, WILLIAM, (Willet,) prop of cabinet and furniture rooms
Dodge, Charles, (Upper Lisle, Broome Co ,) farmer 20¾
Drew, Misses, (Willet,) milliners
Dyer, E J , (Willet,) *(Dyer & Nichols )*
Dyer, J S & Son, (Willet,) merchants
Dyer & Nichols, (Willet,) *(E J Dyer and E F Nichols,)* general merchants
Eaton, Abel, (Willet,) farmer 135
Eaton, John C , (Willet,) farmer 100
Eaton, Peter, (Willet,) farmer 370
Eaton, Ulysses, (Willet,) farmer 100
Eggleston, Samuel, (Upper Lisle, Broome Co ,) farmer 69
Fish, Cornelius D , (Marathon,) farmer 60
Fitzgerald, James C , (Willet,) dealer in patent rights.
Foley, Dennis, (Marathon,) farmer 100
Ford, George, (Willet,) farmer 40
Frolick, George (Marathon,) farmer 150
Fry, Alvirus, (Willet,) tanner
Gage, Daniel, (Willet,) farmer leases 180
Gardiner, Ishmael E , (Willet,) farmer 130
Gardner, William R , (Willet,) prop of saw mill
Grant, Ward, (Willet,) farmer leases 130
Grant, William B , (Willet,) farmer 130
Green, Edward, (Upper Lisle, Broome Co ,) *(with Geo L )* farmer 145
Green, George L , (Upper Lisle, Broome Co ,) *(with Edward,)* farmer 145
Green, Jedediah, (Willet,) sash and blind maker
Greene, Burrel, (Willet,) farmer
Greene, Gilbert, (Willet,) farmer 75
Greene, Henry C , (Willet,) carpenter and joiner
Hall, Owen C , (Willet ) allop physician
Harris, Milton K , (Willet,) blacksmith
Hazard, Harry, (Willet,) farmer 91
Heacock, Hile, (Texas Valley,) farmer 100
Hills, Eliam, (Willet,) farmer 17
Hollenbeck, Nathan, (Willet,) farmer 76

Hopkins, John, (Willet,) tanner
Ingersoll, S Miles, (Willet,) farmer 2½
Isaacs, J J , (Texas Valley,) farmer 60.
Johnson, Abram, (Willet,) farmer 51
Johnson, Abram Jr , (Willet,) farmer 52
Johnson, Elijah, (Willet,) miller
Johnson, Phineas, (Texas Valley,) farmer 199
Jones, Aslle, (Upper Lisle, Broome Co ,) farmer 103
Jones, Edward F , (Willet,) farmer leases 40
Jones, Enoch, (Willet,) farmer 42
Jones, John, (Willet,) farmer leases 34
Jones, Ogden, (Willet,) *(with William,)* farmer 100
Jones, Thomas, (Willet,) carpenter and joiner
Jones, William, (Willet,) *(with Ogden,)* farmer 100
Kelly, Casper D , (Upper Lisle, Broome Co ,) *(with Dewitt B ,)* farmer 250
Kelly, Dewitt B , (Upper Lisle, Broome Co ,) *(with Casper D ,)* farmer 250
KEYES, LESLIES L , (Willet,) cabinet maker
Kingsley, Washington Rev., (Willet,) Baptist minister
Landers, Garry S , (Upper Lisle, Broome Co ,) *(with Marcellus,)* farmer 400
Landers, Marcellus, (Upper Lisle, Broome Co ,) *(with Garry L ,)* farmer 400
Larr, William, (Willet,) blacksmith
Leroy, Silas, (Willet,) blacksmith
Maine, Wesley M , (Willet,) farmer 54½
Marvin, Luther, (Smithville Flats, Chenango Co ,) farmer leases 25
Marvin, William, (Willet,) wagon maker,
Meacham, Dexter, (Upper Lisle, Broome Co ,) farmer 150
Meacham Isaac, (Upper Lisle, Broome Co ,) farmer 50
Meacham Randall S , (Willet,) farmer 80
Meacham, Thomas, (Willet,) carpenter and joiner
Metzgar, Joseph, (Texas Valley,) farmer 120
Morey, Luman, (Willet,) farmer 155
Morgan, Peter, (Smithville Flats, Chenango Co ,) farmer 38
Newcomb, Curtis, (Willet,) farmer leases 240
Newcomb, Samuel E , (Willet,) farmer 240
Nichols, E F , (Willet,) *(Dyer & Nichols,)* merchant
Nichols, Sisson, (Willet,) shoemaker
Palmer, S C , (Willet,) farmer leases 50
Patridge, Eli, (Upper Lisle, Broome Co ,) farmer leases 103
Payce, Charles D , (Willet,) farmer 140
Pember, Luther, (Upper Lisle, Broome Co ,) farmer 43.
Perkins, George J , (Upper Lisle, Broome Co ,) farmer leases 102
Perkins, Samuel, (Willet,) mechanic
Perkins, Wilham, (Willet,) farmer 69
Roby, Fran E , (Upper Lisle, Broome Co ,) farmer 78
Rose, Josiah H , (Willet,) tailor
Rowley, Harteon A , (Texas Valley,) farmer 70
Salisbury, Eben, (Willet,) farmer 90
Salisbury, Enos, (Willet,) farmer 90

Salisbury, Geo , (Upper Lisle, Broome Co ,) prop of saw mill and farmer 40
Sawdey, Asa, (Marathon,) farmer 100
Smith, Josephine, (Upper Lisle, Broome Co ,) farmer 100.
Sowl, Charles W , (Marathon,) farmer leases 125
Steinberg, William, (Willet,) farmer 120
Storms, Thomas, (Willet,) farmer leases 60
Strongh, Franklin, (Texas Valley,) farmer 92½
Sweet, Asel, (Smithville Flats, Chenango Co ,) farmer
Sweet, W C , (Willet,) farmer 12
Talbut, Almon, (Upper Lisle, Broome Co ,) stone mason and farmer 50
Tarbel, Simon, (Willet,) farmer leases 100
Tennant, Elijah, (Willet,) farmer 102
Tennant, Thomas (Willet,) farmer
Todd, Hiram, (Willet,) farmer 60
Ulrick, Stephen L , (Smithville Flats, Chenango Co ,) farmer leases 59

Valentine, Edgar, (Marathon,) (*with Roscoe,*) farmer 104
Valentine, Roscoe, (Marathon,) (*with Edgar,*) farmer 104
Webb, William, (Smithville Flats, Chenango Co ,) farmer 80
Wightman, William, (Willet,) farmer 73
Wilcox, Eben, (Upper Lisle, Broome Co ,) farmer 100.
Wilcox, John, (Willet,) farmer 75
Wiles, A Mrs , (Texas Valley,) farmer 50
Wiles, David A , (Willet,) post master and general merchant
Williams, Samuel A , (Upper Lisle, Broome Co ,) farmer 115
Wilson, Daniel L , (Willet,) farmer leases 80
Wilson, Harry, (Willet,) farmer 231
Yarns, George W , (Upper Lisle, Broome Co ,) farmer leases 40
Yarns, Thomas, (Marathon,) farmer leases 20

---

# PUBLISHER'S NOTICES.

**The Reynold's Steel Tempering Works,** Reynolds, Barber & Co , Proprietors, at Auburn, are largely engaged in the manufacture of Reaper and Mower Knives, Plane Irons, Chisels, &c The process by which they temper steel is a peculiar one, and as patented by Mr Reynolds, is the result of over forty years labor This gentleman always worked on the plan that tempering steel was simply changing it from a *fibrous* to a *granular* state He certainly has succeeded in producing a finer granulation (temper) than has ever before been produced Messrs Reynolds, Barber & Co , control the patents for these processes, and are applying them successfully in all their manufactures — Their establishment is capable of turning out an immense amount of work, yet their orders are now, and have been for some months, accumulating far in advance of their present ability to supply, a circumstance which they will not long allow to be the case We predict that the time is not far distant when all Mower and Reaper Factories and farmers will use their improved sections See their advertisement on page 6, fronting the Introduction

**Charles W. Kinne,** proprietor of the Machine Cooperage establishment, Cortland, N Y , publishes a card on colored page 133, setting forth his work, to which we take pleasure in calling the attention of the public For twenty-five years this establishment has been in operation, and by introducing the most approved machinery Mr Kinne is able to furnish the best of work at reasonable rates

**Chas. Tremain & Co.,** manufacturers of Rag, Book, News, Tea and Wrapping Paper, at Manlius, publish a card on page 146 Publishers and paper dealers will find them fair and honorable men to purchase from In the manufacture of *book* and *news*, they use only domestic stock, which is conceded to be superior to imported rags They employ experienced paper makers only, and having improved machinery, they can insure a superior article in all cases We use their paper in the publication of our directories

**E. A. Shumway's** Wholesale and Retail Paper Warehouse, Syracuse, is always supplied with a large assortment of Paper, Stationery and Printers' Materials, which he will furnish to the trade or to consumers on as good terms as any house in Central New York Mr S understands the wants of the public and will spare no pains to suit his customers Dealers and others will do well to give him a call before purchasing elsewhere See card, page 186

**The Gazette and Banner,** published by Charles P Cole, at Cortland Village, is an eight page paper, too well known to need recommendation from us For several years it has been a welcome visitor to many homes, and it is the purpose of the proprietor to spare no pains to make it a first-class family paper Its large circulation renders it a valuable advertising medium in the County See advertisement on page 194

# LODGES, ASSOCIATIONS &C.

## CORTLAND VILLAGE

**Cortland Chapter, No. 194, R. A. M.**—Chartered February 1866

### CHARTER MEMBERS

Roswell R Bourne,  
Samuel Adams,  
George L Warren,  
John W Oagood,  
G W Davenport,  

R. W Bourne,  
W H Crane,  
Horace Dibble,  
—— Gillett  

### FIRST ELECTED OFFICERS

D C McGraw, H P,  
A Sager, K  
George L Warren, S  
John W Oagood, C H  
Alvah D Waters, P S.  

Dewitt Apgar, R A C  
Horace Dibble, T  
W D Tisdale, Sec  
G W Davenport, 3d V  
S R Hunter, 2d V  
Charles W Kinne, 1st V  

### PRESENT OFFICERS

D C McGraw, H P  
A Sager K  
H O Gillett, S  
G L Warren, C H  
A D Watters, P S  
W D Tisdale, R A C,  

R E Hill, 3d V  
S R Hunter, 2d V  
K W Holmes, 1st V.  
H Dibble, T  
F Freeman, Sec  
O Hitchcock, Tyler  

Number of members 40   Meet 2nd and 4th Wednesday of each month, in Masonic Hall

——

**Lincoln Lodge, No. 119, I. O. of G. T.**—Lodge organized Oct 24th, 1866  
Number of Charter Members, 10

### OFFICERS OF FIRST QUARTER

N W Green, W C T  
Ruth Baker, W V T  
W Bridgeford, W S  
B P Bergren, W F S  

P J Bergren, W T  
Eliza Baker, W G  
Moses Wright, W Sent.  

Number of members Sept 1st, 1868, 170

### PRESENT OFFICERS

George L Waters, W C T  
Hellen M Willett, W V T  
John T Pratt, W S  
W Bridgeford, W F S  
P J Bergren, W T  
Clinton Hale, W M  
Vira McClara, W G  

John Krebs, W Sent  
F H Kenedy, W Chap  
Axie Gazley, W A S  
Hannah Barnea, W D M.  
Hattie Hentie, R H S.  
Julia Grover, L H S  
W W Gale, P W C T  

Regular meeting every Friday evening, at Squire's Hall

**Young Men's Christian Association of Cortland.**—Was organized April, 1868  The objects of this Association are the development of Christian character and the promotion of Evangelical Religion, the cultivation of Christian sympathy and the improvement of the mental, moral and spiritual condition of young men
  Regular meeting every Monday evening, at Squire's Hall

OFFICERS

Adolphns F Tanner, Pres
Henry C Smith, Vice Pres

Roe A Smith, Treas
Chas W Collins, Cor Sec'y
J D Fredricks, Rec Sec'y

BOARD OF MANAGERS

A F Tanner,
H C Smith,
Roe A Smith,
C W. Collins,

J D Fredricks,
Henry F Benton,
Wm H Myres
Alvin Rounseville

---

## HARFORD

**Evening Star Lodge, No. 200, I. O. of G. T.,** located at Harford, was organized February 18th, 1867, by B E. Admonds, District Deputy, and now contains 130 members in good standing  The following are the names of the

CHARTER MEMBERS

Lyman Tanner,
A Johnson,
Samuel Steele,
Josiah H Brown,
Alpha Clark,
Francis B Edmonds,
Robert Purvies,
Maurice Hemingway,
B D Heath,
Wm J Mills,
James D Purple,
Mrs S Steele,
Mrs A. D. Hemingway,

Mrs Wm J. Mills,
Mrs J H. Brown,
Mrs F. B. Edmonds,
Mrs P A. Johnson,
Emma M Holden,
Lorana W Clark,
Mrs. Alpha Clark,
Polly V Baker,
Mrs L Sweetland,
Ellen Moore,
Almyra Tanner,
Mary A. Hemingway,
Sarah A Bradley

OFFICERS—FIRST TERM

J H Brown, W C T
Emma Holden, W V. T
W J. Mills, W C
J D Purple, W S
Mrs A D Hemingway, W. A. S
Maurice Hemingway, W. F. S
Lorana Clark, W T

Lyman Tanner, W M
Mary A Hemingway, W. D. M
P A Johnson, W I G
Francis B Edmonds, W O G
Mrs L. C Steele, W R S.
Almyra Tanner, W L S
Mrs M Clark, P. W. C T

# PUBLISHER'S NOTICES.

**Joseph Watson,** Homer, N Y, is prepared to supply all orders for Monuments, Headstones, Mantles, Table Tops, and anything else in that line, at short notice He deals in all kinds of Granite and will furnish monuments at reasonable rates Designs of various kinds in American and Italian marble can be obtained at all times Mr Watson gives his personal attention and supervision to all work, and the public may rest assured that it will be executed in a satisfactory manner See card, page 124

**W. H. Van Slyck,** Bill Poster and Paper Hanger, Cortland, N Y, is prepared to execute all jobs after the most approved style, whether it be a circus bill upon the side of a barn, upon the fences or in satin paper upon the walls of a lady's parlor Give him a call His card appears on page 150

**Albert G. Smith,** manufacturer and dealer in Boots, Shoes, Rubbers, Leather and Findings, Marathon, N Y, publishes a card on page 150 If you want a good pair of boots for yourself, a pair of those fine gaiters for your wife, or a pair of those copper-toed boots for Johnny, call at Smith's and get them At the same time take along a pair of those Rubbers, which you will need in wet weather

**The Cortland County Republican,** published by J R Dixon, Editor and Proprietor, Homer, N Y, is one of the best family newspapers in the County It not only contains a summary of the news, but its columns are replete with articles calculated to instruct and to instil into the minds of its readers sound principles, which, if followed out, will make them wiser and better Book and Job Printing executed at the same office, in the best manner See card, page 120

**Howe's Never-Failing Ague Cure and Tonic Bitters, and Howe's Concentrated Syrup,** are prepared under the personal supervision of Dr C B Howe, the proprietor, at Seneca Falls, N Y, for ague and fever, and all periodic diseases, rheumatism, paralysis, etc The "Ague Cure" has produced wonderful cures The "Syrup," for the blood, liver, skin, digestive and uterine organs, has cured many cases of scrofula, cancer, tumors, goiter, salt rheum, scaldhead, and many other diseases too numerous to mention in this place See card, page 20

**W. J. Bonner,** dealer in Hats, Caps and Furs, has recently opened a store on the east side of Main street, Homer, N Y, where the most durable and elegant styles of hats and caps may be found and at reasonable prices Young gentlemen are especially invited to examine the fine styles and rich array of goods Mr Bonner may be found at his post at all seasonable hours, where he will show you a full assortment of goods and at prices defying competition See card, colored page 151

**J. C. Gray,** dealer in Watches, Jewelry, Silver and Plated Ware, Musical Instruments &c, publishes a card on page 134 which no one can read without feeling that there is the place to purchase In addition to standard articles of ornament and use, Mr Gray keeps a great variety of Fancy Goods, Toys, Fishing Tackle, &c, and does Repairing in all its branches Photographing in all its branches and of the best kind done at this establishment That person must be highly favored who can do better than to call at Gray's, Marathon, N Y

**James M. Haight,** Taxidermist and Naturalist, East Homer, Cortland Co, N Y, possesses rare skill in preparing Birds and all kinds of Animals in such a manner as to make them appear as "natural as life" Persons having birds or quadrupeds which they wish preserved, will do well to call on Mr. Haight, as he has no superior in these parts His card appears on page 186

**Mrs. George A. Adams,** Pine street, Homer, N Y, manufactures Hair Jewelry, Flowers, Switches, &c Mrs A is an expert at the business, and those having hair which they wish manufactured, will do well to give her a call Cloak and Dress making carried on at the same place See card, page 192

**Oscar Wildey,** dealer in Dry Goods, West Main Street, Marathon, N Y, keeps a large assortment of all goods found in a first-class store His stock of dress goods, cloaks, trimmings, and all goods for either gentlemen's or ladies' wear, is very large, and the *one price system* is fully carried out. Mr Wildey has a thorough acquaintance with his business, and by keeping an eye on the market is able to buy at low figures, and as he is satisfied with small profits, his customers have the benefit of his shrewd business talent Give him a call His card appears on page 158

**J. Burt,** General Merchant, east side of Main street, Homer, N Y, desires to tender his thanks to his friends for their past favors and solicits a continuance of the same His old friends and the public generally may rest assured that in the future as in the past he will show himself worthy of their patronage His assortment of goods is large and no pains will be spared to satisfy the requirements of his customers See card, page 140

**E. L. Baker, M. D.,** Eclectic Physician and Surgeon, Marathon, N Y, publishes a card on page 132 Dr Baker gives special attention to surgical and chronic diseases, and from education and experience he is prepared to minister to the wants of the afflicted and treat all cases according to the most approved methods Give him a call at the Carley House

# Cortland County Table of Distances

## Showing the Air-Line Distances

### Between the Villages, in Miles & Tenths of Miles.

Column headings (reading across the top):

Cincinnatus · Cortland · Cuyler · Freetown Corners · Harfo'c. · Homer · Hunt's Corners · Little York · Lower Cincinnatus · Marathon · McGrawville · Preble · Scott · Solon · South Cortland · South Harford · Taylor · Texas Valley · Truxton · Union Valley · Virgil · Willett.

**VILLAGES**

- Cincinnatus,
- Cortland,
- Cuyler,
- Freetown Corners,
- Harford,
- Homer,
- Hunt's Corners,
- Little York,
- Lower Cincinnatus,
- Marathon,
- McGrawville,
- Preble,
- Scott,
- Solon,
- South Cortland,
- South Harford,
- Taylor Valley,
- Texas Valley,
- Truxton,
- Union Valley,
- Virgil,
- Willett.

## REASONS FOR BUYING ALL

# MUSICAL GOODS

### At the Wholesale Music Store of

# REDINGTON & HOWE,

## No. 2 Wieting Block, Salina St., Syracuse, N. Y.

1st —Purchasers find in our store much the largest stock of Piano Fortes, Organs, Melodeons and Musical Merchandise to be met with any where in the State, outside of New York City   We offer another advantage ·  New York City Houses keep only one Maker's instruments or their own.   Here you see eighteen   ·

2d —You can see the instrument you wish to buy, and know exactly its tone  Persons at their homes are often in doubt whether to buy a Piano, Organ or Melodeon   There are always great varieties in tone and finish

3d.—You can compare each instrument with those of several other makers, thereby judging what will suit you best.

4th.—You will find *first class* instruments   We are no experimental manufacturers   We select our entire stock from good reliable makers who are not ashamed to own their work, and will not allow the name of a dealer to be placed on their name boards as the manufacturer   We have no interest in any factory and no reason to recommend any instrument except for its reliability

5th —We have experts in each department to test *thoroughly* all goods we sell  The purchases we make are only of instruments selected expressly for our trade.

6th —We warrant perfect satisfaction to every purchaser   We have always done this through a successful business experience of twelve years before coming to Syracuse

7th —As we buy much more largely than any other house in the State, we buy cheaper.   We give our customers the benefit of this   You save money

8th —We have the best wholesale facilities, so that we supply all classes of dealers at the lowest New York and Boston prices   We have the only *Wholesale* Agency for the Steinway Piano Forte in Central or Western New York.   We can of course, retail at the lowest prices

9th —We employ only the best tuners, who will see to the reliability of instruments after they leave our Ware Rooms   Our traveling agents will also assist in caring for instruments.

10th —If you want *low priced* instruments, you will find them here cheaper then elsewhere   We can sell you at a profit and charge you only what the retail dealers *pay* for their goods.

11th —Our buying facilities enable us to purchase a lower grade of instruments of large Eastern Factories, (which manufacture from two to four hundred instruments per month,) at a less price than the actual first cost of constructing the same, at any factory (Piano, Organ or Melodeon) in Central New York

12th —Our speciality is *first-class* goods   On no other can we maintain permanently our large business   We shall tell you therefore, candidly, the grade of instruments, if we offer you any other than first quality

13th —We can furnish you unequaled opportunities for exchanging instruments; new for new, or old for new

14th.—The commercial standing of our house, furnishes you the strongest security for the reliability of the instruments, we, or our agents, sell you , and for the value of our warrant, (which we give you in addition to the warrant of the manufacturers )

15th —You are cordially invited to call at any time and examine and hear the instruments, (players always in attendance,) whether desiring to buy or not.  Come and see for yourselves what are the best instruments.  Or write to

### REDINGTON & HOWE, No. 2 Wieting Block,
#### Opposite Main Entrance to Syracuse House.

# NOTICES OF THE PRESS.

(From The Syracuse Daily Standard )

## The Mammoth Musical Emporium of Redington & Howe.

For some time we have designed an account of this immense establishment, that our readers might be posted in regard to one of the leading business establishments of our city, and which has been brought so rapidly to magnitude by the well directed tact and indomitable energy of its proprietors

The store No 2 Wieting Block, is one of the largest and most elegant on the main thoroughfare, and right in the very centre of the business part of the town   As we pass along the street, and more especially on entering the store, the eye is attracted by the elaborate and tastefully arranged exhibit in the show window of all the smaller class of musical instruments, &c , that make as an attractive a display as any window on South Salina Street.  As we enter, glancing to the right, the eye quickly runs over a large array of Guitars, Violins, and all varieties of musical instruments and wares, on shelves, hanging up, and in cases   Upon the counter of this department is a Burdett Reed Organ, in a most elaborately carved case, worth $1,500   It is a beauty   Next, upon the same side, we come to a long counter, behind which the shelves are loaded with Sheet Music   Prof T H Hinton supervises this department ; the best guarantee that the assortment is not only well selected but complete   The opposite side of the store is crowded with Steinway and Dunham Pianos, the sides being lined with the unequaled Vox Humana Organs: with a large variety of Piano and Melodeon covers, and stools added above

Passing by the center arch we come to rows and  rows more of Pianos, Organs and Melodeons, of all varieties and styles   On the right is the department for Music Books,—a branch to which this house gives the most prompt attention-  Drawers the entire length of the store (140 feet) are devoted to the storage of Violin and Guitar strings, Accordeons, Harmonicas, Piano Polish, and multitude of the different wares to be found in a complete music store, for the wholesale as well as retail trade   And still above, we find more Piano and Melodeon stools, cords of Violins, Guitars, Banjos, Drums, &c , &c   Goods are also stored in the basement—the whole size of the main store—finished and lighted for the purpose

In glancing through this great establishment one  particularly notices the large stock and *variety* of Piano Fortes, Organs and Melodeons, numbering more than fifty different kinds   The speciality of the proprietors is first-class instruments—on which the public can rely implicitly as being worthy in every way of confidence   This is an important matter for purchasers   Many dealers do not hesitate to tell buyers that second grade instruments are first class   Sometimes small dealers are really ignorant of what is a first class instrument   Others are themselves manufacturers of second quality instruments, and of course are bound to call their own as good as any made   Sometimes, also, they sell second and third rate goods as first grade for outrageous profits, calculating on only a brief business career in each place they visit   We say then, be careful to buy first class goods, and at a house where they are sure to have such

Messrs. Redington & Howe, in a twelve years business history, have earned an unblemished reputation for giving perfect satisfaction to their customers. This they accomplish by *knowing* that everything sent out by them is exactly what it is represented to be.  Besides, they are independent of any particular factory, and therefore the better fitted to judge between different makers While R & H. make a speciality of first class goods, they are enabled through their great advantages in buying, to sell second and third grade instruments at cheaper rates than any house in Central or Western New York They buy at the large factories east, at a price actually less than the small makers can manufacture. The proof of the matter is in the trying We say, go to Redington & Howe's and see what their facilities are. Their establishment is well worth a visit, even if one does not wish to buy anything All will be made welcome.

(From the Syracuse Daily Courier and Union )

THE IMMENSE MUSICAL ESTABLISHMENT OF REDINGTON & HOWE —The enterprising wholesale Music Dealers of our city, Messrs Redington & Howe, have just closed a most successful business year Their sales have been immense—something entirely unparalleled in the history of the Music trade in Central New York They have deserved their increasing success. Their store is the most magnificent emporium between New York and Chicago. Their stock would supply a dozen ordinary city music stores Theirs is the only strictly wholesale Music House in the State outside of New York City. They have even some advantages over the Metropolitan houses. Our Syracuse wholesale store keeps constantly on hand, the Pianos; Organs and Melodeons, of several different makers, (a total of eighteen, with over fifty different varieties,) while New York houses keep only one maker's instruments Besides business expenses are much less in Syracuse than in New York ; consequently Redington & Howe are diverting much wholesale trade from New York, and building up for themselves a mammoth business in supplying *dealers.* The question is sometimes asked, whether other dealers cannot buy in New York, as cheaply as Redington & Howe. The dealers have thoroughly satisfied *themselves* that they cannot, for there is not a house in Central New York that will agree to take the great quantities of Musical Goods that Redington & Howe buy. Consequently, others *have* to buy on a higher tariff. It is on the same principle that Stewart of New York forced a neighboring house to withdraw He could sell at a profit, cheaper than his competitor could buy. Messrs Redington & Howe, have similar purchasing facilities. Indeed, they can justly be called the 'Stewarts' of the Music trade in Central New York.

We are glad, also, to notice that Redington & Howe do a *first class* business in the Pianos, Organs and Melodeons they furnish Their principal stock is composed of first grade instruments. These they advertise and recommend because they *know* their reliability. This house can furnish second class instruments cheaper than any other establishment in Central New York. (for the reason of buying cheaper,) so that if purchasers want a *low-priced* instrument, Redington & Howe's is the place to procure it. We advise our readers not to buy *any* instrument without first seeing or writing to Redington & Howe They will also tell honestly the quality of the goods

Another point : this house is financially responsible for all they recommend. Besides having the largest capital in the Music business in Central New York, they are backed up by as much more as they choose to call upon

For everything in the musical line, go to Redington & Howe, No. 2 Wieting Block.

(From The Rochester Daily Union )

"The House of Redington & Howe is attracting the attention of the trade everywhere, on account of their superior facilities for wholesaling the acknowledged first-class Pianos, Organs and Melodeons, as well as every variety of Musical Merchandise

From the Syracuse Daily Journal

They have a musical emporium second to none west of New York city. In saying this we do but simple justice to Messrs. Redington & Howe, who occupy one of the largest stores in Central New York, fitted up with an especial view to the accommodation of their rapidly increasing business The various departments of the musical business have each received proper attention, and each is conducted with a view to meet the demands and cater to the tastes of a most fastidious public  First and foremost, Messrs Redington & Howe have in their Piano Department a full line of the various makes of Pianos, thus restricting purchasers to no particular make of Piano, but affording them unusual facilities for the comparing of the various instruments.  They have in their Organ and Melodeon Department all of the most approved Instruments manufactured, and offer inducements superior to any establishment, to persons desirous of purchasing this kind of instruments.  In this, as in the Piano trade, Messrs Redington & Howe have the exclusive State agency for the sale of certain makes of Pianos, Organs and Melodeons, and all business connected with such instruments passes through their hands, thus giving them a chance to furnish at lower rates than any other establishment outside of the manufacturers.

This statement is established beyond a doubt, from the fact that the manufacturers of the best grades of instruments refuse to furnish smaller dealers with instruments as low as they do those dealers whom they designate as their wholesale agents  The fact is well known and conceded by all persons that any article can be manufactured at less cost where the manufacturers are turning out hundreds of such articles monthly than they can be made by manufacturers who make on a smaller scale.  This would lead to the conclusion that this line of goods can be sold by Messrs R & H. at the lowest possible figures.

In the smaller instrument department their stock embraces the most complete and varied assortment ever opened in Central New York, with instruments from the various leading manufactories of this and other States  The sheet music department of this firm is one of the especial features of their trade, and to enable them to be first and foremost in the introduction of all new and popular sheet music, they have secured the services of our well known townsman, Professor T. H. Hinton, who superintends this department.  His well known capability, is the surest guarantee of the manner in which this branch of their trade is conducted  In this department at all times may be found all the latest vocal and instrumental gems issued in New York, Philadelphia and Boston  which will be received so as to enable Messrs Redington & Howe to offer them to the public simultaneous with their appearance in the Eastern cities.  The department of general musical merchandise has been supplied with everything pertaining in any wise to music, and which assortment they keep fully supplied.

The immense musical emporium of Messrs R. & H  is open at all times to musicians and the public generally as a place where they can call at all hours of the day and examine for themselves the various features of a well conducted and stocked musical establishment  The acknowledged leadership in the musical business has secured for them the ticket-selling of all operas, concerts and other first class entertainments given in our city

From the Daily Journal Oct., 24th, 1868

SOMETHING NEW AND BEAUTIFUL.—Messrs Redington & Howe have just received a newly patented Burdett organ, with what we should call a Fairy Bell accompaniment  By means of a stop the effect of a beautiful music box or Mandoline is added  The organ is a perfect gem—worthy of a special visit to their store.

This house is always foremost in introducing to the public in Central New York the various really valuable improvements that appear in musical instruments  They are just as careful to reject the humbugs, and have actually declined the agency of several pianos and organs which less informed dealers here have since adopted and are trying to sell

The immense business acquaintance of Redington & Howe, together with their high reputation in New York, Boston and Chicago, as the strongest and most energetic house in New York State (outside of the city), secures to them the first choice in regard to the agency of any manufacturers of musical instruments in the United States

Their Mammoth trade enables them to buy cheaper than any other Central New York House, as they buy so much more largely  While their principal trade is in *first class* articles, they are able to furnish second or third grade instruments, cheaper than the first cost of manufacture in this city.  They buy of large eastern factories, which, on account of operating on a larger basis, can manufacture much cheaper than small concerns  And R. & H  buy very closely, because buying so much,  On this account they can and do *sell* cheaper—qualities of the goods being considered, than any other house.  For this reason parties in Albany, Troy, Utica, Rochester and Buffalo are sending to Redington & Howe for instruments.

We advise our readers to call there—No 2 Wieting block—by all means, before buying any musical instrument or merchandise

### (From The Northern Christian Advocate, Auburn.)

" This is an old House, and has the best kind of a record for prompt business ability and for reliable and honorable dealing  They secure perfect satisfaction to all customers, whether wholesale or retail.  Their facilities are the best of any establishment in Central or Western New York. and their prices correspondingly liberal. Pastors, Churches, Sabbath Schools and families will do well to correspond with or visit this House  Redington & Howe are known to us and we can recommend them as reliable dealers "

### (From The Auburn Daily Advertiser )

" A prompt, honorable House, who have the best facilities in Western New York for the Music Business, and who secure satisfaction to all customers '

### (From The Oswego Daily Palladium )

" They are thorough, honorable business men, with a larger capital and better facilities than any House in the State, outside of New York City.  They keep the best instruments manufactured, and are fully responsible for the warrant they give of perfect satisfaction  We are certain that our citizens will do well to visit or correspond with this House "

### From the Syracuse Daily Journal, Nov , 14th, 1868

MUCH MUSIC.—We had no adequate idea of the magnitude of Redington & Howe's transactions in musical instruments until permitted the other day to see their order book.  We were surprised at the number of instruments making their way over the country.  We noticed especially a single order recently sent, which surpasses the entire yearly business of many retail establishments.  The order was for one hundred and seven Burdett organs and melodeons, having an aggregate value of over $20,000.  We now see why Redington & Howe pay the only wholesale dealer's license in the music line, assessed by "Uncle Sam" in Central New York  They sell such large quantities because they can sell cheaper than any other dealers, (as low, if neccessary, as their competitors buy or manufacture their goods )  They are also well known to be entirely reliable and honorable in their transactions

## Numbers, Description and Prices,
### OF THE
# DUNHAM PIANO-FORTE.

No. 1—7 Octave.—Rosewood.  Large front round corners, moulding on plinth, octagon legs, carved lyre, scroll desk .$550

No. 2—7 Octave—Rosewood.  Large front round corners, carved legs and lyre, scroll desk.... ... .. .... .. .  575

No. 3—7 Octave.—Rosewood.  Large front round corners, serpentine and fancy moulding on plinth, Gothic legs, carved lyre, scroll desk, beveled top  . . ... .... .  600

No. 4—7 Octave.—Rosewood.  Large front round corners, serpentine and fancy moulding on plinth, carved legs and lyre, scroll desk, beveled top ...  .. ... ..  625

No. 5—7 Octave.—Rosewood.  Four round corners, pearl and serpentine mouldings on plinth, carved legs and lyre, scroll desk, beveled top.  ...  .......  ........ 650

No. 6—7¼ Octave.—Rosewood.  Large front round corners, serpentine and fancy mouldings on plinth, carved legs, and lyre, scroll desk, beveled top....  .... ...  725

No. 7—7¼ Octave—Rosewood.  Four large round corners, pearl and serpentine mouldings on plinth, richly carved legs and lyre, etc  . .... . .......... .... .. .... 750

No 8—7¼ Octave.—Rosewood.  Four large round corners, heavy mouldings on rim and plinth, rich serpentine moulding on plinth, rich carved legs and lyre, scroll desk, beveled top ..  ......  . . . .  ... 800

No. 9—7¼ Octave.—Rosewood.  Same style of case as No. 8, with agraffe arrangements throughout....  . .... 900

No. 10—7 Octave.—Rosewood.  Upright or Boudoir Piano .  550

No 11—7 Octave.—Rosewood.  Large Grand Piano, French repeating action, richly carved legs, lyre, etc  ......1200

No 12—7¼—Octave.—Rosewood   Same style of case as No. 11 1500

## TO THE PUBLIC.

The great combination of improvements attained in the Dunham Piano-Forte in regard to tone, touch, power, equality, durability and workmanship, has built for it a reputation which, to-day, stands unrivalled in every section of the country, and has also elicited from the most eminent professors, critics, connoisseurs, and the most energetic of our competitors, the unanimous opinion that the Dunham Piano can not be excelled.

Being confident that the production of a good article is the best and surest road to success, we have always aimed for perfection in our manufactures, regardless of cost.  The patronage which such a course of business has gained for us, without the meretricious aid of Medals or Foreign Decorations, has proven satisfactory to us beyond our most sanguine expectations, and placed us in the highest position of the Piano-Forte trade.

While claiming as we do, without the fear of contradiction, for our house, the honor of first introducing to the American public this last great era of Piano-Forte improvement, which has given to American Pianos the highest honors, and whose perfections have astonished the world, we would state that the First Grand Square Piano made by us some fifteen years since, served as the model for the great improvement in American Piano Fortes.

We also own the patent, now expired, for the cross or Over-Strings, which is now in general use—so popular has it become, and so pecuniarily satisfactory has it proved to us, that we freely gave it to the world.

The Agraffe arrangement we have used in Pianos for a period of thirty years

## MERITS OF THE DUNHAM PIANO-FORTE.

Its Durability has become a proverb.

Thousands of them can be found in use, which have required no repairs, other than tuning, during a period of thirty years

In Workmanship, It cannot be surpassed if equaled.

The best materials and the most accomplished workmen, only are employed in its construction

In Power, Solidity, Purity, and Equality of Tone, it has no compeer.

It is pronounced by the elite of the musical profession, and the dilettanti the most perfect Piano made.

As a Safe Investment, it is the best.

Dealers throughout the country, who have sold thousands of them during our business career, have never had one returned for being defective, nor have they, during a period of nearly twenty years, been called on to pay five dollars for repairs on the whole number sold

It can be sold after years of use, for nearly, if not quite, its original cost.

We have orders for any quantity of them, at an advance of 33⅓ per cent over any other make of half its age.

It is warranted in the most satisfactory manner.

The commercial standing of our house is sufficient guarantee that any claim will meet with instant liquidation

The Juries of the Universal Exposition of Paris, admit that American Pianos are the best, therefore Americans must be the best judges. Convinced that such is the fact, we have always striven to meet their critical requirements, and their approbation and patronage has been our reward, and we shall continue to manufacture such Instruments as will command the **HIGHEST POSITION IN THE ART**, regardless of Foreign Medals or Royal Decorations.

### DUNHAM & SONS.

# THE DUNHAM PIANO-FORTE.

In asking attention to the preceding circular of the manufacturers we add a few

## REASONS FOR BUYING A DUNHAM PIANO

This establishment is the oldest in the country and possessed of the most valuable experience, taking the lead in important improvements. (They were the inventors of the Overstrung Bass and own the Patent )

They have the largest capital of any establishment, without exception.

Their workmanship is the most perfect and durable possible

Their scales are the most perfect.

NOTE—We ask attention to the following criticism from Watson's Art Journal

" Their new square is one of the most beautiful instruments we ever heard In depth, purity, and grandeur of tone, it can hardly be equaled , its touch is exquisitely sensitive ; the registers are perfectly equalized , it sings with a wonderful purity of vibration, and the quality of its sound is refined, limpid and melodious  and at the same time, great in sonority and  brilliance

It is truly a perfect Piano.

The house of Dunham has also been among the intellectual leaders of Piano improvers, and this new Piano is another step in advance, which will still further enhance its reputation."

The Action of the Dunham is perfect

These Pianos have a peculiar timbre of tone, clear and melodeous, preferred by the majority of musicians to *that of any other Piano whatever.*

The price is more reasonable than that of any other first-class maker

Finally the house is of the most honorable character and ensure beyond the possibility of doubt the *most perfect satisfaction* to every owner of one of the Dunham Pianos.

*A most important improvement* has just been introduced by Messrs. Dunham & Sons' in the construction of the Upright or Boudoir Piano.

The large size of the Full Scale Square Piano has always been an objection from the amount of standing room required for the instrument   The Upright form has always been preferred and is the popular style in Europe and among the older musical nations

While possessing a quality of tone so peculiarly its own and generally preferred to the other grades of Pianos, an objection has always been raised to its general use on account of its complicated action  Messrs Dunham & Sons have removed this great objection in the new

## *Dunham  Upright  Grand.*

This Piano has all the merits of the compactness and beauty of form of the Upright pattern and employs at the same time the simple action of the Square Piano.

The arrangement of the Scale in the Dunham Upright is diagonal instead of perpendicular,  thereby giving an immense advantage in *power and beauty of tone,* as well as in the arrangement of the action.  In full, round, rich power

### IT EQUALS A FULL SIZED CONCERT GRAND !

with an indescribable sweetness that the Grand does not possess.

Another most important feature is  *the wonderful cheapness in price* as compared with the same quality and quantity of tone in any other form.

We are the Manufacturer's Special Agents for the State of New York and portions of some other States, and supply dealers of all grades, as well as retail customers, at the Factory Prices

REDINGTON & HOWE

MUSIC PUBLISHERS AND DEALERS.

# THE STEINWAY PIANOS.

As these wonderful instruments are so well known, we do not take the space to re-produce their price list, (ranging from $650, to $1800.)
These Piano-Fortes have twice taken the first prize over all the Pianos of the World, and are universally acknowledged to be the best that are made.
We sell them at wholesale and retail at lowest factory prices, being the manufacturers exclusive agents in this vicinity

REDINGTON & HOWE.

# THE CHICKERING PIANO

has long stood at the Head   We are dealers in these magnificent instruments    Prices from $550, upward.

# The Hallet, Davis & Co., Piano.

This standard instrument maintains its well established superiority. The Compeer and only Boston rival of the Chickering, (having several times taken the first prize over its world renowned neighbor,) it is furnished by the manufacturers at a very small margin of profit   It is sold wonderfully low for such a complete first-class Piano Forte, affording customers a large saving of money.   When we consider its extremely reasonable price, in connection with its unsurpassed quality and durability, and the unexcelled perfection and beauty of its scales, this Piano is UNRIVALLED.
Prices from $450, upward.   We supply the Trade.

# THE BRADBURY PIANO,

is well known to be of superior merit.   We have them at Wholesale and Retail   Prices from $575, to $1,000

# THE CENTRAL PIANO-FORTE COMPANY'S PIANO,

Manufactured by an association of workmen from Steinway's factory, so closely resembles the Steinway, as to be called the Steinway's Compeer.   We sell these to the Trade on very favorable terms   Retail Prices $545, and upwards

## HINTS ON THE PRESERVATION OF THE PIANO

It is evident that if the Piano is to remain in good order for many years, good care must be taken of it. The instrument should be closed when not in use, in order to prevent the collection of dust, pins, etc., on the sound-board; however, it must not be closed for a period of several months or longer, but be opened occasionally, and the daylight allowed to strike the keys, or else the ivory may turn yellow

Any hard substance, no matter how small, dropped inside the Piano, will cause a rattling, jarring noise

It is in every case desirable that an india-rubber or cloth should protect the instrument from bruises and scratches, as well as dampness

The Piano should not be placed in a damp room, or left open in a draught of air—dampness is its most dangerous enemy, causing the strings and turning pins to rust, the cloth used in the construction of the keys of action, to swell, whereby the mechanism will move sluggishly, or often stick altogether This occurs chiefly in the summer season, and the best Pianos, made of the most thoroughly seasoned material, are necessarily the most affected by dampness, the absorption being more rapid  Extreme heat is scarcely less injurious.  The Piano should not be placed very near to an open fire or a heated stove, nor over close to the hot air from furnaces now in general use

Moths are very destructive to the cloth and felt used in the Piano, and may be kept out of it by placing a lump of camphor, wrapped in soft paper, in the inside corner, care being taken to renew it from time to time

Many persons are unaware of the great importance of having their Pianos kept in order and only tuned by a *competent tuner*.  A new Piano should be tuned at least every three or four months, during the first year, and at longer intervals afterward

## *How to Unpack a Piano.*

Take out the screws holding the lid of the box, remove the lid, take out the Piano legs and lyre, remove the board across the inside box.  Place two benches or strong wide chairs, which should be covered with a quilt or other soft substance, alongside the box where the back of the Piano is, slide the Piano toward the end where the legs were—about six inches, have the Piano lifted out by four persons, one at each corner, and set it on the two benches or chairs on its back

Unscrew the cross-boards on each end of the bottom, and put the lyre and legs on, which are numbered 1, 2, 3, 4, for their respective places.  Have the four persons lift the Piano off the benches and set it down so that the four legs will touch the floor at the same time.  Unlock the instrument (the key will be found tied to the lyre,) and wipe off the dust lightly with a soft silk handkerchief, or piece of buck-skin

## *Purchasing Musical Instruments.*

There is, probably, no article of household equipment, the construction of which the majority of purchasers know so little of as pianos  There are few articles that are used so continuously, and for the length of time that pianos are, hence the importance of durability  The finest case may cover a fifth rate interior, a fine tone piano when new may subsequently prove to be made of cheap material that fails after a few years use.

Cheap Pianos with which the country is flooded, are invariably the most expensive in the end, i. e., if we estimate loss of tone and constant annoyance by the instrument being out of repair, of any account.  It is wisest therefore, for purchasers to get their instruments of dealers, if they are to be found, who are known as practical men, both musically and mechanically, as well as honorable.—*Ogdensburg Daily Journal*

# THE BURDETT ORGANS.

## REDINGTON & HOWE,

Are happy to announce that they have secured the State Agency for the above Organs. Our own opinion agrees with the acknowledgement of all leading Musicians as to the great superiority of the Burdett Organ, with its present patented improvements.

A careful examination of these Instruments will convince any lover of the *beautiful* in music, that these organs contain more purity of tone—more variety of expression—more power, than any other Organ known.

We would call especial attention to their last great improvements, the COMBINATION ORGAN of Mr Burdett, and the wonderful VOX CELESTE STOP, the CAMPANELLA ATTACHMENT of Mr R M Carpenter, together with his IMPROVED VOX HUMANA TREMOLO. Also, the improved HARMONIC ATTACHMENT, (doubling the power;) the PATENT MANUAL SUB-BASS, (giving a wonderful depth and volume of tone,) the ORCHESTRAL SWELL, the DOUBLE BLOW PEDALS, and others.

### THE COMBINATION ORGAN

Has one and a half Banks of Keys, with four Sets of Reeds, tuned in a manner to give the greatest variety possible in a Reed instrument.

We have only space to mention one peculiar and beautiful stop in the Combination Organ, the effect of which heretofore has never been heard in a Reed Organ.

### THE VIOLINCELLO STOP,

used for solos alone, is most entrancing when used with the Vox Humana. It seems almost to speak words—certainly it speaks to the heart of every listener. No one should fail to make inquiry about this Organ.

### THE VOX CELESTE STOP

Is a new and most valuable improvement, which brings into use an extra set of reeds, which, by their peculiar arrangement and method of tuning, produces a wonderfully beautiful string quality of tone, with a most astonishing power, surpassing all the previous efforts of the inventor. This admirable improvement, which has created such a sensation among Organ makers, as well as with the Musical Public, is found only in the Burdett Organ.

### THE CAMPANELLA ATTACHMENT,

The latest and best of all Mr. Carpenters inventions, now for the first time placed before the public, will, when listened to, tell its own sweet story. The Campanella is a stop resembling the tinkling of Fairy Bells, or the rippling waters of a fountain, making music so sweet and harmonious, that it passes Æolian-like over the senses—as passes the music of a Harp at night touched by Fairy fingers. This enchanting stop should certainly be heard by all lovers of music. The patent has been applied for by Mr. Carpenter, the inventor.

### THE VOX HUMANA TREMOLO

of Mr R. M Carpenter, so much admired by musicians every where, needs only a word. It has already become a Household Glory, and no Organ is complete without the beauty it imparts to the tone. This stop should not be confounded with Mr Carpenter's former invention. It is an *improved* Vox Humana—has no third pedal—is perfectly noiseless in its operation—has no clock work to get out of order—is entirely simple in construction—is found only in the Burdett Organ—and when once heard, delights and fascinates the listener.

We invite the most rigid scrutiny of these Organs by Dealers, the Profession and the Musical Public, to prove the justice of the title acknowledged to them as THE BEST ORGAN IN THE WORLD.

We have constantly on hand a large stock of these Excelsior Instruments. We supply all classes of dealers, as well as retail customers, at the lowest Factory rates. Agents will soon be found at all principal points.

Satisfaction warranted in all transactions. Send for Illustrated Catalogue.

REDINGTON & HOWE,
General Agents, No 2, Weiting Block, Syracuse, N Y

*handwritten text at top*

## PRICE LIST OF THE

# BURDETT ORGANS,

### Containing R. W. Carpenter's Improved Vox Humana,

### Patented, June 1st, 1867.

**One Set of Reeds.**

| | | | |
|---|---|---|---|
| 1. | Four Octave—in paneled Walnut Case, with Vox Humana, 1 stop, | | $135 |
| 2 | Five Octave—in paneled Walnut Case,   "   "   1 " | | 165 |
| 3 | The same—in elegant Rosewood Case,   "   "   1 " | | 200 |
| 4. | Six Octave—in paneled Walnut Case,   "   "   1 " | | 190 |
| 5 | The same—in elegant Rosewood Case,   "   "   1 " | | 235 |

**Two Sets of Reeds.**

| | | | |
|---|---|---|---|
| 6. | Four Octave—in paneled Walnut Case, with Vox Humana, 1 stop, | | 165 |
| 7 | Five Octave—in paneled Walnut Case,   "   "   1 " | | 195 |
| 8 | The same—in elegant Rosewood Case,   '   '   1 | | 225 |
| 9 | Five Octave—in paneled Walnut Case with manual Sub Bass, and Vox Humana, 2 stops,..   ..   ..   .   . | | 225 |
| 10 | The same—in elegant Rosewood Case, 2 stops, | | 255 |
| 11 | Five Octave—with Harmonic Attachment and Manual Sub Bass and Vox Humana, 3 stops, .   ...   .. | | 250 |
| 12. | The same—in elegant Rosewood Case, with Vox Humana, 3 stops, | | 275 |
| 13 | Six Octave—in paneled Walnut Case,   '   "   1 " | | 240 |
| 14. | The same—in elegant Rosewood Case,   "   "   1 " | | 270 |
| 15 | Six Octave—in paneled Walnut Case, with Harmonic Attachment, Manual Sub Bass, and Vox Humana, 3 stops,...   .   . | | 285 |

**Two and a Half Sets of Reeds.**

| | | | |
|---|---|---|---|
| 16 | Five Octave—in paneled Walnut Case, with Manual Sub Bass, Harmonic Celeste, and Vox Humana, 3 stops,   . | | 250 |
| 17 | The same—in elegantly carved case, with Vox Humana, 3 stops, | | 280 |
| 18 | Five Octave—in paneled Walnut Case, with Harmonic Attachment, Manual Sub Bass, Harmonic Celeste, and Vox Humana, 4 stops, | | 275 |

**Three Sets of Reeds.**

| | | | |
|---|---|---|---|
| 19 | Five Octave—with Harmonic Attachment, Manual Sub Bass, and Vox Humana, 3 stops, .   .   .. | | 400 |
| 20 | The same—with 1½ Octaves of Pedal Bass instead of Manual Sub Bass 8 stops,   . | | 450 |

**Six Sets of Reeds.**

| | | | |
|---|---|---|---|
| 21. | Five Octave—two Keyboards with Manual Sub Bass, Harmonic Celeste and Vox Humana, 12 stops,. | | 550 |
| 21 | The same—with 1½ Octaves of Pedal instead of Manual Sub Bass, | | 570 |

The Combination Organ, with one and one-half banks of keys, four sets of reeds,   .   ...   .   .   .   ..   - $845

Campanella Attachment—on the different styles of Organs— $25 extra.

Messrs. Burdett & Co , are also manufacturing two styles of Organs with less expensive cases, (5 Octave single reed, and 5 Octave double reed,) called the National Organ   These will be sold much cheaper, thereby obviating any necessity for customers to buy second grade Organs, because desiring to purchase at a low price

*Styles 1 to 15 inclusive, are furnished, if required, without the improved Vox Humana, at $25 less than the printed prices,

## MELODEONS.

### PORTABLE CASE.

| | | | |
|---|---|---|---|
| 41 | Five Octave—Single Reed, Walnut Case, | | 95 |
| 42 | Five Octave—Single Reed, Rosewood Case,   . | | 110 |

### PIANO CASE.

| | | | |
|---|---|---|---|
| 46. | Five Octave—Single Reed, Rosewood Case,   .. | | 150 |
| 50. | Six Octave—Single Reed, Rosewood Case,   . | | 180 |

☞ The Walnut Instruments are also furnished in elegantly carved Cases, at an advance of $30 on the above prices

# THE ESTEY ORGANS.

This Veteran House (established in 1846) holds its rank at the head, and are now finishing every month hundreds of Organs and Melodeons, which are a just credit to American skill and enterprise.

The vast amount of patronage received, has been secured more by the actual merits of the instrument, than by extensive advertising and the pretentious parade of their wares before the public. They have employed and retained, from the first, some of the finest mechanics and inventors of the age, and have adopted, and patented more valuable improvements, than any other establishment in the land. As the result, their instruments stand unrivalled by anything found in this country or in Europe, as is admitted by all impartial judges. The most eminent Pipe-Organ builders and performers—the last to discover excellence in reed tones—pronounce them much superior to others.

They possess the following improvements:

THE PATENT HARMONIC ATTACHMENT is an octave coupler used on a single manual, and doubles the power of the instrument without increasing its size or number of reeds. Thus, by the use of this improvement, an Organ containing two sets of reeds is instantly made equivalent to one of four; and a tri-reed equals an instrument of six sets of reeds, making the MOST POWERFUL instrument of its size yet known in this country.

THE PATENT MANUAL SUB-BASS brings into use an independent set of large and powerful SUB-BASS REEDS, which are played with the ordinary keys and controlled by a stop. The manner in which this set of reeds is placed upon the air chamber increases the volume of tone at least one-third. This new and valuable invention requires no extra room, and has all the effect of pedal bass, and can be used by any ordinary performer.

THE PATENT KNEE-SWELL, whereby the player has complete control over the instrument, obtaining a perfect CRESCENDO or DIMINUENDO, more beautiful than the Automatic Swell, or any other ever before used.

THE PATENT ORGAN BELLOWS greatly enhances the power and quality of the tone without increasing the size of the case.

THE PATENT REED BOARD, whereby the tone is greatly improved, rendering it more like a Pipe Organ than is found in any other instrument. This important improvement is covered by two patents.

## THE PATENT VOX HUMANA TREMOLO.

In attempting to describe the effect of this stop, we are at a loss for language: its beauties cannot be written, but must be heard to be appreciated. By this stop an ordinary performer can produce an effect which requires a lifetime of practice for an artist upon the Violin.

It changes entirely the reed-tone, giving the sympathetic sweetness of the HUMAN VOICE, making it so melodious and pure that it never fails to enchant the appreciative listener.

The Tremolo is produced by means of a REVOLVING FAN placed just back of the swell, which imparts to the tone a charming wave-like effect hitherto unknown in instrumental music.

## THE VOX JUBILANTE

Is a new and beautiful stop, peculiar to the ESTEY ORGANS. The character of the tone is marked and wonderfully effective, giving a style of music hitherto unattained in instruments of this class. This is accomplished by an extra set of reeds, ingeniously arranged, and adjusted to meet this special, and hitherto unsupplied want. It is considered by competent judges a great success.

Send for Illustrated Catalogue, giving accurate pictures of the styles.

REDINGTON & HOWE,

Wholesale Agents.

## Popularity of the Dunham Piano.

We are sometimes asked why the Dunham Piano Forte has not been more prominently before the public for the last eight years. We give the reason At the commencement of the late war, the Dunham, senior. concluded to decrease the very large manufacturing done by himself, so long as public attention should be so completely absorbed in the stirring events then transpiring, consequently he diminished his force employed and sent during the war the greater portion of his pianos to the Canadian Provinces (Where the demand for the Dunham Pianos call for more than five hundred instruments every year)

At the conclusion of the war, he associated with him two sons as partners, built a new factory, and the firm of JOHN B. DUNHAM & SONS are now manufacturing very largely.

The high opinion of their pianos entertained by Piano Dealers is evinced by the great desire of the principal houses to secure the Dunham agency

## Leiter Brother's Jewelry House.

These gentlemen occupy a portion of the shelf and counter room in our store with a very fine stock of well assorted Jewelry and Silver Ware. Their connections with a New York Importing House enable them to sell at wholesale and retail cheaper than any House west of New York City

## Situations for Music Teachers.

We keep a registry of Music Teachers in Central New York. Also a list of those desiring locations.

We can, therefore, always put parties in any town or village in correspondence with good reliable music teachers. who can be secured at reasonable rates We charge nothing either to the teachers or the public. We act cheerfully without pay, as we desire to extend our acquaintance.

Teachers should send us their name, terms, &c, when desiring a new field of employment. Individuals wishing teachers are invited to write us freely at any time

## Wieting Hall.

The largest, best, most central and most popular Hall in the city, can be leased for Concerts, Lectures and all varieties of first class entertainments.

Particulars can be learned in our office

## Correspondence Invited.

It is impossible in our present limits to give full particulars of our trade and varieties of musical goods we sell. We invite, therefore, inquiries by mail, or otherwise in regard to any department of the music business, We can send to any address, circulars with fuller details than our catalogue admits of, or forward written information We do so with pleasure

REMEMBER that it costs no more to write one thousand miles to us than five miles to some smaller House

REMEMBER that we save you much more than cost of freight on what you buy of us. We guarantee to do it.

REMEMBER that unless you are satisfied with our treatment to you *you have nothing to pay*

## ONE PRICE ONLY!

# D. W. CARR,

### DEALER IN FOREIGN AND DOMESTIC

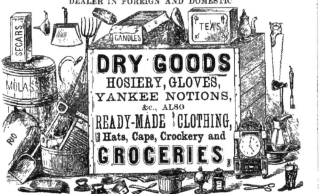

**DRY GOODS**
HOSIERY, GLOVES,
YANKEE NOTIONS,
&c., ALSO
**READY-MADE CLOTHING,**
Hats, Caps, Crockery and
**GROCERIES,**

## McGRAW BLOCK, MAIN STREET,
# McGRAWVILLE, N. Y.

## Dodge & Lord

MANUFACTURERS OF

# MELODEONS

AND

# REED
# Organs,

Of every description and in the various styles of finish, and containing all modern patent improvements known to the trade, such as TREMOLO, SUB-BASS, COMBINATION VALVE, PATENT KNEE SWELL AND OCTAVE COUPLER. Styles adapted to the **PARLOR, SCHOOLS, CHURCHES, LECTURE ROOMS AND LODGES,** and containing from one to four Sets of Reeds, or more, as desired.

The usual discount to clergymen, churches and the trade. Also retail customers will here find the advantages of cheapness of material and light expenses, as compared with those of city manufacture. All work warranted first-class, and for a term of FIVE YEARS. Factory, Hintermister Block, 21 State St., opposite Watkins' Exchange,

## ITHACA, N. Y.
### A. M. Williams, 25 Warren St., Syracuse, Agent.

# GREGG IRON WORKS,

## TRUMANSBURG, TOMPKINS CO., N. Y.

## GREGG, PLYER & CO.,

### MANUFACTURERS OF

# THAYER'S IRON MOWER.

It is all Iron, very strong and durable, warranted less draft than any other Mower. Will work the knives at any angle. The cutter-bar joint is around the Pitman Shaft, and is entirely different from other machines. See circulars giving full description of this Mower.

## Sharp's Patent Wheel Horse Rakes,

### With cleaners between each tooth.

## SHARP'S IMPROVED REVOLVING-AXLE RAKE.

The teeth of these Rakes are of the best Pittsburg Steel, work independent, dump easy, and done with the horse standing or walking.

## Grain Threshing Machines, Large Combined Clover Threshing Machines, Warranted the Best in Use,

**Horse Powers, Wood Planing Machines, Circular Wood Saws, Drag Saws, &c**

CPSIA information can be obtained
at www.ICGtesting.com
Printed in the USA
BVHW082322111219
566319BV00006B/400/P